MACBETH

Major Literary Characters

CHELSEA HOUSE PUBLISHERS

Major Literary Characters

DAVID COPPERFIELD
Charles Dickens, *David Copperfield*

ROBINSON CRUSOE
Daniel Defoe, *Robinson Crusoe*

DON JUAN
Molière, *Don Juan*
Lord Byron, *Don Juan*

HUCK FINN
Mark Twain, *The Adventures of Tom Sawyer, Adventures of Huckleberry Finn*

CLARISSA HARLOWE
Samuel Richardson, *Clarissa*

HEATHCLIFF
Emily Brontë, *Wuthering Heights*

ANNA KARENINA
Leo Tolstoy, *Anna Karenina*

MR. PICKWICK
Charles Dickens, *The Pickwick Papers*

HESTER PRYNNE
Nathaniel Hawthorne, *The Scarlet Letter*

BECKY SHARP
William Makepeace Thackeray, *Vanity Fair*

LAMBERT STRETHER
Henry James, *The Ambassadors*

EUSTACIA VYE
Thomas Hardy, *The Return of the Native*

TWENTIETH CENTURY

ÁNTONIA
Willa Cather, *My Ántonia*

BRETT ASHLEY
Ernest Hemingway, *The Sun Also Rises*

HANS CASTORP
Thomas Mann, *The Magic Mountain*

HOLDEN CAULFIELD
J. D. Salinger, *The Catcher in the Rye*

CADDY COMPSON
William Faulkner, *The Sound and the Fury*

JANIE CRAWFORD
Zora Neale Hurston, *Their Eyes Were Watching God*

CLARISSA DALLOWAY
Virginia Woolf, *Mrs. Dalloway*

DILSEY
William Faulkner, *The Sound and the Fury*

GATSBY
F. Scott Fitzgerald, *The Great Gatsby*

HERZOG
Saul Bellow, *Herzog*

JOAN OF ARC
William Shakespeare, *Henry VI*
George Bernard Shaw, *Saint Joan*

LOLITA
Vladimir Nabokov, *Lolita*

WILLY LOMAN
Arthur Miller, *Death of a Salesman*

MARLOW
Joseph Conrad, *Lord Jim, Heart of Darkness, Youth, Chance*

PORTNOY
Philip Roth, *Portnoy's Complaint*

BIGGER THOMAS
Richard Wright, *Native Son*

CHELSEA HOUSE PUBLISHERS

Major Literary Characters

MACBETH

Edited and with an introduction by
HAROLD BLOOM

CHELSEA HOUSE PUBLISHERS
New York ◇ Philadelphia

Jacket illustration: Oil painting of Macbeth and the three Witches
by George Romney (ca. 1780) (From the art collection of The
Folger Shakespeare Library). *Inset:* First page of *Macbeth* from the First Folio
(1623). With permission from The Folger Shakespeare Library.

Chelsea House Publishers

Editor-in-Chief   Remmel T. Nunn
Managing Editor   Karyn Gullen Browne
Picture Editor   Adrian G. Allen
Art Director   Maria Epes
Manufacturing Manager   Gerald Levine

Major Literary Characters

Senior Editor   S. T. Joshi
Copy Chief   Richard Fumosa
Designer   Maria Epes

Staff for MACBETH

Picture Researcher   Wendy P. Wills
Assistant Art Director   Noreen Romano
Production Manager   Joseph Romano
Production Coordinator   Marie Claire Cebrian

7 9 8 6

Library of Congress Cataloging-in-Publication Data

Macbeth / edited and with an introduction by Harold Bloom.
p.   cm.—(Major literary characters)
Includes bibliographical references (p.   ) and index.
ISBN 0-7910-0923-8.—ISBN 0-7910-0978-5 (pbk.)
1. Shakespeare, William, 1564–1616. Macbeth.   2. Macbeth, King of Scotland,
11th cent., in fiction, drama, poetry, etc.   I. Bloom, Harold.
II. Series.
PR2823.M229   1991
822.3'3—dc20
90-2459
CIP

CONTENTS

THE ANALYSIS OF CHARACTER

Harold Bloom

"Character," according to our dictionaries, still has as a primary meaning a graphic symbol, such as a letter of the alphabet. This meaning reflects the word's apparent origin in the ancient Greek *charactēr*, a sharp stylus. *Charactēr* also meant the mark of the stylus' incisions. Recent fashions in literary criticism have reduced "character" in literature to a matter of marks upon a page. But our word "character" also has a very different meaning, matching that of the ancient Greek *ēthos*, "habitual way of life." Shall we say then that literary character is an imitation of human character, or is it just a grouping of marks? The issue is between a critic like Dr. Samuel Johnson, for whom words were as much like people as like things, and a critic like the late Roland Barthes, who told us that "the fact can only exist linguistically, as a term of discourse." Who is closer to our experience of reading literature, Johnson or Barthes? What difference does it make, if we side with one critic rather than the other?

Barthes is famous, like Foucault and other recent French theorists, for having added to Nietzsche's proclamation of the death of God a subsidiary demise, that of the literary author. If there are no authors, then there are no fictional personages, presumably because literature does not refer to a world outside language. Words indeed necessarily refer to other words in the first place, but the impact of words ultimately is drawn from a universe of fact. Stories, poems, and plays are recognizable as such because they are human utterances within traditions of utterances, and traditions, by achieving authority, become a kind of fact, or at least the sense of a fact. Our sense that literary characters, within the context of a fictive cosmos, indeed are fictional personages is also a kind of fact. The meaning and value of every character in a successful work of literary representation depend upon our ideas of persons in the factual reality of our lives.

Literary character is always an invention, and inventions generally are indebted to prior inventions. Shakespeare is the inventor of literary character as we know it; he reformed the universal human expectations for the verbal imitation of personality, and the reformation appears now to be permanent and uncannily inevitable. Remarkable as the Bible and Homer are at representing personages, their characters are relatively unchanging. They age within their stories, but their habitual modes of being do not develop. Jacob and Achilles unfold before us, but without metamorphoses. Lear and Macbeth, Hamlet and Othello severely modify themselves not only by their actions, but by their utterances, and most of all through *overhearing themselves,* whether they speak to themselves or to others. Pondering what they themselves have said, they will to change, and actually do change, sometimes extravagantly yet always persuasively. Or else they suffer change, without willing it, but in reaction not so much to their language as to their relation to that language.

I do not think it useful to say that Shakespeare successfully imitated elements in our characters. Rather, it could be argued that he compelled aspects of character to appear that previously were concealed, or not available to representation. This is not to say that Shakespeare is God, but to remind us that language is not God either. The mimesis of character in Shakespeare's dramas now seems to us normative, and indeed became the accepted mode almost immediately, as Ben Jonson shrewdly and somewhat grudgingly implied. And yet, Shakespearean representation has surprisingly little in common with the imitation of reality in Jonson or in Christopher Marlowe. The origins of Shakespeare's originality in the portrayal of men and women are to be found in the *Canterbury Tales* of Geoffrey Chaucer, insofar as they can be located anywhere before Shakespeare himself. Chaucer's savage and superb Pardoner overhears his own tale-telling, as well as his mocking rehearsal of his own spiel, and through this overhearing he is emboldened to forget himself, and enthusiastically urges all his fellow-pilgrims to come forward to be fleeced by him. His self-awareness, and apocalyptically rancid sense of spiritual fall, are preludes to the even grander abysses of the perverted will in Iago and in Edmund. What might be called the character trait of a negative charisma may be Chaucer's invention, but came to its perfection in Shakespearean mimesis.

The analysis of character is as much Shakespeare's invention as the representation of character is, since Iago and Edmund are adepts at analyzing both themselves and their victims. Hamlet, whose overwhelming charisma has many negative components, is certainly the most comprehensive of all literary characters, and so necessarily prophesies the labyrinthine complexities of the will in Iago and Edmund. Charisma, according to Max Weber, its first codifier, is primarily a natural endowment, and implies a primordial and idiosyncratic power over nature, and so finally over death. Hamlet's uncanniness is at its most suggestive in the scene of his long dying, where the audience, through the mediation of Horatio, itself is compelled to meditate upon suicide, if only because outliving the prince of Denmark scarcely seems an option.

Shakespearean representation has usurped not only our sense of literary character, but our sense of ourselves as characters, with Hamlet playing the part of the largest of these usurpations. Insofar as we have an idea of human disinterestedness, we tend to derive it from the Hamlet of Act V, whose quietism has about it a ghostly authority. Oscar Wilde, in his profound and profoundly witty dialogue, "The Decay of Lying," expressed a permanent insight when he insisted that art shaped every era, far more than any age formed art. Life imitates art, we imitate Shakespeare, because without Shakespeare we would perish for lack of images. Wilde's grandest audacity demystifies Shakespearean mimesis with a Shakespearean vivaciousness: "This unfortunate aphorism about art holding the mirror up to Nature is deliberately said by Hamlet in order to convince the bystanders of his absolute insanity in all art-matters." Of *Hamlet*'s influence upon the ages Wilde remarked that: "The world has grown sad because a puppet was once melancholy." "Puppet" is Wilde's own deconstruction, a brilliant reminder that Shakespeare's artistry of illusion has so mastered reality as to have changed reality, evidently forever.

The analysis of character, as a critical pursuit, seems to me as much a Shakespearean invention as literary character was, since much of what we know about how to analyze character necessarily follows Shakespearean procedures. His hero-villains, from Richard III through Iago, Edmund, and Macbeth, are shrewd and endless questers into their own self-motivations. If we could bear to see Hamlet, in his unwearied negations, as another hero-villain, then we would judge him the supreme analyst of the darker recalcitrances in the selfhood. Freud followed the pre-Socratic Empedocles, in arguing that character is fate, a frightening doctrine that maintains the fear that there are no accidents, that overdetermination rules us all of our lives. Hamlet assumes the same, yet adds to this argument the terrible passivity he manifests in Act V. Throughout Shakespeare's tragedies, the most interesting personages seem doom-eager, reminding us again that a Shakespearean reading of Freud would be more illuminating than a Freudian exegesis of Shakespeare. We learn more when we discover Hamlet in the Freudian Death Drive, than when we read *Beyond the Pleasure Principle* into *Hamlet*.

In Shakespearean comedy, character achieves its true literary apotheosis, which is the representation of the inner freedom that can be created by great wit alone. Rosalind and Falstaff, perhaps alone among Shakespeare's personages, match Hamlet in wit, though hardly in the metaphysics of consciousness. Whether in the comic or the modern mode, Shakespeare has set the standard of measurement in the balance between character and passion.

In Shakespeare the self is more dramatized than theatricalized, which is why a Shakespearean reading of Freud works out so well. Character-formation after the passing of the Oedipal stage takes the place of fetishistic fragmentings of the self. Critics who now call literary character into question, and who proclaim also the death of the author, invariably also regard all notions, literary and human, of a stable character as being mere reductions of deeper pre-Oedipal desires. It becomes clear that the fortunes of literary character rise and fall with the prestige of normative conceptions of the ego. Shakespeare's Iago, who wars against being, may be the first deconstructionist of the self, with his proclamation of "I am not what I am." This constitutes the necessary prologue to any view that would regard a fixed ego as a virtual abnormality. But deconstructions of the self are no more modern than Modernism is. Like literary modernism, the decentered ego came out of the Hellenistic culture of ancient Alexandria. The Gnostic heretics believed that the psyche, like the body, was a fallen entity, mechanically fashioned by the Demiurge or false creator. They held however that each of us possessed also a spark or pneuma, which was a fragment of the original Abyss or true, alien God. The soul or psyche within every one of us was thus at war with the self or pneuma, and only that sparklike self could be saved.

Shakespeare, following after Chaucer in this respect, was the first and remains still the greatest master of representing character both as a stable soul and a wavering self. There is a substance that endures in Shakespeare's figures, and there is also a quicksilver rendition of the unsettling sparks. Racine and Tolstoy, Balzac and Dickens, follow in Shakespeare's wake by giving us some sense of pre-Oedipal sparks or drives, and considerably more sense of post-Oedipal character and personality, stabilizations or sublimations of the fetish-seeking drives. Critics like Leo Bersani and René Girard argue eloquently against our taking this mimesis as the only proper work of literature. I would suggest that strong fictions of the self, from the Bible through Samuel Beckett, necessarily participate in both modes, the sublimation of desire, and the persistence of a primordial desire. The mystery of Hamlet or of Lear is intimately invested in the tangled mixture of the two modes of representation.

Psychic mobility is proposed by Bersani as the ideal to which deconstructions of the literary self may yet guide us. The ideal has its pathos, but the realities of literary representation seem to me very different, perhaps destructively so. When a novelist like D. H. Lawrence sought to reduce his characters to Eros and the Death Drive, he still had to persuade us of his authority at mimesis by lavishing upon the figures of *The Rainbow* and *Women in Love* all of the vivid stigmata of normative personality. Birkin and Ursula may represent antithetical and uncanny drives, but they develop and change as characters pondering their own pronouncements and reactions to self and others. The cost of a non-Shakespearean representation is enormous. Pynchon, in *The Crying of Lot 49* and *Gravity's Rainbow*, evades the burden of the normative by resorting to something like Christopher Marlowe's art of caricature in *The Jew of Malta*. Marlowe's Barabas is a marvelous rhetorician, yet he is a cartoon alongside the troublingly equivocal Shylock. Pynchon's personages are deliberate cartoons also, as flat as comic strips. Marlowe's achievement, and Pynchon's, are beyond dispute, yet they are like the prelude and the postlude to Shakespearean reality. They do not wish to engage with our hunger for the empirical world and so they enter the problematic cosmos of literary fantasy.

No writer, not even Shakespeare or Proust, alters the available stock that we agree to call reality, but Shakespeare, more than any other, does show us how much of reality we could encounter if only we retained adequate desire. The strong literary representation of character is already an analysis of character, and is part of the healing work of a literary culture, which implicitly seeks to cure violence through a normative mimesis of ego, *as if it were stable,* whether in actuality it is or is not. I do not believe that this is a social quest taken on by literary culture, but rather that we confront here the aesthetic essence of what makes a culture *literary,* rather than metaphysical or ethical or religious. A culture becomes literary when its conceptual modes have failed it, which means when religion, philosophy, and science have begun to lose their authority. If they cannot heal violence, then literature attempts to do so, which may be only a turning inside out of the critical arguments of Girard and Bersani.

I conclude by offering a particular instance or special case as a paradigm for the healing enterprise that is at once the representation and the analysis of literary character. Let us call it the aesthetics of being outraged, or rather of successfully representing the state of being outraged. W. C. Fields was one modern master of such representation, and Nathanael West was another, as was Faulkner before him. Here also the greatest master remains Shakespeare, whose Macbeth, himself a bloody outrage, yet retains our imaginative sympathy precisely because he grows increasingly outraged as he experiences the equivocation of the fiend that lies like truth. The double-natured promises and the prophecies of the weird sisters finally induce in Macbeth an apocalyptic version of the stage actor's anxiety at missing cues, the horror of a phantasmagoric stage fright of missing one's time, of always reacting too late. Macbeth, a veritable monster of solipsistic inwardness but no intellectual, counters his dilemma by fresh murders, that prolong him in time yet provoke him only to a perpetually freshened sense of being outraged, as all his expectations become still worse confounded. We are moved by Macbeth, however estrangedly, because his terrible inwardness is a paradigm for our own solipsism, but also because none of us can resist a strong and successful representation of the human in a state of being outraged.

The ultimate outrage is the necessity of dying, an outrage concealed in a multitude of masks, including the tyrannical ambitions of Macbeth. I suspect that our outrage at being outraged is the most difficult of all our affects for us to represent to ourselves, which is why we are so inclined to imaginative sympathy for a character who strongly conveys that affect to us. The Shrike of West's *Miss Lonelyhearts* or Faulkner's Joe Christmas of *Light in August* are crucial modern instances, but such figures can be located in many other works, since the ability to represent this extreme emotion is one of the tests that strong writers are driven to set for themselves.

However a reader seeks to reduce literary character to a question of marks on a page, she will come at last to the impasse constituted by the thought of death, her death, and before that to all the stations of being outraged that memorialize her own drive towards death. In reading, she quests for evidences that are strong representations, whether of her desire or her despair. Such questings constitute the necessary basis for the analysis of literary character, an enterprise that always will survive every vagary of critical fashion.

EDITOR'S NOTE

This book gathers together a representative selection of the best criticism that has been devoted to Macbeth, considered as a major literary character. I am much indebted to S. T. Joshi for his erudite care and skill in assisting my editing of this volume.

My introduction centers upon our obsessive interest in Macbeth's proleptic imagination, which dominates us even as it tyrannizes over him. A selection of excerpts from the main traditions of Macbeth criticism follows, starting with William Warner in 1606, and continuing through such major interpreters as Dr. Johnson, Hazlitt, and Coleridge on to Victor Hugo and Georg Brandes. Modern commentary commences with Sigmund Freud in 1915 and proceeds with crucial readings by G. Wilson Knight and Harold C. Goddard, among other scholarly critics.

Full-scale critical essays begin here with A. C. Bradley, still the most useful of characterological critics, whose interpretation emphasizes the hero-villain's mounting horror of self. Wayne C. Booth, rightly esteemed as a scholar of prose fiction, centers upon the persistence of our sympathy for Macbeth, while John Holloway stresses philosophical perspectives that illuminate the protagonist as their moral icon. In the context of public justice, C. J. Sisson sees Macbeth as undone as much by his best qualities as by his defects.

Elizabeth Nielsen centers upon Macbeth's tragic glory, a grandeur that thwarts most post-Shakespearean actors, while Robert B. Heilman suggests a limitation (which I do not feel) in the tyrant's supposed failure to judge himself. A more dialectical reading, admirably balanced, is offered by Wilbur Sanders, who shows us the "unknown fear" that hovers in the tragedy's movements between despair and affirmation.

The dialectical context of order and disorder is invoked by Alan Hobson, after which P. Rama Moorthy sets forth a Macbeth who embodies "life-in-death." Carolyn Asp argues that the hero-villain is victimized by a stereotype of false masculinity, while Lisa Low goes so far as to speak of our acquired "Macbethness," of which we free ourselves by necessity.

A vision of Macbeth as being unable to extricate his own sexual passion for

Lady Macbeth from murderous ambition is given us by Kay Stockholder, after which this volume concludes with Barbara Everett's very different stress upon Macbeth's authenticity as a husband, since he and Lady Macbeth, however ironically, indeed are Shakespeare's most thoroughly married couple.

INTRODUCTION

Macbeth is the culminating figure in the sequence of what might be called Shakespeare's Grand Negations: Richard III, Iago, Edmund, Macbeth. He differs from his precursors in lacking their dark intellectuality, and their manipulative power over other selves. But he surpasses them in imagination, in its High Romantic sense, even though that is hardly a faculty in which they are deficient. His imagination is so strong that it exceeds even Hamlet's, so strong indeed that we can see that it *is* imagination, rather than ambition or the Witches, that victimizes and destroys Macbeth. The bloodiest tyrant and villain in Shakespeare, Macbeth nevertheless engages our imaginations precisely because he is so large a representation of the dangerous prevalence of the imagination. The tragedy *Macbeth* constitutes an implicit self-critique of the Shakespearean imagination, and therefore also of a crucial element in your own imagination, whoever you are.

Not even Hamlet dominates his play as Macbeth does; he speaks about one third of the text as we have it. Compared to him, the other figures in the drama take on a common grayness, except for Lady Macbeth, and she largely vanishes after the middle of Act III. No Shakespearean protagonist, again not even Hamlet, is revealed to us so inwardly as Macbeth. Shakespeare quite deliberately places us under a very paradoxical stress: we intimately accompany Macbeth in his interior journey, and yet we attempt to refuse all identity with Macbeth; an impossible refusal, since his imagination becomes our own. We are contaminated by Macbeth's fantasies; perhaps someday our critical instruments will be keen enough so that we will comprehend just how much Sigmund Freud's theories owe to precisely Macbethian contamination. I myself am inclined to place *The Tragedy of Macbeth* foremost among Shakespeare's works, above even *Hamlet* and *Lear,* because of the unique power of contamination manifested by its protagonist's fantasy-making faculty. Everything that Macbeth says, particularly to himself, is notoriously memorable, yet I would assign a crucial function to a passage in Act I that defines the exact nature of Macbeth's imagination:

> Present fears
> Are less than horrible imaginings.
> My thought, whose murder yet is but fantastical,

I

> Shakes so my single state of man that function
> Is smothered in surmise, and nothing is
> But what is not.

What does Macbeth mean by "single" here? Perhaps "alone" or "unaided," perhaps "total," but either way the word indicates vulnerability to phantasmagoria. To smother function or thought's ordinary operation by surmise, which is antici-pation but not action, is to be dominated by what might be called the *proleptic* imagination, which is Macbeth's great burden and his tragedy. Though the murder of Duncan is still a pure prolepsis, Macbeth has but to image an act or event and instantly he is on the other side of it, brooding retrospectively. The negations of Iago and Edmund were willed nihilisms, but Macbeth's imagination does the work of his will, so that "nothing is / But what is not." Macbeth represents an enormous enhancement of that element in us that allows us to see Shakespeare acted, whether in the theatre, or the mind's eye of the reader, without protesting or denying the illusion. It is not that Macbeth has faith in the imagination, but that he is enslaved to his version of fantasy. Brooding on Macduff's absence from court, Macbeth sums up his proleptic mode in one powerful couplet:

> Strange things I have in head that will to hand,
> Which must be acted ere they may be scanned.

He seems to know already that he seeks to murder every member of Macduff's family, yet he will not truly have the knowledge until the massacre is accomplished, as though the image in his head is wholly independent of his will. This is the burden of his great soliloquy at the start of Act I, Scene vii, with its Hamlet-like onset:

> If it were done when 'tis done, then 'twere well
> It were done quickly. If th'assassination
> Could trammel up the consequence, and catch,
> With his surcease, success; that but this blow
> Might be the be-all and the end-all—here,
> But here, upon this bank and shoal of time,
> We'd jump the life to come.

"Bank and shoal of time" is a brilliant trope, whether or not it is Shakespeare's, since "shoal" there is a scholarly emendation, and perhaps Shakespeare wrote "school," which would make "bank" into a schoolbench. Scholars tell us also that "jump" here means "hazard," but I think Macbeth means both: to leap and to risk, and I suspect that Shakespeare actually wrote "shoal." The metaphor is superbly characteristic of precisely how Macbeth's imagination works, by leaping over present time and over a future act also, so as to land upon the other bank of time, looking back to the bank where he stood before action. The soliloquy ends with the same figuration, but now broken off by the entry of Lady Macbeth. Vaulting and overleaping, Macbeth's ambition, which is another name for the proleptic aspect of his imagination, falls upon the other side of his intent, which is to say, the other bank both of his aim and his meaning:

> I have no spur
> To prick the sides of my intent, but only
> Vaulting ambition, which o'erleaps itself
> And falls on th'other—

The intent is a horse all will, but Macbeth's imagination again falls on the other side of the will, and dominates the perpetually rapt protagonist, who is condemned always to be in a kind of trance or phantasmagoria that governs him, yet also is augmented by every action that he undertakes. Though Shakespeare doubtless gave full credence to his Witches, weird or wayward demiurges of the Gnostic cosmos of *Macbeth,* they may also be projections of Macbeth's own rapt state of prolepsis, his inability to control the temporal elements of his imagination. The Witches embody the temporal gap between what is imagined and what is done, so that they take the place of Macbeth's Will. We could not envision Iago or Edmund being sought out by the Witches, because Iago and Edmund will their own grand negations, or indeed will to become grand negations of every value. Macbeth imagines his negations, and becomes the grandest negation of them all.

Why then do we sympathize with Macbeth's inwardness, in spite of our own wills? He shares Hamlet's dark side, but is totally without Hamlet's intellect. It is almost as though Shakespeare deliberately cut away Hamlet's cognitive gifts while preserving Hamlet's sensibility in the immensely powerful if purely involuntary imagination of Macbeth. Hamlet interests us for reasons very different from why we interest ourselves; Macbeth precisely is interesting to us exactly as we are interesting, in our own judgment. We know Macbeth's inwardness as we know our own, but Hamlet's vast theatre of mind remains an abyss to us. Both Macbeth and Lady Macbeth are well aware that in murdering Duncan they are slaying the good father. We share their Oedipal intensity (which becomes her madness) if not their guilt. The primal act of imagination, as Freud had learned from Shakespeare, is the ambitious act of desiring the father's death. The first part of Macbeth's appeal to us is his rapt state of being or Oedipal ambition, but the second part, even more appealing, is his power of representing an increasing state of being outraged, outraged by time, by mortality, and by the equivocation of the fiend that lies like truth.

William Hazlitt shrewdly observed of Macbeth that: "His energy springs from the anxiety and agitation of his mind." I would add that, as the drama advances, the principal agitation is the energy of being outraged by the baffling of expectations. Increasingly obsessed with time, Macbeth fears becoming an actor who always misses his cue, and constantly learns that the cues he was given are wrong. The energy that stems from an adroit representation of a state of being outraged is one that imbues us with a remarkable degree of sympathy. I recall watching a television film of Alec Guinness playing the last days of Hitler, portrayed accurately as progressing to a greater intensity of being outraged from start to end. One had to keep recalling that this *was* a representation of Hilter in order to fight off an involuntary sympathy. Our common fate is an outrage: each of us must die. Shakespeare, implicating us in Macbeth's fate, profoundly associates the proleptic imagination with the sense of being outraged, nowhere more than in Macbeth's extraordinary refusal to mourn the death of his afflicted wife. All of Western literature does not afford us an utterance so superbly outraged as this, or one that so abruptly jumps over every possible life to come:

> She should have died hereafter;
> There would have been a time for such a word.
> Tomorrow, and tomorrow, and tomorrow
> Creeps in this petty pace from day to day,
> To the last syllable of recorded time;
> And all our yesterdays have lighted fools
> The way to dusty death. Out, out, brief candle!
> Life's but a walking shadow, a poor player
> That struts and frets his hour upon the stage
> And then is heard no more. It is a tale
> Told by an idiot, full of sound and fury
> Signifying nothing.

Dr. Samuel Johnson was so disturbed by this speech that initially he wished to emend "such a word" to "such a world." Upon reflection, he accepted "word," but interpreted it as meaning "intelligence," in the sense that we say we send "word" when we give intelligence. Macbeth, outraged yet refusing to mourn, perhaps begins with the distancing observation that his wife would have died sooner or later anyway, but then centers ironically upon the meaninglessness now, for him, of such a word as "hereafter," since he *knows* that quite literally there will be no tomorrow for him. In the grim music of the word "tomorrow" he hears his own horror of time, his proleptic imagining of all of remaining life, and not just for himself alone. Recorded time, history, will end with the last syllable of the word "tomorrow," but that will refer to a tomorrow that will not come. If all our yesterdays have existed to light "fools" (presumably meaning "victims") the way to a death that is only ourselves (Adam being created from the dust of red clay), then the brief candle of Lady Macbeth's life just as well has gone out. By the light of that candle, Shakespeare grants Macbeth an outraged but astonishing vision of life as an actor in a Shakespearean play, rather like *The Tragedy of Macbeth.* The best in this kind are but shadows, but life is not one of the best, being a bad actor, strutting and fretting away his performance, and lacking reverberation in the memories of the audience after they have left the theatre. Varying the figurative identification, Macbeth moves life's status from bad actor to bad drama or tale, composed by a professional jester or court fool, an idiot indulged in his idiocy. The story is either meaningless or a total negation, signifying nothing because there is nothing to signify. Theatrical metaphors are more fully appropriate for Shakespeare himself than for the tyrant Macbeth, we might think at first, but then we remember that Macbeth's peculiar imagination necessarily has made him into a poetic dramatist. Iago and Edmund, nihilistic dramatists, manipulated others, while Macbeth has manipulated himself, leaping over the present and the actions not yet taken into the scenes that followed the actions, as though they already had occurred.

Critics of Macbeth always have noted the terrible awe he provokes in us. Sublime in himself, the usurper also partakes in the dreadful sublimity of the apocalyptic cosmos of his drama. When Duncan is slain, lamentings are heard in the air, great winds blow, owls clamor through the night, and behave like hawks, killing falcons as if they were mice. And Duncan's horses break loose, warring against men, and then devour one another. It is as though the daemonic underworld of the Weird Sisters and Hecate had broken upwards into Duncan's realm, which in some sense they had done by helping to spur on the rapt Macbeth. Shakespeare's protagonist plays a fearful price for his sublimity, and yet as audience and readers we do not wish Macbeth to be otherwise than the grand negation he becomes. I think this is because Macbeth is not only a criticism of our imaginations, which are as guilty and Oedipal as his own, but also because Macbeth is Shakespeare's critique of his own tragic imagination, an imagination beyond guilt.

—H. B.

CRITICAL EXTRACTS

WILLIAM WARNER

One *Makebeth,* who had traitrously his sometimes Souereigne slaine,
And like a Monster not a Man vsurpt in *Scotland* raigne,
Whose guiltie Conscience did it selfe so feelingly accuse,
As nothing not applide by him, against himselfe he vewes;
No whispring but of him, gainst him all weapons feares he borne,
All Beings iointly to reuenge his Murthres thinks he sworne,
Wherefore (for such are euer such in selfe-tormenting mind)
But to proceed in bloud, he thought no safetie to find.
All Greatnesse therefore, saue his owne, his driftings did infest * * * *
One *Banquho,* powrefulst of the Peers, in popular affection
And prowesse great, was murthred by his tyrannous direction.
Fleance therefore this *Banquhos* sonne fled thence to Wales for feare,
Whome *Gruffyth* kindly did receiue, and cherisht nobly there.

—WILLIAM WARNER, *A Continuance of Albions England,* 1606,·Book 15, Ch. 94

SAMUEL JOHNSON

This play is deservedly celebrated for the propriety of its fictions, and solemnity, grandeur, and variety of its action; but it has no nice discriminations of character, the events are too great to admit the influence of particular dispositions, and the course of the action necessarily determines the conduct of the agents.

The danger of ambition is well described; and I know not whether it may not be said in defence of some parts which now seem improbable, that, in Shakespeare's time, it was necessary to warn credulity against vain and illusive predictions.

The passions are directed to their true end. Lady Macbeth is merely detested;

7

and though the courage of Macbeth preserves some esteem, yet every reader rejoices at his fall.

—SAMUEL JOHNSON, *The Plays of William Shakespeare*
(London: J. & R. Tonson, 1768), Vol. 6, p. 484

W. RICHARDSON

In the character of Macbeth, we have an instance of a very extraordinary change. ⟨...⟩ He is exhibited to us valiant, dutiful to his sovereign, mild, gentle, and ambitious: but ambitious without guilt. Soon after, we find him false, perfidious, barbarous, and vindictive. All the principles in his constitution seem to have undergone a violent and total change. Some appear to be altogether reduced or extirpated; others monstrously overgrown. Ferocity is substituted instead of mildness, treasonable intentions instead of a sense of duty. His ambition, however, has suffered no diminution: on the contrary, by having become exceedingly powerful, and by rising to undue pretentions, it seems to have vanquished and suppressed every amiable and virtuous principle. But, in a conflict so important, and where the opposing powers were naturally vigorous, and invested with high authority, violent must have been the struggle, and obstinate the resistance. Nor could the prevailing passion have been enabled to contend with virtue, without having gained, at some former period, an unlawful ascendancy. Therefore, in treating the history of this revolution, we shall consider how the usurping principle became so powerful; how its powers were exerted in its conflict with opposing principles; and what were the consequences of its victory.

⟨...⟩ Ambition grown habitual and inveterate in the soul of Macbeth, suggests the idea of assassination. The sense of virtue, compassion, and other kindred principles, are alarmed, and oppose. His ruling passion is repulsed, but not enfeebled. Resigning himself to the hope of profiting by some future emergency, he renounces the idea of violence. A difficulty appears: it renews, rouses, and inflames his ambition. The principles of virtue again oppose; but, by exercise and repetition, they are, for a time enfeebled. They excite no abhorrence; and he reflects, with composure, on his design. But, in reflecting, the apprehension of danger, and the fear of retribution alarm him. He abandons his purpose; is deemed irresolute: not less innocent for not daring to execute what he dares to desire, he is charged with cowardice. Impatient of the charge, and indignant; harrassed by fear, by the consciousness of guilt, and by humanity struggling to resume her influence, he rushes headlong on his bane.

—W. RICHARDSON, "On the Character of Macbeth," *A Philosophical Analysis
and Illustration of Some of Shakespeare's Remarkable Characters*
(London: J. Murray, 1780), pp. 48–50, 71–72

JOHN PHILIP KEMBLE

Ambition is the impulse that governs every action of Richard ⟨III⟩'s life; he attains the crown by dissimulation, that owns no respect for virtue; and by cruelty, which entails no remorse on the valour, that wou'd maintain his ill-acquir'd dignity. Ambition is the predominant vice of Macbeth's nature; but he gratifies it by hypocrisy, that reveres virtue too highly to be perfectly itself; and by murders, the recollection whereof, at times, renders his valour, useless by depriving him of all sense, but that of his enormous wickedness. Richard's character is simple, Macbeth's is mix'd. Richard is only intrepid, Macbeth intrepid, and feeling. Richard's mind not being diverted by reflection from the exigencies of his situation, he is always at full leisure to display his valour; Macbeth, distracted by remorse, loses all apprehension of danger in the contemplation of his guilt; and never recurs to his valour for support, till the enemy's approach rouzes his whole soul, and conscience is repell'd by the necessity for exertion.

—JOHN PHILIP KEMBLE, *Macbeth Reconsidered; an Essay: Intended as an Answer to Part of the* Remarks on Some of the Characters of Shakspeare (London: T. & J. Egerton, 1786), pp. 35–36

WILLIAM HAZLITT

This tragedy is alike distinguished for the lofty imagination it displays, and for the tumultuous vehemence of the action; and the one is made the moving principle of the other. The overwhelming pressure of preternatural agency urges on the tide of human passion with redoubled force. Macbeth himself appears driven along by the violence of his fate like a vessel drifting before a storm: he reels to and fro like a drunken man; he staggers under the weight of his own purposes and the suggestions of others; he stands at bay with his situation; and from the superstitious awe and breathless suspense into which the communications of the Weïrd Sisters throw him, is hurried on with daring impatience to verify their predictions, and with impious and bloody hand to tear aside the veil which hides the uncertainty of the future. He is not equal to the struggle with fate and conscience. He now 'bends up each corporal instrument to the terrible feat'; at other times his heart misgives him, and he is cowed and abashed by his success. 'The deed, no less than the attempt, confounds him.' His mind is assailed by the stings of remorse, and full of 'preternatural solicitings.' His speeches and soliloquies are dark riddles on human life, baffling solution, and entangling him in their labyrinths. In thought he is absent and perplexed, sudden and desperate in act, from a distrust of his own resolution. His energy springs from the anxiety and agitation of his mind. His blindly rushing forward on the objects of his ambition and revenge, or his recoiling from them, equally betrays the harassed state of his feelings. ⟨. . .⟩

The leading features in the character of Macbeth are striking enough, and they form what may be thought at first only a bold, rude, Gothic outline. By comparing it with other characters of the same author we shall perceive the absolute truth and identity which is observed in the midst of the giddy whirl and rapid career of events. Macbeth in Shakespear no more loses his identity of character in the fluctuations of fortune or the storm of passion, than Macbeth in himself would have lost the identity of his person. Thus he is as distinct a being from Richard III. as it is possible to imagine, though these two characters in common hands, and indeed in the hands of any other poet, would have been a repetition of the same general idea, more or less exaggerated. For both are tyrants, usurpers, murderers, both aspiring and ambitious, both courageous, cruel, treacherous. But Richard is cruel from nature and constitution. Macbeth becomes so from accidental circumstances. Richard is from his birth deformed in body and mind, and naturally incapable of good. Macbeth is full of 'the milk of human kindness,' is frank, sociable, generous. He is tempted to the commission of guilt by golden opportunities, by the instigations of his wife, and by prophetic warnings. Fate and metaphysical aid conspire against his virtue and his loyalty. Richard on the contrary needs no prompter, but wades through a series of crimes to the height of his ambition from the ungovernable violence of his temper and a reckless love of mischief. He is never gay but in the prospect or in the success of his villainies: Macbeth is full of horror at the thoughts of the murder of Duncan, which he is with difficulty prevailed on to commit, and of remorse after its perpetration. Richard has no mixture of common humanity in his composition, no regard to kindred or posterity, he owns no fellowship with others, he is 'himself alone.' Macbeth is not destitute of feelings of sympathy, is accessible to pity, is even made in some measure the dupe of his uxoriousness, ranks the loss of friends, of the cordial love of his followers, and of his good name, among the causes which have made him weary of life, and regrets that he has ever seized the crown by unjust means, since he cannot transmit it to his posterity—

> For Banquo's issue have I fil'd my mind—
> For them the gracious Duncan have I murther'd,
> To make them kings, the seed of Banquo kings.

In the agitation of his mind, he envies those whom he has sent to peace. 'Duncan is in his grave; after life's fitful fever he sleeps well.'—It is true, he becomes more callous as he plunges deeper in guilt, 'direness is thus rendered familiar to his slaughterous thoughts,' and he in the end anticipates his wife in the boldness and bloodiness of his enterprises, while she for want of the same stimulus of action, 'is troubled with thick-coming fancies that rob her of her rest,' goes mad and dies. Macbeth endeavours to escape from reflection on his crimes by repelling their consequences, and banishes remorse for the past by the meditation of future mischief. This is not the principle of Richard's cruelty, which displays the wanton malice of a fiend as much as the frailty of human passion. Macbeth is goaded on to acts of violence and retaliation by necessity; to Richard, blood is a pastime.—There are other decisive differences inherent in the two characters. Richard may be regarded as a man of the world, a plotting, hardened knave, wholly regardless of every thing but his own ends, and the means to secure them.—Not so Macbeth. The superstitions of the age, the rude state of society, the local scenery and customs, all give a wildness and imaginary grandeur to his character. From the strangeness of the events that surround him, he is full of amazement and fear; and stands in doubt between the world of reality and the world of fancy. He sees sights not shown to mortal eye, and hears unearthly music. All is tumult and disorder within and without his mind; his purposes recoil upon himself, are broken and disjointed; he is the double thrall of his passions and his evil destiny. Richard is not a character either of imagination or pathos, but of pure self-will. There is no conflict of opposite feelings in his breast. The apparitions which he sees only haunt him in his sleep; nor does he live like Macbeth in a waking dream. Macbeth has considerable energy and manliness of character; but then he is 'subject to all the skyey influences.' He is sure of nothing but the present moment. Richard in the busy turbulence of his projects never loses his self-possession, and makes use of every circumstance that happens as an instrument of his long-reaching designs. In his last extremity we can only regard him as a wild beast taken in the toils: while we never entirely lose our concern for Macbeth; and he calls back all our sympathy by that fine close of thoughtful melancholy—

> My way of life is fallen into the sear,
> The yellow leaf; and that which should accompany old age,
> As honour, troops of friends, I must not look to have;
> But in their stead, curses not loud but deep,
> Mouth-honour, breath, which the poor heart
> Would fain deny, and dare not.

—WILLIAM HAZLITT, Characters of Shakspear's Plays
(London: C. H. Reynell, 1817)

SAMUEL TAYLOR COLERIDGE

Macbeth stands in contrast throughout with *Hamlet;* in the manner of opening more especially. In the latter, there is a gradual ascent from the simplest forms of conversation to the language of impassioned intellect,—yet the intellect still remaining the seat of passion: in the former, the invocation is at once made to the imagination and the emotions connected therewith. Hence the movement throughout is the most rapid of all Shakspeare's plays; and hence also, with the exception of the disgusting passage of the Porter (Act ii. sc. 3.), which I dare pledge myself to demonstrate to be an interpolation of the actors, there is not, to the best of my remembrance, a single pun or play on words in the whole drama. I have previously given an answer to the thousand times repeated charge against Shakspeare upon the subject of his punning, and I here merely mention the fact of the absence of any puns in *Macbeth,* as justifying a candid doubt at least, whether even in these figures of speech and fanciful modifications of language, Shakspeare may not have followed rules and principles that merit and would stand the test of philosophic examination. And hence, also, there is an entire absence of comedy, nay, even of irony and philosophic contemplation in *Macbeth,*—the play being wholly and purely tragic. For the same cause, there are no reasonings of equivocal morality, which would have required a more leisurely state and a consequently greater activity of mind;—no sophistry of self-delusion,—except only that previously to the dreadful act, Macbeth mistranslates the recoilings and ominous whispers of conscience into prudential and selfish reasonings, and, after the deed done, the terrors of remorse into fear from external dangers,—like delirious men who run away from the phantoms of their own brains, or, raised by terror to rage, stab the real object that is within their reach:—whilst Lady Macbeth merely endeavours to reconcile his and her own sinkings of heart by anticipations of the worst, and an affected bravado in confronting them. In all the rest, Macbeth's language is the grave utterance of the very heart, conscience-sick, even to the last faintings of moral death. It is the same in all the other characters. The variety arises from rage, caused ever and anon by disruption of anxious thought, and the quick transition of fear into it.

—SAMUEL TAYLOR COLERIDGE, "Notes on *Macbeth*" [1819], *Literary Remains,*
ed. Henry Nelson Coleridge (London: William Pickering, 1836),
Vol. 2, pp. 235–36

H. N. HUDSON

Now, in Macbeth and Lady Macbeth the Weird Sisters find minds pre-configured and pre-attempered to their influences; and their success seems owing to the fact, that the hearts of their victims were already open to welcome and entertain their suggestions. Macbeth, by his great qualities, his valour, his able conduct and admirable success, has won for himself not only the highest rank but one in the kingdom but the first place in the confidence and affection of his sovereign. What principles his great actions have hitherto sprung from, whether from loyalty or ambition, is uncertain: if from loyalty, then he is probably satisfied; if from ambition, he is only inflamed, and the height he has reached prepares him for projects to mount up higher. This point, so uncertain to us, is known to the Weird Sisters. They look not only into the seeds of time but into the seeds of Macbeth's character; and they are enabled to cast his horoscope and predict his fortune, partly by what they see before him, and partly by what they see within him. At his meeting with them Macbeth's mind, unstaid by principle, flushed with recent victory, and thirsting for glory the more for the glory he has just been winning, is in a proper state for generating or receiving superstitious impressions, especially if those impressions offer any encouragement to his ruling passion. They have but to engage his faith in their predictions; and this readily follows from the condition in which they find him.

Critics have differed a good deal as to the origin of Macbeth's purpose to usurp the crown by murdering the king. That this purpose originates with Macbeth himself, I can find no room for doubt. The promise of the throne by the Weird Sisters is no more an instigation to murder for it, than the promise of wealth in similar circumstances would be an instigation to steal for it. To a truly honest, upright man such a promise, in so far as he trusted in it, would obviously preclude the motives to theft; and his argument at worst would be, that inasmuch as he was destined to be rich he had nothing to do but sit still and wait for the riches to come. If, however, he were already a thief at heart, and restrained from actual thieving only by prudential regards, he would naturally construe the promise of wealth into a promise of impunity in theft, and accordingly go to stealing. Such appears to be the case with Macbeth. Having just received two promises, namely, that he should be thane of Cawdor and that he should be king, he proceeds forthwith to argue against the probability of either event; as men often argue against what they wish to find true. His argument is this:—

> The thane of Cawdor lives,
> A prosperous gentleman; and, to be king,
> Stands not within the prospect of belief,
> No more than to be Cawdor.

Now, he has just fought and defeated the thane of Cawdor as a rebel and a traitor, and therefore knows that in all probability his life and title are forfeit to the state; and he seems to spy a sort of hope that he may be Cawdor sure enough; and if so, then why not king? Presently, however, come messengers from the king to greet him thane of Cawdor; and this literal fulfilment of one promise confirms at once his faith in the other promise: this, trusted home, at once "enkindles him unto the crown." Upon this confirmation the pre-existing elements of his character immediately gather and fashion themselves into the purpose in question. The assurance of the crown becomes to him only an assurance of impunity in crime. Thus—

> Oftentimes, to win us to our harm,
> The instruments of darkness tell us truths;
> Win us with honest trifles, to betray us
> In deepest consequences.

The Weird Sisters, then, put nothing into Macbeth, but only bring out what was already there. They seem drawn to him, indeed, by the secret sympathy which evil naturally has with evil:—

> By the pricking of their thumbs,
> Something wicked this way comes;

and it is this knowledge that invites their prophetic greeting. They saw the seeds of murder sleeping within him, and ready to germinate into purpose as soon as breathed upon by the hope of success and impunity. To inspire him with this hope was all they had to do,—a task made easy by the fact, that men are apt to believe what they so earnestly desire to have true; and no sooner have they opened upon him the prospect of success than the germs of wickedness within him forthwith begin to sprout and grow.

> Two truths are told,
> As happy prologues to the swelling act.
> Of the imperial theme.—
> This supernatural soliciting
> Cannot be ill, cannot be good:—If ill,
> Why hath it given me earnest of success,
> Commencing in a truth?

If good, why do I yield to that suggestion,
Whose horrid image doth unfix my hair,
And make my seated heart knock at my ribs,
Against the use of nature?

Some, however, have maintained that the wicked purpose not only originates with Macbeth, but was deliberately formed by him and imparted to his wife before his meeting with the Weird Sisters. On this ground there is nothing for the Weird Sisters to do; and their agency goes rather to perplex and embarrass than facilitate and explain the action that follows. There needed no preternatural agents come from the world of devils to develope a purpose already ripe for execution! It is the very necessity of their predictions that justifies the introducing of them into the play; otherwise their presence would be an obvious superfluity and incumbrance to the drama. The truth, it seems to me, is, that the purpose in question neither originates with the Weird Sisters nor with Macbeth before his meeting with them. Nor does this position at all affect Macbeth's responsibility, or anywise clash with the ordinary laws of human action. Macbeth doubtless had will enough before, but nothing short of supernatural agencies could furnish the motives to develope his will into act. In his lawless ambition, his indomitable lust of power and popularity, the same impulses which have hitherto prompted his heroic exploits,—in these are involved the principles of his subsequent crimes; but his conviction of the impossibility of succeeding in such crimes of course precludes the conditions answering to those principles. In a word, it is not that he lacks the heart, but that Providence ties his hands. Some extraordinary assurances therefore are indispensable, not indeed as the origin or cause, but simply as the occasion of his wicked purpose. Hence the necessity of the Weird Sisters to the rational accomplishment of the poet's design. Without their supernatural disclosures it would be impossible not only for us to account for Macbeth's conduct, but for Macbeth himself to act as he does; so that the existence of such beings is far more probable in reason than such action would be without them. Thus we shall always find, that of two improbabilities Shakspeare uniformly chooses the least; as, for example, in the case before us, to shun the anti-natural, he takes refuge in the supernatural: whenever he goes above nature, it is to avoid going against her.

With Macbeth, then, the conviction of impossibility has hitherto kept the general desire from passing into the definite resolve. *I cannot* hangs like a mill-stone about the neck of *I would,* holding it down out of the sight of others and even of himself; for he never conceives himself capable of such a horrid intent until, to his amazement, he finds himself actually harbouring it. He is a man of great powers as well as strong passions: and with his wise foresight and circumspection, with his "large discourse looking before and after," he knows that such an undertaking is like going to war with the nature of things; that without some miraculous intervention the consequences must in all probability recoil upon himself; and this knowledge, though it does not preclude the wish, effectually precludes the attempt. In short, he "is afraid to be the same in his own act and valour as he is in desire;" "would not play false, and yet would wrongly win;" and "rather fears to do the deed than wishes it undone." Thus his indwelling germs of sin are kept from budding and blossoming out into conscious thought and purpose. But this conviction of impossibility, though the chief, is not the only restraint upon his ambition:—

> He's here in double trust:
> First, as I am his kinsman and his subject,
> Strong both against the deed; then, as his host,
> Who should against his murderer shut the door,
> Not bear the knife myself. Besides, this Duncan
> Hath borne his faculties so meek, hath been
> So clear in his great office, that his virtues
> Will plead like angels, trumpet-tongued, against
> The deep damnation of his taking off.

Here we see he has moral as well as prudential objections to crime; motives of duty as well as of interest against it; and though neither his virtue nor his prudence alone is an overmatch for his ambition, both of them together are. What is necessary, therefore, in order to set his ambition free, is to obviate his prudential objections, to nullify his motives of interest, and quiet his apprehension of the consequences. It is on this principle that the Weird Sisters proceed. Their preternatural insight both of what is in the future and of what is in him, teaches them how and where he is vulnerable. By throwing the security of fate around him, by convincing him of the safety and practicability of the undertaking, they reconcile his circumspection with his ambition, and bribe his reason into the service and support of his passion.

Herein lies the difference between Banquo and Macbeth. The former shrinks from the guilt of crime, and therefore borrows no encouragement from assurances of success; the latter shrinks from the danger of crime, and therefore rushes into it as soon as such assurances are given him. Banquo's ambition is restrained by principle; Macbeth's by prudence: with the one therefore the revelations of fate preclude the motives to crime; with the other those revelations themselves become the motives to crime. Macbeth's starting upon hearing the predictions of the Weird Sisters is but the bursting of a germ of wickedness into conception; and his subsequent starting upon the fulfilment of one of their predictions is but the bursting of that conception into resolution. Banquo starts not in either case, because he has no such germs of wickedness for them to work upon; so that "he neither begs nor fears their favour nor their hate." Macbeth hears their prophetic greeting with terror, because it awakens in him thoughts of crime; Banquo hears it with composure, because in him it only awakens resolutions of virtue. Thus the self-same thing is often a temptation to one man and a warning to another; where the former sees a prize to be sought, the latter sees only a snare to be shunned. The Weird Sisters now harp Macbeth's wish aright, as they afterwards harp his fear; and they at once engage his faith and awaken his fears by realizing him to himself and showing him what he is. Macbeth kisses the confirmation from which Banquo recoils. It is the greedy fish that snatches at the bait.

> If chance will have me king, why, chance may crown me,
> Without my stir,

is but the momentary recoil of Macbeth's conscience from a suggestion which he lacks the will to oppose. He thus tries to arm himself against prospective and preventive remorse. The truth is, chance but awakens in him the "black and deep desires" which have hitherto been kept asleep by chance. His virtue is altogether a dependent, conditional virtue; a reverse of circumstances therefore reverses the entire scope and drift of his action. He is rather guilty of tempting the Weird Sisters than of being tempted by them; at least he tempts them to tempt him.

Macbeth is surprised and terrified at his own hell-begotten conception. There is nothing in the play more profound or more natural than this. The Weird Sisters have brought fire, as it were, to the characters traced as with sympathetic ink upon his soul; and he shudders with horror as he reads the darkening and deepening, but hitherto unsuspected inscription.

> The thought, whose murder yet is but fantastical,
> Shakes so his single state of man, that function
> Is smothered in surmise; and nothing is,
> But what is not.

Like others, he knows not, suspects not, the innate and essential evil of his heart until prospect awakens it into purpose or occasion develops it into performance. Engrossed in the pursuit of glory, he has taken his ideas of himself from public opinion; and of course dreams not that his heart is a nest of cockatrice's eggs till opportunity hatches out the serpents into the eye of consciousness: he knows not what he is capable of doing until he ascertains from the perfectest report what is possible to be done. Hitherto his ambition and his imagination have kept billing and cooing each other on; now they are brought into conflict, and his imagination shudders at the deeds which his ambition persuades. Without strict and constant self-examination we cannot know what we *are* except by what we *do;* and doubtless many of us would tremble at ourselves, were some preternatural assurance of success and impunity to unfold our latent capabilities of evil into conscious thought and purpose. The truth is, we know not how frail a thing our boasted virtue is, nor how much we are indebted for it, frail as it is, to the kindliness of favouring circumstances. How many of us rush into crime with all the chances of detection and punishment before us; if all those chances were removed, how many more of us would rush into crime! It almost makes one shudder to think of it! On the whole, the precept, "Keep thy heart diligently, for out of it are the issues of life," is nearly as wise, I suspect, as any thing that has yet come from the mouth of infidelity.

But, though Macbeth has the wickedness to originate, he lacks the firmness to execute, the design of murdering the king. His strength and irritability both of understanding and of imagination are more than a match for his ambition; and his infirmity and vacillation of purpose is but a struggle between them. He foresees many dangers and imagines many more. It is not so much the guilt, however, as the failure of the undertaking that he fears. The very height to which his ambition is vaulting makes him fear it will overleap itself; and his apprehensions of defeat prevent his forming any plans to insure success. He is to run for a prize of glory, and he dare not start in the race lest he should lose the prize by overrunning.

> If it were done, when 'tis done, then 'twere well
> It were done quickly: If the assassination
> Could trammel up the consequence, and catch,
> With his surcease, success; that but this blow
> Might be the be-all and the end-all here,
> But here, upon this bank and shoal of time,
> We'd jump the life to come. But, in these cases,
> We still have judgment here; that we but teach
> Bloody instructions, which, being taught, return
> To plague the inventor: This even-handed justice
> Commends the ingredients of our poison'd chalice
> To our own lips.

The truth is, Macbeth has not faith enough in the Weird Sisters to overcome the suggestions of experience and the terrors of imagination; he cannot bring himself to trust their word against the natural and ordinary course of things. "*If we should fail*"—this is the point whereon he sticks; and he must not only believe in the practicability of the undertaking, but see his way clear through it before he can venture upon it. By a miracle he has been called to an act which he wishes done, yet fears to do; and he thinks that nothing less than a perpetual miracle can tie up the consequences of such an act. The question with him is, from whence is this latter miracle to come? Thus his mind is held in suspense between the miracle which invites him to the deed and the unknown miracle which is to avert its consequences from himself.

—H. N. HUDSON, "Macbeth," *Lectures on Shakspeare* (New York:
Baker & Scribner, 1848), Vol. 2, pp. 151–61

VICTOR HUGO

To say "Macbeth is ambition," is to say nothing. Macbeth is hunger. What hunger? The hunger of the monster, always possible in man. Certain souls have teeth. Do not arouse their hunger.

To bite at the apple is a fearful thing. The apple is named "Omnia," says Filesac, that doctor of the Sorbonne who confessed Ravaillac. Macbeth has a wife whom the chronicle calls Gruoch. This Eve tempts this Adam. Once Macbeth has taken the first bite, he is lost. The first thing that Adam produces with Eve is Cain; the first thing that Macbeth accomplishes with Gruoch is murder.

Covetousness easily becoming violence, violence easily becoming crime, crime easily becoming madness: this progression is in Macbeth. Covetousness, Crime, Madness—these three night-hags have spoken to him in the solitude, and have invited him to the throne. The cat Gray-malkin has called him: Macbeth will be cunning; the toad Paddock has called him: Macbeth will be horror. The unsexed being, Gruoch, completes him. It is done; Macbeth is no longer a man. He is no longer anything but an unconscious energy rushing wildly toward evil. Henceforth, no notion of right; appetite is everything. The transitory right of royalty, the eternal right of hospitality—Macbeth murders both. He does more than slay them: he ignores them. Before they fell bleeding under his hand, they already lay dead within his soul. Macbeth begins by this parricide,—the murder of Duncan, his guest; a crime so terrible that, as a consequence, in the night when their master is stabbed, the horses of Duncan become wild again. The first step taken, the ground begins to crumble; it is the avalanche. Macbeth rolls headlong; he is precipitated; he falls and rebounds from one crime to another, ever deeper and deeper. He undergoes the mournful gravitation of matter invading the soul. He is a thing that destroys. He is a stone of ruin, a flame of war, a beast of prey, a scourge. He marches over all Scotland, king as he is, his barelegged kernes and his heavily armed gallow-glasses slaughtering, pillaging, massacring. He decimates the thanes, he murders Banquo, he murders all the Macduffs except the one that shall slay him, he murders the nobility, he murders the people, he murders his country, he murders "sleep." At length the catastrophe arrives,—the forest of Birnam moves against him. Macbeth has infringed all, overstepped all, destroyed all, violated all; and this desperation ends in arousing even Nature. Nature loses patience, Nature enters into action against Macbeth, Nature becomes soul against the man who has become brute force.

This drama has epic proportions. Macbeth represents that frightful hungry creature who prowls throughout history—in the forest called brigand, and on the throne, conqueror. The ancestor of Macbeth is Nimrod. These men of force, are they forever furious? Let us be just; no. They have a goal, which being attained, they stop. Give to Alexander, to Cyrus, to Sesostris, to Caesar—what?—the world; they are appeased. Geoffrey St. Hilaire said to me one day: "When the lion has eaten, he is at peace with Nature." For Cambyses, Sennacherib, Genghis Khan, and the like, to have eaten is to possess the whole earth. They would calm themselves down in the process of digesting the human race.

—VICTOR HUGO, William Shakespeare [1864], tr. Melville B. Anderson
(Chicago: A. C. McClurg, 1887), pp. 240–42

P. W. CLAYDEN

The character of Macbeth is, I venture to suggest, nearly related to that of Hamlet, though so wonderfully different in its development. Hamlet is a man under the power of a tyrannous imagination, but with a sensitive conscience. Macbeth is also subject to the sway of his imagination, but he has no conscience. Hence Hamlet's imagination is a source of strength to him, but Macbeth's imagination is to him a source of weakness. Of a large intellectual nature, with vast power to do and dare, his imagination is his master. In the honest part of his life that imagination was allowed to dwell on scenes of sin, to picture to itself the means by which he might in a few sudden leaps reach the throne; and this dalliance with guilty thoughts, this playing with a criminal design, so familiarised him with it that it grew at length to be his master, and he became a criminal at its bidding. In such a nature there must at first have been a conscience; but his imagination had smothered it, and all that remained within him now was the dim echo of a diviner voice than that of his ambition or his pride. Satisfied with a phrase, contented by a well-turned expression, silenced by a metaphor, conscience was now a merely intellectual thing, its moral function was abnegated, and its rightful authority lost. But the echo of its voice remained, and dwelling in his fancy were vague words and phrases, meaningless now, but haunting his thoughts and wandering amid his images of terror, like the ghost of that better nature he had slain. He therefore presents himself to us during the short acquaintance we have with him in the action of the play as a brave man who is a coward, a man of large poetic mind who is a murderer and a tyrant, a great soul lost, one who might have been a hero and is nothing but a villain.

—P. W. CLAYDEN, "Macbeth and Lady Macbeth," *Fortnightly Review* 8, No. 2 (August 1867): 163

EDWARD DOWDEN

There is a line in the play of *Macbeth,* uttered as the evening shadows begin to gather on the day of Banquo's murder, which we may repeat to ourselves as a motto of the entire tragedy, "Good things of day begin to droop and drowse." It is the tragedy of the twilight and the setting-in of thick darkness upon a human soul. We assist at the spectacle of a terrible sunset in folded clouds of blood. To the last, however, one thin hand's-breadth of melancholy light remains—the sadness of the day without its strength. Macbeth is the prey of a profound world-weariness. And while a huge *ennui* pursues crime, the criminal is not yet in utter blackness of night. When the play opens, the sun is already dropping below the verge. And as at sunset strange winds arise, and gather the clouds to westward with mysterious pause and stir, so the play of *Macbeth* opens with movement of mysterious, spiritual powers, which are auxiliary of that awful shadow which first creeps, and then strides across the moral horizon. ⟨. . .⟩

Shakspere does not believe in any sudden transformation of a noble and loyal soul into that of a traitor and murderer. At the outset Macbeth possesses no real fidelity to things that are true, honest, just, pure, lovely. He is simply not yet in alliance with the powers of evil. He has aptitudes for goodness, and aptitudes for crime. Shakspere felt profoundly that this careless attitude of suspense or indifference between virtue and vice cannot continue long. The kingdom of heaven suffers violence, and the violent take it by force. Those who lack energy of goodness, and drop into a languid neutrality between the antagonist spiritual forces of the world must serve the devil as slaves, if they will not decide to serve God as freemen.

But beside the vague yet mastering inspiration of crime received from the witches, there is the more definite inspiration received from his wife. Macbeth is excitably imaginative, and his imagination alternately stimulates, and enfeebles him. The facts in their clear-cut outline disappear in the dim atmosphere of surmise, desire, fear, hope, which the spirit of Macbeth effuses around the fact. But his wife sees things in the clearest and most definite outline. Her delicate frame is filled with high-strung nervous energy. With her to perceive is forthwith to decide, to decide is to act. Having resolved upon her end a practical logic convinces her that the means are implied and determined. Macbeth resolves, and falters back from action; now he is restrained by his imagination, now by his fears, now by his lingering velleities towards a loyal and honourable existence. He is unable to keep in check or put under restraint any one of the various incoherent powers of his nature, which impede and embarrass each the action of the other. Lady Macbeth gains, for the time, sufficient strength by throwing herself passionately into a single purpose, and by resolutely repressing all that is inconsistent with that purpose. Into the service of evil she carries some of the intensity and energy of asceticism,—she cuts off from herself her better nature, she yields to no weak paltering with conscience. "I have given suck," she exclaims, "and know how tender 'tis to love the babe that milks me;" she is unable to stab Duncan because he resembles her father in his sleep; she is appalled by the copious blood in which the old man lies, and the horror of the sight clings to her memory; the smell of the blood is hateful to her and almost insupportable; she had not been without apprehension that her feminine nature might fail to carry her through the terrible ordeal, through which she yet resolved that it should be compelled to pass. She must not waste an atom of her strength of will, which has to serve for two murderers,—for her husband as well as for herself. She puts into requisition with the aid of wine and of stimulant words the reserve of nervous force which lay unused. No witches have given her "Hail;" no airy dagger marshals her the way that she is going; nor is she afterwards haunted by the terrible vision of Banquo's gory head. As long as her will remains her own she can throw herself upon external facts and maintain herself in relation with the definite, actual surroundings, it is in her sleep, when the will is incapable of action, that she is persecuted by the past which perpetually renews itself, not in ghostly shapes, but by the imagined recurrence of real and terrible incidents.

The fears of Lady Macbeth upon the night of Duncan's murder are the definite ones, that the murderers may be detected, that some omission in the pre-arranged plan may occur, that she or her husband may be summoned to appear before the traces of their crime have been removed. More awful considerations would press in upon her and overwhelm her sanity, but that she forcibly repels them for the time:

> These deeds must not be thought
> After these ways; so, it will make us mad.

To her the sight of Duncan dead is as terrible as to Macbeth; but she takes the dagger from her husband; and with a forced jest, hideous in the self-violence which it implies, she steps forth into the dark corridor:

> If he do bleed
> I'll gild the faces of the grooms withal
> For it must seem their guilt.

"A play of fancy here is like a gleam of ghastly sunshine striking across a stormy landscape." The knocking at the gate clashes upon her overstrained nerves and thrills her; but she has determination and energy to direct the actions of Macbeth, and rouse him from the mood of abject depression which succeeded his crime. A white flame of resolution glows through her delicate organisation, like light through an alabaster lamp:

> Infirm of purpose!
> Give me the daggers: the sleeping and the dead
> Are but as pictures: 'tis the eye of childhood
> That fears a painted devil.

If the hold which she possesses over her own faculties should relax for a moment all would be lost. For dreadful deeds anticipated and resolved upon, she has strength, but the surprise of a novel horror, on which she has not counted, deprives her suddenly of consciousness; when Macbeth announces his butchery of Duncan's grooms the lady swoons,—not in feigning but in fact,—and is borne away insensible.

Macbeth wastes himself in vague, imaginative remorse:

> Will not great Neptune's ocean wash this blood
> Clean from my hand? No, this my hand will rather
> The multitudinous seas incarnadine,
> Making the green one red.

Thus his imagination serves to dissipate the impression of his conscience. What is the worth of this vague, imaginative remorse? Macbeth retained enough of goodness to make him a haggard, miserable criminal; never enough to restrain him from a crime. His hand soon became subdued to what it worked in,—the blood in which it paddled and plashed. And yet the loose incoherent faculties ever becoming more and more disorganised and disintegrated somehow held together till the end. "My hands are of your colour," exclaims Lady Macbeth; "but I shame to wear a heart so white. A little water clears us of this deed." Yet it is she who has uttered no large words about "the multitudinous seas," who will rise in slumbery agitation, and with her accustomed action eagerly essay to remove from her little hand its ineffaceable stain, and with her delicate sense sickened at the smell of blood upon it, which "all the perfumes of Arabia will not sweeten;" and last, will loosen the terrible constriction of her heart with a sigh that longs to be perpetual. It is the queen, and not her husband who is slain by conscience.

Yet the soul of Macbeth never quite disappears into the blackness of darkness. He is a cloud without water, carried about of winds; a tree whose fruit withers, but not even to the last quite plucked up by the roots. For the dull ferocity of Macbeth is joyless. All his life has gone irretrievably astray, and he is aware of this. His suspicion becomes uncontrollable; his reign is a reign of terror; and as he drops deeper and deeper into the solitude and the gloom, his sense of error and misfortune, futile and unproductive as that sense is, increases. He moves under a dreary cloud, and all things look gray and cold. He has lived long enough, yet he clings to life; that which should accompany old age "as honour, love, obedience, troops of friends," he may not look to have. Finally his sensibility has grown so dull that even the intelligence of his wife's death,—the death of her who had been bound to him by such close communion in crime,—hardly touches him, and seems little more than one additional incident in the weary, meaningless tale of human life:

> She should have died hereafter;
> There would have been a time for such a word.
> To-morrow, and to-morrow, and to-morrow,
> Creeps in this petty pace from day to day
> To the last syllable of recorded time;
> And all our yesterdays have lighted fools
> The way to dusty death. Out, out, brief candle!
> Life's but a walking shadow, a poor player
> That struts and frets his hour upon the stage,
> And then is heard no more; it is a tale
> Told by an idiot, full of sound and fury,
> Signifying nothing.

This world-weariness, which has not the energy of Timon's despair, is yet less remote from the joy and glory of true living than is the worm-like vivacity of Iago. Macbeth remembers that he once knew there was such a thing as human goodness. He stands a haggard shadow against the handsbreadth of pale sky which yields us sufficient light to see him. But Iago rises compact with fiend-like energy, seen brightly in the godless glare of hell. The end of Macbeth is savage, and almost brutal—a death without honour or loveliness. He fights now not like "Bellona's bridegroom lapp'd in proof," but with a wild and animal clinging to life:

> They have tied me to a stake; I cannot fly,
> But, bear-like, I must fight the course.

His followers desert him; he feels himself taken in a trap. The powers of evil in which he had trusted turn against him and betray him. His courage becomes a desperate rage. We are in pain until the horrible necessity is accomplished.

Shakspere pursues Macbeth no farther. He does not follow him with yearning conjecture, as Mr. Browning follows the murderer of his poem, *The Ring and the Book,*

Into that sad obscure sequestered state,
Where God unmakes but to re-make the soul
He else made first in vain.

Our feet remain on solid Scottish earth. But a new and better era of history dawns. Macbeth and Siward's son lie dead; but the world goes on. The tragic deeds take up their place in the large life of a country. We suffer no dejection; "the time is free." Sane and strong, we expect the day when Malcolm will be crowned at Scone.

—EDWARD DOWDEN, *Shakspere: A Critical Study of His Mind and Art*
(London: H. S. King, 1875), pp. 244, 250–56

RICHARD G. MOULTON

⟨...⟩ Macbeth is essentially the practical man, the man of action, of the highest experience, power, and energy in military and political command, accustomed to the closest connection between willing and doing. His is one who in another age would have worked out the problem of free trade, or unified Germany, or engineered the Suez Canal. On the other hand, he has concerned himself little with things transcendental; he is poorly disciplined in thought and goodness; prepared for any emergency in which there is anything to be *done,* yet a mental crisis or a moral problem afflicts him with the shock of an unfamiliar situation. This is by no means a generally accepted view: amongst a large number of readers the traditional conception of Macbeth lingers as a noble disposition dragged down by his connection with the coarser nature of his wife. According to the view here suggested the nobility of Macbeth is of the flimsiest and most tawdry kind. The lofty tone he is found at times assuming means no more than virtuous education and surroundings. When the purely practical nature is examined in reference to the qualities which belong to the intellectual life, the result is not a blank but ordinariness: the practical nature will reflect current thought and goodness as they appear from the outside. So Macbeth's is the morality of inherited notions, retained just because he has no disposition to examine them; he has all the practical man's distrust of wandering from the beaten track of opinion, which gives the working politician his prejudice against doctrinaires, and has raised up stout defenders of the Church amongst men whose lives were little influenced by her teaching. And the traditionary morality is more than merely retained. When the seed fell into stony ground forthwith it sprang up *because* it had no deepness of earth: the very shallowness of a man's character may lend emphasis to his high professions, just as, on the other hand, earnestness in its first stage often takes the form of hesitation. So Macbeth's practical genius takes in strongly what it takes in at all, and gives it out vigorously. But that the nobility has gone beyond the stage of passive recognition, that it has become absorbed into his inner nature, there is not a trace; on the contrary, it is impossible to follow Macbeth's history far without abundant evidence that real love of goodness for its own sake, founded on intelligent choice or deep affection, has failed to root a single fibre in his nature.

—RICHARD G. MOULTON, "Macbeth, Lord and Lady," *Shakespeare as a Dramatic Artist* (Oxford: Clarendon Press, 1885; 3rd. ed. 1893), pp. 147–49

SIR HENRY IRVING

⟨Macbeth's⟩ hypocrisy runs through the play. There is no stronger instance of it than when, in the presence of his wife, he pathetically pictures the aspect of the murdered King and the innocent attendants, whose faces he and his "dearest partner of greatness" had smeared with blood. This is certainly a little too much for Lady Macbeth, for she faints and is carried away. He was a poet with his brain—the greatest poet that Shakespeare has ever drawn—and a villain with his heart, and the mere appreciation of his own wickedness gave irony to his grim humor, and zest to his crime. He loved throughout to paint himself and his deeds in the blackest pigments, and to bring to the exercise of his wickedness the conscious deliberation of an intellectual voluptuary. All through the play his darkest deeds are heralded by high thoughts told in the most glorious word-painting, so that, after a little, the reader or the hearer comes to understand that excellence of poetic thought is but a suggestion of the measure of the wickedness that is to follow.

—SIR HENRY IRVING, "The Character of Macbeth," *Werner's Magazine* 18, No. 2 (February 1896): 98

GEORG BRANDES

There is much to indicate that an unbroken train of thought led Shakespeare from *Hamlet* to *Macbeth*. The personality of Macbeth is a sort of counterpart to that of Hamlet. The Danish prince's nature is passionate, but refined and thoughtful. Before the deed of vengeance which is imposed upon him he is restless, self-reproachful, and self-tormenting; but he never betrays the slightest remorse for a murder once committed, though he kills four persons before he stabs the King. The Scottish thane is the rough, blunt soldier, the man of action. He takes little time for deliberation before he strikes; but immediately after the murder he is attacked by hallucinations both of sight and hearing, and is hounded on, wild and vacillating and frenzied, from crime to crime. He stifles his self-reproaches and falls at last, after defending himself with the hopeless fury of the "bear tied to the stake."

Hamlet says:—

And thus the native hue of resolution
Is sicklied o'er with the pale cast of thought.

Macbeth, on the contrary, declares (iv. 1)—

> From this moment
> The very firstlings of my heart shall be
> The firstlings of my hand.

They stand at opposite poles—Hamlet, the dreamer; Macbeth, the captain, "Bellona's bridegroom." Hamlet has a superabundance of culture and of intellectual power. His strength is of the kind that wears a mask; he is a master in the art of dissimulation. Macbeth is unsophisticated to the point of clumsiness, betraying himself when he tries to deceive. His wife has to beg him not to show a troubled countenance, but to "sleek o'er his rugged looks."

Hamlet is the born aristocrat: very proud, keenly alive to his worth, very self-critical—too self-critical to be ambitious in the common acceptation of the word. To Macbeth, on the contrary, a sounding title is honour, and a wreath on the head, a crown on the brow, greatness. When the Witches on the heath, and another witch, his wife in the castle, have held up before his eyes the glory of the crown and the power of the sceptre, he has found his great goal—a tangible prize in this life, for which he is willing to risk his welfare in "the life to come." Whilst Hamlet, with his hereditary right, hardly gives a thought to the throne of which he has been robbed, Macbeth murders his king, his benefactor, his guest, that he may plunder him and his sons of a chair with a purple canopy.

And yet there is a certain resemblance between Macbeth and Hamlet. One feels that the two tragedies must have been written close upon each other. In his first monologue (i. 7) Macbeth stands hesitating with Hamlet-like misgivings:—

> If it were done, when 't is done, then 't were well
> It were done quickly: if the assassination
> Could trammel up the consequence, and catch
> With his surcease success; that but this blow
> Might be the be-all and the end-all here,
> But here, upon this bank and shoal of time,—
> We'd jump the life to come.—But in these cases
> We still have judgment here

Hamlet says: Were we sure that there is no future life, we should seek death. Macbeth thinks: Did we not know that judgment would come upon us here, we should care little about the life to come. There is a kinship in these contradictory reflections. But Macbeth is not hindered by his cogitations. He pricks the sides of his intent, as he says, with the spur of ambition, well knowing that it will o'erleap itself and fall. He cannot resist when he is goaded onward by a being superior to himself, a woman.

Like Hamlet, he has imagination, but of a more timorous and visionary cast. It is through no peculiar faculty in Hamlet that he sees his father's ghost; others had seen it before him and see it with him. Macbeth constantly sees apparitions that no one else sees, and hears voices that are inaudible to others.

When he has resolved on the king's death he sees a dagger in the air:—

> Is this a dagger which I see before me,
> The handle toward my hand? Come, let my clutch thee:—
> I have thee not, and yet I see thee still.
> Are thou not, fatal vision, sensible
> To feeling, as to sight? or art thou but
> A dagger of the mind, a false creation,
> Proceeding from the heat-oppressed brain?

Directly after the murder he has an illusion of hearing:—

> Methought I heard a voice cry, "Sleep no more!
> Macbeth does murder sleep."

And, very significantly, Macbeth hears this same voice give him the different titles which are his pride:—

> Still it cried, "Sleep no more!" to all the house:
> "Glamis hath murder'd sleep, and therefore Cawdor
> Shall sleep no more, Macbeth shall sleep no more!"

Yet another parallel shows the kinship between the Danish and the Scottish tragedy. It is in these dramas alone that the dead leave their graves and reappear on the scene of life; in them alone a breath from the spirit-world reaches the atmosphere of the living. There is no trace of the supernatural either in *Othello* or in *King Lear*.

—GEORG BRANDES, *William Shakespeare: A Critical Study,* tr. William Archer
and Mary Morison (London: William Heinemann, 1898), Vol. 2, pp. 94–96

STOPFORD A. BROOKE

Macbeth is the bold soldier of a rude time. We must not apply to his actions, if we would conceive him as Shakespeare conceived him, the standards of our time, especially in the matter of killing. He was accustomed to slaughter, and the mere slaying of Duncan, Banquo, and Fleance was nothing to him. When a man stood opposed to the aims of a soldier of that date, unless he had like Banquo a delicate conscience, he slew his enemy at once, in the shortest and surest way. Stone dead has no fellow. Killing was Macbeth's trade; assassination of an obstacle caused him no remorse. But though mere killing or murder did not trouble his mind, it did trouble him when it violated his code of honour. The killing of Duncan, under the circumstances, was such a violation. In that famous speech beginning

> If it were done when 'tis done,

he does not dwell on the guilt of murder, but first on the penalties which follow it. These he fears; if there were no punishment, no return of blood for blood, here on this earth, it is little I would think of the life to come. I'd take the risk of that.

Then, secondly, he dwells on the dishonour to him of the murder. To slay one who is in my castle in double trust violates all the laws of honour. Duncan is my kinsman, I am his subject, and he has done me kindness. Duncan is my guest, under the shelter of my roof. This is not the cry of conscience, but of the common code of honour. Then he thinks again of the consequences. Duncan has been so good, so gentle a king that his virtues will plead like trumpet-tongued angels against my deed, and pity for his fate awake the tears of the world. This too is not his personal conscience speaking; it is partly that it jars honour to slay so excellent a chief, and partly it is fear of the results.

This sense of honour in Macbeth, frequently a man's only conscience, disappears altogether after the murder of Duncan. He has irredeemably violated it, and it never has another shred of influence upon him. Moreover, since nothing isolates a man like the loss of honour, Macbeth is henceforth separated by Shakespeare from the whole of his world, except from his comrade in the murder. He is isolated also from his earlier self, from the honourable soldier that he was; he is an outlaw to himself.

To know my deed were best not know myself.

And the loss of his honour makes him absolutely reckless. No crime, after his great crime, in which he murdered his own honour, seems more than a trifle to him. He dooms, in savage petulance, the wife and children of Macduff to an innocent and useless death.

On the whole, if we would see Macbeth clearly we must not dwell on his conscience, of which so much is made, but on his sense of honour. They are, of course, related to one another, but the realm of each is quite distinct. Were it conscience that troubled him he would have been pictured by Shakespeare as a victim of remorse, like Lady Macbeth. There is no remorse in him, but there is the wild, indifferent recklessness which comes to one who is conscious that he has shut himself out from his fellows by a fatal act of dishonour. And when we think of this, that pathetic statement of his case in Act V, which is not at all the cry a remorseful conscience would make, seems naturally in harmony with his self-consciousness. It is what a dishonoured gentleman, even now, might say

I have liv'd long enough: my way of life
Is fall'n into the sear, the yellow leaf;
And that which should accompany old age,
As honour, love, obedience, troops of friends,
I must not look to have; but, in their stead,
Curses, not loud but deep, mouth-honour, breath
Which the poor heart would fain deny, and dare not.

Again, Macbeth is described by a modern critic as the type of the practical man, not imaginative; who knows himself; who knows his purpose, and goes straight to it by the shortest way. I do not think any description can be further from the reality, *before his murder of Duncan.* Even after the murder this description is only partially true. I suppose his wife was aware of his character, and this was not her view of him. The very contrary was her experience. 'Infirm of purpose,' she cries, at the very top of the event, 'give me the daggers.'

> Art thou afeard
> To be the same in thine own act and valour
> As thou art in desire? Would'st thou have that
> Which thou esteem'st the ornament of life
> And live a coward in thine own esteem,
> Letting 'I dare not' wait upon 'I would'
> Like the poor cat i' the adage?

This is not the swift-acting, practical man. He hovers to and fro; now ambition seizes him, now fear. He wants much, but dreads to take the straight way to it. He's soft by nature in one part of him, and lets the weaker part of him tyrannise over his bolder thoughts. He needs his wife's quicker, bolder, more practical nature to heighten him into audacious, rapid action. This is her view of his character; and till after the murder, it is the character Shakespeare meant him to have. That is plain from Lady Macbeth's description of him in her first speech in the play.

> Glamis thou art, and Cawdor; and shalt be
> What thou art promis'd. Yet do I fear thy nature;
> It is too full of the milk o' human-kindness
> To catch the nearest way; thou wouldst be great,
> Art not without ambition, but without
> The illness should attend it; what thou wouldst highly,
> That wouldst thou holily; wouldst not play false,
> And yet wouldst wrongly win; thou'dst have, great Glamis,
> That which cries, 'Thus thou must do, if thou have it';
> And that which rather thou dost fear to do
> Than wishest should be undone. Hie thee hither,
> That I may pour my spirits in thine ear,
> And chastise with the valour of my tongue
> All that impedes thee from the golden round,
> Which fate and metaphysical aid doth seem
> To have thee crown'd withal.

All through the murder scene Macbeth remains this character. He wavers, through over-thinking of it, before the deed; now cold, now all on fire. He needs his wife's scorn to spur him to the act. He piles up extravagant words about it till he feels himself that he is chilling by words his purpose. He loses his head in the horror of the murder, when it is done, considering it too deeply for sanity. His brain is sick; every noise appals him. The blood of his hands seems to stain the universe. He is lost in fear; he thinks he will never sleep again. His wife is tender to him, but is shamed for his white heart. This is not the practical, swift, purposeful man, but one wildly troubled by imagination, doubling and trebling, through a host of images, the terror and hate of what he has done.

Imagination—that is his trouble! I do not know whether this salient element in his character has been much dwelt on. It ought to be. We cannot understand Macbeth without realising it. Indeed, it is this lively, shaping, various imagination, continually multiplying new aspects of anything to be done, or that has been done, which is at the root of his hesitations, his fears, his outbursts of agony. His wife has none of it, but brings her impulsive common-sense to meet it, check it, and dissolve it. Her cool reasoning face to face with the imagination which has overwhelmed his intellect is one of the most remarkable and dramatic contrasts Shakespeare has conceived. She pulls him out of fantasy into reality. He slips back; she drags him out again.

Macbeth, as Shakespeare saw him, was instinct with imagination. Had he not been a soldier and cousin of the king, had he lived in a less rude time, and in a private gentleman's condition, he might have had the poet's name. Everything he says in this play is poetically said, cast in keen imagination's mould, thought and form equally good; and rising easily, at times of great emotion, into words equal to the emotion. The conception, for example, of all the oceans of the world incarnadined by the blood on his hand is equally magnificent in passion, conception, and execution. Even his common phrases are couched in poetry. The ideal his imagination laid before him was to be king, to wear the golden top of sovereignty. In comparison with this ideal and its imaginative charm, all its material advantages were as nothing in his mind. Lady Macbeth alludes to these. He does not.

Before, during, and after the murder, this imagination, blown into a white heat by the intense passion of the hour, is so alive and powerful that it doubles the horror of the murder. It lifts it out of a vulgar assassination into the archetype of all terrible, soul-shaking murders. It flies from heaven to earth and down to hell. It sees an air-drawn dagger, 'a metaphysical dagger of the working soul,' pointing him to Duncan's chamber. It blackens all Nature with his thought. It drags in the remotest things to increase the terror of the present—Hecate, Tarquin whose strides towards his design are like those of withered murder with her sentinel the wolf. In the very midst of his slaughter he hears a voice, 'Sleep no more! Macbeth does murder sleep,' and at the word his imagination takes fire, and runs away from the horror of the moment into all the poetry of sleep—strange island of peaceful imagination in this sea of murder—

>   the innocent sleep,
> Sleep that knits up the ravell'd sleave of care,
> The death of each day's life, sore labour's bath,
> Balm of hurt minds, great nature's second course,
> Chief nourisher in life's feast,—

There speaks the natural poet. Lady Macbeth, who has none of this imagination, cannot comprehend this divagation. 'What do you mean?' she says. 'Who was it that thus cried?' He is the same throughout. He adds more than an imaginative, I may say an artist's, touch to everything he says. Matter, passion, and form are equally good. He is always mixing up his deeds and himself with the whole of Nature. In his mind Nature, dark Nature, sympathises with him. The heavens, the solid earth, the sea, are companions of this thoughts. He makes them his by universalising himself into them, and with them—a common element in poets. Even at the end when, driven to bay, he feels that all is over, and meets his coming fate with reckless courage and weariness of life, he is still poetic in the hours of his loneliness. Few soliloquies are richer in imagination and humanity than his are in the fifth act.

We cannot understand Shakespeare's Macbeth till we realise this element of poetic imagination in him. It lifts him above the brutal murderer. Yet it makes his ruthlessness more abominable. The artist who is bloodthirsty and cruel is not unknown to history. Art and savagery are often ugly lovers.

—STOPFORD A. BROOKE, *"Macbeth," On Ten Plays of Shakespeare*
(London: Constable, 1905), pp. 196–201

MAURICE MAETERLINCK

And, now, what exactly are Macbeth and his gloomy consort? Are they the titanic monsters celebrated, for instance, by Paul de Saint-Victor, the most brilliant commentator that the French romantic movement gave us? I think that we must first, energetically and once for all, reject any interpretation of this kind, the falsest and least defendable of any. But, to go to the other extreme, do they represent simply normal humanity tempted beyond its strength by a more commanding hazard than those which assail ourselves? Are they greater or smaller than we, more intelligent or nearer to the ancestral darkness? Were they free or drawn on by irresistible powers? Was it on the heath or in their own hearts that the three witches lived? Are they to be hated or pitied? Is their soul only a blighted field, hedged with crimes and filled with mean thoughts, or does it contain fine, noble spaces? Is Macbeth the horrid butcher, the man of impulse, with the glance more brutal and quicker than the fist, the shaggy, stubborn barbarian of the primitive legends, or do we not find in him a saddened poet, a stumbling dreamer, endowed with a sickly sensibility, a Hamlet who has strayed into the realms of action, a little prompter, but at bottom quite as irresolute and nearly as pensive as his brother of Elsinore, a sort of less sensual and more sombre Mark Antony? And is Lady Macbeth the dry, mannish fury, the harsh, rough, vain mistress of Inverness Castle, the detestable business-woman, inflexible, self-contained, unfeeling, crafty, treacherous and colder than the steel of the dagger which she wields, or rather shall we not see in her the wife who loves too well under the stifled words, the victim too severely punished for a horrible thought born in wedlock? Shall we remember the monstrous smile of welcome to the unfortunate Duncan, or the inconceivable distress displayed nightly at Dunsinane; the bloody daggers, or the lamp that reveals the weakness of a soul worn to the death by secret tears? Is she better or worse, more interesting or more hateful, than her husband? And have we settled the features of her face? Is she black as the raven which she quotes at the approach of her prey? Is she tall and sombre, bony and muscular, haughty and insolent, or delicate and fair, short and sinuous, voluptuous and fond? Have we to do with the psychology of murder, the tragedy of remorse and unrecognised justice? Is it a study of destiny or of the poisoning of a soul by its own thoughts? We know nothing of the matter; we can discuss it endlessly, maintain all this or all that; and it is exceedingly probable that Shakspeare himself would be incapable of defining the two beings that have come from his wonderful hands. It is as difficult to behold them in the written tragedy as it would be did they live among us. They project on every side beyond the poem that tries to encompass them. We think we know them; but they are constantly surprising us. We feel that they are prepared for the most extraordinary reversals. Macbeth sacrificing himself for Malcolm, his wife giving her life to save the son of Lady Macduff: neither would be out of keeping with the mysterious depths of the existence which the drama bestows upon them. And this is due, not to a lack of precision in the drawing, but to the astonishing vitality of the work itself. In truth, the heroes have not finished living; they have not spoken their last word nor made their last movement. They are not yet separated from the general basis of all existence. We cannot judge them nor go round them, because a whole piece of them is still connected with the future. They are incomplete, not from the smaller side of the drama, but from the side of infinity. Characters which we grasp in their entirety, which we analyse with certainty, are already dead. It seems, on the contrary, as if Macbeth and his wife cannot remain motionless in the lines and words that create them. They shift them, stir them with their breath; they pursue their destiny in them and modify their form and meaning. They develop and expand in them as in a vital and nourishing atmosphere, whence they receive the influence of the passing years and centuries and derive unexpected thoughts and sentiments, new greatness and new strength.

—MAURICE MAETERLINCK, "The Tragedy of *Macbeth*," tr. Alexander Teixeira de Mattos, *Fortnightly Review* 93, No. 4 (April 1910): 699–701

SIGMUND FREUD

Shakespeare's *Macbeth* is a *pièce d'occasion*, written for the accession of James, who had hitherto been King of Scotland. The plot was ready-made, and had been handled by other contemporary writers, whose work Shakespeare probably made use of in his customary manner. It offered remarkable analogies to the actual situation. The 'virginal' Elizabeth, of whom it was rumoured that she had never been capable of childbearing and who had once described herself as 'a barren stock', in an anguished outcry at the news of James's birth, was obliged by this very child-lessness of hers to let the Scottish king become her successor. And he was the son of that Mary Stuart whose execution she, though reluctantly, had decreed, and who, despite the clouding of their relations by political concerns, was yet of her blood and might be called her guest.

The accession of James I. was like a demonstration of the curse of unfruitfulness and the blessings reserved for those who carry on the race. And Shakespeare's *Macbeth* develops on the theme of this same contrast. The three Fates, the 'weird sisters', have assured him that he shall indeed be king, but to Banquo they promise that *his* children shall obtain possession of the crown. Macbeth is incensed by this decree of destiny; he is not content with the satisfaction of his own ambition, he desires to found a dynasty and not to have murdered for the benefit of strangers. This point is overlooked when Shakespeare's play is regarded only as a tragedy of ambition. It is clear that Macbeth cannot live for ever, and thus there is but one way for him to disprove that part of the prophecy which opposes his wishes—namely, to have children himself, children who can succeed him. And he seems to expect them from his vigorous wife:

> Bring forth men-children only!
> For thy undaunted mettle should compose
> Nothing but males. . . .   (Act I. Sc. 7.)

And equally it is clear that if he is deceived in this expectation he must submit to destiny; otherwise his actions lose all purpose and are transformed into the blind fury of one doomed to destruction, who is resolved to destroy beforehand all that he can reach. We watch Macbeth undergo this development, and at the height of the tragedy we hear that shattering cry from Macduff, which has often ere now been recognized to have many meanings and possibly to contain the key to the change in Macbeth:

> He has no children!   (Act IV. Sc. 3.)

Undoubtedly that signifies 'Only because he is himself childless could he murder my children'; but more may be implied in it, and above all it might be said to lay bare the essential motive which not only forces Macbeth to go far beyond his own true nature, but also assails the hard character of his wife at its only weak place. If one looks back upon *Macbeth* from the culmination reached in these words of Macduff's, one sees that the whole play is sown with references to the father-and-children relation. The murder of the kindly Duncan is little else than parricide; in Banquo's case, Macbeth kills the father while the son escapes him; and he kills Macduff's children because the father has fled from him. A bloody child, and then a crowned one, are shown him by the witches in the conjuration-scene; the armed head seen previously is doubtless Macbeth's own. But in the background arises the sinister form of the avenger, Macduff, who is himself an exception to the laws of generation, since he was not born of his mother but ripp'd from her womb.

It would be a perfect example of poetic justice in the manner of the talion if the childlessness of Macbeth and the barrenness of his Lady were the punishment for their crimes against the sanctity of geniture—if Macbeth could not become a father because he had robbed children of their father and a father of his children, and if Lady Macbeth had suffered the unsexing she had demanded of the spirits of murder. I believe one could without more ado explain the illness of Lady Macbeth, the transformation of her callousness into penitence, as a reaction to her childlessness, by which she is convinced of her impotence against the decrees of nature, and at the same time admonished that she has only herself to blame if her crime has been barren of the better part of its desired results.

In the *Chronicle* of Holinshed (1577), whence Shakespeare took the plot of *Macbeth,* Lady Macbeth is only once mentioned as the ambitious wife who instigates her husband to murder that she may herself be queen. Of her subsequent fate and of the development of her character there is no word at all. On the other hand, it would seem that there the change in Macbeth to a sanguinary tyrant is motivated just in the way we have suggested. For in Holinshed ten years pass between the murder of Duncan, whereby Macbeth becomes king, and his further misdeeds; and in these ten years he is shown as a stern but righteous ruler. It is not until after this period that the change begins in him, under the influence of the tormenting apprehension that the prophecy to Banquo will be fulfilled as was that of his own destiny. Then only does he contrive the murder of Banquo, and, as in Shakespeare, is driven from one crime to another. Holinshed does not expressly say that it was his childlessness which urged him to these courses, but there is warrant enough—both time and occasion—for this probable motivation. Not so in Shakespeare. Events crowd breathlessly on one another in the tragedy, so that to judge by the statements made by the persons in the play about one week represents the duration of time assigned to it. This acceleration takes the ground from under our attempts at reconstructing the motives for the change in the characters of Macbeth and his wife. There is no time for a long-drawn disappointment of their hopes of offspring to enervate the woman and drive the man to an insane defiance; and it remains impossible to resolve the contradiction that so many subtle interrelations in the plot, and between it and its occasion, point to a common origin of them in the motive of childlessness, and that yet the period of time in the tragedy expressly precludes a development of character from any but a motive contained in the play.

What, however, these motives can have been which in so short a space of time could turn the hesitating, ambitious man into an unbridled tyrant, and his steely-hearted instigator into a sick woman gnawed by remorse, it is, in my view, impossible to divine. I think we must renounce the hope of penetrating the triple obscurity of the bad preservation of the text, the unknown intention of the dramatist, and the hidden purport of the legend. But I should not admit that such investigations are idle in view of the powerful effect which the tragedy has upon the spectator. The dramatist can indeed, during the representation, overwhelm us by his art and paralyse our powers of reflection; but he cannot prevent us from subsequently attempting to grasp the psychological mechanism of that effect. And the contention that the dramatist is at liberty to shorten at will the natural time and duration of the events he brings before us, if by the sacrifice of common probability he can enhance the dramatic effect, seems to me irrelevant in this instance. For such a sacrifice is justified only when it merely affronts probability, and not when it breaks the causal connection; besides, the dramatic effect would hardly have suffered if the time-duration had been left in uncertainty, instead of being expressly limited to some few days.

One is so unwilling to dismiss a problem like that of *Macbeth* as insoluble that I will still make another attempt, by introducing another comment which points towards a new issue. Ludwig Jekels, in a recent Shakespearean study, thinks he has divined a technical trick of the poet, which might have to be reckoned with in *Macbeth,* too. He is of opinion that Shakespeare frequently splits up a character into two personages, each of whom then appears not altogether comprehensible until once more conjoined with the other. It might be thus with Macbeth and the Lady; and then it would of course be futile to regard her as an independent personage and seek to discover her motivation without considering the Macbeth who completes her. I shall not follow this hint any further, but I would add, nevertheless, a remark which strikingly confirms the idea—namely, that the stirrings of fear which arise in Macbeth on the night of the murder, do not develop further in him, but in the Lady. It is he who has the hallucination of the dagger before the deed, but it is she who later succumbs to mental disorder; he, after the murder, hears the cry from the house: 'Sleep no more! Macbeth does murder sleep . . .', and so 'Macbeth shall sleep no more', but we never hear that King Macbeth could not sleep, while we see that the Queen rises from her bed and betrays her guilt in somnambulistic wanderings. He stands helpless with bloody hands, lamenting that not great Neptune's ocean can wash them clean again, while she comforts him: 'A little water clears us of this deed'; but later it is she who washes her hands for a quarter of an hour and cannot get rid of the blood-stains. 'All the perfumes of Arabia will not sweeten this little hand.' Thus is fulfilled in her what his pangs of conscience had apprehended; she is incarnate remorse after the deed, he incarnate defiance— together they exhaust the possibilities of reaction to the crime, like two disunited parts of the mind of a single individuality, and perhaps they are the divided images of a single prototype.

—SIGMUND FREUD, "Some Character-Types Met With in Psycho-Analytic Work"
(1915), *Collected Papers,* tr. Joan Riviere (New York: Basic Books, 1959),
Vol. 4, pp. 328–33

LEVIN L. SCHÜCKING

Macbeth is a character at variance with himself, drawn in opposite directions by conflicting tendencies. For this reason numerous critics speak of the struggle which he has to carry on against his own conscience. But against this view it has been very properly objected that conscience speaks only with a very small voice in Macbeth's bosom, conscience, of course, meaning here the moral reaction of a person against the motives of his own conduct, not the fear of the consequences or the mortification produced by them. It is true that Macbeth is not without a sense of honour, and the meanness of his crime dawns upon him when he reflects, before murdering his guest, the old King Duncan, that

> he's here in double trust:
> First, as I am his kinsman and his subject,
> Strong both against the deed; then, as his host,
> Who should against his murderer shut the door,
> Not bear the knife myself.   (I, vii, 12)

It is undeniable that what looks like a part of his better nature appears here and also in the passage where a stirring of gratitude seems to act as a check to his dark designs:

> We will proceed no further in this business:
> He hath honour'd me of late. . . .   (I, vii, 31)

The more probable explanation is, however, that these are mere transitory emotions in the great volcanic upheaval of his soul and not really firm convictions which, in the struggle between good and bad instincts, have gradually been undermined and overthrown. What always occupies the foreground of his thoughts is the fear of the consequences, the idea

> If it were done, when 't is done, then 't were well
> It were done quickly.   (I, vii, 1)

In the reasons for Macbeth's hesitation the selfish element predominates. The deed itself is not abhorrent to him on moral grounds. Nor is his fear of the consequences in the life after death due to any stirrings of conscience, as Siburg has rightly maintained against Vischer (*Shakespeare Vorträge,* ii, 80). What we find there are cool deliberations whether the deed is advisable nor not, shrewd reflections that, as a rule, retribution overtakes the evil-doer already in this life:

> . . . that we but teach
> Bloody instructions, which, being taught, return
> To plague th' inventor.   (I, vii, 7)

Caution warns him that the violent death of the kind old king will arouse in his subjects a measure of compassion most dangerous to the murderer; he becomes apprehensive that he may lose the popularity newly won by his victories; and other more or less practical considerations flash through his mind.

Are we to suppose, then, that Macbeth's mental process is merely a cool, businesslike calculation? Certainly not; but neither is the contrary true, namely, that his is a struggle between good and bad instincts. In reality he is fighting against his own weakness; and it is just in this that we recognize the peculiar Shakespearean quality of the character.

In his original source, Holinshed's *Chronicles,* Shakespeare found a man who was credited with the highest warlike achievements, but whose hardness and cruelty, unusual even for that period, are several times mentioned. Had he dealt with this character more than a decade earlier it would most probably have become a thick-skinned brute of the stamp of Richard III; for, like Schiller, Shakespeare might have said of himself: "The older I get the more my stock of caricatures diminishes." By this time he had passed the youthful stage in which he, like every other man, gets his views of reality from the study of models; he is observing life itself more closely and drawing directly from it; he is especially attracted by hidden psychological correspondences. This makes him study his original in quite a different way; he finds in it that the prophecy of the fatal sisters goes on rankling in the King's mind, and also that the murder of King Duncan is due principally to the instigation of his ambitious wife. It is here that we must look for the germ from which sprang the conception of the character of a man of unusual bravery who yet does not initiate his own actions, but receives and must receive the decisive impulse from without, consequently a man who is dependent on his human environment, in certain aspects a weak man. We can now understand that this problem begins to exert a much greater attraction for Shakespeare at a time when he himself and the public have grown tired of purely historical subjects. Moreover, a sharp contrast of this sort producing cross-currents in a complex mind is what interests him most in this period of his dramatic activity: inborn weakness and the desire for action in Hamlet, tenderest love and the desire to kill in Othello, the supreme strength of the conqueror of the world and doting feebleness in Antony.

In Macbeth we may see, if we choose, a special family likeness to Hamlet, but certainly not his counterpart, as Brandes, copying Gervinus (iii, p. 307 seq.), would make him (p. 592). It was Gervinus who first stamped the figure of Macbeth with a character which has been accepted by the most notable among his successors. According to him Macbeth is "a man of the ancient energy of the heroic races," a "heathenish and savage" fellow, he has "the simple and unaffected nature of the true soldier." We find the same view in Ulrici (ii, 113), to whom he appears as a heroic character of ancient Northern strength and endurance; in Kreyssig, who calls him "a simple nature full of primitive energy and robust virility," an "unbroken and un-spoiled character" (p. 151 seq.); and finally in Brandes, who has largely incorporated Kreyssig's ideas in his own work, and who describes him as a rude, simple warrior, a man of action, whose inclination is to strike and not to engage in long delibera-tions.

It is interesting to see how these interpreters account for the terrors that haunt Macbeth. The explanation they give is simple enough: these states are due to the "paralysing power of his imagination" (Gervinus, p. 132). "He is bold, he is ambitious, he is a man of action," says H. Cuningham (in the introduction to the "Arden" edition, xlv), "but he is also, within limits, a man of imagination. Through his vivid imagination he is kept in touch with supernatural impressions and is liable to supernatural fears." Almost the same view was taken by Ulrici (p. 109) of Macbeth's fear of failure, which he attributes to his quick and uncontrollable imagination. But is not this reversing the natural order of things—i.e., mixing up the cause and the effect? Surely there can be no doubt that terrifying visions are produced by fear, not *vice versa!* It is weakness that sees spectres, not strength. Sir Walter Raleigh (1909, p. 17) likewise depicts Macbeth as a character chiefly dominated by imagi-nation, and for this reason puts him in the same category with Richard II and

Hamlet. We know, however, that those two figures also are remarkable for their weakness of will (cf. p. 168 seq.). In itself, as experience shows, imagination is not incompatible with strength. Imaginative people, on the contrary, may act with the utmost temerity. A man, however, in whose imagination terrifying images predominate may safely be regarded as the very opposite of a heroic character of ancient Northern strength and endurance.

The truth is, this whole conception is based upon a misunderstanding. It is due to an excessive contemplation of the warlike achievements and personal bravery of the man, and it confounds physical and moral courage. Macbeth certainly is a lion on the field of battle; open and visible dangers leave him unmoved. But this is not incompatible with the fact that, at heart, he is greatly dependent on other people, is always a prey to fear, and feels himself helpless in every moral conflict into which his own actions lead him. This weakness grows out of a nervous disposition which under the influence of strong impressions may produce highly morbid mental states. Naturally these have also been noticed by the critics of Macbeth, for the most part, however, only in those cases where they assume quite grotesque forms, as, for example, when immediately before the murder of Duncan Macbeth is terrified by the image of a bloody dagger hovering in the air in front of his eyes. A more attentive observer, however, will receive a correct impression of Macbeth's character at his very first appearance. To him and Banquo the weird sisters appear on the empty heath and salute him with the threefold title. Their greeting does not cause him any surprise or astonishment, but evidently makes him give such a perceptible start and sends such a shudder through his frame that Banquo, wondering what is the matter, asks him:

Good sir, why do you start, and seem to fear
Things that do sound so fair?   (I, iii)

If we inquire what is the reason of this tremendous effect produced by the prophetic words upon his whole being, we are told by the critics (Kreyssig, ii, 150 v. Friesen, iii, 162 seq.) that it is the sudden revelation, which like a flash of lightning illuminates his soul, of all his secret and slumbering wishes. This is true enough; but the same experience would affect another type of character in quite a different way. Even if a train of thought ending in the idea of a crime were set going in the mind of a criminal he would not necessarily be seized by such a sudden fright, unless he habitually suffered from what the Germans call *Furcht vor der eigenen Courage*. This, indeed, is the mental condition of Macbeth.

It is only after Banquo, perfectly cool and self-possessed, has taken his turn in asking information of the unearthly creatures about his own future and has received his answer that Macbeth recovers from his shock and once more addresses them, but in vain. They disappear, and he is again alone with Banquo. His whole mind is filled with what he has heard. But it is characteristic of him that he does not dare openly to confess what is going on within him. From the very beginning we find something close and suspicious in the man. As Siburg very cleverly remarks, his real motive in observing to Banquo, "Your children shall be kings," is to make his companion repeat once more the dazzling promise. When Banquo promptly replies, "You shall be king," he quickly adds,

> And thane of Cawdor too; went it not so?

betraying by his eagerness how little he is thinking of Banquo's future and how much he is occupied with his own fate. This first impression of Macbeth is confirmed and completed by the soliloquy which soon follows. Whereas Banquo has remained perfectly calm at the quick fulfilment of the first prophecy, Macbeth shows the excessive irritability of his nervous system by getting into an extreme state of excitement. We see that the very first emergence of the criminal thought marks the beginning of the fight against his nerves; he speaks of that suggestion

> Whose horrid image doth unfix my hair
> And make my seated heart knock at my ribs
> Against the use of nature.   (I, iv, 135)

The emotion, evidently, is so strong that his whole appearance is changed. He is so little able to control himself that his companions, of whom he is entirely oblivious, notice his state and Banquo with great astonishment calls attention to his "rapt" expression (I, iii, 57 and 142), which v. Friesen rightly likens to that of a man who is drunk. The excuse which he then offers them contains an untruth:

> Give me your favour: my dull brain was wrought
> With things forgotten.   (I, iii, 149)

Like all weak characters, Macbeth is a liar. Therefore, when Banquo immediately before the murder scene reminds him of the three weird sisters he replies, disagreeably moved by this thought at this moment: "I think not of them" (II, i, 21). The enormous irritability from which Macbeth suffers leaves its traces on his countenance, which, to the great vexation of his wife, again and again most distinctly reflects the inner workings of his mind. Again and again she is obliged to warn him to put on a different expression (I, iv, 62 seq.; III, ii, 27). When he thinks he sees the ghost of Banquo he completely loses control over his features, and his face becomes so contorted that his wife in a mixture of fear and rage shouts at him:

> Shame itself!
> Why do you make such faces?   (III, iv, 66)

The critics (Gervinus, Brandes, etc.) find in his inability to control his facial expression an indication of a straightforward and natural character. But we may be certain that Macbeth, who, as we have seen, was not afraid of a lie, would willingly and without any scruples have changed the appearance of his face had he been able to do so. The fact of the matter is, however, that here, as in all other cases, he is a victim of his nerves. No doubt of their diseased condition can arise when we find him suffering from unmistakable hallucinations of the visual and auditory organs, when he sees the bloody dagger, hears voices after the murder, and finally is confronted with the ghost of Banquo, his victim, sitting upon his own chair. The words with which on this last occasion Lady Macbeth addresses the alarmed guests,

Sit, worthy friends. My lord is often thus,
And hath been from his youth: pray you, keep seat;
The fit is momentary: upon a thought
He will again be well, (III, iv, 53)

sound like an excuse invented for the moment, and this may be really the case; but, after all, there is nothing absolutely impossible in the explanation, though it is certain that the fearful excitement consequent upon the second murder has once more caused his natural tendencies to break out with unusual violence.

As Macbeth takes so little account of his nerves we should not be surprised if he fell a victim to them, as he occasionally seems to be on the point of doing, especially as he is tormented by sleeplessness (III, iv). But in the end he becomes master of his over-excited nerves, though not of his inner unrest, which drives him on from crime to crime. He grows accustomed to wickedness, his mind is hardened and at last completely blunted, whereas his wife, who, hard as she is, has over-taxed her nature, goes the opposite way. He himself has the feeling that his frenzied excitement is principally called forth by his inexperience of his murderous trade.

My strange and self-abuse
Is the initiate fear, that wants hard use:
We are yet but young in deed,

he says (III, iv, 142) with a certain cynical humour. Finally, however, when he is brought to bay like a wild beast and has to fight for his life, his personal courage once more appears and sends the calm of a firm resolve through his whole nature. We know that weak men often, when no choice remains to them, cast behind them all hesitation and irresolution. Macbeth becomes conscious of the great change which has taken place within him, as we see from the words:

I have almost forgot the taste of fears.
The time has been, my senses would have cool'd
To hear a night-shriek; and my fell of hair
Would at a dismal treatise rouse, and stir
As life were in 't. I have supp'd full with horrors:
Direness, familiar to my slaughterous thoughts,
Cannot once start me. (V, v, 9)

But this reflection and the courage with which he faces his end cannot conceal from us the extraordinary weakness and lack of assurance which are prominent features of his character. Against these, rather than against any good part of his nature, he struggles. Critics who are unwilling to abandon their belief in the essential nobility of his nature have desperately tried to save their theory by discrediting his words about himself. Henry Cuningham, for instance, says (p. xlv) that Macbeth's character is not understood either by himself or by Lady Macbeth; his better nature incorporates itself in images which alarm and terrify instead of speaking to him in the language of moral ideas and commands. This process of disguising his better self, however, quite apart from the psychological improbability, is so complicated and puzzling that we can hardly credit a popular dramatist with employing it. Moreover, we have to ask why this better nature of the hero does not appear on any other occasion. These undeniable facts render improbable any view except the one we have taken. The strongly marked, single ambitious impulses of Macbeth are not co-ordinated into one great and continued effort of will. This peculiarity Shakespeare, true to his usual technique, several times describes in plain words, for example when Macbeth is blamed for being "infirm of purpose" (II, ii, 51), and when he himself speaks of having "no spur to prick the sides of my intent, but only vaulting ambition" (I, vii, 26), thus comparing himself to a lazy horse requiring to be spurred. We could not imagine a clearer demonstration of this weakness than his wishing, in the very moment when the murder of King Duncan has been effected, that it had never been committed (II, ii, 73).

—LEVIN L. SCHÜCKING, *Character Problems in Shakespeare's Plays*
(London: George G. Harrap & Co., 1922), pp. 71–80

G. WILSON KNIGHT

The central human theme—the temptation and crime of Macbeth—is ⟨. . .⟩ easy of analysis. The crucial speech runs as follows:

> Why do I yield to that suggestion,
> Whose horrid image doth unfix my hair,
> And makes my seated heart knock at my ribs
> Against the use of nature? Present fears
> Are less than horrible imaginings.
> My thought whose murder yet is but fantastical
> Shakes so my single state of man that function
> Is smother'd in surmise, and nothing is
> But what is not.   (I. iii. 134)

These lines, spoken when Macbeth first feels the impending evil, expresses again all those elements I have noticed in the mass-effect of the play: questioning doubt, horror, fear of some unknown power; horrible imaginings of the supernatural and 'fantastical'; an abysm of unreality; disorder on the plane of physical life. This speech is a microcosm of the *Macbeth* vision: it contains the germ of the whole. Like a stone in a pond, this original immediate experience of Macbeth sends ripples of itself expanding over the whole play. This is the moment of the birth of evil in *Macbeth*—he may have had ambitious thoughts before, may even have intended the murder, but now for the first time he feels its oncoming reality. This is the mental experience which he projects into action, thereby plunging his land, too, in fear, horror, darkness, and disorder. In this speech we have a swift interpenetration of idea with idea, from fear and disorder, through sickly imaginings, to abysmal darkness, nothingness. 'Nothing is but what is not': that is the text of the play. Reality and unreality change places. We must see that Macbeth, like the whole universe of this play, is paralysed, mesmerized, as though in a dream. This is not merely 'ambition'—it is fear, a nameless fear which yet fixes itself to a horrid image. He is helpless as a man in a nightmare: and this helplessness is integral to the conception— the will-concept is absent. Macbeth may struggle, but he cannot fight: he can no more resist than a rabbit resists a weasel's teeth fastened in its neck, or a bird the serpent's transfixing eye. Now this evil in Macbeth propels him to an act absolutely evil. For, though no ethical system is ultimate, Macbeth's crime is as near absolute as may be. It is therefore conceived as absolute. Its dastardly nature is emphasized clearly (I. vii. 12–25): Duncan is old, good; he is at once Macbeth's kinsman, king, and guest; he is to be murdered in sleep. No worse act of evil could well be found. So the evil of which Macbeth is at first aware rapidly entraps him in a mesh of events: it makes a tool of Duncan's visit, it dominates Lady Macbeth. It is significant that she, like her husband, is influenced by the Weird Sisters and their prophecy. Eventually Macbeth undertakes the murder, as a grim and hideous duty. He cuts a sorry figure at first, but, once embarked on his allegiant enterprise of evil, his grandeur grows. Throughout he is driven by fear—the fear that paralyses everyone else urges him to an amazing and mysterious action of blood. This action he repeats, again and again.

By his original murder he isolates himself from humanity. He is lonely, endures the uttermost torture of isolation. Yet still a bond unites him to men: that bond he would 'cancel and tear to pieces'—the natural bond of human fellowship and love. He further symbolizes his guilty, pariah soul by murdering Banquo. He fears everyone outside himself but his wife, suspects them. Every act of blood is driven by fear of the horrible disharmony existent between himself and his world. He tries to harmonize the relation by murder. He would let 'the frame of things disjoint, both the worlds suffer' (III. ii. 16) to win back peace. He is living in an unreal world, a fantastic mockery, a ghoulish dream: he strives to make this single nightmare to rule the outward things of his nation. He would make all Scotland a nightmare thing of dripping blood. He knows he cannot return, so determines to go o'er. He seeks out the Weird Sisters a second time. Now he welcomes disorder and confusion, would let them range wide over the earth, since they range unfettered in his own soul:

> . . . though the treasure
> Of nature's germens tumble all together,
> Even till destruction sicken; answer me
> To what I ask you.   (IV. i. 58)

So he addresses the Weird Sisters. Castles, palaces, and pyramids—let all fall in general confusion, if only Macbeth be satisfied. He is plunging deeper and deeper into unreality, the severance from mankind and all normal forms of life is now abysmal, deep. Now he is shown Apparitions glassing the future. They promise him success in terms of natural law; no man 'of woman born' shall hurt him, he shall not be vanquished till Birnam Wood come against him. He, based firmly in the unreal, yet thinks to build his future on the laws of reality. He forgets that he is trafficking with things of nightmare fantasy, whose truth is falsehood, falsehood truth. That success they promise is unreal as they themselves. So, once having cancelled the bond of reality he has no home: the unreal he understands not, the real condemns him. In neither can he exist. He asks if Banquo's issue shall reign in Scotland: most horrible thought to him, since, if that be so, it proves that the future takes its natural course irrespective of human acts—that prophecy need not have been interpreted into crime: that he would in truth have been King of Scotland without his own 'stir' (I. iii. 144). Also the very thought of other succeeding and prosperous kings, some of them with 'twofold balls and treble sceptres' (IV. i. 121), is a maddening thing to him who is no real king but only monarch of a nightmare realm. The Weird Sisters who were formerly as the three Parcae, or Fates, foretelling Macbeth's future, now, at this later stage of his story, become the Erinyes, avengers of murder, symbols of the tormented soul. They delude and madden him with their apparitions and ghosts. Yet he does not give way, and raises our admiration at his undaunted severance from good. He contends for his own individual soul against the universal reality. Nor is his nightmare fear of his life—he goes on 'till destruction sicken' (IV. i. 60): he actually does 'go o'er'—is not lost in the stream of blood he elects to cross. It is true. He wins his battle. He adds crime to crime and emerges at last victorious and fearless:

> I have almost forgot the taste of fears:
> The time has been, my senses would have cool'd
> To hear a night-shriek; and my fell of hair
> Would at a dismal treatise rouse and stir
> As life were in't; I have supp'd full with horrors;
> Direness, familiar to my slaughterous thoughts,
> Cannot once start me.   (V. v. 9)

Again, 'Hang those that talk of fear!' (V. iii. 36) he cries, in an ecstasy of courage. He is, at last, 'broad and general as the casing air' (III. iv. 23).

This will appear a strange reversal of the usual commentary; it is, however, true and necessary. Whilst Macbeth lives in conflict with himself there is misery, evil, fear: when, at the end, he and others have openly identified himself with evil, he faces the world fearless: nor does he appear evil any longer. The worst element of his suffering has been that secrecy and hypocrisy so often referred to throughout the play (I. iv. 12; I. v. 64; III. ii. 34; V. iii. 27). Dark secrecy and night are in Shakespeare ever the badges of crime. But at the end Macbeth has no need of secrecy. He is no longer 'cabin'd, cribb'd, confined, bound in to saucy doubts and fears' (III. iv. 24). He has won through by excessive crime to an harmonious and honest relation with his surroundings. He has successfully symbolized the disorder of his lonely guilt-stricken soul by creating disorder in the world, and thus restores balance and harmonious contact. The mighty principle of good planted in the nature of things then asserts itself, condemns him openly, brings him peace. Daylight is brought to Macbeth, as to Scotland, by the accusing armies of Malcolm. He now knows himself to be a tyrant confessed, and wins back that integrity of soul which gives us:

> I have lived long enough: my way of life
> Is fallen into the sere, the yellow leaf ...   (V. iii. 22)

Here he touches a recognition deeper than fear, more potent than nightmare. The delirious dream is over. A clear daylight now disperses the imaginative dark that has eclipsed Scotland. The change is remarkable. There is now movement, surety and purpose, colour: horses 'skirr the country round' (V. iii. 35), banners are hung out on the castle walls (V. v. 1), soldiers hew down the bright leaves of Birnam (V. iv. 5). There is, as it were, a paean of triumph as the *Macbeth* universe, having struggled darkly upward, now climbs into radiance. Though they oppose each other in fight, Macbeth and Malcolm share equally in this relief, this awakening from horror. Of a piece with this change is the fulfilment of the Weird Sisters' prophecies. In bright daylight the nightmare reality to which Macbeth has been subdued is insubstantial and transient as sleep-horrors at dawn. Their unreality is emphasized by the very fact that they are nevertheless related to natural phenomena: they are thus parasitic on reality. To these he has trusted, and they fail. But he himself is, at the last, self-reliant and courageous. The words of the Weird Sisters ring true:

> Though his bark cannot be lost
> Yet it shall be tempest-toss'd.   (I. iii. 24)

Each shattering report he receives with redoubled life-zest; and meets the fate marked out by the daylight consciousness of normal man for the nightmare reality of crime. Malcolm may talk of 'this dead butcher and his fiend-like queen' (V. vii. 98). We, who have felt the sickly poise over the abysmal deeps of evil, the hideous reality of the unreal, must couch our judgement in a different phrase.

—G. WILSON KNIGHT, "Macbeth and the Metaphysic of Evil,"
The Wheel of Fire (1930; 4th rev. ed. London: Methuen, 1949), pp. 152–57

STEPHEN SPENDER

I do not know whether any Shakespearean critic has ever pointed out the significant part played by ideas of time in *Macbeth*.

One often hears quoted:

> Come what may
> Time and the hour runs through the roughest day.

Actually the tragedy of Macbeth is his discovery that this is untrue.

Macbeth and Lady Macbeth are as haunted as James Joyce and Proust by the sense of time. After she has received his letter describing the meeting with the witches, Lady Macbeth's first words to her husband are:

... Thy letters have transported me beyond
The ignorant present, and I feel now
The future in the instant.

Their trouble is though that the future does not exist in the instant. There is
another very unpleasant instant preceding it which has to be acted on—the murder
of Duncan.

In the minds of Macbeth and Lady Macbeth there are, after the prophetic
meeting with the weird sisters, three kinds of time: the time before the murder, the
time of the murder of Duncan, and the enjoyable time afterwards when they reap
the fruits of the murder. Their problem is to keep these three times separate and
not to allow them to affect each other. If they can prevent their minds showing the
sense of the future before the murder, and of the past, after it, they will have
achieved happiness. As soon as the murder has been decided on, Lady Macbeth
scents the danger:

Your face, my thane, is as a book where men
May read strange matters: to beguile the time,
Look like the time.

How little Macbeth succeeds in this, we gather from his soliloquy before the
murder:

If it were done—when 'tis done—then 'twere well
If it were done quickly: if the assassination
Could trammel up the consequence, and catch
With his surcease, success: that but this blow
Might be the be-all and the end-all here,
But here upon this bank and shoal of time,
We'ld jump the life to come. But in these cases
We still have judgement here; that we but teach
Bloody instructions, which, being taught, return
To plague th' inventor.

Macbeth certainly has good reason to fear 'even-handed justice.' But, I think, the
second part of this speech is only a rationalization of his real fear, as unconvincing
in its way as Hamlet's reasons against self-murder. The real fear is far more terrible:
it is a fear of the extension into infinity of the instant in which he commits the
murder. 'The bank and shoal of time' is time that has stood still; beyond it lies the
abyss of a timeless moment.

He loses his nerve, but Lady Macbeth rallies him:

When you durst do it, then you were a man;
And, to be more than what you were you would
Be so much more the man. Nor time nor place
Did then adhere, and yet you would make both:
They have made themselves, and that their fitness now
Does unmake you.

She forces his mind upon the conjunction of time and place which may never occur again. They never do, indeed, recur. The murder of Banquo is ill-timed, Malcolm escapes, everything is botched, and Macbeth swears that after this he will carry out those crimes which are the 'firstlings of his heart.'

The soliloquy in which Macbeth sees the dagger before him is the first of his hallucinations. Yet the delusion is not complete. He is able to dismiss it from his mind, and he does so by fixing down the time and place, in order to restore his mind to sanity.

> There's no such thing:
> It is the bloody season which informs
> Thus to mine eyes. Now o'er the one half world
> Nature seems dead.

He reminds himself of the exact time of night, and this calms him. He invokes the hour, and he invokes the place, with a reason: to relegate this moment preceding the murder to the past from which it cannot ever escape into a future. As some people say, 'I will remember this moment for the rest of my life,' Macbeth tries to say, 'I will uproot this moment from my memory.'

> Thou sure and firm-set earth,
> Hear not my steps, which way they walk, for fear
> Thy very stones prate of my whereabout,
> And take the present horror from the time
> Which now suits with it.

He is more afraid of the associations of the stones than any evidence they may actually reveal to living witnesses.

Immediately after the murder we are left in no doubt that Macbeth and Lady Macbeth have failed in their main purpose of killing in memory the moment of the murder itself.

Macbeth tells his wife how he could not say 'Amen' to the prayer of the man in his sleep. 'Amen' is the conclusion of prayer, which is inconcludable. 'Methought I heard a voice cry, "Sleep no more! Macbeth does murder sleep." '

There is no 'Amen' nor night of sleep which will ever end that moment which opens wider and wider as the play proceeds. Macbeth's speech in the next scene is a naif deception, which happens also to be the truth wrung from his heart:

> Had I but lived an hour before this chance,
> I had lived a blessed time.

With this he tries to fob off his followers. Meanwhile, one is left in some doubt as to Lady Macbeth's state of mind. The Sleepwalking scene is a shocking revelation which shows that the moment when she smeared the faces of the grooms has died no more for her than has the murder for Macbeth. 'Here's the smell of blood still.' The ailment of indestructible time is revealed by Macbeth to the doctor:

Canst thou not minister to a mind diseased;
Pluck from the memory a rooted sorrow;
Raze out the written troubles of the brain;
And with some sweet oblivious antidote
Cleanse the stuft bosom of that perilous stuff
Which weighs upon the heart?

Thus, after the murder the past comes to life again and asserts itself amid the general disintegration. An old man appears on the stage to compare the horrors of the past with the monstrosities of the present. Ross says:

By the clock 'tis day,
And yet dark night strangles the travelling lamp.

The present disgorges the past. The horror of not being able to live down his deeds is symbolized by the appearance of Banquo's ghost. Macbeth looks back on a time when the past was really past and the present present:

The time has been
That, when the brains were out, the man would die,
And there an end.

There is no end within the control of Macbeth. In the fourth act, we even have a feeling that everything has stopped. The play seems to spread out, burning up and destroying a wider and wider area, without moving forward.

'To-morrow, and to-morrow and to-morrow' is not merely the speech of a disillusioned tyrant destroyed by the horror which he has himself created; it has a profound irony, coming from Macbeth's mouth, because he of all people ought to have been able to make to-morrow different from to-day and yesterday. But all his violence has done is to create a deathly sameness.

—STEPHEN SPENDER, "Time, Violence and Macbeth," *Penguin New Writing*
No. 3 (February 1941): 120–25

H. B. CHARLTON

Holinshed gives to Shakespeare the main traits of Macbeth's personality and the main sequence of the incidents of Macbeth's life. But in one significant episode, particularly significant for his purpose, Shakespeare supplements Holinshed's record of Macbeth by bringing into it details of a similar episode in which another of Holinshed's Scottish kings had been involved. The chronicler records that Macbeth coveted the crown, and how

the woords of the three weird sisters also (of whom before ye have heard) greatlie incouraged him hereunto, but speciallie his wife lay sore upon him to attempt the thing, as she that was verie ambitious, burning in unquenchable desire to beare the name of a queene. At length therefore [as the record forthwith and summarily puts it], communicating his purposed intent with his trustie friends, amongst whome Banquho was the chiefest, upon confidence of their promised aid, he slue the king at Enverns [Inverness]. (Boswell Stone, *Shakspere's Holinshed* (1896), p. 25.)

That is all that is told of the murder. But Shakespeare wanted to see more of the inward stirrings within the murderer, the promptings which preceded the murder and the reactions as the deed itself was being performed. He found material which he could employ in another chapter of the chronicle, where Holinshed tells of another Scottish regicide, Donwald, who slew King Duff, and, like Macbeth, had been goaded to the murder 'through setting on of his wife.' This Donwald felt that the king had slighted his family, and so

> conceived such an inward malice towards the king (though he shewed it not outwardlie at the first) that the same continued still boiling in his stomach, and ceased not, till through setting on of his wife, and in revenge of such unthank-fulnesse, hee found meanes to murther the king within the foresaid castell of Fores where he used to soiourne. [King Duff] oftentimes used to lodge in his house [Donwald's castle at Forres] without anie gard about him, other than the garrison of the castell which was wholie at his [Donwald's] commandement.

So Donwald's wife 'ceassed not to travell with him', and counselled him to make Duff away, showing him 'the meanes wherby he might soonest accomplish it'.

> Donwald thus being the more kindled in wrath by the words of his wife, determined to follow hir advise in the execution of so heinous an act. Wherupon devising with himselfe for a while, which way hee might best accomplish his curssed intent, at length gat opportunitie.

On the last day of the king's stay with them, when he had retired 'into his privie chamber, onelie with two of his chamberlains, who having brought him to bed, came foorth againe', Donwald and his wife 'had preapred diverse delicate dishes and sundrie sorts of drinks for their reare supper or collation'; they invited the chamberlains to the 'blanketting',

> whereat they sate up so long, till they had charged their stomachs with such full gorges that their heads were no sooner got to the pillow, but asleepe they were so fast, that a man might have remooved the chamber over them, sooner than to have awaked them out of their droonken sleepe.

This was Donwald's opportunity, though he had not cast himself to be the actual murderer.

> Then Donwald, though he abhorred the act greatlie in heart, yet through instigation of his wife hee called foure of his servants whom he had made privie to his wicked intent before...[and they] speedilie going about the murther...secretlie cut his [the king's] throte as he lay sleeping, without anie buskling at all.

They disposed of the corpse according to an arranged plan. Meanwhile

> Donwald, about the time that the murther was in dooing, got him amongst
> them that kept the watch, and so continued in companie with them all the
> residue of the night. But in the morning when the noise was raised in the king's
> chamber how the king was slaine . . . he with the watch ran thither as though
> he had knowne nothing of the matter, and breaking into the chamber . . . he
> foorthwith slue the chamberleins, as guiltie of that heinous murther.

Here, clearly, is an account of an act of regicide which Shakespeare could easily fit
into his *Macbeth:* its facts fill out the detail of incident which Holinshed had not
attached to his Macbeth story, and, still more, it suggests lines of enquiry into the
murderer's motive. Donwald had some grounds for resentment; his wife fostered
and nourished them; he himself 'abhorred the act greatlie in heart', and he planned
for the deed itself to be done by suborned assassins. The whole situation is charged
with promptings to stir Shakespeare's imagination to those psychological explorations which reproduced his own Macbeth.

Holinshed's Macbeth is hardly harassed at all by inner perturbations and
doubts. He is a natural leader 'of such valiant and hardie men of warre as the Scots
were': 'he was a valiant gentleman and one that if he had not beene somewhat
cruell of nature, might have beene thought most worthie the government of a
realme.' He complained bitterly against Duncan's 'softnes and overmuch slacknesse
in punishing offendors.' When, at the king's request, he took charge of a punitive
expedition against rebels who also regarded Duncan as 'a faint-hearted milkesop,
more meet to governe a sort of idle monks in some cloister' than to rule a kingdom,
he was utterly ruthless, 'remitting no peece of his cruel nature' in the barbarous
measures he employed. Returning with Banquo from a later expedition in which he
had 'made such slaughter on all sides without anie resistance that it was a woonder-
full matter to behold', he met 'three women in strange and wild apparell, ressem-
bling creatures of elder world', and heard their prophecies. In reply to Banquo's
questioning after their prophesying, the first of the witches answered Banquo:

> Yes, we promise greater benefits unto thee than unto him, for he shall reigne
> in deed, but with an unluckie end, neither shall he leave anie issue behind him
> to succeed in his place, where contrarilie thou in deed shalt not reigne at all,
> but of thee those shall be borne which shall governe the Scotish kingdome by
> long order of continuall descent.

When two of these prophecies had come true,

> Mackbeth revolving the thing in his mind, began even then to devise how he
> might atteine to the kingdome: but yet he thought with himself that he must
> tarie a time, which should advance him thereto (by the divine providence) as
> it had come to passe in his former preferment.

There is a complacent resignation to the Almighty's rule in this, which is utterly
different from the self-cowed inertia of Macbeth's:

If chance will have me king, why, chance may crown me
Without my stir. (*Macbeth* I. iii. 143)

But shortly afterwards, Duncan promoted his elder son Malcolm prince of Cumberland 'as it were thereby to appoint him his successor in the kingdome'. Macbeth was sore troubled by this—and apparently it would seem to have been an attempt to forestall the old laws of the realm, which barred succession to a minor. So regarding this as a 'just quarrell', and encouraged by the words of the witches, and still more pushed on by his wife's ambition, he murdered Duncan. He was confirmed in the kingship, and for some years ruled diligently and well, suppressing evil-doers, causing 'young men to exercise themselves in vertuous maners, and men of the church to attend their divine service according to their vocations', so that, in sum, the country enjoyed 'the blisseful benefit of good peace and tranquilitie'.

> To be briefe such were the woorthie dooings and princelie acts of this Mackbeth in the administration of the realme, that if he had atteined thereunto by rightfull means, and continued in uprightnesse of justice as he began, till the end of his reigne, he might well have beene numbred amongest the most noble princes that anie where had reigned.... But this was but a counterfet zeale of equitie shewed by him, partlie against his naturall inclination, to purchase thereby the favour of the people. Shortlie after, he began to shew what he was, in stead of equitie practising crueltie.... The pricke of conscience (as it chanceth ever in tyrants, and such as atteine to anie estate by unrighteous means) caused him ever to feare, least he should be served of the same cup, as he had ministered to his predecessor.

So he plotted to murder Banquo and Fleance. 'By the helpe of almightie God reserving him to better fortune', Fleance escaped.

> After the contrived slaughter of Banquho nothing prospered with the foresaid Makbeth: for in maner everie man began to doubt his owne life, and durst unneth appeare in the kings presence; and even as there were manie that stood in feare of him, so likewise stood he in feare of manie, in such sort that he began to make those awaie by one surmized cavillation or other, whom he thought most able to worke him anie displeasure. At length he found such sweetnesse by putting his nobles thus to death, that his earnest thirst after bloud in this behalfe might in no wise be satisfied.

The whole story thus told, Holinshed has no difficulty in recognising its fitness with the eternal scheme of things.

> In the beginning of his reigne he accomplished manie woorthie acts, verie profitable to the common-wealth (as ye have heard) but afterward, by the illusion of the divell, he defamed the same with most terrible crueltie.

But when Shakespeare took the story into drama, he made Macbeth an intelligible embodiment of the human spirit, and Macbeth's world a universe whose operative principles could be seen in action as an inevitable and a necessary order.

—H. B. CHARLTON, *Shakespearian Tragedy* (Cambridge: Cambridge University Press, 1948), pp. 155–60

EUGENE M. WAITH

In *Macbeth,* more clearly than in *Hamlet,* there is an explicit contrast between two ideals of manhood. Macbeth is a soldier whose valor we hear praised throughout the play. To the "bleeding Sergeant" he is "brave Macbeth," to Duncan "valiant cousin, worthy gentleman"; Ross calls him "Bellona's bridegroom." To be courageous is to be "manly," as the soldier understands that word, and hence at the end of the play, when Macduff reveals the fatal circumstances of his birth, Macbeth says that the news has "cow'd my better part of man," to which Macduff replies, "Then yield thee, coward" (V, viii, 18, 23). After the death of the hero physical valor is given final emphasis in a speech of Ross to Siward:

> Your son, my lord, has paid a soldier's debt.
> He only liv'd but till he was a man,
> The which no sooner had his prowess confirm'd
> In the unshrinking station where he fought
> But like a man he died.   (V, viii, 39–43)

In all these comments there is implied one ideal—the soldier's, or as Plutarch says, the Roman's ideal—of what it is to be a man. Lady Macbeth clearly subscribes to it when she urges her husband to "screw his courage to the sticking place." In her speeches she makes explicit the contrast between the sexes which underlies this concept of manhood. To strengthen her resolve she appeals to the spirits to "unsex me here":

> Come to my woman's breasts
> And take my milk for gall. . . .   (I, v, 48–9)

She fears that Macbeth has too much of the "milk of human kindness," and he himself says to her,

> Bring forth men-children only;
> For thy undaunted mettle should compose
> Nothing but males.   I, vii, 72–4)

Thus not to be a man is to be effeminate.

In this same scene, however, Macbeth introduces another antithesis—that of man and beast. When Lady Macbeth taunts him for his cowardice, he replies,

Who dares do more is none.
I dare do all that may become a man.   (I, vii, 46–7)

That Lady Macbeth understands his implication is clear from her scoffing question:

What beast was't then
That made you break this enterprise to me?   (I, vii, 47–8)

The important point is that Macbeth's distinction rests, as we can see from his soliloquy at the opening of the scene, upon his awareness of the moral nature of man. His mental torment grows out of the conflict between the narrow concept of man as the courageous male and the more inclusive concept of man as a being whose moral nature distinguishes him from the beasts. The first is that debased ideal of manhood censured by Milles, while the second is the "reall excellencie of humaine Nature" based on "another kinde of strength and courage, then that which is proper to brute Beasts onely."

Shakespeare keeps the two concepts before us throughout the play. The pangs of Macbeth's conscience after the murder (note his inability to say "amen") are no more than effeminate or childish fears to Lady Macbeth (II, ii). In urging his hired assassins to the murder of Banquo, Macbeth echos his wife, contrasting patience and piety with the manhood necessary to perform the bloody deed (III, i). When Banquo's ghost brings on Macbeth's "fit," Lady Macbeth asks him, "Are you a man?" And then:

O, these flaws and starts
(Impostors to true fear) would well become
A woman's story at a winter's fire....
What, quite unmann'd in folly?   (III, iv, 63–5, 73)

Macbeth says, "What man dare I dare" (III, iv. 99).

In the puzzling scene (IV, iii) in which Malcolm tests Macduff, Macbeth's formidable antagonist is established as the exact antithesis of the sort of man Lady Macbeth admires. When Malcolm accuses himself of all Macbeth's sins, Macduff demonstrates his "truth and honor" by his horrified rejection of Malcolm, and thus reveals the moral qualifications of "true" manhood. Then, when Ross tells him of the murders of Lady Macduff and of his children, Macduff appears so overwhelmed by grief that Malcolm says to him, "Dispute it like a man." His reply is most significant:

I shall do so;
But I must also feel it as a man.
I cannot but remember such things were
That were most precious to me. Did heaven look on
And would not take their part? Sinful Macduff,
They were all struck for thee! Naught that I am,
Not for their own demerits, but for mine,
Fell slaughter on their souls.   (IV, iii, 220–7)

Macduff is a complete man: he is a valiant soldier, ready to perform "manly" deeds, but is neither ashamed of "humane" feelings nor unaware of his moral responsibilities. This combination is emphasized in his next speech, where he shows clearly that his admirable sensibility does not make him womanish:

> O, I could play the woman with mine eyes
> And braggart with my tongue! But, gentle heavens,
> Cut short all intermission. Front to front
> Bring thou this fiend of Scotland and myself.
> Within my sword's length set him. If he scape,
> Heaven forgive him too!   (IV, iii, 230–5)

Malcolm's comment is: "This tune goes manly."

The development of Macbeth's character is a triumph for Lady Macbeth's ideal, for conscience is stifled, and Macbeth, like Hamlet, becomes increasingly "bloody, bold and resolute." His deliberate decision, against the dictates of his better judgment, to be a "man" in this narrow sense of the word is one of the most important manifestations of the evil which dominates the entire play: to his subjects Macbeth now seems a devil. Shakespeare's insistence upon this narrowing of character is also a commentary on Macbeth's ambition. In "the swelling act of the imperial theme," the hero becomes fatally diminished. The final stage of the development is revealed in Macbeth's speeches at the time of Lady Macbeth's death. Here we are confronted by the supreme irony that when she dies, tortured by the conscience she despised, Macbeth is so perfectly hardened, so completely the soldier that she wanted him to be, that he is neither frightened by the "night-shriek" nor greatly moved by the news of her death. Death has no meaning for him, and life is

>   a tale
> Told by an idiot, full of sound and fury,
> Signifying nothing.   (V, v, 26–8)

Though Macduff's announcement that he was "untimely ripp'd" from his mother's womb causes Macbeth to falter, he dies a courageous soldier, and hence, according to that narrower definition, "like a man." It is appropriate that his death is immediately followed by the last statement of the soldierly standard of values in the tribute Ross pays to Siward's son: "Like a man he died." But on the battlefield is Macduff, who is even more of a man—a soldier who fights only in a good cause, and in whose nature valor is not the sole virtue.

—EUGENE M. WAITH, "Manhood and Valor in Two Shakespearean Tragedies,"
ELH 17, No. 4 (December 1950): 265–68

HAROLD C. GODDARD

How did Shakespeare have the audacity to center a tragedy around a murderer and tyrant, a man so different in his appeal to our sympathies from a Romeo, a Brutus, or a Hamlet? He had done something of the sort before in *Richard III*, but

Richard is more nearly a melodramatic and theatrical than a strictly tragic success. Doubts remain in many minds whether such a creature could ever have existed. But Macbeth is at bottom any man of noble intentions who gives way to his appetites. And who at one time or another has not been that man? Who, looking back over his life, cannot perceive some moral catastrophe that he escaped by inches? Or did not escape. *Macbeth* reveals how close we who thought ourselves safe may be to the precipice. Few readers, however, feel any such kinship with Macbeth as they do with Hamlet. We do not expect to be tempted to murder; but we do know what it is to have a divided soul. Yet Hamlet and Macbeth are imaginative brothers. The difference is that Macbeth begins more or less where Hamlet left off.

> Now might I do it pat, now he is praying,

says the latter, meditating the death of the King,

> And now I'll do 't. And so he goes to heaven;
> And so am I reveng'd. *That would be scann'd.*

> Strange things I have in head, that will to hand,
> Which must be acted *ere they may be scann'd,*

says Macbeth, plotting the destruction of the Macduffs. The two couplets seem written to match each other. Yet Hamlet had to go down only a corridor or so from the praying King to commit a deed, the killing of Polonius, of which Macbeth's couplet is a perfect characterization.

> My strange and self-abuse,

says Macbeth, unstrung at the sight of Banquo's ghost,

> Is the initiate fear that wants hard use:
> We are yet but young in deed.

Deeds, he divines, are the only opiates for fears, but their defect as a remedy is the fact that the dose must be increased with an alarming rapidity.

> O, from this time forth,

cried Hamlet, shamed at the sight of the efficient Fortinbras,

> My thoughts be bloody, or be nothing worth!

The Macbeth-in-Hamlet meant *deeds,* but there was enough of the original Hamlet still left in him to keep it "thoughts." But bloody thoughts are the seed of bloody deeds, and Macbeth, with the very accent of the Fortinbras soliloquy, says, without Hamlet's equivocation,

> from this moment
> The very firstlings of my heart shall be
> The firstlings of my hand.

The harvest of this creed is of course a complete atrophy of heart.

> The time has been my senses would have cool'd
> To hear a night-shriek,

he says when that atrophy has overtaken him,

> and my fell of hair
> Would at a dismal treatise rouse and stir
> As life were in 't.

That is Macbeth gazing back, as it were, into his Hamletian past ("Angels and ministers of grace defend us!"), quite as Hamlet looks forward into his Macbethian future. In that sense the rest was not silence.

Hamlet is to Macbeth somewhat as the Ghost is to the Witches. Revenge, or ambition, in its inception may have a lofty, even a majestic countenance; but when it has "coupled hell" and become crime, it grows increasingly foul and sordid. We love and admire Hamlet so much at the beginning that we tend to forget that he is as hot-blooded as the earlier Macbeth when he kills Polonius and the King, cold-blooded as the later Macbeth or Iago when he sends Rosencrantz and Guildenstern to death. If in *Othello* we can trace fragments of a divided Hamlet transmigrated into Desdemona and Iago, in *Macbeth* an undivided Hamlet keeps straight onward and downward in Macbeth himself. The murderer of Duncan inherits Hamlet's sensibility, his nervous irritability, his hysterical passion, his extraordinary gifts of visualization and imaginative expression; and under the instigating influence of his wife the "rashness" and "indiscretion" of the later Hamlet are progressively translated into a succession of mad acts.

It is this perhaps that explains the main technical peculiarity of *Macbeth*, its brevity. It is so short that not a few have thought that what has come down to us is just the abbreviated stage version of a much longer play. As it stands, it has no "beginning" in the Aristotelian sense, scarcely even a "middle." It is mostly "end." The hero has already been tempted before the opening of the action. We do not know how long he has been turning the murder over in his mind before he broaches the matter to his wife, in a decisive scene which is recapitulated in half a dozen lines near the end of Act I and which occurred before Macbeth encountered the Weird Sisters. This is exactly the way Dostoevsky manages it in *Crime and Punishment,* where Raskolnikov is represented as having lain for days on his bed "thinking" before the story actually opens, and we learn only retrospectively of his meeting the previous winter with the officer and student in the tavern who echo his innermost guilty thoughts and consolidate his fatal impulse precisely as the Weird Sisters do Macbeth's. If the novelist abstains from attempting a detailed account of the period when the crime was being incubated, is it any wonder that the dramatist does, especially when he has already accomplished something resembling this seemingly impossible dramatic representation of inaction in the first two acts of *Hamlet?* Why repeat it? When we consider *Macbeth* as a separate work of art, what its author did or didn't do in another work has of course nothing to do with it. But when we consider the plays, and especially the Tragedies, as chapters of a greater whole, it has everything to do with it. What may be a disadvantage, or even a flaw, from the point of view of the man witnessing *Macbeth* for the first time in the theater may be anything but that to a reader of all the Tragedies in order. And the truth of the statement is in no wise diminished if we hold that Shakespeare himself was largely unconscious of the psychic relationship of his plays.

Viewed in the context of his other works, *Macbeth* is Shakespeare's Descent into Hell. And since it is his *Inferno*, it is appropriate that the terrestrial and celestial parts of his universe should figure in it slightly.

Explorations of the underworld have been an unfailing feature of the world's supreme poetry. From the Greek myths and Homer, to go no farther back or further afield, through the Greek dramatists and the theological-religious visions of Dante and Milton, on to the symbolic poems and prophecies of Blake and the psychological-religious novels of Dostoevsky, we meet wide variations on a theme that remains basically the same. All versions of it, we are at last in a position to recognize, are attempts to represent the psychic as distinguished from the physical world. The difference in nomenclature should not blind us to the identity of subject. We could salvage vast tracts of what is held to be the obsolete wisdom of the world if we would recognize that fact. Wisdom does not become obsolete.

—HAROLD C. GODDARD, *"Macbeth," The Meaning of Shakespeare*
(Chicago: University of Chicago Press, 1951), pp. 495–98

IRVING RIBNER

Macbeth is not like Richard a scourge of God whose evil course is a necessary element in a larger merciful divine scheme. He is rather, like Othello, a man of potential goodness, in whose fall we are made to feel our common frailty and our fellowship with him in sin. His soliloquies inform the supreme illusion of reality in his characterization, and we see him not as an abstract symbol of evil in whose destruction we may rejoice, but rather as a fellow human in whose fall there is terrible waste and a view of the fate of which we ourselves are capable. There is also in the fall of Macbeth a heroic quality, for we admire the greatness of the man in spite of all, and we sense the courage of his devotion to his sinful moral choice, demonic though that devotion may be. In this there is a suggestion of the paradox which Shakespeare is to develop in his final Roman plays.

Shakespeare's movement from *Othello* to *Lear* had, in part, been from the range of a circumscribed domestic tragedy to one embracing the entire scheme of creation. *Macbeth* is a large universal tragedy like *Lear,* but it also includes the domestic qualities of *Othello;* these are most evident in the relation between Macbeth and his wife, whose tragedy we feel more intensely than we can the political tragedy which falls upon Scotland. This domestic tragedy is carefully sub-ordinated to the larger conception of which it is but a part. To make clear the cosmic scope of *Macbeth* Shakespeare further developed the technique he had used in *Lear*. The tragedy is cast simultaneously on the planes of man, the state, the family and the physical universe; each is thrown into chaos by the sin of Macbeth, and evil is allowed to work itself out on each of these corresponding planes.

Although there is no redemption for the fallen hero as in *King Lear*, Shakespeare's final statement is not one of despair, for the play asserts divine order and purpose. There can be little doubt of the final damnation of 'this dread butcher and his fiend-like queen' (V.viii.69), but the audience comes to feel that Macbeth is destroyed by counter-forces which he himself, through his very dedication to evil, sets in motion. The very violence of his tyranny causes Macduff and Malcolm to oppose him. His very trust in the witches, which starts him on his evil course, leads also to his final destruction. The total emotional and intellectual impact of the play reveals good through divine grace emerging out of evil and triumphant at the end with a promise of rebirth.

Othello and Lear in their falls parallel the fall of Adam, and like Adam they are able to learn from their disasters the nature of evil and thus attain a victory in defeat. The destruction of Macbeth reflects the fall of Satan himself, and the play is full of analogies to make this parallel clear. Like Satan, Macbeth is aware from the first of the evil he embraces, and like Satan he will not renounce his free-willed moral choice once it has been made. It is fitting that this evil be symbolized by ambition, for this was the sin of Satan. For Shakespeare, as it had been for Aquinas, ambition was an aspect of pride, a rebellion against the will of God and the order of nature. Macbeth, through love of self, sets his own will against divine will, chooses a lesser finite good—kingship and power—rather than the infinite good of God's order.

The ambitious man will strive to rise higher on the great chain of being than the place God has appointed him. To do so he must break the bond which ties him to God and to the rest of humanity. It is of this bond that Macbeth speaks immediately before the murder of Banquo:

> Come, seeling night,
> Scarf up the tender eye of pitiful day;
> And with thy bloody and invisible hand
> Cancel and tear to pieces that great bond
> Which keeps me pale!   (III.ii.48–52)

This is the bond which ties Macbeth to humanity and enjoins him to obey the natural law of God which he has already broken in his murder of Duncan, but which still keeps him pale, in the undiminished terror of the act he has already committed and of that he is about to commit. It is the bond of nature which Cordelia had invoked and Lear rejected. Macbeth is aware of the implications of this bond as Lear in his folly is not; he is calling upon the Satanic forces of darkness to sever it and thus enable him again to defy the laws of man and God, to murder his friend and his guest.

That Macbeth's crime is opposed to the order and harmony of the universe is supported by the imagery of planting and husbandry, of feasting and conviviality, by the pleasant evocation of the calmness and beauty of nature as Duncan and Banquo enter the dread castle walls (I.iv.1–9). Duncan himself stands for the fruitful aspects of nature; he is like Timon the source of the goodness of life, of all that Macbeth may hope to attain:

> I have begun to plant thee, and will labour
> To make thee full of growing.   (I.iv.28–29)

The murder of Duncan strikes at all which makes life good, fruitful, beautiful. Macbeth cuts off the source of his own being, and this is echoed in Lady Macbeth's 'Had he not resembled / My father as he slept, I had done 't' (II.ii.13–14), for this line, upon which so many fantastic theories have been spun, is not primarily a literal statement; it is choral commentary to emphasize the father symbolism with which Duncan is endowed.

Macbeth's sin, like Satan's, is a deliberate repudiation of nature, a defiance of God. All of the natural forces which militate against the deed are evoked by Macbeth himself:

>   He's here in double trust;
> First, as I am his kinsman and his subject,
> Strong both against the deed; then, as his host,
> Who should against his murderer shut the door,
> Not bear the knife myself. Besides, this Duncan
> Hath borne his faculties so meek, hath been
> So clear in his great office, that his virtues
> Will plead like angels, trumpet-tongued, against
> The deep damnation of his taking-off;
> And pity, like a naked new-born babe,
> Striding the blast, or heaven's cherubim, horsed
> Upon the sightless couriers of the air,
> Shall blow the horrid deed in every eye,
> That tears shall drown the wind. I have no spur
> To prick the sides of my intent, but only
> Vaulting ambition, which o'erleaps itself
> And falls on the other.   (I.vii.12–28)

Macbeth knows that by defying God's natural order he forfeits his own claim to manhood:

> I dare do all that may become a man;
> Who dares do more is none.   (I.vii.46–47)

Because he willingly embraces damnation, the way of redemption is closed to him, and he must end in destruction and despair. In denying nature Macbeth cuts off the source of redemption. Once he has given his 'eternal jewel' to the 'common enemy of man', he must abide by the contract he has made. This is a tragedy about damnation in Christian terms; Macbeth and the audience are always aware of this. ⟨. . .⟩

The specific act of evil occurs on two levels, the state and Macbeth's own 'single state of man' (I.iii.140); the crime is ethical and political, for Macbeth murders not only his kinsman and guest, but his king as well, and its immediate end is to replace a divinely sanctioned monarchy with a tyranny built on usurpation. Once evil is unleashed, it corrupts all of creation, not only man and the state, but the family and the physical universe as well. Shakespeare explores the process of corruption on these four interrelated planes.

That the physical universe has been thrown out of harmony is made clear in the speech of Lennox which immediately follows Duncan's murder:

> The night has been unruly: where we lay,
> Our chimneys were blown down; and, as they say,
> Lamentings heard i' the air; strange screams of death,
> And prophesying with accents terrible
> Of dire combustion and confused events
> New hatch'd to the woeful time: the obscure bird
> Clamour'd the livelong night: some say, the earth
> Was feverous and did shake.   (II.iii.59–66)

This confusion in nature is stressed again in the brief exchange between Ross and a nameless old man. The strange phenomena which Ross describes are all perversions of physical nature which indicate that one man's crime has thrown the entire universe out of harmony:

> Thou seest, the heavens, as troubled with man's act,
> Threaten his bloody stage: by the clock, 'tis day,
> And yet dark night strangles the travelling lamp:
> Is't night's predominance, or the day's shame,
> That darkness does the face of earth entomb,
> When living light should kiss it?   (II.iv.4–9)

The order of nature is reversed, the sun blotted out. On the animal plane, a falcon is killed by a mousing owl, and most horrible of all:

> And Duncan's horses—a thing most strange and certain—
> Beauteous and swift, the minions of their race,
> Turn'd wild in nature, broke their stalls, flung out,
> Contending 'gainst obedience, as they would make
> War with mankind.   (II.iv.14–18)

Man by his sin has forfeited his dominion over nature; horses turn against their natural master, and 'they eat each other.'

This corruption in nature contains within itself the means of restoring harmony; in the working out of evil is implicit a rebirth of good. Shakespeare uses the very perversion of nature, in the form of a moving forest and a child unborn of mother to herald the downfall of the tyrant and thus to restore the physical universe to its natural state of perfection. That the forest does not really move, and that Macduff was only technically so born are of no significance, for Shakespeare is giving us not scientific fact but thematic symbol.

Upon the state, Macbeth unleashes the greatest political evils of which Shakespeare's audience could conceive, tyranny, civil war, and an invading foreign army. The tyranny of Macbeth's reign, in which:

> each new morn
> New widows howl, new orphans cry, new sorrows
> Strike heaven on the face, that it resounds
> As if it felt with Scotland and yell'd out
> Like syllable of dolour. (IV.iii.4–8)

is set off by the initial description of the gentility and justice of Duncan's previous rule, with a king still firm enough to overcome the threats both internal and external with which the opening scenes of the play are concerned. Holinshed, on the contrary, had stressed Duncan's 'feeble and slothful administration' and he had, by way of contrast, praised Macbeth for the excellence of at least the first ten years of his reign.

The disorder in the state, as it works out its course, is also the source of its own extinction and the restoration of political harmony. The very tyranny of Macbeth arouses Macduff against him, causes Malcolm to assert the justice of his title, and perhaps most significantly, causes the saint-like English king, Edward the Confessor, to take arms against Macbeth. In Act IV, Scene ii is described King Edward's curing of scrofula by touch. This is Shakespeare's means of underscoring the saintliness of Edward and of illustrating that he is an emissary of God, an instrument of supernatural Grace, designed to cleanse the unnatural evil in the state, just as he removes evil from individual man. Macbeth's very tyranny has made him 'ripe for shaking, and the powers above / Put on their instruments' (IV.iii.237–8).

The family relationship between Macbeth and his wife steadily deteriorates. At the beginning of the play they are one of the closest and most intimate couples in all literature. She is 'my dearest partner in greatness' (I.v.10–11), and much as it harrows him to think of its implications, he sends her immediate word of the witches' prophecy, so that she may not 'lose the dues of rejoicing' (I.v.11–12). The very terror of the murder scene emphasizes the closeness of the murderers. But as the force of evil severs Macbeth from the rest of humanity, it breaks also the bond which ties him to his wife. He lives more and more closely with his own fears into which she cannot intrude, as the banquet scene illustrates. She cannot see the ghost which torments her husband.

The gradual separation of man and wife first becomes apparent just before the murder of Banquo. No longer does Macbeth confide in her: 'Be innocent of the knowledge, dearest chuck, / Till thou applaud the deed' (III.ii.45–46). At the play's beginning they plan the future together; at the end each dies alone, and when the news of her death comes to Macbeth, he shows little concern:

She should have died hereafter;
There would have been a time for such a word.   (V.v.17–18)

This theme of family disintegration is repeated in Macduff's desertion of his wife and children.

On the disintegration of Macbeth the man, Shakespeare lavishes his principal attention. He is careful to paint his hero in the opening scenes as a man of great stature, the saviour of his country, full of the 'milk of human kindness'. Macbeth has natural feelings which link him to his fellow men and cause him to view with revulsion the crime to which ambition prompts him. Once the crime is committed these feelings are gradually destroyed, until at the end of the play he is, like Timon of Athens, unnatural man, cut off from humanity and from God. As his link with humanity weakens, so also does his desire to live, until at last he sinks into total despair, the medieval sin of *Acedia,* which is the surest evidence of his damnation.

Macbeth's extraordinary powers of imagination are not the cause of his destruction; they could not be so viewed within any meaningful moral system. It is to indicate Macbeth's strong moral feelings that Shakespeare endows his hero with ability to see all of the implications of his act in their most frightening forms before the act itself is committed. Imagination enables Macbeth emotionally to grasp the moral implications of the deed he contemplates, to participate imaginatively, as does the audience, in the full horror of the crime. Macbeth is fully aware of God's moral system with its 'even-handed justice', which 'Commends the ingredients of our poison'd chalice / To our own lips' (I.vii.10–12). His soliloquy in contemplation of Duncan's murder (I.vii.1–28) is designed to underscore his feelings of kinship with the moral order before he commits his crime.

As he prepares to enact the deed he dreads, he calls in another soliloquy for the suppression of these feelings within him. In a devilish incantation he calls for darkness and the extinction of nature, conjuring the earth itself to look aside while he violates the harmonious order of which he and it are closely related parts:

> Now o'er the one half-world
> Nature seems dead, and wicked dreams abuse
> The curtain'd sleep; witchcraft celebrates
> Pale Hecate's offerings, and wither'd murder,
> Alarum'd by his sentinel, the wolf,
> Whose howl's his watch, thus with his stealthy pace,
> With Tarquin's ravishing strides, towards his design
> Moves like a ghost. Thou sure and firm-set earth,
> Hear not my steps, which way they walk, for fear
> Thy very stones prate of my whereabout,
> And take the present horror from the time,
> Which now suits with it.   (II.i.49–60)

The figure of the wolf is appropriate, for here Macbeth allies himself with the destroyer of the innocent lamb, symbolic of God, just as he allies himself with the ravisher Tarquin, the destroyer of chastity, symbolic in the Renaissance of the perfection of God.

That Macbeth cannot say 'amen' immediately after the murder is a sign of his alienation from God. He will sleep no more, for sleep is an aspect of divine mercy which offers man escape from worldly care. Steadily Macbeth moves farther and farther from God and his fellow men, and his bond with nature is weakened. After the murder of Duncan he is committed to an unnatural course from which he cannot retreat:

> For mine own good,
> All causes shall give way: I am in blood
> Stepp'd in so far that, should I wade no more,
> Returning were as tedious as go o'er.   (III.iv.135–8)

He has become the centre of his own little world, for which 'all causes shall give way'. Now Macbeth is ready to seek the witches out, and their words lead him to the most horrible excess of all, the wanton murder of Macduff's family. At the beginning of the play, evil had come to Macbeth unsought; he had followed its promptings in order to attain definite ends, and not without strong misgivings. At the end he embraces evil willingly and without fear, for no other purpose than the evil act itself.

The divided mind and the fear felt by the early Macbeth were the signs of his kinship with man and God, but by the fifth act:

> I have almost forgot the taste of fears:
> The time has been, my senses would have cool'd
> To hear a night-shriek; and my fell of hair
> Would at a dismal treatise rouse and stir
> As life were in't: I have supp'd full with horrors;
> Direness, familiar to my slaughterous thoughts,
> Cannot once start me.   (V.v.9–15)

With the loss of human fear, Macbeth must forfeit also those human qualities which make life liveable: 'that which should accompany old age, / As honour, love, obedience, troops of friends' (V.iii.24–25). There is nothing left for him but the despair of his 'To-morrow and to-morrow' speech (V.v.19–28). Even with this unwillingness to live, in itself a denial of the mercy of God, Shakespeare will not allow to Macbeth the heroic gesture of suicide which he grants to Brutus and Othello. Macbeth will not 'play the Roman fool' (V.viii.1). His spiritual destruction must be reflected in an ignominious physical destruction, and the play ends with the gruesome spectacle of the murderer's head held aloft in triumph. One man has been damned. But when we reflect upon the play in its totality we see that in spite of this there is order and meaning in the universe, that good may be reborn out of evil. We experience that feeling of reconciliation which is the ultimate test of tragedy.

—IRVING RIBNER, "The Operation of Evil: *Timon of Athens* and *Macbeth*,"
Patterns in Shakespearian Tragedy (London: Methuen, 1960),
pp. 154–57, 162–67

WILLIAM ROSEN

Of all Shakespeare's tragic figures, Macbeth is the most isolated. The tragic lovers have one another. Hamlet can reveal himself to Horatio; Othello, to the villainous Iago. Lear has the company of the faithful Kent, the Fool, Edgar, Gloucester. Timon has Flavius. Coriolanus has a friend in Menenius, and though he rejects him, he does not reject his mother, for it is her pleading which makes him give up his attack on Rome. But Macbeth turns completely inward upon himself. His wife's question, "Why do you keep alone?" sounds the thematic note of isolation which Shake-speare renders in a carefully developed pattern of dramatic action.

Macbeth cannot find kinship even with his wife, the one person who shares his guilt. And after refusing to divulge to her the details of future plans, he willfully cuts himself off from his own humanity:

> Come, seeling night,
> Scarf up the tender eye of pitiful day,
> And with thy bloody and invisible hand
> Cancel and tear to pieces that great bond
> Which keeps me pale!   (III.ii.46)

Invoking the powers of darkness, he would shut himself off from light, and suppress all feelings of pity, lest it interfere with the carrying out of his unnatural acts. The bond he would cancel and tear to pieces is Fleance and Banquo's lease on life, but there is the suggestion that it is also the bond of human fellowship which Macbeth must cast off before he can destroy, with deliberate calculation, another human being.

Free of the outer sanctions of social and moral doctrines, Macbeth derives authority from himself alone. His own pragmatic standards determine what is good and what is evil; consequently, good is that which affords him freedom from fear of the living. As Macbeth retreats from the light of day and the natural feelings that join people together in bonds of sympathy and trust, there is nobody he can depend upon completely. When he sends the two malcontent murderers to attack Banquo and Fleance, his mistrust of others is highlighted—he sends a third man to spy upon the two.

It is impossible, however, to murder all the living; and this is the import of Fleance's escape from death. That Banquo's son still lives is sufficient testimony that crime will be opposed, that it cannot succeed in making good of bad and friends of foes. Once again our view is not of man in conflict with society, the external world; our vision is of Macbeth confronting himself:

> But now I am cabin'd, cribb'd, confin'd, bound in
> To saucy doubts and fears.   (III.iv.24)

Macbeth might advise his wife to assume the Machiavellian pose, to make the "faces vizards to our hearts, / Disguising what they are" (III.ii.34), but he uncovers to an audience the reality behind the mask. Of *King Lear* Melville wrote that, "Tormented into desperation, Lear the frantic king tears off the mask, and speaks the sane madness of vital truth." In unmasking himself to his audience, Macbeth also articulates vital truth, of a different kind, the reverse of Lear's truth, but no less of a discovery of what is beneath the seeming. Macbeth uncovers dark truths unchangeable: that if a man strikes out at law and nature, law and nature recede, leaving him to his aloneness; and though he possess crown and sceptre, there is no joy.

—WILLIAM ROSEN, *"Macbeth," Shakespeare and the Craft of Tragedy*
(Cambridge, MA: Harvard University Press, 1960), pp. 84–86

MARIAN BODWELL SMITH

Macbeth, the particular man whose dram of evil has corrupted his whole substance, is, if not Everyman, then every man who denies his kinship with humanity by saying, "For mine own good, all causes shall give way," even though he knows in his heart that such good can only be evil. His tragedy results from a double usurpation, for Macbeth is not only a usurper of a throne, but one in whose breast Friar Lawrence's "two . . . opposed kings . . . grace and rude will" are encamped, and whose plant of life begins to shrivel into death as soon as the "worser is predominant." Yet, as usually in Shakespearean tragedy, there is a faint and relieving glimmer of hope for the individual as well as for the state even in the dark world of *Macbeth*. Even this man is not seen as totally depraved, though the play presents a treatment of absolute evil, the rejection of God's Providence and reliance upon the powers of Satan, which, according to James I's *Daemonologie,* was the unforgivable sin against the Holy Ghost. But the imagery of darkness in the play is shot with light, and though we have seen the protagonist decline from the praise of "golden opinions" to the epithet of "dead butcher," he is not permitted to lose his human dignity entirely. In his last fight he is shown as retaining something of his original courage, even though the inroads of brutalizing fear have turned fortitude into desperation. His unwillingness to charge his soul with more of Macduff's blood is an indication that he retains also some vestiges of moral sensitivity. Courage and sensitivity are the pillars of his character which frame the story of his downfall. However far astray internal evil and external circumstance have driven him he remains a man, though a man who has dedicated his goodness to the service of evil, who has turned his soul, and his world, upside down. In this, the inverted Morality Play pattern of *Macbeth*, Evil, not Grace, has won the battle for a man's soul, but the harrowing of Scotland's hell is at hand.

—MARIAN BODWELL SMITH, *Dualities in Shakespeare* (Toronto:
University of Toronto Press, 1966), p. 187

TERENCE EAGLETON

Macbeth centres around a single action—the murder of Duncan—which, like the action of Coriolanus and Antony, is seen as self-defeating. The whole structure of the play makes this clear: Scotland moves from health to sickness and back into health, Malcolm replaces Duncan, and the wheel comes full circle without Macbeth having made any permanent achievement. The energy he expends in trying to secure his position contrasts ironically with this lack of attainment: his actions are cancelled out by the circular movement of the play, and he becomes a momentary aberration in Scotland's history, an aberration without lasting consequence: the history rights itself and continues. Macbeth's action in killing Duncan is marred by a literal sterility: he will have no sons to make his achievement permanently fruitful. But the action is inherently sterile, too, and it is this paradox which the play builds on: an action intended as creative, self-definitive, is in fact destructive, self-undoing.

Macbeth becomes king of Scotland between the end of Act II and the beginning of Act III, but in achieving the status which he saw previously as ultimate, he finds that his troubles have in fact only just begun: he spends the rest of the play fighting to secure his role. He fights to *become* what, objectively, he is: to clear up and tidy the straggling consequences of his action and settle down in the achieved and perfected definition of kingship:

> To be thus is nothing,
> But to be safely thus.   (III, 1)

The idea of a perfected, completely achieved act is insistent in the play: Macbeth upbraids the witches as 'imperfect speakers', and his reaction to the news of Fleance's escape focusses his frustration as continually falling short of full achievement:

> I had else been perfect,
> Whole as the marble, founded as the rock,
> As broad and general as the casing air,
> But now I am cabin'd, cribb'd, confin'd, bound in
> To saucy doubts and fears.   (III, 3)

Every action done to attain security mars itself: every act has a built-in flaw, a consequence which escapes, like Fleance, from the control of the actor and returns to plague him. Macbeth cannot achieve a pure act, a wholeness: his actions unravel themselves, and he longs for a pure act as he longs for the sleep which 'knits up the ravell'd sleave of care':

> If it were done, when 'tis done, then 'twere well
> It were done quickly. If th'assassination
> Could trammel up the consequence, and catch,
> With his surcease, success; that but this blow
> Might be the be-all and the end-all here—
> But here upon this bank and shoal of time—
> We'd jump the life to come. But in these cases
> We still have judgment here, that we but teach
> Bloody instructions, which being taught return
> To plague th'inventor.   (I, 7)

Macbeth wants the action without the consequences, without the uncontrollable, multiplying effects; he dreams of an action which contains and controls all its results within itself. He also wants achievement without the process of reaching it, as Lady Macbeth sees:

> Thou wouldst be great;
> Art not without ambition, but without
> The illness should attend it. What thou wouldst highly,
> That wouldst thou holily; wouldst not play false,
> And yet wouldst wrongly win.   (I, 4)

But the irony implicit in all action is precisely that any achievement involves a process of reaching and a process of results, and both processes can destroy what is attained. Macbeth wants the static, permanent status of kingship without the fluid, temporal process of actions necessary to win and secure it; he finds that kingship is for him only a process, not the complete definition it was for Duncan. Having become king officially by killing Duncan, he finds that he has achieved nothing: there is always another step to be taken before he is *really* king, secure in his role, and each step taken undoes what he has won because each step breeds more de-structive consequences. He is not allowed to become what he is, to be, authenti-cally, king; he spends all his time and energy in consolidating his position and is therefore unable to enjoy kingship at all. He is a man pursuing his own act, chasing himself; his action in killing Duncan both makes and mars him, as drink, according to the Porter, makes and mars a man.

Macbeth's condition is imaged especially in the recurrent metaphor of ill-fitting robes. When Ross and Angus greet him with the title of Cawdor he asks why they dress him in borrowed robes, and Banquo's aside when Macbeth is 'rapt' after the witches' promise captures the significance of this:

> New honours come upon him,
> Like our strange garments, cleave not to their mould
> But with the aid of use.   (I, 3)

A role or title can be laid externally on a man, but he must then make it his own, moulding it like new clothes to his own shape so that it is authentic, not external any longer. It is not enough to be Cawdor or king in a merely objective way, as in *Measure for Measure* it is not enough to conform externally to the law; Macbeth sees that he must become, genuinely, what he is officially, authenticate his new name so that he can live it by habit, as in the Last Comedies virtue is a habitual living of the law. The importance of names and titles is stressed in the play: Macbeth is given, ceremonially, the former title of Cawdor; Macduff, discovering the murder of Duncan, says it is a deed which tongue and heart 'cannot conceive nor name'; the witches perform 'a deed without a name'; Macbeth is a 'tyrant, whose sole name blisters our tongues', as Malcolm says. In all these cases, names have a peculiarly creative power: things without names are beyond the reach of human meanings, part of the nothingness of the evil lying at the edges of the human community. To receive a name is to be something positive, to have a sanctioned place within the community.

Macbeth's murder of Duncan is a falling from such a place within the community to the pure negativity of evil, the area of nameless deeds. Before the murder, Macbeth's authentic life consists in serving Duncan, and the service is not an external, mechanical obedience but a living self-expression: he wants no reward for his allegiance because

> The service and the loyalty I owe,
> In doing it, pays itself.   (I, 4)

He needs no external payment, but is paid by the deed itself; the circularity here is that of the fusion of authentic and responsible action, not the self-destroying circularity which is Macbeth's later condition. It is in Duncan's service that Macbeth finds personal joy: 'The rest is labour, which is not us'd for you' (I, 4). In destroying Duncan, Macbeth is destroying himself: his own life and peace is in Duncan's possession, and the murder is thus an act of self-violence. It is a self-destroying act, one done to achieve a happiness lost in the very moment of trying to attain it; his action, like his ambition, 'o'er-leaps itself, And falls on the other' (I, 7). In destroying Duncan he is being inauthentic, less than himself: he overreaches himself, falling away from his own positive life into negativity:

> I dare do all that may become a man;
> Who dares do more is none.   (I, 7)

To overreach one's limits is to be less than oneself, to undo oneself; authentic living consists in staying freely within these limits of nature, recognising them as creative. To try to be more than human is to be an animal: evil is a kind of failure, a meaninglessness. This is what Lady Macbeth cannot see: to her a man can create his own limits, pushing them out to suit his ambition:

> When you durst do it, then you were a man;
> And to be more than what you were, you would
> Be so much more the man.   (I, 7)

Macbeth takes her advice and goes beyond the limits of humanity in an attempt to be more fully human; in trying to achieve a title he goes beyond all names, all definitions, into the negation of evil and chaos. Lady Macbeth cannot see that limits are not what restrict humanity but what make it what it is, as a name creates in defining, in limiting. 〈. . .〉

Macbeth's attempts to create meaning from a world which Duncan's death drained of value degenerate finally into the peace of embracing chaos, accepting meaninglessness: life is a succession to tomorrows, a tale told by an idiot, and having recognised this he can fight till the flesh is hacked from his bones, trying to the last. He will at least die in harness, enjoying action for its own sake, spending himself freely in his final moments. He can find comfort in absurdity, as he finds constancy in inconstancy:

> Come what come may,
> Time and the hour runs through the roughest day.   (I, 3)

There is no final answer in this for Shakespeare, any more than there is in *Antony and Cleopatra;* Macbeth, like Antony, undoes himself in rejecting social responsibility, and whatever value can be forcibly created from the rejection must be inevitably marginal. The main exploration must still be towards a way of discovering a mode of social responsibility which can fully contain and express individual drives of the power and depth of those we see at work in *Macbeth,* and this will mean moving beyond a kind of energy which is formidable in its human strength, but negative at root.

—TERENCE EAGLETON, *"Macbeth," Shakespeare and Society: Critical Studies in Shakespearean Drama* (New York: Schocken Books, 1967), pp. 130–35, 137–38

MAYNARD MACK, JR.

The quality in Macbeth that most engages us is not, I think, his acute imagination, though this has often been proposed. More accurately, it is his deep, almost inarticulate sense of levels beyond our limited experience to which his imagination gives him, and us, some sort of intuitive access. Everything, for the Macbeth of the first two or even three acts, has reverberations, has *mana.* Everything, moreover, vibrates for him somewhere outside the world of time and beyond the human senses as well as within them, and therefore shakes him (the phrase is Hamlet's) "with thoughts beyond the reaches of our souls." For playgoers, probably the best remembered evidence of this faculty in Macbeth is the murder scene itself, where the reverberations that reach him from the owl, the cricket, the blood, and the voice crying "Sleep no more" are altogether lost on his wife. She cuts through the anxieties caused by his inability to say "Amen" and by his imagined murdering of sleep with the practical advice, "Go, get some water, / And wash this filthy witness from your hand" (II.ii.45–46). Leaving to return the daggers, she confidently adds,

> If he do bleed,
> I'll gild the faces of the grooms withal,
> For it must seem their guilt.   [II.ii.54–56]

As the assured tone and grim pun on "gilt" suggest, she is unworried by the blood except as it may be a "witness."

But as soon as she has left, and the knocking offstage has announced, as De Quincey was the first to see, the emergence of some sort of nemesis from within but also from beyond the temporal, he looks at his hands uncomprehendingly: "What hands are here?" (58) and then, in a new key echoes her command.

> Will all great Neptune's ocean wash this blood
> Clean from my hand? No, this my hand will rather
> The multitudinous seas incarnadine,
> Making the green one red.   [II.ii.59–62]

Again her easy literalism is replaced with a wildly imaginative apprehension of a kind of reality in which blood has moral and not simply literal status. Then this too is set aside by her confident repetition as she returns from replacing the daggers: "A little water clears us of this deed: / How easy is it then!" (66–67). We have met with the washing image before. It occurs at crucial moments in both *Richard II* and *Hamlet.* Obviously, for Shakespeare it had the usual connections with Christian purification from sin, but also a special connection with tragic insight. Here, in *Macbeth,* it can hardly be coincidental that the only time we see Lady Macbeth reveal any internal stress or strain (in the sleepwalking scene) the washing reappears—and in Macbeth's sense of it: "Out, damned spot! out, I say!"—"What, will these hands ne'er be clean?"—"Here's the smell of blood still: all the perfumes of Arabia will not sweeten this little hand" (V.i.34–35).

Macbeth's intense consciousness of something that lies beyond the pale of our normal Aristotelian city—where, as Auden says, "Euclid's geometry / And Newton's mechanics would account for our experience, / And the kitchen table exists because I scrub it"—becomes apparent on our first acquaintance with him.

> If good, why do I yield to that suggestion
> Whose horrid image doth unfix my hair,
> And make my seated heart knock at my ribs,
> Against the use of nature? Present fears
> Are less than horrible imaginings.
> My thought, whose murther yet is but fantastical,
> Shakes so my single state of man,
> That function is smother'd in surmise,
> And nothing is, but what is not.   [I.iii.134–42]

These lines are remarkable, as everyone remembers, both for their intuition of some profound inner assault by anarchic forces on his humanity, his "single state of man," and for their apprehension of a buried life within that can under the proper stimulation rise to efface the life of which he is routinely conscious: "And nothing is, but what is not." How far Shakespeare has come in his exploration of the unexplorable may be seen by looking momentarily back to *Hamlet.* The Prince's first soliloquy, like Macbeth's here, immediately opens his character to our view. But there what we see is a man musing on external events in the face of which he must set a clear limit on his actions, "but I must hold my tongue." Here something altogether different happens. As the external reality, Macbeth's new title, Thane of Cawdor, fades almost from his view, his introspections dominate completely—possess him as if he were simply their instrument. It is the difference between thoughts aroused by external and those aroused by internal "events"—thoughts which in fact become their own events. Not his new title but "horrible imaginings" and a "horrid image" take over his consciousness, while out of his internal agitation dawns suddenly the fully developed, if still fantastical, will to murder. There has been nothing to prepare us for this; it seems to be Shakespeare's way of indicating that some mysterious world and life are carrying on their own business beneath the surface of Macbeth's public character.

The difference between this genesis of the idea of king killing and its genesis in *Hamlet* is also revealing. There, too, the "command" comes suddenly and surprisingly. That something requires revenge is mentioned in the Ghost's sixth line, and the actual command—"Revenge his foul and most unnatural murther"—is our first indication that a crime has been committed. But again the distinction is what matters. Between the external, visible Ghost in *Hamlet* and the mysterious inner impulse in *Macbeth,* the gulf is wide. Even if we argue that Hamlet's Ghost is simply symbolic of his own internal desire and need for vengeance, this must not blind us to the vast difference in tone, dramatic effect, and meaning between hearing a father's ghost command his son to avenge his murder and hearing the will to murder, fully formed in all its horrid particulars, surge up from within. It will not do to say that in *Macbeth* Shakespeare merely does by internal means what in *Hamlet* he does externally, for though this is partly true, the way things are done in the theater is, inevitably, a large part of what they mean.

Macbeth, then, appeals to us, even as he repels us, by his unspoken and perhaps unspeakable intuitions of a life within himself and beyond himself to which we too respond, and tremble as we do. What he experiences seems to go much deeper than the predictable hypocrisies of the villain, whether stage or real. When he participates, for a moment, in Duncan's world, falling into its idiom—"The service and the loyalty I owe, / In doing it, pays itself" (I.iv.22–23)—and imagining his duties to Duncan as "children and servants" (25), we have no right to be sure, as too many critics have been, that he is merely hypocritical. Much more plausibly that world is yet a possibility for Macbeth, a potentiality in him, like the valorous service he has just shown in battle against the invaders, the "milk of human kindness" in him to which his wife calls attention, and the scruples that beset him in his soliloquy outside the banqueting chamber at Inverness—not to mention the moral sensitivities that after the murder enable his ears to hear the voice crying sleep no more and his eyes to see the murder sticking to his hands along with the blood. Yet always from somewhere inside him (though also outside him, as the Sisters attest, for they are as visible to us and to Banquo as to him) comes the other urgency, and it floods in now, powerfully, as Duncan speaks to create Malcolm his heir.

> Stars, hide your fires!
> Let not light see my black and deep desires;
> The eye wink at the hand; yet let that be,
> Which the eye fears, when it is done, to see.   [I.iv.50–53]

—MAYNARD MACK, JR., "The Voice in the Sword," *Killing the King: Three Studies in Shakespeare's Tragic Structure* (New Haven: Yale University Press, 1973), pp. 156–60

JAMES L. CALDERWOOD

Macbeth is self-constitutive. He creates himself by means of action. He is what he has done, and he knows what he is. But that knowledge must be suppressed for him to continue to function. Thus in *Macbeth* we have the absence or concealment of what we know to be present—the hero's true self and a world of order and meaning that disappeared with Duncan's death and will reappear with Macbeth's death. In *Hamlet,* however, we have the presence of what is absent. For instance, instead of concealing the absence, the delay of Hamlet's revenge, Shakespeare advertises it so insistently—by means of Hamlet's self-recriminations, the ghost's reminder, and the parallel cases of the undelaying Fortinbras and Laertes—that during the middle of the play we seem to have not an absence of revenge but a presence of not-revenge. Not only does the play keep announcing what it is not, a conventional revenge tragedy, but the hero follows the same practice, repeatedly asserting not who he is but who he is not. He is not, he informs us at one time or another, the passionate player who weeps for Hecuba, the dispassionate stoic Horatio, the dutiful son of a murdered father, the compliant son and heir of a murderous stepfather, the lover of Ophelia, the bluff and warlike Fortinbras, or the headlong man of honor Laertes. Most of all, he is not what he once was, the "expectancy and rose of the fair state, / The glass of fashion and the mold of form," the Danish courtier-prince of whom Castiglione might have written. Nor, on the other hand, is he a madman, except perhaps north-northwest. In a world whose operant principle is "seems," Hamlet cannot "be," not at least until he comes to the graveyard, where death "is" and men and maids are "not." There, in the presence of the Great Negative, he can at last affirm his identity: "This is I, / Hamlet, the Dane!"

Macbeth, on the other hand, emerges from Duncan's bedchamber to ask in a guilty whisper, "Is this I, Macbeth, with these hangman's hands?" It is indeed, and he averts his gaze. To be sure, Macbeth plays innocent and Hamlet plays mad. But Macbeth knows what he is apart from his role, whereas Hamlet does not; he is compact of many identities and nonidentities and is reluctant to yield any of them in favor of the one the ghost has commanded him to assume. Thus Hamlet moves toward self-knowledge and Macbeth from it. Nevertheless, Macbeth experiences a moment that is correlative to, though radically different from, Hamlet's proclamation of self-identity, his "This is I." It occurs even before Birnam Wood comes to Dunsinane, when Macbeth arborealizes his plight:

> I have lived long enough. My way of life
> Is fallen into the sear, the yellow leaf,
> And that which should accompany old age,
> As honor, love, obedience, troops of friends,
> I must not look to have; but, in their stead,
> Curses, not loud but deep, mouth-honor, breath,
> Which the poor heart would fain deny, and dare not.   (V.iii.22–28)

"Hell," Thomas Hobbes said, "is truth seen too late." The sight of it causes Oedipus to blind himself, Lear to go mad, and a prematurely aged Macbeth to mourn for the self he might have been—the Macbeth who died with Duncan. In this and the "Tomorrow" soliloquy, Macbeth attains to a promontory of consciousness from which he looks back and sees how what he might have been has shriveled into what he now is. What he sees in those speeches is appalling, and yet the act of seeing is an achievement of a high order. "When all that is within him," as Menteith says, "does condemn / Itself for being there" (V.ii.23–24), Macbeth must be more loathe to reenter the chambers of his self than he was to reenter those of the dead Duncan ("Look on it again I dare not" [II.ii.50]). But he does. At the worst of times he has the courage to face not only the circling enemies without but the far greater enemy within, to reckon up his losses ("honor, love, obedience, troops of friends") and his gains ("curses," "mouth-honor") and to admit in his soul sickness, "This is I, Macbeth."

Macbeth's *anagnorisis* is a recognition of meaninglessness, of the great "de-meaning" he has wrought in the world and himself. He ends roughly where Hamlet begins, except that unlike the earthly Hamlet, he has dreadfully earned his sorrows. Yet he earns more than those at the end. His willingness to acknowledge "all that is within" is a major reason why he transcends the level of melodramatic villain and achieves tragic stature. That stature is enhanced by the fact that neither here nor further on, when the world closes about him more menacingly, does he cast about for scapegoats. Although he might with considerable justice have glanced in the direction of the witches and certainly of his wife, he speaks only of his own failures. But if his sense of failure implies a complexity of character that elevates him above melodrama, it does not carry him so high that he yields his role as tragic hero for that of a morality-play character. Without minimizing his crimes, he nevertheless keeps the fine line between tragic *anagnorisis* and Christian confession and peni-tence. Indeed, the very enormity of his crimes, he seems to realize, sets him well beyond the shores of conventional mercy—so deeply plunged in evil that returning were even more tedious than go o'er.

It is part of the tragic irony of the ending that as Macbeth sees himself for what he is and carries that image into battle like a wound ("But get thee back! My soul is too much charged / With blood of thine already"), and thus exhibits the self-division that marks him off from simple villainy, his enemies advance on him to kill nothing more in their view than a "cursed usurper" and a "butcher" (V.viii.55, 70). In some degree, of course, he shares their judgment—and so transcends their judgment. It is the fate of tragic heroes to be isolated in self-division and nuance as the world they have injured returns to an oblivious but healing wholeness.

—JAMES L. CALDERWOOD, *"Macbeth:* Counter-*Hamlet," Shakespeare Studies* 17 (1985): 115–17

MICHAEL GOLDMAN

Macbeth is a brave soldier, an active physical man—but the most striking thing about him is his imagination. Here the term applies in its most literal sense—Macbeth possesses an image-making faculty of nightmarish power. We get, in this play, as full a portrait of the workings of a human mind as we do in *Hamlet,* but Macbeth has none of Hamlet's interest in analysis. He doesn't tend to think abstractly, and he doesn't *like* to think about his situation in any form. But he cannot help thinking about it in images. When he is about to commit a murder, the image of a bloody dagger comes up before him unbidden; it is so vivid he thinks it is real. He wishes it would go away, but it will not. This is not a supernatural apparition, but, as he calls it, a dagger of the mind—the product of his imagination.

What is particularly important is that Macbeth's imagination is a moral imagination. The images it registers most vividly have to do with the moral status of Macbeth's acts and desires. It is especially sensitive to evil, and it confronts Macbeth with vivid and terrible pictures that express the moral repulsiveness of what he is doing. As the play progresses, his typical response to his imaginings is to try to act, and to act instead of thinking and feeling. Macbeth, in fact, would much rather do something evil than imagine its moral meaning. But the more he acts, the more vividly he sees the moral horror.

Shakespeare gives the images that throng Macbeth's mind a powerful histrionic setting by having Macbeth use them both to explore and to discover his new emotions. In this, he behaves very much like an actor rehearsing a role. For *Macbeth* shows us a man not only betraying and murdering his king, but learning to perform the act, as an actor might. That is, he uncovers in himself what a modern actor might call his motivation. But this term, though natural enough, is misleading. For what the actor playing a murderer and traitor must discover is not some nuance of intention—not why Macbeth wants to kill Duncan—but rather, a convincing capacity for the act. He must discover what it is *like* to be able to commit such a crime, to have desires and proclivities and mental activity large enough to propel him into the act. And this is exactly what Macbeth, in the early scenes, discovers in himself.

Macbeth observes carefully and with surprise the psychic readjustments by which he becomes a criminal. His first soliloquy allows the actor to develop the capacity for Macbeth's grand passion—for murdering Duncan and for *intending* to murder Duncan—as part of his performance. And of course it involves us in this development and makes it part of the central material of the play. In this speech, Macbeth maps and explores his new mental topography:

> Why do I yield to that suggestion
> Whose horrid image doth unfix my hair
> And make my seated heart knock at my ribs
> Against the use of nature? Present fears
> Are less than horrible imaginings . . .   (I, iii, 134–38)

The histrionic imagery here allows the actor to build up a complex state of mind step by step. Macbeth begins with an imagined picture and a reaction to it. He fights against, questions, and gradually becomes absorbed in this picture of himself doing murder, a picture which is both his and not his, ambiguously placed by his vocabulary neither quite inside him nor outside him—it is a "suggestion" (or, more obscurely, the image of a suggestion), to which he "yields." The image in his mind frightens him, and the actor is given specific terms in which to explore his fear: heart beating violently, scalp tingling, and that jumpy, up-and-down movement of breath and thought which L. C. Knights has aptly described as a "sickening see-saw."

The process by which Macbeth explores the capacity for evil that has appeared, as if out of nowhere, in his mind may be traced to its full extent in the dagger speech. Again the actor is allowed to develop his feelings through a series of investigations and discoveries:

> Is this a dagger which I see before me,
> The handle toward my hand? Come, let me clutch thee.
> I have thee not, and yet I see thee still.
> Art thou not, fatal vision, sensible
> To feeling as to sight, or art thou but
> A dagger of the mind, a false creation . . . ? (II, i, 33–38)

Like the image of murder which springs to his mind when he hears that he is Thane of Cawdor, the dagger is something Macbeth examines with close attention to physical detail. And the process of exploration itself becomes a theme for startled discovery:

> I see thee yet, in form as palpable
> As this which now I draw.
> Thou marshal'st me the way that I was going. (40–42)

To confirm the reality of his "false creation," Macbeth draws his own dagger, and then, staring at the knife he holds, realizes what his exploration has led to. The vision has placed a weapon in his hand, drawn him a step further toward murder. The actor is still supported by the step-by-step exploratory method, but now it is moving him from feeling to action, a development which will be expanded in the next several lines.

Like the prophecies he has heard from the witches, the dagger strikes Macbeth as both a cunning trap and an extraordinary revelation—a kind of supernatural solicitation:

> Mine eyes are made the fools o'th'other senses,
> Or else worth all the rest. (44–45)

Now he begins to project the terrible instigation, the dagger in his mind, outward into the world around him. Once more he ambiguously defines the source of the image which obsesses him. He locates his murderous "creation" not in his mind but in a deceptively objectified future—the "business" he must soon perform has created the vision:

> It is the bloody business which informs
> Thus to mine eyes. (48–49)

The phrase almost acknowledges—but also helps to obscure—the mental origin of the dagger.

Next comes the decisive movement outside Macbeth's mind:

> Now o'er the one half world
> Nature seems dead, and wicked dreams abuse
> The curtained sleep; witchcraft celebrates
> Pale Hecate's offerings; and withered murder,
> Alarumed by his sentinel, the wolf,
> Whose howl's his watch, thus with his stealthy pace,
> With Tarquin's ravishing strides, towards his design
> Moves like a ghost.   (49–56)

What is striking here is that, as Macbeth thrusts the thickness in his thought out into nature, he converts it into yet another image, which allows him to develop his murderous propensities further. He transforms his passion into action first by imagining a figure he calls "murder," and then by imitating the very image he has projected. The bloody business now informs all nature, and through it moves the figure of Murder, whose movements Macbeth copies. The references to Murder's "pace" and "stride" lead naturally to Macbeth's own steps:

> Thou sure and firm-set earth
> Hear not my steps, which way they walk, for fear
> Thy very stones prate of my whereabout,
> And take the present horror from the time,
> Which now suits with it.   (56–60)

The psychological and mimetic process by which a man can become a murderer has been very thoroughly laid out, both for the actor and the audience.

At this point, the histrionic complexity of the speech can be felt in a single word:

> Whiles I threat, he lives.   (60)

What process of articulation in the previous lines has allowed Macbeth to describe them as a *threat?* Surely it is a movement like the one just described, the projection of his murderous design outward into the world. He sees his speech as a step toward murder, a threat. And though he can now dismiss what he has just said as merely verbal ("Words to the heat of deeds too cold breath gives"), the speech has quite literally gotten him moving. Moreover, it has done so by transforming him into the image of murder he has projected. Macbeth has made his choice. He is now an embodiment of the very atmosphere of horror he has described.

The interplay here between imagination and action is characteristic of the role. Projection—the forcing of material that horrifies him outward into the world—is Macbeth's basic method of defending himself against his thoughts. It is also his typical basis for action. Even his familiar habit of trying to "outrun" his imaginings by acting on them is a version of this mechanism. Macbeth goes out and makes a murder in order to stop thinking about one.

—MICHAEL GOLDMAN, "Speaking Evil: Language and Action in *Macbeth*,"
Acting and Action in Shakespearean Tragedy (Princeton:
Princeton University Press, 1985), pp. 101–5

JOHN TURNER

Why does Macbeth kill Duncan? The familiar isolation of ambition by way of an answer does not begin to match the metaphoric richness of Macbeth's soliloquies in Acts I and II, and these are the only reliable guide that we have to his motives and their significant connections with the world. Ambition doesn't usually feel like *that*, we might say. A sentence from Wordsworth, describing the neo-Shakespearean villain of his own play *The Borderers*, establishes the keynote: 'he finds his temptation in strangeness. He is unable to suppress a low hankering after the *double entendre* in vice.' The strangeness in Macbeth's mind has been well described by Wilson Knight: 'He himself is hopelessly at a loss, and has little idea as to why he is going to murder Duncan. He tries to fit names to his reasons—"ambition", for instance—but this is only a name.' *Macbeth* is a study of ambivalence in a total society; and the reason why its hero cannot articulate his motives is that they appertain to the disowned aspect of his own ambivalence. Fair is foul, and foul is fair: Macbeth is unable to resist the desire which is the secret face of prohibition, and which has been driven to speak perversely—'in a double sense' (V.viii.20), with the *double entendre* of vice—precisely because it is secret. It has become disowned and unable to involve itself creatively in life. Macbeth kills Duncan for the sake of what the play calls 'mischief', for the fascinating pleasure that he finds in doing what most he believes to be wrong. The corollary of this, of course, is that Duncan is killed because he is believed to be good. He falls victim to the tragic paradox that, by the perverse logic of ambivalence, in anathematizing temptation and making it seem unnatural he activates it against himself. He succumbs to the contradictions which he himself has helped to create in the minds of his subjects— contradictions whose material base, of course, lies deep in the military dependence of the warring feudal state upon the loyalty of its aristocratic families.

It is on the heath, by the battlefield, that the sisters tempt Macbeth, seeking (it seems) to exploit the dependence of the gentle weal upon war; for it is there and now, in this most marginal place and time, that Macbeth and his country are most vulnerable. As René Girard puts it, 'a special sort of impurity clings to the warrior returning to his homeland, still tainted with the slaughter of war'. When he returns home and re-enters his castle, however, he finds the sisters' temptation redoubled upon him by his wife:

> Art thou afeard
> To be the same in thine own act and valour,
> As thou art in desire?   (I.vii.39–41)

This is the very dream of omnipotence, to destroy the distinctions between heart and hand, desire and deed; and, as Lady Macbeth persuades her husband to act against the king he should defend, she aims to destroy too the distinctions that Duncan had so laboriously drawn between peace and war. What is more, her temptation, like the charms of the sisters, is highly sexualized, in a way that spells destruction for all the gentle courtesies through which Duncan tries to discipline the extended family of his kingdom. For the unruliness of sexuality, the waywardness of what the porter calls lechery, is felt throughout *Macbeth;* and it is just this unruliness that Lady Macbeth seeks to arouse in her husband by the *double entendre* of her references to act, valour and desire. Duncan, when he addressed her as the wife of the Thane of Cawdor (I.vi.20ff.) had, by the intricate dance of his pronouns, distinguished woman from man, family from family, subject from king, each in its rightful place; but here, within the family, fuelled by those same sexual energies that might keep a family and state together, we find a fierce, competitive, highly sexualized spirit bent upon particular ambition and set against the general good, aroused against it precisely because it is good. Sexual and soldierly excitements fuel one another, promiscuously mixed in the mind of Lady Macbeth, and the extended family loyalties of trust by which Duncan had tried to secure his state against the hazards of war and peace are doomed to disappear. Not even his expressed wish to have been Macbeth's 'purveyor' (I. 22) can contain the desire to turn his kingdom upside-down, and he will be murdered by the captain who is his cousin.

The murder is a *folie à deux,* created between Macbeth and his wife where neither alone would have done it; and it strikes to the heart of all that they hold sacred in their society. It is the one great central act of violation that, as all the metaphors of child-murder, rape, blasphemy and drunkenness reveal, evokes all the other acts of violation that they can imagine; for they share with their king a common imaginative commitment to the language of the sacramental. There is one crucial difference, however. Duncan's language tends to *realize* the people around him, offering them the time and place to fulfil themselves voluntarily through their responses to him. But, when Macbeth speaks of the wicked dreams that abuse the curtained sleep, of the celebrations of Witchcraft or the preparations of Murther, his images depend for their intensity upon a superstitious *derealization* of the world. His earlier idealization of Duncan—his virtues pleading 'like angels, trumpet-tongu'd, against/The deep damnation of his taking-off' (I.vii.19–20)—shows the same hallucinatory quality. He has lost his hold upon those courtesies through which other people can exert their discipline, and has been led instead into a state of rapt introversion, a private theatricality of the moral imagination which is a form of self-estrangement. Even in the self-examinations of his conscience, we sense the contamination of excitement upon him. So it is that the hallucinated dagger with its gouts of blood—perfect emblem of the desire and the aversion which are the twin faces of his ambivalence—comes to serve the stronger passion and marshall him the way that he was going.

All that the Macbeths can conceive of love and tenderness points them irresistibly towards Duncan in his bedchamber.

> I have given suck, and know
> How tender 'tis to love the babe that milks me:
> I would, while it was smiling in my face,
> Have pluck'd my nipple from his boneless gums,
> And dash'd the brains out, had I so sworn
> As you have done to this. (I.vii.54–9)

Through such troubled sensuous poetry, they are daring to express themselves in the perverse creations of debauchery, and finding (as Iago finds) that the immediate juxtaposition of images of goodness and evil, of tenderness and cruelty, of vulnerability and savagery, generates emotions of great violence. Macbeth, his energies roused, relishes the dramatization of himself as 'wither'd Murther' (II.i.52) and as Tarquin about to ravish Lucrece; and the metaphor of rape is a revealing one. Duncan's lying-asleep at Macbeth's mercy in his castle is an emblem of trust, of everything that both would have their civilization to be; and yet trust excites betrayal, debt exploitation, weakness violence, and faith faith-breach. The murder of Duncan is no mere political assassination. It is the very worst thing imaginable: 'most sacrilegious Murther' (II.iii.68), violating all the bonds between man, nature and God. And hence—its hour come round at last—the fascination that it holds.

'O horror! horror! horror!' cries Macduff, forced suddenly to face the physical reality, the moral atrocity and the full imaginative implications of Duncan's death. 'Tongue nor heart cannot conceive, nor name thee!' (II.iii.64–5). The thanes too are seized by the contamination of the excitement caused by the murder, and for a moment Macduff glimpses into the strangeness of a world in which he has lost all bearings. Then suddenly he finds the language he wants, an old language aroused to an assimilation of the horror he has just seen. 'Confusion now hath made his masterpiece!' (l. 67), he cries, and the elegiac note is prophetic. He senses what Macbeth most deeply fears, that the future will only bring anti-climax. 'All is but toys: renown, and grace, is dead' (l. 94), Macbeth will say. It is true in the fullest sense that 'Treason has done his worst' (III.ii.24)—which by the paradox of ambivalence has also been the best, a masterpiece. A terrible pornographic beauty has been born:

> Here lay Duncan,
> His silver skin lac'd with his golden blood;
> And his gash'd stabs look'd like a breach in nature
> For ruin's wasteful entrance. (II.iii.111–14)

But nothing that Macbeth can do in the future will ever be able so fully to absorb his imagination again. The king has been killed; and what's done cannot be redone.

The period of Macbeth's kingship has two antithetically related aspects, embodied at the end of the play in the alternating scenes of Act V: the degeneration of Macbeth and his wife, and the gathering resistance of the thanes under Malcolm and Macduff. I want briefly to outline them both. First, the degeneration of the Macbeths—a development which is a deepening not of debt and trust but of fear,

mistrust, suspicion. This mistrust has its political expression in the rapid establishment of a tyranny where one man's security is bought with the aid of a network of
paid informers and hired assassins, and where even the assassins are watched in
'mistrust' (III.iii.2). 'There's not a one of them, but in his house/I keep a servant fee'd'
(III.iv.130–1): the keynote is not gratitude but contempt—the contempt reserved
for those one fears or uses and akin to self-contempt in the generally degraded
view it holds of all mankind. Macbeth does not adventure upon relationship; where
Duncan visited his thanes, Macbeth must stay put in Dunsinane. The mistrust has its
family expression too in the widening separation between husband and wife; their
lack of issue comes to seem emblematic of the sterility into which their desires have
brought their marriage. Their relationship begins to fail even as conspiracy. Macbeth
embarks upon a course of debauchery in violence which he cannot bring himself to
share with his wife. 'Be innocent of the knowledge, dearest chuck' (III.ii.45), he says
to her with grotesque tenderness whilst awaiting Banquo's murder, and in so doing
he condemns her to an isolation which leads eventually to her suicide.

But it is perhaps the psychological exploration of mistrust that is most remarkable in the play, as we watch Macbeth himself disintegrate within the disintegration of his kingdom and his family. 'For mine own good', he says, 'All causes shall
give way' (III.iv.134–5). His hubris is a vain attempt to code the moral universe in
his own desires in order to secure himself against his fears; and as the play goes on,
he falls increasingly into the mistrustful anxieties of the paranoid cycle, where the
magical sense of omnipotence is haunted by its fellow-contrary nightmare of impotence. As in *King Lear,* the single state of man falls into extremes which (to quote
King James once more) 'although they seeme contrarie, yet growing to the height,
runne euer both in one'. The copresence of these two extremes is embodied with
great dramatic economy in the *double entendre* of the sisters' second group of
prophecies, which torture Macbeth with the hope that that which it is impossible to
prevent (his defeat) will be indeed prevented by that which is—again—impossible
(the movement of Birnam Wood to Dunsinane, the existence of a man not born
of woman). For Macbeth, these gnomic gobbets torn from the book of the black
arts serve as fetishes; tantalizingly untrustworthy as they are, they encourage him to
plunge on through his 'initiate fear' (III.iv.142) into a reckless debauchery of wrong-
doing. But, in the manner of fetishes, they cannot adequately replace those reci-
procities of love and trust which Macbeth has already put to the sword; they can
do no more than afford a displaced ground upon which the subsequent conflict
between desire and terror can be acted out to its inescapable conclusion. Finally,
the contamination of this violent conflict infects Macbeth totally; the diminishing
returns of his perversity wither him into the image of the 'wither'd Murther' that he
had at first invoked; and then, played out, he is killed, a haunting after-image of the
soldier in Act I, fighting fiercely still but for what he no longer believes in.

The process of Macbeth's disintegration is complemented by the integration of
the thanes' resistance to him. They resist as they must; but we should not think
simply of the opposition between them. There is identity as well as difference, and
the language of the thanes suggests how deeply they are united with Macbeth in the

strife which divides them; for the violence of emotion aroused by the murder of Duncan has caused a general moral panic throughout the community.

> Alas, poor country!
> Almost afraid to know itself. It cannot
> Be call'd our mother, but our grave; where nothing,
> But who knows nothing, is once seen to smile;
> Where sighs, and groans, and shrieks that rent the air
> Are made, not mark'd; where violent sorrow seems
> A modern ecstasy. . . .   (IV.iii.164–70)

Here is the same contamination of excitement and theatricality of imagination that we found in Macbeth, as Rosse attempts to picture the masterpiece of confusion that he sees in Scotland.

Yet, as Macduff found an old language to save himself from strangeness when he spoke of 'most sacrilegious Murther', so too do the thanes in their attempt to help their poor country reknow itself. It is an excited, often superstitious language, anathematizing Evil and the inversion of Good and sentimentalizing both because of the excitements that they feel. Their army will 'dew the sovereign flower, and drown the weeds' (V.ii.30), Macbeth is simply 'the tyrant' (l.11) and Malcolm 'the med'cine of the sickly weal' (l. 27): Macbeth is the source of all contamination in the realm, it seems, and to kill him has become a sacred necessity; and a regular use of images of purification and purgation accordingly marks the sacrificial way in which the thanes approach their military mission.

> Well; march we on,
> To give obedience where 'tis truly ow'd:
> Meet we the med'cine of the sickly weal;
> And with him pour we, in our country's purge,
> Each drop of us.   (V.ii.25–9)

Yet the emotions in Macduff, for one, are clearly not always of this sacrificial cast. 'Revenges burn in them' (l. 3), says Menteth of Malcolm and his military command-ers, including 'the good Macduff' (l. 2). The language of purification is no doubt psychologically and politically valuable to restrain the violent energies of the civil war in which the play (as it began) is ending; and yet it is a language inadequate to what we see. There is a real sense in which Macbeth has become, despite all his tyranny, a scapegoat, bearing all the violence in his society, unifying it by his death and thereby preventing the thanes from understanding those political contradictions and psychological ambivalences that have caused the violence in which they are even now implicated. Duncan perceived the kind of violence by which he was threatened but could not accommodate it in either his language or his statecraft; Macbeth perceived the kind of violence by which he was threatened but could not accommodate its power to excite; but the thanes do no more than name the violence by which they are threatened 'Macbeth' and try to restore the world as it was before.

This desire on the part of the thanes to restore the world that had already failed them serves by contrast to reinforce the aristocratic heroism of Macbeth, a heroism not of service but of hubris.

> I am in blood
> Stepp'd in so far, that, should I wade no more,
> Returning were as tedious as go o'er. (III.iv.135–7)

Macbeth does not return, he goes over; he dares those perverse extremes of experience which he cannot resist. With a warrior's recklessness and a thane's conscience, he commits himself to the conflicts that they entail, and in so doing he draws out everything previously disavowed in his society. In daring that which was most forbidden, he sets in train a violent civil conflict that will change it decisively; he becomes the heroic destroyer of a heroic age.

—JOHN TURNER, "The Tyrannical Kingship of Macbeth," *Shakespeare: The Play of History* by Graham Holderness, Nick Potter, and John Turner (Iowa City: University of Iowa Press, 1987), pp. 136–43

CRITICAL ESSAYS

A. C. Bradley

MACBETH

Macbeth, the cousin of a King mild, just, and beloved, but now too old to lead his army, is introduced to us as a general of extraordinary prowess, who has covered himself with glory in putting down a rebellion and repelling the invasion of a foreign army. In these conflicts he showed great personal courage, a quality which he continues to display throughout the drama in regard to all plain dangers. It is difficult to be sure of his customary demeanour, for in the play we see him either in what appears to be an exceptional relation to his wife, or else in the throes of remorse and desperation; but from his behaviour during his journey home after the war, from his *later* conversations with Lady Macbeth, and from his language to the murderers of Banquo and to others, we imagine him as a great warrior, somewhat masterful, rough, and abrupt, a man to inspire some fear and much admiration. He was thought 'honest,' or honourable; he was trusted, apparently, by everyone; Macduff, a man of the highest integrity, 'loved him well.' And there was, in fact, much good in him. We have no warrant, I think, for describing him, with many writers, as of a 'noble' nature, like Hamlet or Othello;[1] but he had a keen sense both of honour and of the worth of a good name. The phrase, again, 'too much of the milk of human kindness,' is applied to him in impatience by his wife, who did not fully understand him; but certainly he was far from devoid of humanity and pity.

At the same time he was exceedingly ambitious. He must have been so by temper. The tendency must have been greatly strengthened by his marriage. When we see him, it has been further stimulated by his remarkable success and by the consciousness of exceptional powers and merit. It becomes a passion. The course of action suggested by it is extremely perilous: it sets his good name, his position, and even his life on the hazard. It is also abhorrent to his better feelings. Their defeat in the struggle with ambition leaves him utterly wretched, and would have kept him so, however complete had been his outward success and security. On the other hand, his passion for power and his instinct of self-assertion are so vehement that no inward misery could persuade him to relinquish the fruits of crime, or to advance from remorse to repentance.

From *Shakespearean Tragedy* (London: Macmillan, 1904), pp. 351–65.

In the character as so far sketched there is nothing very peculiar, though the strength of the forces contending in it is unusual. But there is in Macbeth one marked peculiarity, the true apprehension of which is the key to Shakespeare's conception.[2] This bold ambitious man of action has, within certain limits, the imagination of a poet,—an imagination on the one hand extremely sensitive to impressions of a certain kind, and, on the other, productive of violent disturbance both of mind and body. Through it he is kept in contact with supernatural impressions and is liable to supernatural fears. And through it, especially, come to him the intimations of conscience and honour. Macbeth's better nature—to put the matter for clearness' sake too broadly—instead of speaking to him in the overt language of moral ideas, commands, and prohibitions, incorporates itself in images which alarm and horrify. His imagination is thus the best of him, something usually deeper and higher than his conscious thoughts; and if he had obeyed it he would have been safe. But his wife quite misunderstands it, and he himself understands it only in part. The terrifying images which deter him from crime and follow its commission, and which are really the protest of his deepest self, seem to his wife the creations of mere nervous fear, and are sometimes referred by himself to the dread of vengeance or the restlessness of insecurity.[3] His conscious or reflective mind, that is, moves chiefly among considerations of outward success and failure, while his inner being is convulsed by conscience. And his inability to understand himself is repeated and exaggerated in the interpretations of actors and critics, who represent him as a coward, cold-blooded, calculating, and pitiless, who shrinks from crime simply because it is dangerous, and suffers afterwards simply because he is not safe. In reality his courage is frightful. He strides from crime to crime, though his soul never ceases to bar his advance with shapes of terror, or to clamour in his ears that he is murdering his peace and casting away his 'eternal jewel.'

It is of the first importance to realise the strength, and also (what has not been so clearly recognised) the limits, of Macbeth's imagination. It is not the universal meditative imagination of Hamlet. He came to see in man, as Hamlet sometimes did, the 'quintessence of dust'; but he must always have been incapable of Hamlet's reflections on man's noble reason and infinite faculty, or of seeing with Hamlet's eyes 'this brave o'erhanging firmament, this majestical roof fretted with golden fire.' Nor could he feel, like Othello, the romance of war or the infinity of love. He shows no sign of any unusual sensitiveness to the glory or beauty in the world or the soul; and it is partly for this reason that we regard him with more of awe than of pity. His imagination is excitable and intense, but narrow. That which stimulates it is, almost solely, that which thrills with sudden, startling, and often supernatural fear.[4] There is a famous passage late in the play (V. v. 10) which is here very significant, because it refers to a time before his conscience was burdened, and so shows his native disposition:

> The time has been, my senses would have cool'd
> To hear a night-shriek; and my fell of hair
> Would at a dismal treatise rise and stir
> As life were in't.

This 'time' must have been in his youth, or at least before we see him. And, in the drama, everything which terrifies him is of this character, only it has now a deeper and a moral significance. Palpable dangers leave him unmoved or fill him with fire. He does himself mere justice when he asserts he 'dare do all that may become a man,' or when he exclaims to Banquo's ghost,

> What man dare, I dare:
> Approach thou like the rugged Russian bear,
> The arm'd rhinoceros, or the Hyrcan tiger;
> Take any shape but that, and my firm nerves
> Shall never tremble.

What appals him is always the image of his own guilty heart or bloody deed, or some image which derives from them its terror or gloom. These, when they arise, hold him spell-bound and possess him wholly, like a hypnotic trance which is at the same time the ecstasy of a poet. As the first 'horrid image' of Duncan's murder—of himself murdering Duncan—rises from unconsciousness and confronts him, his hair stands on end and the outward scene vanishes from his eyes. Why? For fear of 'consequences'? The idea is ridiculous. Or because the deed is bloody? The man who with his 'smoking' steel 'carved out his passage' to the rebel leader, and 'unseam'd him from the nave to the chaps,' would hardly be frightened by blood. How could fear of consequences make the dagger he is to use hang suddenly glittering before him in the air, and then as suddenly dash it with gouts of blood? Even when he *talks* of consequences, and declares that if he were safe against them he would 'jump the life to come,' his imagination bears witness against him, and shows us that what really holds him back is the hideous vileness of the deed:

> He's here in double trust;
> First, as I am his kinsman and his subject,
> Strong both against the deed; then, as his host,
> Who should against his murderer shut the door,
> Not bear the knife myself. Besides, this Duncan
> Hath borne his faculties so meek, hath been
> So clear in his great office, that his virtues
> Will plead like angels, trumpet-tongued, against
> The deep damnation of his taking-off;
> And pity, like a naked new-born babe,
> Striding the blast, or heaven's cherubim, horsed
> Upon the sightless couriers of the air,
> Shall blow the horrid deed in every eye,
> That tears shall drown the wind.

It may be said that he is here thinking of the horror that others will feel at the deed—thinking therefore of consequences. Yes, but could he realise thus how horrible the deed would look to others if it were not equally horrible to himself?

It is the same when the murder is done. He is well-nigh mad with horror, but it is not the horror of detection. It is not he who thinks of washing his hands or getting his nightgown on. He has brought away the daggers he should have left on the pillows of the grooms, but what does he care for that? What *he* thinks of is that, when he heard one of the men awaked from sleep say 'God bless us,' he could not say 'Amen'; for his imagination presents to him the parching of his throat as an immediate judgment from heaven. His wife heard the owl scream and the crickets cry; but what *he* heard was the voice that first cried 'Macbeth doth murder sleep,' and then, a minute later, with a change of tense, denounced on him, as if his three names gave him three personalities to suffer in, the doom of sleeplessness:

> Glamis hath murdered sleep, and therefore Cawdor
> Shall sleep no more, Macbeth shall sleep no more.

There comes a sound of knocking. It should be perfectly familiar to him; but he knows not whence, or from what world, it comes. He looks down at his hands, and starts violently: 'What hands are here?' For they seem alive, they move, they mean to pluck out his eyes. He looks at one of them again; it does not move; but the blood upon it is enough to dye the whole ocean red. What has all this to do with fear of 'consequences'? It is his soul speaking in the only shape in which it can speak freely, that of imagination.

So long as Macbeth's imagination is active, we watch him fascinated; we feel suspense, horror, awe; in which are latent, also, admiration and sympathy. But so soon as it is quiescent these feelings vanish. He is no longer 'infirm of purpose': he becomes domineering, even brutal, or he becomes a cool pitiless hypocrite. He is generally said to be a very bad actor, but this is not wholly true. Whenever his imagination stirs, he acts badly. It so possesses him, and is so much stronger than his reason, that his face betrays him, and his voice utters the most improbable untruths[5] or the most artificial rhetoric.[6] But when it is asleep he is firm, self-controlled and practical, as in the conversation where he skilfully elicits from Banquo that information about his movements which is required for the successful arrangement of his murder.[7] Here he is hateful; and so he is in the conversation with the murderers, who are not professional cut-throats but old soldiers, and whom, without a vestige of remorse, he beguiles with calumnies against Banquo and with such appeals as his wife had used to him.[8] On the other hand, we feel much pity as well as anxiety in the scene (I. vii.) where she overcomes his opposition to the murder; and we feel it (though his imagination is not specially active) because this scene shows us how little he understands himself. This is his great misfortune here. Not that he fails to realise in reflection the baseness of the deed (the soliloquy with which the scene opens shows that he does not). But he has never, to put it pedantically, accepted as the principle of his conduct the morality which takes shape in his imaginative fears. Had he done so, and said plainly to his wife, 'The thing is vile, and, however much I have sworn to do it, I will not,' she would have been helpless; for all her arguments proceed on the assumption that there is for them no such point of view. Macbeth does approach this position once, when, resenting the accusation of cowardice, he answers,

> I dare do all that may become a man;
> Who dares do more is none.

She feels in an instant that everything is at stake, and, ignoring the point, overwhelms him with indignant and contemptuous personal reproach. But he yields to it because he is himself half-ashamed of that answer of his, and because, for want of habit, the simple idea which it expresses has no hold on him comparable to the force it acquires when it becomes incarnate in visionary fears and warnings.

Yet these were so insistent, and they offered to his ambition a resistance so strong, that it is impossible to regard him as falling through the blindness or delusion of passion. On the contrary, he himself feels with such intensity the enormity of his purpose that, it seems clear, neither his ambition nor yet the prophecy of the Witches would ever without the aid of Lady Macbeth have overcome this feeling. As it is, the deed is done in horror and without the faintest desire or sense of glory,—done, one may almost say, as if it were an appalling duty; and, the instant it is finished, its futility is revealed to Macbeth as clearly as its vileness had been revealed beforehand. As he staggers from the scene he mutters in despair,

> Wake Duncan with thy knocking! I would thou could'st.

When, half an hour later, he returns with Lennox from the room of the murder, he breaks out:

> Had I but died an hour before this chance,
> I had lived a blessed time; for from this instant
> There's nothing serious in mortality:
> All is but toys: renown and grace is dead;
> The wine of life is drawn, and the mere lees
> Is left this vault to brag of.

This is no mere acting. The language here has none of the false rhetoric of his merely hypocritical speeches. It is meant to deceive, but it utters at the same time his profoundest feeling. And this he can henceforth never hide from himself for long. However he may try to drown it in further enormities, he hears it murmuring,

> Duncan is in his grave:
> After life's fitful fever he sleeps well:

or,

> better be with the dead:

or,

> I have lived long enough:

and it speaks its last words on the last day of his life:

> Out, out, brief candle!
> Life's but a walking shadow, a poor player

That struts and frets his hour upon the stage
And then is heard no more: it is a tale
Told by an idiot, full of sound and fury,
Signifying nothing.

How strange that this judgment on life, the despair of a man who had knowingly made mortal war on his own soul, should be frequently quoted as Shakespeare's own judgment, and should even be adduced, in serious criticism, as a proof of his pessimism!

It remains to look a little more fully at the history of Macbeth after the murder of Duncan. Unlike his first struggle this history excites little suspense or anxiety on his account: we have now no hope for him. But it is an engrossing spectacle, and psychologically it is perhaps the most remarkable exhibition of the *development* of a character to be found in Shakespeare's tragedies.

That heart-sickness which comes from Macbeth's perception of the futility of his crime, and which never leaves him for long, is not, however, his habitual state. It could not be so, for two reasons. In the first place the consciousness of guilt is stronger in him than the consciousness of failure; and it keeps him in a perpetual agony of restlessness, and forbids him simply to droop and pine. His mind is 'full of scorpions.' He cannot sleep. He 'keeps alone,' moody and savage. 'All that is within him does condemn itself for being there.' There is a fever in his blood which urges him to ceaseless action in the search for oblivion. And, in the second place, ambition, the love of power, the instinct of self-assertion, are much too potent in Macbeth to permit him to resign, even in spirit, the prize for which he has put rancours in the vessel of his peace. The 'will to live' is mighty in him. The forces which impelled him to aim at the crown re-assert themselves. He faces the world, and his own conscience, desperate, but never dreaming of acknowledging defeat. He will see 'the frame of things disjoint' first. He challenges fate into the lists.

The result is frightful. He speaks no more, as before Duncan's murder, of honour or pity. That sleepless torture, he tells himself, is nothing but the sense of insecurity and the fear of retaliation. If only he were safe, it would vanish. And he looks about for the cause of his fear; and his eye falls on Banquo. Banquo, who cannot fail to suspect him, has not fled or turned against him: Banquo has become his chief counsellor. Why? Because, he answers, the kingdom was promised to Banquo's children. Banquo, then, is waiting to attack him, to make a way for them. The 'bloody instructions' he himself taught when he murdered Duncan, are about to return, as he said they would, to plague the inventor. *This* then, he tells himself, is the fear that will not let him sleep; and it will die with Banquo. There is no hesitation now, and no remorse: he has nearly learned his lesson. He hastens feverishly, not to murder Banquo, but to procure his murder: some strange idea is in his mind that the thought of the dead man will not haunt him, like the memory of Duncan, if the deed is done by other hands.[9] The deed is done: but, instead of peace descending on him, from the depths of his nature his half-murdered conscience rises; his deed confronts him in the apparition of Banquo's Ghost, and the horror of the night of his first murder returns. But, alas, *it* has less power, and *he* has more will. Agonised and trembling, he still faces this rebel image, and it yields:

> Why, so: being gone,
> I am a man again.

Yes, but his secret is in the hands of the assembled lords. And, worse, this deed is as futile as the first. For, though Banquo is dead and even his Ghost is conquered, that inner torture is unassuaged. But he will not bear it. His guests have hardly left him when he turns roughly to his wife:

> How say'st thou, that Macduff denies his person
> At our great bidding?

Macduff it is that spoils his sleep. He shall perish,—he and aught else that bars the road to peace.

> For mine own good
> All causes shall give way: I am in blood
> Stepp'd in so far that, should I wade no more,
> Returning were as tedious as go o'er:
> Strange things I have in head that will to hand,
> Which must be acted ere they may be scann'd.

She answers, sick at heart,

> You lack the season of all natures, sleep.

No doubt: but he has found the way to it now:

> Come, we'll to sleep. My strange and self abuse
> Is the initiate fear that wants hard use:
> We are yet but young in deed.

What a change from the man who thought of Duncan's virtues, and of pity like a naked new-born babe! What a frightful clearness of self-consciousness in this descent to hell, and yet what a furious force in the instinct of life and self-assertion that drives him on!

He goes to seek the Witches. He will know, by the worst means, the worst. He has no longer any awe of them.

> How now, you secret, black and midnight hags!

—so he greets them, and at once he demands and threatens. They tell him he is right to fear Macduff. They tell him to fear nothing, for none of woman born can harm him. He feels that the two statements are at variance; infatuated, suspects no double meaning; but, that he may 'sleep in spite of thunder,' determines not to spare Macduff. But his heart throbs to know one thing, and he forces from the Witches the vision of Banquo's children crowned. The old intolerable thought returns, 'for Banquo's issue have I filed my mind'; and with it, for all the absolute

security apparently promised him, there returns that inward fever. Will nothing
quiet it? Nothing but destruction. Macduff, one comes to tell him, has escaped him;
but that does not matter: he can still destroy:[10]

> And even now,
> To crown my thoughts with acts, be it thought and done:
> The castle of Macduff I will surprise;
> Seize upon Fife; give to the edge o' the sword
> His wife, his babes, and all unfortunate souls
> That trace him in's line. No boasting like a fool;
> This deed I'll do before this purpose cool.
> But no more sights!

No, he need fear no more 'sights.' The Witches have done their work, and after
this purposeless butchery his own imagination will trouble him no more.[11] He has
dealt his last blow at the conscience and pity which spoke through it.

   The whole flood of evil in his nature is now let loose. He becomes an open
tyrant, dreaded by everyone about him, and a terror to his country. She 'sinks
beneath the yoke.'

> Each new morn
> New widows howl, new orphans cry, new sorrows
> Strike heaven on the face.

She weeps, she bleeds, 'and each new day a gash is added to her wounds.' She is
not the mother of her children, but their grave;

> where nothing,
> But who knows nothing, is once seen to smile:
> Where signs and groans and shrieks that rend the air
> Are made, not mark'd.

For this wild rage and furious cruelty we are prepared; but vices of another kind
start up as he plunges on his downward way.

> I grant him bloody,
> Luxurious, avaricious, false, deceitful,
> Sudden, malicious,

says Malcolm; and two of these epithets surprise us. Who would have expected
avarice or lechery[12] in Macbeth? His ruin seems complete.

   Yet it is never complete. To the end he never totally loses our sympathy; we
never feel towards him as we do to those who appear the born children of
darkness. There remains something sublime in the defiance with which, even when
cheated of his last hope, he faces earth and hell and heaven. Nor would any soul
to whom evil was congenial be capable of that heart-sickness which overcomes him
when he thinks of the 'honour, love, obedience, troops of friends' which 'he must

not look to have' (and which Iago would never have cared to have), and contrasts
with them

> Curses, not loud but deep, mouth-honour, breath,
> Which the poor heart would fain deny, and dare not,

(and which Iago would have accepted with indifference). Neither can I agree with
those who find in his reception of the news of his wife's death proof of alienation
or utter carelessness. There is no proof of these in the words,

> She should have died hereafter;
> There would have been a time for such a word,

spoken as they are by a man already in some measure prepared for such news, and
now transported by the frenzy of his last fight for life. He has no time now to feel.[13]
Only, as he thinks of the morrow when time to feel will come—if anything comes,
the vanity of all hopes and forward-lookings sinks deep into his soul with an infinite
weariness, and he murmurs,

> To-morrow, and to-morrow, and to-morrow,
> Creeps in this petty pace from day to day
> To the last syllable of recorded time,
> And all our yesterdays have lighted fools
> The way to dusty death.

In the very depths a gleam of his native love of goodness, and with it a touch of
tragic grandeur, rests upon him. The evil he has desperately embraced continues to
madden or to wither his inmost heart. No experience in the world could bring him
to glory in it or make his peace with it, or to forget what he once was and Iago and
Goneril never were.

NOTES

[1] The word is used of him (l. ii. 67), but not in a way that decides this question or even bears on it.
[2] This view, thus generally stated, is not original, but I cannot say who first stated it.
[3] The latter, and more important, point was put quite clearly by Coleridge.
[4] It is the consequent insistence on the idea of fear, and the frequent repetition of the word, that have principally led to misinterpretation.
[5] E.g. l. iii. 149, where he excuses his abstraction by saying that his 'dull brain was wrought with things forgotten,' when nothing could be more natural than that he should be thinking of his new honour.
[6] E.g. in l. iv. This is so also in ll. iii. 114 ff., though here there is some real imaginative excitement mingled with the rhetorical antitheses and balanced clauses and forced bombast.
[7] III. i. Lady Macbeth herself could not more naturally have introduced at intervals the questions 'Ride you this afternoon?' (l. 19), 'Is't far you ride?' (l. 24), 'Goes Fleance with you?' (l. 36).
[8] We feel here, however, an underlying subdued frenzy which awakes some sympathy. There is an almost unendurable impatience expressed even in the rhythm of many of the lines; e.g.:

> Well then, now
> Have you consider'd of my speeches? Know
> That it was he in the times past which held you
> So under fortune, which you thought had been
> Our innocent self: this I made good to you

> In our last conference, pass'd in probation with you,
> How you were borne in hand, how cross'd, the instruments,
> Who wrought with them, and all things else that might
> To half a soul and to a notion crazed
> Say, 'Thus did Banquo.'

This effect is heard to the end of the play in Macbeth's less poetic speeches, and leaves the same impression of burning energy, though not of imaginative exaltation, as his great speeches. In these we find either violent, huge, sublime imagery, or a torrent of figurative expressions (as in the famous lines about 'the innocent sleep'). Our impressions as to the diction of the play are largely derived from these speeches of the hero, but not wholly so. The writing almost throughout leaves an impression of intense, almost feverish, activity.

[9] See his first words to the Ghost: 'Thou canst not say I did it.'

[10]   For only in destroying I find ease
>   To my relentless thoughts.   (*Paradise Lost*, ix. 129.)

Milton's portrait of Satan's misery here, and at the beginning of Book IV., might well have been suggested by *Macbeth*. Coleridge, after quoting Duncan's speech, I. iv. 35ff., says: 'It is a fancy; but I can never read this, and the following speeches of Macbeth, without involuntarily thinking of the Miltonic Messiah and Satan.' I doubt if it was a mere fancy. (It will be remembered that Milton thought at one time of writing a tragedy on Macbeth.)

[11] The immediate reference in 'But no more sights' is doubtless to the visions called up by the Witches; but one of these, the 'blood-bolter'd Banquo,' recalls to him the vision of the preceding night, of which he had said,

>   You make me strange
> Even to the disposition that I owe,
> When now I think you can behold such *sights*,
> And keep the natural ruby of your cheeks,
> When mine is blanch'd with fear.

[12] 'Luxurious' and 'luxury' are used by Shakespeare only in this older sense. It must be remembered that these lines are spoken by Malcolm, but it seems likely that they are meant to be taken as true throughout.

[13] I do not at all suggest that his love for his wife remains what it was when he greeted her with the words 'My dearest love, Duncan comes here to-night.' He has greatly changed; she has ceased to help him, sunk in her own despair; and there is no intensity of anxiety in the questions he puts to the doctor about her. But his love for her was probably never unselfish, never the love of Brutus, who, in somewhat similar circumstances, uses, on the death of Cassius, words which remind us of Macbeth's:

> I shall find time, Cassius, I shall find time.

For the opposite strain of feeling cf. Sonnet 90:

> Then hate me if thou wilt; if ever, now,
> Now while the world is bent my deeds to cross.

Wayne C. Booth
MACBETH AS TRAGIC HERO

Put even in its simplest terms, the problem Shakespeare gave himself in *Macbeth* was a tremendous one. Take a good man, a noble man, a man admired by all who know him—and destroy him, not only physically and emotionally, as the Greeks destroyed their heroes, but also morally and intellectually. As if this were not difficult enough as a dramatic hurdle, while transforming him into one of the most despicable mortals conceivable, maintain him as a tragic hero—that is, keep him so sympathetic that, when he comes to his death, the audience will pity rather than detest him and will be relieved to see him out of his misery rather than pleased to see him destroyed. Put in Shakespeare's own terms: take a "noble" man, full of "conscience" and "the milk of human kindness," and make of him a "dead butcher," yet keep him an object of pity rather than hatred. If we thus artificially reconstruct the problem as it might have existed before the play was written, we see that, in choosing these "terminal points" and these terminal intentions, Shakespeare makes almost impossible demands on his dramatic skill, although at the same time he insures that, if he succeeds at all, he will succeed magnificently. If the trick can be turned, it will inevitably be a great one.

One need only consider the many relative failures in attempts at similar "plots" and effects to realize the difficulties involved. When dramatists or novelists attempt the sympathetic-degenerative plot, almost always one or another of the following failures or transformations occurs: (1) The feeling of abhorrence for the protagonist becomes so strong that all sympathy is lost, and the play or novel becomes "punitive"—that is, the reader's or spectator's chief pleasure depends on his satisfaction in revenge or punishment. (2) The protagonist is never really made very wicked, after all; he only *seems* wicked by conventional (and, by implication, unsound) standards and is really a highly admirable reform-candidate. (3) The protagonist reforms in the end and avoids his proper punishment. (4) The book or play itself becomes a "wicked" work; that is, either deliberately or unconsciously the artist makes us side with his degenerated hero against "morality." If it is deliberate, we have propaganda works of one kind or another, often resembling the second

From *Journal of General Education* 6, No. 1 (October 1951): 17–25.

type above; if it is unconscious, we get works whose immorality (as in pornographic or sadistic treatments of the good-girl-turned-whore, thief, or murderess) makes them unenjoyable as literature unless the reader or spectator temporarily or permanently relaxes his own standards of moral judgment. Any of these failures or transformations can be found in conjunction with the most frequent failure of all: the degeneration remains finally unexplained, unmotivated; the forces employed to destroy the noble man are found pitifully inadequate to make his fall seem credible.

Even in works which are somewhat successful, there is almost always some shrinking from a fully responsible engagement with the inherent difficulties. For example, in *Tender Is the Night,* which is in many ways strikingly similar to *Macbeth,* Fitzgerald waters down the effect in several ways. Dick Diver, Fitzgerald's "noble" man, is destroyed, but he is destroyed only to helplessness—to unpopularity and drunkenness and poverty; he becomes a "failure." The signs of his destruction are never grotesque acts of cruelty or wickedness of the kind committed by Macbeth or of a kind which for the modern reader would be analogous in their unsympathetic quality. Rather, he speaks more sharply to people than he used to; he is no longer charming. This is indeed pitiful enough, in its own way, but it is easy enough, too, especially when the artist chooses, as Fitzgerald does, to report the final demoralization of the hero only vaguely and from a great distance: one never *sees* Dick Diver's final horrible moments as one sees Macbeth's. So that, at the end of his downward path, Diver has been more sinned against than sinning, and we have no obstacles to our pity. But, on the other hand, since the fall has not been nearly so great, our pity that the fall should have occurred at all is attenuated, compared with the awfulness of the last hours of Macbeth. Other attenuations follow from this one. If the fall is not a very great one, the forces needed to produce it need not be great (although one might argue that even in *Tender Is the Night* they should have been greater, for credibility). Nicole and a general atmosphere of gloom and decay are made to do a job which in *Macbeth* requires some of the richest degenerative forces ever employed. If, then, comparison on these structural points is just, in spite of the strong differences between the works, it indicates that in point of difficulties faced—or, one should say, created—Shakespeare in *Macbeth* has it all over Fitzgerald, as he has it all over anyone else I know of who has attempted this form.[1]

I

A complete study of how *Macbeth* is made to succeed in spite of—or rather because of—the difficulties is perhaps beyond the capacities of any one reader. It is certainly impossible here. But the major devices employed—one never knows how "consciously"—by Shakespeare can be enumerated and discussed quite simply.

The first step in convincing us that Macbeth's fall is a genuinely tragic occurrence is to convince us that there was, in reality, a fall: we must believe that Macbeth was once a man whom we could admire, a man with great potentialities. One way to convince us would have been to show him, as Fitzgerald shows Dick Diver, in action as an admirable man. But, although this is possible in a leisurely novel, it would, in a play, have wasted time needed for the important events, which begin only with Macbeth's great temptation at the conclusion of the opening battle. Thus the superior choice in this case (although it would not necessarily always be so) is to begin your representation of the action with the first real temptation to the fall and to use testimony by other characters to establish your protagonist's prior goodness. We are thus given, from the beginning, sign after sign that Macbeth's greatest nobility was reached at a point just prior to the opening of the play. When the play begins, he has already coveted the crown, as is shown by his excessively nervous reaction to the witches' prophecy; it is indeed likely that he has already considered foul means of obtaining it. But, in spite of this wickedness already present to his mind as a possibility, we have ample reason to think Macbeth a man worthy of our admiration. He is "brave" and "valiant," a "worthy gentleman"; Duncan calls him "noble Macbeth." These epithets have an ironic quality only in retrospect; when they are first applied, one has no reason to doubt them. Indeed, they are true epithets, or they would have been true if applied, say, only a few days or months earlier.

Of course, this testimony to his prior virtue given by his friends in the midst of other business would not carry the spectators for long with any sympathy for Macbeth if it were not continued in several other forms. We have the testimony of Lady Macbeth (the unimpeachable testimony of a "bad" person castigating the goodness of a "good" person):

> Yet do I fear thy nature;
> It is too full o' the milk of human kindness
> To catch the nearest way. Thou wouldst be great,
> Art not without ambition, but without
> The illness should attend it. What thou wouldst highly,
> That wouldst thou holily; wouldst not play false,
> And yet wouldst wrongly win.

No verbal evidence would be enough, however, if we did not see in Macbeth himself signs of its validity, since we have already seen many signs that he is *not* the good man that the witnesses seem to believe. Thus the best evidence we have of his essential goodness is his vacillation before the murder. Just as Raskolnikov is tormented and just as we ourselves—virtuous theater viewers—would be tormented, so Macbeth is tormented before the prospect of his own crime. Indeed, much as he wants the kingship, he decides in Scene 3 against the murder:

> If chance will have me King, why, chance may crown me,
> Without my stir. . . .

And when he first meets Lady Macbeth he is resolved not to murder Duncan. In fact, as powerful a rhetorician as she is, she has all she can do to get him back on the course of murder.[2]

In addition, Macbeth's ensuing soliloquy not only weighs the possible bad practical consequences of his act but shows him perfectly aware, in a way an evil man would not be, of the moral values involved:

> He's here in double trust:
> First, as I am his kinsman and his subject,
> Strong both against the deed; then, as his host,
> Who should against his murderer shut the door,
> Not bear the knife myself. Besides, this Duncan
> Hath borne his faculties so meek, hath been
> So clear in his great office, that his virtues
> Will plead like angels, trumpet-tongued, against
> The deep damnation of his taking-off. . . .

In this speech we see again, as we saw in the opening of the play, Shakespeare's wonderful economy: the very speech which shows Macbeth to best advantage is the one which shows the audience how very bad his contemplated act is, since Duncan is blameless. One need only think of the same speech if it were dealing with a king who *deserves* to be assassinated or if it were given by another character commenting on Macbeth's action, to see how right it is as it stands.

After this soliloquy Macbeth announces again to Lady Macbeth that he will not go on ("We will proceed no further in this business"), but her eloquence is too much for him. Under her jibes at his "unmanliness," he progresses from a kind of petulant, but still honorable, boasting ("I dare do all that may become a man;/Who dares do more is none"), through a state of amoral consideration of mere expediency ("If I should fail?"), to complete resolution, but still with a full understanding of the wickedness of his act ("I am settled . . . this terrible feat"). There is never any doubt, first, that he is bludgeoned into the deed by Lady Macbeth's superior rhetoric and force of character and by the pressure of unfamiliar circumstances (including the witches) and, second, that even in the final decision to go through with it he is extremely troubled by a guilty conscience ("*False* face must hide what the *false* heart doth know"). In the entire dagger soliloquy he is clearly suffering from the realization of the horror of the "bloody business" ahead. He sees fully and painfully the wickedness of the course he has chosen, but not until after the deed, when the knocking has commenced, do we realize how terrifyingly alive his conscience is: "To know my deed, 't were best not know myself./Wake Duncan with thy knocking! I would thou couldst!" This is the wish of a "good" man who, though he has become a "bad" man, still thinks and feels as a good man would.

To cite one last example of Shakespeare's pains in this matter, we have the testimony to Macbeth's character offered by Hecate (III, 5):

> And which is worse, all you have done
> Hath been but for a wayward son,
> Spiteful and wrathful, who, as others do,
> Loves for his own ends, not for you.

This reaffirmation that Macbeth is not a true son of evil comes, interestingly enough, immediately after the murder of Banquo, at a time when the audience needs a reminder of Macbeth's fundamental nobility.

The evil of his acts is thus built upon the knowledge that he is not a naturally evil man but a man who has every potentiality for goodness. This potentiality and its frustration are the chief ingredients of the tragedy of Macbeth. Macbeth is a man whose progressive external misfortunes seem to produce, and at the same time seem to be produced by, his parallel progression from great goodness to great wickedness. Our emotional involvement (which perhaps should not be simplified under the term "pity" or "pity and fear") is thus a combination of two kinds of regret: (1) We regret that any potentially good man should come to such a bad end: "What a pity that things should have gone this way, that things should *be* this way!" (2) We regret even more the destruction of this particular man, a man who is not only morally sympathetic but also intellectually and emotionally interesting. In eliciting both these kinds of regret to such a high degree, Shakespeare goes beyond his predecessors and establishes trends which are still working themselves out in literature. The first kind—never used at all by classical dramatists, who never employed a genuinely degenerative plot—has been attempted again and again by modern novelists. Their difficulty has usually been that they have relied too completely on a general humane response in the reader and too little on a realized prior height or potentiality from which to fall. The protagonists are shown succumbing to their environment—or, as in so many "sociological" novels, already succumbed—and the reader is left to himself to infer that something worth bothering about has gone to waste, that things might have been otherwise, that there is any real reason to react emotionally to the final destruction. The second kind—almost unknown to classical dramatists, whose characters are never "original" or "fresh" in the modern sense—has been attempted in ever greater extremes since Shakespeare, until one finds many works in which mere *interest* in particular characteristics completely supplants emotional response to *events* involving men with interesting characteristics. The pathos of Bloom, for example, is an attenuated pathos, just as the comedy of Bloom is an attenuated comedy; one is not primarily moved to laughter or tears by events involving great characters, as in *Macbeth,* but rather one is primarily interested in details about characters. It can be argued whether this is a gain or a loss to literature, when considered in general. Certainly, one would rather read a modern novel like *Ulysses,* with all its faults on its head, than many of the older dramas or epics involving "great" characters in "great" events. But it can hardly be denied that one of Shakespeare's triumphs is his success in doing many things at once which lesser writers have since done only one at a time. He has all the generalized effect of a classical tragedy. We lament the "bad fortune" of a great man who has known good fortune. To this he adds the much more poignant (at least to us) pity one feels in observing the moral destruction of a great man who has once known goodness. And yet with all this he combines the pity one feels when one observes a highly characterized individual—whom one knows intimately, as it were, in whom one is *interested*—going to destruction. One difference between watching Macbeth go to destruction and watching the typical modern hero, whether in the drama (say, Willy Loman) or in the novel (say, Jake or any other of Hemingway's heroes), is that in *Macbeth* there is some "going." Willy Loman doesn't have very far to fall; he begins the play on the verge of suicide, and at the end of the play he has committed suicide. Even if we assume that the "beginning" is the time covered in the earliest of the flashbacks, we have not "far to go" from there to Willy's destruction. It is true that our contemporary willingness to exalt the potentialities of the average man makes Willy's fall seem to *us* a greater one than it really is, dramatically. But the reliance on convention will, of course, sooner or later dictate a decline in the play's effectiveness. *Macbeth* continues to be effective at least in part because everything necessary for a complete response to a complete action is given to us. A highly individualized, noble man is sent to complete moral, intellectual, and physical destruction.

II

But no matter how carefully the terminal points of the drama are selected and impressed on the spectator's mind, the major problem of how to represent such a "plot" still remains. Shakespeare has the tremendous task of trying to keep two contradictory dynamic streams moving simultaneously: the stream of events showing Macbeth's growing wickedness and the stream of circumstances producing and maintaining our sympathy for him. In effect, each succeeding atrocity, marking another step toward complete depravity, must be so surrounded by contradictory circumstances as to make us feel that, in spite of the evidence before our eyes, Macbeth is still somehow admirable.

The first instance of this is the method of treating Duncan's murder. The chief point here is Shakespeare's care in avoiding any "rendering" or representation of the murder itself. It is, in fact, not even narrated. We *hear* only the details of how the guards reacted and how Macbeth reacted to their cries. We *see* nothing. There is nothing about the actual dagger strokes; there is no report of the dying cries of the good old king. We have only Macbeth's conscience-stricken lament for having committed the deed. Thus what would be an intolerable act if depicted with any vividness becomes relatively bearable when seen only afterward in the light of Macbeth's suffering and remorse. This may seem ordinary enough; it is always convenient to have murders take place offstage. But if one compares the handling of this scene, where the perpetrator must remain sympathetic, with the handling of the blinding of Gloucester, where the perpetrators must be hated, one can see how important such a detail can be. The blinding of Gloucester is not so wicked an act, in itself, as murder. If we had seen, say, a properly motivated Goneril come in from offstage wringing her hands and crying, "Methought I heard a voice cry, 'Sleep no more.' Goneril does put out the eyes of sleep . . . I am afraid to think what I have done," and on thus for nearly a full scene, our reaction to the whole episode would, needless to say, be exactly contrary to what it now is.

A second precaution is the highly general portrayal of Duncan before his murder. It is necessary only that he be known as a "good king," the murder of whom will be a wicked act. He must be the *type* of benevolent monarch. But more particular characteristics are carefully kept from him. There is nothing for us to love, nothing for us to "want further existence for," within the play. We hear of his goodness; we do not see it. We know practically no details about him, and we have little, if any, personal interest in him at the time of his death. All the personal interest is reserved for Macbeth and Lady Macbeth. So, again, the wickedness is played up in the narration but played down in the representation. We must identify Macbeth with the murder of a blameless king, but only intellectually; emotionally we should be concerned as far as is possible only with the *effects on Macbeth.* We *know* that he has done the deed, but we *feel* primarily only his own suffering.

Banquo is considerably more "particularized" than was Duncan. Not only is he also a good man, but we have seen him acting as a good man, and we know quite a lot about him. We saw his reaction to the witches, and we know that he has resisted temptations similar to those of Macbeth. We have seen him in conversation with Macbeth. We have heard him in soliloquy. We know him to be very much like Macbeth, both in valor and in being the subject of prophecy. He thus has our lively sympathy; his death is a personal, rather than a general, loss. Perhaps more important, his murder is actually shown on the stage. His dying words are spoken in our presence, and they are unselfishly directed to saving his son. We are forced to the proper, though illogical, inference: it is more wicked to kill Banquo than to have killed Duncan.

But we must still not lose our sympathy for Macbeth. This is partially provided for by the fact that the deed is much more necessary than the previous murder; Banquo is a real political danger. But the important thing is again the choice of what is represented. The murder is done by accomplices, so that Macbeth is never *shown* in any real act of wickedness. When we see him, he is suffering the torments of the banquet table. Our incorrect emotional inference: the self-torture has already expiated the guilt of the crime.

The same devices work in the murder of Lady Macduff and her children, the third and last atrocity explicitly shown in the play (except for the killing of young Siward, which, being military, is hardly an atrocity in this sense). Lady Macduff is more vividly portrayed even than Banquo, although she appears on the stage for a much briefer time. Her complaints against the absence of her husband, her loving banter with her son, and her stand against the murderers make her as admirable as the little boy himself, who dies in defense of his father's name. The murder of women and children of such quality is wicked indeed, the audience is made to feel. And when we move to England and see the effect of the atrocity on Macduff, our active pity for Macbeth's victims is at the high point of the play. For the first time, perhaps, pity for Macbeth's victims really wars with pity for him, and our desire for his downfall, to protect others and to protect himself from his own further misdeeds, begins to mount in consequence.

Yet even here Macbeth is kept as little "to blame" as possible. He does not do the deed himself, and we can believe that he would have been unable to, had he seen the wife and child as we have seen them. (The Orson Welles movie version contains many grotesque errors of reading, but none worse than showing Macbeth actively engaged on the scene of this crime.) He is much further removed from them than from his other victims; as far as we know, he has never seen them. They are as remote and impersonal to him as they are immediate and personal to the audience, and personal blame against him is thus attenuated. More important, however, immediately after Macduff's tears we shift to Lady Macbeth's scene—the effect being again to impress on us the fact that the punishment for these crimes is always as great as, or greater than, the crimes themselves. Thus all three crimes are followed immediately by scenes of suffering and self-torture. Shakespeare works almost as if he were following a master-rulebook: By your choice of what to represent from the materials provided in your story, insure that each step in your protagonist's degeneration will be counteracted by mounting pity for him.

All this would certainly suffice to keep Macbeth at the center of our interest and sympathy, even with all our mounting concern for his victims. But it is reinforced by qualities in his character separate and distinct from his moral qualities. Perhaps the most important of these is his gift (indirectly Shakespeare's gift, it is true, but we should remember that in his maturer work Shakespeare does not bestow it indiscriminately on all his characters) of expressing himself in great poetry. We naturally tend to feel with the character who speaks the best poetry of the play, no matter what his deeds (Iago would never be misplayed as protagonist if his poetry did not rival, and sometimes surpass, Othello's). When we add to this poetic gift an extremely rich and concrete set of characteristics, over and above his moral qualities, we have a character which is in its own way more sympathetic than any character portrayed in only moral colors could be. Even the powers of virtue gathering about his castle to destroy him seem petty compared with his mammoth sensitivity, his rich despair. When he says:

> my way of life
> Is fall'n into the sere, the yellow leaf;
> And that which should accompany old age,
> As honour, love, obedience, troops of friends,
> I must not look to have,

we feel that he wants these things quite as honestly and a good deal more passionately than even the most virtuous man could want them. And we regret deeply the truth of his conclusion that he "must not look to have" them.

III

If Macbeth's initial nobility, the manner of representation of his atrocities, and his rich poetic gift are all calculated to create and sustain our sympathy for him throughout his movement toward destruction, the kind of mistake he makes in initiating his own destruction is equally well calculated to heighten our willingness to forgive while deploring. On one level it could, of course, be said that he errs simply in being overambitious and underscrupulous. But this is only partly true. What allows him to sacrifice his moral beliefs to his ambition is a mistake of another kind—of a kind which is, at least to modern spectators, more probable or credible than any conventional tragic flaw or any traditional tragic error such as mistaking the identity of a brother or not knowing that one's wife is one's mother. Macbeth knows what he is doing, yet he does not know. He knows the immorality of the act, but he has no conception of the effects of the act on himself or on his surroundings. Accustomed to murder of a "moral" sort, in battle, and having valorously and successfully "carv'd out his passage" with "bloody execution" many times previously, he misunderstands completely what will be the devastating effect on his own character if he tries to carve out his passage in civil life. The murder of Duncan on one level resembles closely the kind of thing Macbeth has done professionally, and he lacks the insight to see the great difference between the two kinds of murder. He cannot foresee that success in the first murder will only lead to the speech "to be thus is nothing; But to be safely thus," and to ever increasing degradation and suffering for himself and for those around him. Even though he has a kind of double premonition of the effects of the deed both on his own conscience and on Duncan's subjects ("If it were done when 't is done, then 't were well . . ."), he does not really understand. If he did understand, he could not do the deed.

This ignorance is made more convincing by being extended to a misunderstanding of the forces leading him to the murder. Macbeth does not really understand that he has two spurs "to prick the sides" of his intent, besides his own vaulting ambition. The first of these is, of course, the witches and their prophecy. A good deal of nonsense has been written about these witches, some in the direction of making them totally responsible for the action of Macbeth and some making them merely a fantastical representation of Macbeth's mental state. Yet they are quite clearly real and objective, since they say and do things which Macbeth could know nothing about—such as their presentation of the ambiguous facts of Macduff's birth and the Birnam wood trick. And equally they are not "fate," alone responsible for what happens to Macbeth. He deliberately chooses from what they have to say only those things which he wishes to hear; and he has already felt the ambition to be king and even possibly to become king through regicide. Dramatically they seem to be here both as a needed additional goad to his ambition and as a concrete instance of Macbeth's tragic misunderstanding. His deliberate and consistent mistaking of what they have to say objectifies for us his misunderstanding of everything about his situation. He should realize that, if they are true oracles, *both* parts of their prophecy *must* be fulfilled. He makes the mistake of acting criminally to bring about the first part of the prophecy, and then acting criminally to prevent the fulfilment of the second part, concerning Banquo. But only if they were not true oracles would the slaying of Duncan be necessary or the slaying of Banquo be of any use. Macbeth tries to pick and choose from their promises, and they thus aid him in his self-destruction.

The second force which Macbeth does not understand, and without which he would find himself incapable of the murder, is Lady Macbeth. She, of course, fills several functions in the play, besides her inherent interest as a character, which is great indeed. But her chief function, as the textbook commonplace quite rightly has it, is to incite Macbeth to the murder of Duncan. Shakespeare has realized the best possible form for this incitation. She does not urge Macbeth with pictures of the pleasures of rewarded ambition; she does not allow his thoughts to remain on the moral aspects of the problem, as they would if he were left to himself. Rather, she shifts the whole ground of the consideration to questions of Macbeth's valor. She twits him for cowardice, plays upon the word "man," making it seem that he becomes more a man by doing the manly deed. She exaggerates her own courage (although significantly she does not offer to do the murder herself), to make him fear to seem cowardly by comparison. Macbeth's whole reputation for bravery seems at last to be at stake, and even questions of success and failure are made to hang on his courage: "But screw your courage to the sticking-place/And we'll not fail." So that the whole of his past achievement seems to depend for its meaning on his capacity to go ahead with the contemplated act. He performs the act, and from that point his final destruction is certain.

His tragic error, then, is at least threefold: he does not understand the forces working upon him to make him commit the deed, neither his wife nor the weird sisters; he does not understand the differences between "bloody execution" in civilian life and in his past military life; and he does not understand his own character—he does not know what will be the effects of the evil act on his own future happiness. Only one of these—the misunderstanding of the witches' prophecy—can be considered similar to, say, Iphigenia's ignorance of her brother's identity. Shakespeare has realized that simple ignorance of that sort will not do for the richly complex degenerative plot. The hero here must be really aware of the wickedness of his act, in advance. The more aware he can be—and still commit the act convincingly—the greater the regret felt by the reader or spectator. Being thus aware, he must act under a special kind of misunderstanding: it must be a misunderstanding caused by such powerful forces that even a good man might credibly be deceived by them into "knowingly" performing an atrocious deed.

All these points are illustrated powerfully in the contrast between the final words of Malcolm concerning Macbeth—"This dead butcher and his fiendlike queen"—and the spectator's own feelings toward Macbeth at the same point. One judges Macbeth, as Shakespeare intends, not merely for his wicked acts but in the light of the total impression of all the incidents of the play. Malcolm and Macduff do not know Macbeth and the forces that have worked on him; the spectator does know him and, knowing him, can feel great pity that a man with so much potentiality for greatness should have fallen so low. The pity is that everything was not otherwise, since it so easily could have been otherwise. Macbeth's whole life, from the time of the first visitation of the witches, is felt to be itself a tragic error, one big pitiful mistake. And the conclusion brings a flood of relief that the awful blunder has played itself out, that Macbeth has at last been able to die, still valiant, and is forced no longer to go on enduring the knowledge of the consequences of his own misdeeds.

NOTES

[1] It should go without saying that in other tragedies Shakespeare faced totally different problems. But the willingness to face big ones rather than little ones is always there (see n. 2, below).

[2] This scene illustrates again what I am saying about the importance of Shakespeare's willingness to give himself difficulties that are worth surmounting. Give yourself a man who has no real objections to an act, and then throw somebody at him to persuade him to that act: the conflict is insignificant, the tension slight, the drama weak. Give yourself an extremely good man and set someone to persuade him to do the most horrible of deeds; inevitably, if you rise to the occasion, you must create a true giant of a rhetorician to accomplish the almost impossible persuasive task: you must create Lady Macbeth. Or, again, suppose you want to write a domestic tragedy, the tragedy of a man who strangles his wife in a jealous rage. You create a man given to jealous rages and a woman who is known to be inclined to infidelity; sure enough, she is unfaithful, and he murders her. Contrast that with Othello, a man *not* inclined to jealousy, married to Desdemona, a woman of spotless reputation, beyond all scandal, and you see that Shakespeare has forced himself, as it were, into big things: primarily Iago.

John Holloway

MACBETH

There is a clear sense, in *Hamlet* and to a lesser extent in *Othello*, that a retributive justice works through human life, and that an order and symmetry may
therefore be seen in the doings of men. In *Macbeth* this is more conspicuous still.
First, it is a substantial part of the whole movement of the action. Moreover, the
action itself is seen in a perspective which extends beyond the doings of men, since
it takes in the environment of Nature within which these doings occur, and from
which in the end they seem to derive their quality. *Macbeth*, that is to say, is a work
which offers the spectator no view of life alone, but a view of life which is part of
a view of the world. In a broad and perhaps old-fashioned sense of the term, it is
a philosophical play as *Hamlet* and *Othello* are not.

What opens up this wider perspective of life is nothing short of the play's total
dynamic; but this includes far more than any mere 'what happens to the characters'
seen in simple terms. The characters, taken in themselves, have to thread their way
through an ampler body of experience proffered to the spectator; and for him, this
ampler body of experience, this poetic richness of the play, is less conspicuous as
chains of imagery which he could list as mere words in his study, than as images in
the true sense, images which seem to people the stage, which have an independent
life in the experience before him. It is in this sense, a sense which takes us beyond
'language' considered by itself, that *Macbeth* is a more than realistic, a truly poetic
play.

At the opening of *Macbeth*, Macbeth himself is the centre of respect and
interest. He is the cynosure, the present saviour of the state.

> ... brave Macbeth—well he deserves that name—
> Disdaining Fortune, with his brandish'd steel
> Which smoked with bloody execution,
> Like *valour's minion*, car'd out his passage ...   (I. ii. 16)

With these vivid words, the absent is present: the minion of valour and disdainer
of Fortune is sharply before our imagination in all the slaughter of civil war. Yet this

From *The Story of the Night: Studies in Shakespeare's Major Tragedies* (London: Routledge & Kegan
Paul, 1961), pp. 57–74.

image of Macbeth is ambivalent. Only a few lines before, in the expolsive opening words of the very first scene (other than that of the witches, no clear part of human life at all), Shakespeare has provided his audience, before their eyes and on stage, with an actual picture that the account of Macbeth in battle, quoted just now, disquietingly resembles:

> What bloody man is that? He can report,
> As seemeth by his plight, of the *revolt*
> The newest state.   (I. ii. 1)

But insofar as we identify Macbeth with the image of a man stained in blood, and his weapon dripping with blood, he is no image merely of a destroyer of revolt. By a more direct and primitive mode of thought, by simple association, he is an image of revolt itself. The doubtful goodness of his disdaining Fortune (of which more must be said later) appears in a new, uneasy light.

This image of the bloody man is so much insisted on in the opening scenes, that it is not enough to call it an image. It is an apparition. It haunts the stage. Ross says that Macbeth was:

> Not afraid of what thyself didst make,
> Strange *images of death*.   (I. iii. 96)

Again, the ambiguous phrasing carries weight. It is the same hideous sight which is the 'horrid image' seen by Macbeth, in imagination, after his meeting with the witches (I. iii. 135); and that we see, in Macbeth himself, when he enters after the murder of Duncan, and invites our contemplation almost as if he were an emblem of violence ('this is a sorry sight', II. ii. 20). Again, it is the same image that we must call to mind when Macbeth says that he will not return to see the spectacle of the murdered Duncan (II. ii. 50); and that Lady Macbeth says she will make the grooms look like; and that Lennox revives once more for us in his account of the grooms ('their hands and faces were all badged with blood'(II. iii. 100). It is 'the great doom's image' that Macbeth himself sees in Duncan lying dead when he tells the lords of the murder (II. iii. 60). This image, kept so much before our imagination that it seems without exaggeration to stalk the stage, is the image with which Macbeth is identified in the very first account we have of him. From the start, he may be valour's minion, but he impresses our minds as the bloody man, the image of death.

The apparition was not coined by Shakespeare. Its force is greater and its meaning clearer than that, for it is a traditional image from the Bible. 'Come foorth thou bloodshedder' ('man of blood' is the gloss: II Sam., 16. 7); or again, 'the Lord wyll abhorre the bloodthirstie and deceitful man' (Ps. 5, 6). Macbeth himself makes the exact verbal connection: he speaks (III. v. 126) of how augurs have 'brought forth / The secret'st *man of blood*'. We must therefore go much further than to say, with Professor Knights, that in the early part of the play the 'theme' of 'the reversal of values' is prominently 'stated'.[1] The play opens with something not static and discursive, but violent, integral to the play, and dynamic: an 'image of revolt', the image of an actual *deed* of overturning, which serves from the start as emblem both of the central character, and of the course of the action.

The double nature of Macbeth is emphasized by a turn of events at the beginning of the play which would be distracting and confusing if it did not serve exactly this purpose. This is the introduction of the Norwegian invaders, who upset Macbeth's victory over the rebel Macdonwald by their inopportune arrival. By itself, this would be wholly distracting. It is only not so, through the significance which is given to it. The new threat of danger to the state is made to underline the conflicting meanings in Macbeth's victory over the rebels. 'From that spring, whence comfort seem'd to come / Discomfort swells', says the Sergeant (I. ii. 25): comparing the event with the coming of clouds that obscure the sun, and bring at first welcome shade, but then unwelcome storm. Both the comparison with the sun (ruler of the sky as the king is of the country), and the Sergeant's later assertion that Macbeth (and also Banquo) respond to the new challenge as if they meant to bring about 'another Golgotha' (I. 41) reinforce the effect. The Norwegians, soon forgotten, free Shakespeare to suggest, even before there is any imputation against Macbeth, that his deliverance of the state is also the opposite of a deliverance.

The nature of Macbeth's conduct, and the experience of ourselves which this makes of the play, are quite misunderstood if he is thought, however, to be an 'image of revolt' merely at the level of civil disobedience. The significance of what he does goes deeper. It must anyhow do this, if only by implication. That rebellion against the lawful king counted as rebellion against God was a commonplace of the time. The idea may be illustrated by many quotations from obvious sources such as the *Mirror for Magistrates* or the Elizabethan *Homilies;* and it simply follows, from the essential correspondence between the order of civil government and the order of nature, which (as everyone knows by now) was one of the basic ideas of Shakespeare's time, and appeared repeatedly in his work. Yet for *Macbeth*, to see this is not to see enough. It is not merely by implication that Macbeth's act of revolt is more than civic, is an ultimate revolt. It is this, clearly and with emphasis, from the start. At its inception, his plot makes his heart knock against his ribs 'against the use of nature' (I. iv. 137); Duncan on his death-bed looks 'like a breach in Nature / For Ruin's wasteful entrance' (a rich line, in which the image of Duncan himself, as bloody man, is transformed into the image of the revolt of which he is victim, and the ruin which must prove its sequel). After Banquo's ghost disrupts the feast. Macbeth thinks of how 'the secret'st man of blood' has been given away:

> Stones have been known to move, and trees to speak;   (III. v. 123)

But the line seems to call up miracles in the past less than it suggests the anti-nature which Macbeth has created, not only in his own mind, in the present. The sense of Macbeth's career as one of revolt against everything in the world is even sustained by lines like those of Ross describing the woes of Scotland:

> good men's lives
> Expire before the flowers in their caps.
> Dying or ere they sicken.   (IV. iii. 171)

This is no vivid Shakespearean innovation: and to find that men are seen in it as among all the earth's other living things is merely to hear its echoes in tradition:

> Thou turnest man to destruction . . . they . . . fade away sodainly lyke the grasse. In the morning it is greene & groweth up: but in the evenyng it is cut downe, dryed up, and wythered. (Ps. 90)

Again, it is no fact of disorder we are offered, but an act; one of giant divergence whose rise and fall preoccupies the spectator from the 'innocent flower' which Lady Macbeth tells her husband to seem like at the outset (I. v. 62), to the 'sere and yellow leaf' into which he finds that his way (or May?) of life has fallen in the autumn of his career. His anit-Nature has had its year, like Nature itself.

The word 'disorder' offers no more than a vague blur in the direction of what this anti-Nature essentially is. From the very opening of the play, when the witches plan 'to meet with Macbeth' (I. i. 8), we have a clear clue, which may be brought into focus by reference to Burton's catalogue of the kinds of evil spirits:

> . . . the fifth kind are cozeners, such as belong to magicians *and witches; their prince is Satan*[2]

One after the other, and with much greater deliberateness than Othello, Lady Macbeth and then Macbeth dedicate themselves formally to evil, and more specifically, to the powers of evil in traditional terms:

> Come, you spirits
> That tend on mortal thoughts, unsex me here . . .
> That no compunctious visitings of nature
> Shake my fell purpose . . . (I. v. 37)

The formalized moment of self-dedication shows as clearly here as it does in Macbeth's own prayer later:

> Now o'er the one half-world
> Nature seems dead . . .
> . . . thou sure and firm-set Earth,
> Hear not my steps . . . (II. i. 49)

But that we are to see it as dedication to the Satanic itself is reserved for a later moment, that of Macbeth's resolution to murder Banquo:

> Come seeling Night . . .
> And with thy bloody and invisible hand
> Cancel and tear to pieces that great bond
> Which keeps me pale . . . (III. ii. 46)

'bloody hand' and 'tear to pieces' resurrect, behind the words 'which keeps me pale', the recurrent apparition of the play: Macbeth's prayer is to be transformed, once for all, into the man of blood. By whose power this is to be done, is made clear in the lines which follow almost immediately:

Good things of day begin to droop and drowse,
While night's black agents to their preys do rouse.

In the last episode of the play, the combat between Macbeth and Macduff, it is
made plain that night's black agents are the fallen angels, the powers of Satan
himself:

> Despair thy charm;
> And let the *angel* which thou still hast served
> Tell thee Macduff was from his mother's womb
> Untimely ripped.   (V. viii. 33)

—and also that at the end Macbeth admits, and defiantly faces, the known reward
of such service:

> lay on, Macduff;
> And *damn'd* be him that first cries 'Hold, enough!'

That the rôle of the Macbeths is one of service to the principle of evil itself has
one consequence which is especially important, because it recurs:

> Though you untie the winds and let them fight
> Against the churches; though the yesty waves
> Confound and swallow navigation up;
> Though bladed corn be lodg'd and trees blown down; (flattened)
> Though castles topple on their warders' heads;
> Though palaces and pyramids do slope
> Their heads to their foundations; though the treasure
> Of nature's germens tumble all together,
> Even till destruction sicken—answer me
> To what I ask you.   (IV. i. 52)

In these words Macbeth 'conjures' the witches (it is again, as that word suggests, a
formalized speech, a recognizable and ritual act), to tell him what he needs to
know, even at the cost of universal destruction. In effect, the lines come near to a
curse upon the whole of Nature. Rebellion has been taken to its full extent.

There is another 'apparition' (as it might be called) besides that of the bloody
man, which haunts this play, and expresses and symbolizes this aspect of Macbeth's
rôle, his journey in the direction of universal chaos. It is that of riders and horses,
and it seems to have gone unnoticed by critics up to now. To register the full
contribution which this image makes to the play, one should call to mind something
of what the armed rider, and indeed the horse itself (that almost extinct animal, at
least in the *milieu* of critics) stood for in Shakespeare's society, as for millennia
before. The armed rider was the surest and swiftest of all human messengers, and
the signal embodiment of violence, warfare, brigandage, revolt. The horse was the
most powerful and valuable of the species which served man, and at the same time,

if it rebelled, the most spirited, mischievous and formidable. Both were deeply ambiguous figures, inviting admiration and fear at once.

How these images contribute to *Macbeth* becomes clearer, in fact, once their contribution to *Lear* is seen as well; but even without anticipating this feature of that play, the facts are plain enough. The oft-quoted horses of Duncan that 'turned wild in nature' and ate each other like monsters (II. iv. 14) should be seen in this light: their monstrous act is the more terrifying because it brings to life what within the world of the play is a permanently latent fear. A passage from the *Homily against Wilful Rebellion* illuminates this episode. When married men revolt, it runs, they leave their wives at home, which is bad enough. It is much worse when the unmarried revolt: 'being now by rebellion set at liberty from correction of laws, they pursue other men's wives and daughters... *worse than any stallions or horses*'.[3] Unexpectedly perhaps for our own time, it is the horse which proves to be the obvious illustration of unbridled violence. The disturbing image runs throughout the play. The crucial scenes of the murder in Macbeth's castle at Inverness are set in the context of the arrival first of the Macbeth's messenger:

> One of my fellows had the speed of him,
> Who, almost dead for breath, had scarcely more
> Than would make up his message.   (I. v. 32)

and then of the furiously galloping Macbeth himself:

> DUNCAN: Where's the Thane of Cawdor?
> We coursed him at the heels and had a purpose
> To be his purveyor; but he rides well,
> And his great love, sharp as his spur, hath holp him
> To his home before us.   (I. iv. 20)

The murderers waiting for Banquo and Fleance hear their horses' hooves as they stand waiting in the dark. 'Hark, I hear horses', says the Third Murderer (III. iii. 8): and Macbeth's earlier 'I wish your horses sure and swift of foot' (III. i. 37) has made it clear that the horses (in imagination, or by theatrical device) are at a gallop. We are to envisage the same before Macbeth's last battle:

> Send out more horses, skirr the country round,
> Hang those that talk of fear   (V. iii. 35)

and it is this sound again which Macbeth hears after his last meeting with the witches:

> Infected be the air whereon they ride;
> And damn'd all those that trust them! I did hear
> The galloping of horse. Who was't came by?   (IV. i. 138)

What he hears, moreover (or so the spectator's impression should run), is not the presumably soundless riding away of the witches, nor merely that of the men who bring him news of Macduff's flight to England. In the last analysis, he hears also those who properly preside unseen at such a meeting; and these are the

> heaven's cherubim hors'd
> Upon the sightless couriers of the air

of his first soliloquy (I. vii. 22). Nor is the word 'hors'd' here wholly figurative: a more literal interpretation of it will bring to mind heavenly cherubim that belong to this context, and that come down from a then universally known passage of scripture:

> And I sawe, and beholde, a white horse, and hee that sate on hym had a bowe, and a crowne was geuen vnto hym, and he went foorth conquering, and for to overcome.... And there went out another horse that was redde: and power was geuen to him that sate thereon to take peace from the earth, and that they should kyl one another.... And I behelde, and loe, a blacke horse: and he that sate on hym hadde a pair of ballances in his hande.... And I looked, and beholde a pale horse, his name that sate on hym was death, and hel folowed with him: and power was geuen vnto them, ouer the fourth part of the earth, to kyl with sworde, & with hunger, and with dearth, and with the beastes of the earth.   (Rev. 6, 2–8)

The horses that Macbeth hears galloping are the Four Horsemen of the Apocalypse: bringing, as they ride over the earth, the disasters which are the proper result of, proper retribution for, human evil.

That the play depicts disorder spreading throughout a whole society ('bleed, bleed poor country': IV. iii. 32) is a commonplace. So is it, indeed, that this is seen as an infringement of the whole beneficent order of Nature; and that nothing less than that whole beneficient order gears itself, at last, to ending the state of evil ('... the pow'rs above / Put on their instruments,' IV. iii. 238). That the coming of Birnam Wood to Dunsinane is a vivid emblem of this, a dumbshow of nature overturning anti-nature at the climax of the play, has gone unnoticed. Professor Knights once suggested that in this scene, 'nature becomes unnatural in order to rid itself of Macbeth', or rather, that it was 'emphasizing the disorder' by showing the forces of good in association with deceit and with the *un*natural.[4] To a contemporary audience, however, the scene must have presented a much more familiar and less unnatural appearance than it does to ourselves. The single figure, dressed in his distinctive costume (one should have Macbeth in his war equipment in mind) pursued by a whole company of others carrying green branches, was a familiar sight as a Maying procession, celebrating the triumph of new life over the sere and yellow leaf of winter. Herrick's 'Corinna's Going a-Maying' brings out not only the gaiety of the occasion, and its intimate connections with procreation and new life even in the human sphere, but also how familiar such scenes must have been in Shakespeare's time and indeed long after:

> There's not a budding youth, or girl, this day
> But is got up, and gone to bring in May.

A deal of youth, ere this, is come
Back, and with white-thorn laden home.
And some have wept, and wooed, and plighted troth,
　　Many a green-gown has been given
　　Many a kiss both odd and even...
Many a jest told of the keys betraying
This night, and locks picked, yet we're not a-Maying.

One should remember that the May procession, with its green branches, survived even in the London Strand until as late as the 1890s.

To a certain extent, Macbeth's career through the play almost invites being seen against the patterns of this primitive kind of ritual. Like any Lord of Misrule, he has (at least in metaphor) his ill-fitting, borrowed robes:

　　　　　　　now does he feel his title
Hang loose about him, like a giant's robe
Upon a dwarfish thief.　　　　　　　　　　　　　　　(V. ii. 20)

Moreover, he has his Feast (III. iv.) that proves only the mockery of a feast. But the interest of these details is increased, if we call to mind that there are certain features of Macbeth's career which not only fall obviously into place here, but also closely resemble moments which have already been distinguished in *Hamlet* and *Othello*. Macbeth's transition from Lord of Misrule and image of revolt to victim of the abiding and restorative forces of life is one, in fact, with that progressive isolation which (like Hamlet and Othello) he clearly undergoes. The sons of Duncan flee him, Fleance flees, Macduff

　　　　　　　denies his person
At our great bidding...　　　　　　　　　　　　　　(III. iv. 128)

and his other followers are shams as well:

There's not a one of them, but in his house
I keep a servant fee'd.　　　　　　　　　　　　　　(III. iv. 131)

In the last Act, Macbeth makes his isolation explicit:

　　...that which should accompany old age,
As honour, love, obedience, troops of friends,
I must not look to have.　　　　　　　　　　　　　(V. iii. 24)

It is this scene which closes with the Doctor's profession that he too would desert if he could; and the last episode before the death of Macbeth himself is the revelation that many of his army abandoned him:

　　...We have met with foes
That strike beside us.　　　　　　　　　　　　　　(V. vii. 28)

Nor is our experience of merely a process whereby the protagonist is isolated. As with Othello, we are invited to recognize, and to dwell on the fact, that this journey of progressive isolation is one with its distinctive end. The protagonist, transformed bit by bit from leader to quarry, must at last stand at bay. Macbeth first registers this phase of his experience in words which resume how it was integral to it to enrol as an enemy against Nature:

> If this which he avouches does appear,
> There is *nor flying hence nor tarrying here;*
> I 'gin to be a-weary of the sun,
> *And wish th' estate o' th' world were now undone.*
> Ring the alarum bell. Blow wind, come wrack . . .   (V. v. 47)

He confirms the coming of the final phase in a passage reminiscent of Othello's 'Here is my butt / And very sea-mark of my utmost sail':

> They have tied me to a stake; I cannot fly,
> But bear-like I must stand the course. . . .   (V. vii. 1)

Nor does the resemblance end there. Macbeth's course, like Othello's, has been from man to monster. Montano's 'O monstrous act' (*Othello*, V. ii. 183) has its exact parallel in the later play; and, as in *Othello*, it comes in the closing lines, when the movement is complete, and significance at its plainest:

> MACDUFF: Then yield thee, coward,
> And live to be the gaze and show o' th' time;
> We'll have thee, *as our rarer monsters are,*
> Painted upon a pole, and underwrit,
> 'Here you may see the tyrant'.   (V. viii. 26)

Finally, Malcolm in his closing speech makes clear what is at issue in the sweeping away of the dominion of the lonely monster, once he has been brought to bay and destroyed. His first thought is to re-establish the social group in all its harmonious plurality, honouring his immediate followers as earls, and

> . . . calling home our exil'd friends abroad.   (V. viii. 66)

Isolation is at once to be replaced by community.

The play also moves forward in another dimension: one more intimate and inward than this of society ridding itself of its own monstrous birth, for it explores Macbeth's growing realization of what he has done. Neither in *Othello* nor in *Macbeth* is there really much question of the protagonist's repenting. In the former play, this is not because of any moral failure on Othello's part, but simply because (though many will be loth to admit it) the crucial questions of right are barely raised. Whether Montano would or should have seen Othello's act as monstrous, even had Desdemona really been confirmed in adultery, is left undiscussed. It is Iago who (in Lodovico's words) is the viper. In calling Othello merely a 'rash and most unfortunate man', Lodovico confirms how Othello's error of *fact* is now so much the central reality, that the moral judgement most interesting to many in our own age is passed over. The repentance of Othello is concentrated, like the awareness of all those with him, upon his disastrous folly, and is not repentance in the moral sense at all. It is quite otherwise in *Macbeth*. Here, attention is indeed concentrated on the protagonist as not foolish but fiendish. In him, however, there is one glimpse only of something like repentance in the full sense. It comes in the closing scene of the play, and we should surely admire how Shakespeare held this final movement of Macbeth's mind in reserve, sustaining our interest, insight and sympathy at the very last:

MACDUFF: Turn hell-hound, turn.
MACBETH: *Of all men else I have avoided thee,*
But get thee back; my soul is too much charged
With blood of thine already.   (V. viii. 3)

Of Macbeth's genuinely beginning to turn from the evil he has done, I can find no clear hint but this; and even this falls somewhat short of repentance proper.

On the side of intellectual response, what Macbeth comes to recognize, and even in a limited sense regret, is his own error; but this process of realization goes further, and takes in more, than might be thought. Macbeth's career is an illustration, of course, of the traditional belief, which is expressed in three different places in scripture, that 'all they that take the sword, shall perish with the sword' (Matth. 26, 52; cf. Gen. 9, 6, and Rev. 13, 10). The central irony is that what Macbeth saw from the start as a mere difficulty in his way is proved, bit by bit, to be inescapable reality, and foreseeable as such;

This even-handed justice
Commends the ingredients of our poison'd chalice
To our own lips . . .   (I. vii. 10)

'From that spring whence comfort seem'd to come / Discomfort swells' proves no truer for Duncan than it does, in turn, for Macbeth. Two prominent speeches set the irony beyond overlooking. The first consists in Macbeth's insincere words at the very moment of success. He is announcing the death of Duncan, and alleging that with this, life has lost all meaning:

Had I but died an hour before this chance
I had lived a blessed time: for from this instant
There's nothing serious in mortality;
All is but toys: renown and grace is dead,
The wine of life is drawn, and the mere lees
Is left this vault to brag of.   (II. iii. 89)

The irony goes further than the fact that, as a moral comment on what Macbeth has just done, this is more than a fitting though empty gesture, because it is the sober truth: what completes that irony is how Macbeth echoes these words, later on, in a speech as sincere as this is insincere:

SEYTON; The Queen, my lord, is dead.
MACBETH: She should have died hereafter;
There would have been a time for such a word.
To-morrow, and to-morrow, and to-morrow,
Creeps in this petty pace from day to day
To the last syllable of recorded time,
And all our yesterdays have lighted fools
The way to dusty death. Out, out, brief candle!
Life's but a walking shadow, a poor player,
That struts and frets his hour upon the stage,
And then is heard no more; it is a tale
Told by an idiot, full of sound and fury,
Signifying nothing.

Whatever may be the exact relation between the first two lines of this speech and the rest, it is clear that the effect of the queen's death is to bring out finally what he has half seen before, when he says

I am in blood
Stepp'd in so far that, should I wade no more,
Returning were as tedious as go o'er.

It is something which also emerges through the irony of Lady Macbeth's account of the murder:

This night's great business . . .
Which shall to all our nights and days to come
Give solely sovereign sway and masterdom.   (I. v. 65)

What looked as if it would endow life with the greatest meaningfulness has deprived it, in the end, of all meaning. What seemed like the beginning of everything was in fact the end of that, and beginning of nothing. The queen's death does not convince so much as remind Macbeth that he now knows this. Nor, driven as he has been by both inner forces ('these terrible dreams / That shake us nightly', III. ii. 18) and outer ('the pow'rs above / Put on their instruments'), is this a reaction to his personal situation alone. His cynicism is general; it is not his own life, but Life, which has come to have no meaning.

Yet this, perhaps, falls short of the exact truth; and it perhaps omits what is vital to the play as a whole. After all, what 'all our yesterdays' lighted were 'fools'; and what they were lighted to was 'dusty death'; and because of the moment when this is said, and the fact that life is seen as one who 'struts and frets his hour', as a tale 'full of sound and fury', it is impossible not to see this speech as going beyond a vision of total choas, to a glimpse, or at least an ironical hint, of retributive order. The fools lit to dusty death are less the innocent simpletons, than men like Macbeth himself. His own thought has already pushed out in this direction. The invocation to the witches was prepared to see 'nature's germens tumble all together / *Even till*

Destruction sicken' (the passage is quoted in full above). Here too Macbeth knows, or half-knows, what is fatal to his cause. That destruction should indeed sicken is a conviction upon which the whole movement of the play is based. When Fortune 'show'd like a rebel's whore', it was glimpsed incompletely. Macbeth 'disdained' her too soon; just as Lady Macbeth spoke too easily of 'Fate' having crowned her husband (I. v. 26), and Macbeth himself spoke too easily, in inviting Fate to 'come into the list' on his side (III. i. 70) against Banquo.

Fate, properly understood, is another kind of thing. To see either it, or Fortune, in these ways, is like seeing only the exposed part of the iceberg. It is the injustice of Fate and Fortune which is even-handed; their justice may come more slowly, but in the end it redresses the balance. And if Macbeth never comes to repent of his actions, he comes at least to comprehend not merely that they brought him no good, but that he could have known this, that he was wrong on a matter of fact, from the start:

> And be these juggling fiends no more believed,
> That palter with us in a double sense,
> That keep the word of promise to our ear
> And break it to our hope.

These are his last words before his final act of animal-like defiance. The fiends are what Burton said: cozeners; and it is a substantial part, not only of Macbeth's response to his ordeal, but also, and still more, of the play's whole action, that fiends are cozeners because Fortune, or Fate, have both this surface meaning, and their true and deeper one.

A passage from Browne's *Religio Medici* makes clear that, once again, Shakespeare has ordered his action upon a belief basic but familiar in his time. Saying that Nature is in effect the Art of God, Browne writes:

> ... this is the ordinary and open way of his Providence ... whose effects we may foretel without an Oracle ... (but) there is another way ... whereof the devil and Spirits have no exact Ephemerides [i.e., calculating tables]; and that is a more particular and obscure method of his Providence, directing the operations of individuals and single essences: this we call *Fortune*, that serpentine and crooked line, whereby he draws those actions his Wisdom intends, in a more unknown and secret way ... surely there are in every man's Life certain rubs, doublings, and wrenches, which pass a while under the effects of chance, but at the last, well examined, prove the meer hand of God ... the lives, not only of men, but of Commonwealths, and the whole World, run not upon an Helix that still enlargeth, but on a Circle, where, arriving to their Meridian, they decline in obscurity, and fall under the Horizon again.
>
> These must not therefore be named the effects of Fortune, but in a relative way, and as we term the works of Nature. It was the ignorance of man's reason that begat this very name, and by a careless term miscalled the

Providence of God: for there is no liberty for causes to operate in a loose and stragling way.[5]

Thus *Macbeth* does not start, as does *Othello*, with something like a plain representation of real life. Its opening scenes are dominated less by the human figures in them, than by emblematic images which embody great and indeed terrible forces running through human life, but which appear before us in detachment from the realistically presented characters. Out of a world dominated by these two images, the powers of evil in the witches, and the emblem of revolt in the man of blood, one of the human characters emerges into prominence. At first, this is a prominence which belongs properly to the chief of the king's lieutenants and the saviour of the state.

Yet even from the start, Macbeth is more than, as it were, a plain historical figure. Through his identification with the image of revolt he becomes an icon of one of the great evil potentialities of life. Then, as it is made progressively clearer that his deed of revolt is a deliberate defiance of the whole work of Nature, and a conscious enlistment under the powers of evil, he becomes identified also with the second of these images, the 'hell-hound' of Act V scene vii: a plainer and more active embodiment of the satanic power than the witches themselves. Macbeth's status as emblem and embodiment of evil is stressed by his formal self-dedication to this as a way of life (Lady Macbeth pursues the same course), and by his ritualized invocation of universal disaster on Nature in pursuit of his own ends. His actions replace the 'bounteous nature' of the kindom under Duncan by a condition of life which, on the level of explicit political affairs, is one of tyranny, fear, spying and continual murder; and at the level of poetic suggestion is one where ordinary life is haunted—no less emphatic word will serve—haunted by the emblematical images of the evil things of night, the armed rider, the violent horses, the Horsemen, even, of the Apocalypse. These spread through the ordinary patterns of life and give it a new quality of unnatural disruption, strangeness and violence.

As the powers of good re-assert themselves, our perspective is shifted once more. We are now invited to see Macbeth's progress through the contours, as it were, of another image, though one again which has had a long history in human thought and society. We are invited to see him as a kind of ritual victim: a scapegoat, a lord of misrule, who has turned life into riot for his limited time, and is then driven out and destroyed by the forces which embody the fertile vitality and the communal happiness of the social group. A vital part of the interest of these closing scenes in Macbeth's own growing consciousness of how what he has done futilely defies these forces, and is sterile and self-destroying.

The element of ritual in the closing scenes, their almost imperceptible relapsing into the contours of a sacrificial fertility ceremony, the expulsion, hunting down and destruction of a man who has turned into a monster, give to the action its final shape. As the action is seen to be turning into this recognizable kind of thing, this activity which has repeatedly been a part of social life, its significance cannot but emerge into final clarity. The suspense and unpredictability which have held the audience's attention so strongly mutate into the working out of a movement which now seems pre-appointed. Macbeth is seen to have strutted and fretted his 'hour'; and both this hour, and what bring it to a close, belong to, and represent, one of the basic contours of life. Both depict for us that 'particular and obscure method of ... Providence' through which the chaos of men's affairs is seen as reposing on an order, and the complexity and entanglement of the play to repose on an underlying form which reflects it.

NOTES

[1] *Explorations* (1946), p. 18.
[2] *Anatomy of Melancholy*, 1.2.1.2.
[3] Homily *Against Disobedience and Wilful Rebellion*, the Third Part (Homilies, 1859 ed., p. 572).
[4] *Explorations*, p. 34.
[5] Browne, *Religio Medici*, the First Part (*Works*, ed. G. Keynes, 1928, Vol. I, pp. 23–4).

C. J. Sisson

PUBLIC JUSTICE: *MACBETH*

In its main lines *Macbeth* seems to offer little difficulty, at first sight at any rate. Malcolm summarizes the case for us at the end of the play. Justice has been done upon 'this dead butcher and his fiend-like queen.' Malcolm was not, of course, an unprejudiced observer. But however partial and incomplete his estimate of the great protagonists of this tragedy, we assent without protest to their downfall. Yet there is a marked difference between Shakespeare's history of *Richard the Third* and his tragedy of *Macbeth*, the difference of pity which suffuses terror. It might seem that Hobbes's facile reduction of pity to transferred self-pity is out of place here at least. The German poet and dramatist Grillparzer sought the solution of the problem in the conception of Macbeth and Lady Macbeth as man and woman in the abstract, types of the universal masculine and the universal feminine in their character and their actions. There is thus a natural sympathy for them in all of us who belong to one or the other sex. This suggestion is really only an over-stressing of one part of the truth concerning these two complete and rounded dramatic portraits of a man and a woman. We are moving steadily away, in spite of stage and film, from the concept of *Hamlet* as the tragedy of a man who cannot make up his mind. We may be tempted by a description of *Macbeth* as the tragedy of a man who has his mind made up for him. But we could not accept this notion in the form 'the tragedy of *man* who always has to have his mind made up for him by a woman.' This would obviously not do as an interpretation of *Macbeth*. Yet there is some truth in this approach, and it has its bearings upon the question of tragic pity or tragic sympathy.

There is a very fine distinction to be made in the initial presentation of Macbeth, in his first response to the prophecies of the witches. The question is whether or no they are playing upon a mind that has already considered and half-formulated desperate and ambitious designs. The tendency of late, in criticism as upon the stage, has been to accept this preparation of Macbeth's mind and nature for temptation. Such an interpretation is in harmony with the conception of tragedy as the outcome of a tragic flaw in character, the flaw here being ambition.

From *Shakespeare's Tragic Justice* (Scarborough, Ontario: W. J. Gage, 1961), pp. 11–27.

It also harmonizes with the general modern inexperience of witchcraft, and leads, with a little experience of its able successor, modern psychology in its more spectacular aspects, to the sophisticated notion that the Witches, along with the Ghost of Banquo, as well as the Dagger, are mere projections of Macbeth's mind, even though Banquo too sees the Witches. It is a common error that to ensure for Shakespeare some significance for reader and stage to-day we must in some measure translate him, in effect, into a modern idiom and atmosphere of thought and experience. Witchcraft, along with the power of evil itself, has sunk to-day to the category of superstitions, of exhibits preserved by history and the Churches of all religions in a kind of museum of an incredible past, to the eyes of all who are narrowly bound within the circle of this limited contemporary world, and who cannot escape from their bonds even by the imagination that suspends disbelief in yielding to dramatic creation. It is a salutary thought that the certain truths of a recent yesterday are the exploded theories of to-day, as with the constitution of matter, and that our cherished certainties of to-day may be the rejected superstitions of to-morrow, in all fields of human thought. The vast majority of readers and spectators of a play of Shakespeare are wisely content to merge themselves in the entrancing exhibition of the universals of human nature, in a setting which their imagination enables them to accept unfettered. The prime fault of a producer of a play of Shakespeare is the refusal to trust his dramatist.

It is well to recall once more that this play moves in the Jacobean age, under a Scottish King who had executed witches for such evil powers and acts as the witches in *Macbeth* boast of on their first appearance. And the scene of the play is set in Scotland, in wild remote country where, as notoriously then in Lancashire, as to-day in Cornwall or even in Warwickshire, such evil phenomena could be observed by believing eyes in full operation. The *Book of Common Prayer* then as now provided in the Litany a prayer for daily use for delivery from 'the crafts and assaults of the devil,' of which witchcraft was one potent instrument. There is no sign of Macbeth's dangerous ambition until after his first interview with the witches. And even then Lady Macbeth diagnoses him coolly as 'not without ambition.'[1]

Much play has been made with the argument that the Weird Sisters do not in fact tempt Macbeth to evil designs upon Duncan, but only prophesy a future in which he rises to the kingship. To the Elizabethan, this is mere hair-splitting, and the law was decisive on the question. To 'imagine' the death of the sovereign, to prophesy evil to the sovereign, was a capital offence, indistinguishable from conspiracy to bring about such disastrous events. The temptation was implicit in the prophecy, as any Elizabethan would understand.

We must moreover consider from an Elizabethan standpoint the nature of the crime in which Macbeth becomes involved, and before which he naturally hesitates. As in *Hamlet*, so here it is not merely murder, it is regicide. But here the King is no usurper. It would be dangerous to conceive, or to present on the stage of James's London, and before James himself and his Court, the story of a nobleman who moved by human passions only, by human motives, could plot and execute this ultimate crime. James, like Duncan, was legitimate King of Scotland. He had seen his father murdered, and the Gowrie Conspiracy aimed at himself as he believed. Gunpowder Plot and its aftermath at that very time were busying the Court of Star Chamber. It was necessary to attribute such a design to more than human engineering. Even where an ordinary felony was concerned, the formal indictment of the accused was couched in the words

deum pre oculis suis non habens sed instigacione diabolica motus et seductus.

The phrase 'moved and *seduced*' by devilish instigation is significant. The crime of Macbeth, like that of Guy Fawkes, was not merely diabolical, not merely the yieldings of Macbeth to temptation. It was the outcome of a diabolical conspiracy, a deliberate assault initiated by the Devil working through his instruments, the Witches. And from this craft and this assault Macbeth is not delivered.

The very first scene of the play presents the Witches, with thunder and lightning, signs of the hellish world of chaos and destruction that lies beneath the perilously balanced order of the universe of man. They are to meet Macbeth presently, a first meeting that *they* are seeking, under orders. It is decisive for the interpretation of the action and significance of the play, as of Macbeth's character. It has been suggested that this first scene requires a previous scene, with Macbeth already preparing for his crime, and that this, with other apparent gaps in the play, illustrates the incompleteness of the surviving text. This to my mind is merely a re-writing of Shakespeare and his play, on the assumption that Macbeth is by nature criminally ambitious and villainous. The only conceivable further introduction to the play as we have it would indeed be a Prologue in Hell. One could almost wish that Shakespeare had done it.

It is this, indeed, that makes it possible for Macbeth to be a truly tragic figure, in the sense that pity and terror are alike aroused and are consistent with submission to the catastrophe. But for this, we should be at a loss to understand Shakespeare's insistence upon the great excellencies of Macbeth in the opening scenes, in which he comes close to the perfection of Hamlet in Ophelia's eyes. A loyal subject, a man of nobility in all things, a great soldier who is yet free from ruthlessness, the picture is almost overdrawn, and certainly has no tinge of irony. It is, with equal certainty, intentional that in this picture King Duncan, the Lords of Scotland, and the soldiers and common people are of one mind about Macbeth. Macbeth was a great prize, worth winning for his own sake as for the issues at stake in the winning. And he proved to be hard to win. 'The more we increase in faith and virtuous living,' wrote Sir John Cheke, 'the more strongly will Satan assault us.' This is the deep significance of the words that Shakespeare puts into Macbeth's mouth immediately after the murder of Duncan:

Had I but died an hour before this chance,
I had lived a blessed time.

We may not take these words, with what follows, as hypocritical, designed merely to meet the situation and to mislead. They do so, of course. But they spring directly out of Macbeth's true nature, which he has outraged in his desperate deed.

Yet there is that in Macbeth's nature that promises success in the assault upon him. The deeply poetic and imaginative cast of his mind, no rare thing in great captains, makes him receptive to all that is metaphysical, not of this world of reality, to hallucination as to the Weird Sisters. This it is and not the preparation of his own previous thoughts, that makes him amenable to their influence, where Banquo the practical man holds aloof in sceptical questioning. William Perkins in his *Cases of Conscience*[2] specifically names imagination as a contributory factor to the seductions of evil. It might well seem then that Macbeth's virtues and the exceptional qualities of his mind set him in the rank of true heroes of tragedy, and are the source of the tragic pity that is a component part of our acceptance of his fate, without any questioning of the verdict of justice. So, over and over again, an Elizabethan felon on the very scaffold declares, even as he confesses to devilish instigation, penitent, burdened by his conscience, that he is satisfied with the operation of the law. The responsibility is his, and justice must be done lest that chaos return which is the absence of all justice. There remains for such a felon the hope and trust in God's final mercy.

I said that Macbeth was hard to win. From Holinshed onwards the influence of Lady Macbeth was crucial. 'His wife lay sore upon him to attempt the thing.' And Donwald, whose story contributed to Shakespeare's version of the *Macbeth* story, 'abhorred the act greatly in heart, yet through instigation of his wife' agreed to murder King Duff. In the five stages of submission to temptation which the divines recognise,[3] reception, enticement, consent, commission, and habit, the fatal dividing line comes with consent, with the formation of purpose. Up to this point, even a Saint Paul might yield, but no further. And it is at this point that Macbeth's resistance is overcome, and overcome by Lady Macbeth.

Not that this could be pleaded in mitigation for Macbeth in any Elizabethan court. On the contrary, critically-minded Elizabethans with a bowing acquaintance with Aristotle would probably diagnose one of Macbeth's tragic flaws as being unnatural submissiveness to a woman's will. When Adam put up this plea in Milton's *Paradise Lost* to God the Son, he met with a pretty smart rebuke. And Spenser deals at considerable length and with great severity with the submission of Sir Artegall himself, the Knight of Justice, to the Amazon Radigund. The condemnation is none the less because Adam was moved by love and Artegall by love of beauty and by magnanimity. The relations between Macbeth and Lady Macbeth are indeed the key to this play, and they strongly affect the operation of tragic justice on a level far above the simpler logic of *hamartia*. It helps if we shift the emphasis of our thought from the tragedy of Macbeth to the tragedy of Lady Macbeth, and in so doing move as far away from the concept of a 'fiend-like queen' as we have moved from that of a 'dead butcher.'

Is there anywhere in literature a more rounded or a more affecting picture of the intimacy and mutual confidence of husband and wife? There is an amazing touch in the Sleep-walking scene, when Lady Macbeth mutters to herself and to the absent, remote Macbeth who haunts her waking dreams:

Wash your hands, put on your night-gown; look not so pale. I tell you yet again, Banquo's buried; he cannot come out on's grave.

'I tell you *yet again.'* How often have these two talked together once they were alone; how often has she had to reassure him, strengthen him, give her courage to him. We seem to know far more than the play has time to show us explicitly in action and dialogue. Or see how Shakespeare shows us Lady Macbeth working upon Macbeth before his dread decision to murder Duncan. As Professor Kittredge once put it vividly, she uses three arguments, the three stock arguments of a woman with a man, especially of a wife with a husband. 'You would do it if you dared—but you daren't.' 'You would do it if you loved me—but you don't.' And finally, 'If I were a man, I'd do it myself.' 'I am settled,' says Macbeth—and no wonder! The essential normality of the Macbeth we are so clearly shown fits him for a close and intimate partnership with a woman. He attaches a high value to the social amenities, to love, to honour, to 'troops of friends,' to 'golden opinions from all sorts of people.' We might fancy that we see something of Shakespeare himself in this, as in his merciful humanity as a soldier, and in his sensitive, over-active imagination. To such a man his inevitable Eve, who is essentially feminine even in her rejection of her femininity, remote indeed from that Goneril who bullied the Duke of Albany. Lady Macbeth's being was bound up with Macbeth's at all points. Her ambition is all for him, and she stands by his side, doing violence to her own nature until it breaks under the strain. And here, in this great play, we diverge from all formal, official, theological analyses of human action.

The most tragic aspect of the whole play may well seem to be that in which we may look upon it as the loss of their paradise by these two, a more poignant tragedy than Milton's. For in the end of the poem Adam and Eve unparadised pass through the gates hand in hand, taking their solitary way together. Dante too, relegating Paolo and Francesca to the Inferno befitting their sin, leaves them still in company. Francesca is still and for ever with him 'who never from me shall be parted,' as the winds of hell blow them to and fro. But Shakespeare was more ruthless. The crime of Macbeth and Lady Macbeth brings separation between them, gradually, fatally, finally. And this separation develops, widens, and is made complete in measure as retribution approaches and at last overwhelms them. They meet their fates severally, and in a terrible solitude and darkness of the spirit with an unpassable gulf fixed between them.[4]

This separation is amazingly portrayed in the play. It arises in a measure out of the character of Macbeth; it runs parallel to the development of this character; and it is one of the fundamental causes of the shattering of Lady Macbeth's mind and spirit. Once the initial, decisive crime is committed, and Macbeth has gone over to the powers of evil, he begins to withdraw himself into the fastnesses of his own darkening mind, into a solitary world of his own thoughts, imagination, and will. 'All causes shall give way.' Surely the beginning of this separation is marked already in Act II. Sc. 2, as soon as the murder is committed. Lady Macbeth, meeting him, cries out, *'My husband!'* But he answers grimly, 'I have done the deed,' She is wrapped up in him from beginning to end. But he is already deep in the deed. For her the murder, and their ambitions, are part and parcel of their common life. But Macbeth does not think of it in terms of husband and wife. He keeps his own counsel for the manner and time of the slaying of Banquo and Fleance, lost in his own imaginings, in Act III. Sc. 2. She is already at arm's length from him. The decision is his alone, and he is no longer under her guidance and tutelage. She still shares his burden with him and is his partner, as far as Act III. Sc. 4, in the Banquet scene, when the appalling effect on Macbeth of the apparition of Banquo's ghost threatens to make him betray himself, and she strives to save the situation. 'Are you a man?' is her cry again. She was still his 'sweet remembrancer' just before this, but these are the last words of love she was to hear from him. From now on she is an intruder upon his dark and secret thoughts, as the end of this scene plainly shows. What is apparently dialogue is mainly soliloquy interrupted by abrupt questions.

And from that night on, as far as the play shows, they never meet again; the separation is complete. In Act IV. Sc. I Macbeth is alone; he is taking counsel with the Witches now, and his counsel is not shared with Lady Macbeth, who, be it observed, never comes into contact with the Witches. She is, indeed, a subsidiary force in the seducing of Macbeth. In Act V. Sc. I she is alone, walking in her sleep, speaking strange matters, her thoughts and her words beyond her control. It is an amazing scene of virtuosity in the portrayal of a nervous breakdown, as we should now call it. Lady Macbeth is capable of terrific self-control in emergency, stronger than Macbeth. Her faint in Act II. Sc. 3, a genuine faint, occurs when the crisis has come, has been met, and is over. Macbeth is now doing very well. She is not needed further, and she gives way to the strain. A very woman in all ways, she is never more so than in her physical revulsion from blood. In this scene, her fainting follows hot upon Macbeth's vivid evocation of images of blood. In her sleep-walking her ruined mind is haunted by the gush of the old man Duncan's blood, and nauseated by the smell of blood upon her uncleansable hands.

Macbeth has no need of her now. She will never be needed again. And she is entirely dependent upon him and identified with him. The purpose and springs of her life are broken. The temporary physical weakness of the earlier scene is transformed into the permanent breakdown of her mind and spirit. In her sleep-walking her thoughts are still on him, and she lives over once again the scenes in which their life came to this pass, addressing herself throughout and solely to him. We hear how in her sleep she writes letters, to whom if not to Macbeth, 'since his majesty went into the field'? She must seek to share her thoughts, her fears; she must express them or perish. Her separation in soul from Macbeth has closed her only normal outlet. Macbeth was out and about, busy with his wars, in his true element, a soldier at his trade. But she was cooped up, powerless, unoccupied. If it is not good for man to be alone, it is infinitely worse for a woman, repugnant to the more social structure of her nature, the purpose and conditions of her exist-ence. How much more if to this is added an outcast solitariness of spirit, with no warm heart to nestle into.

So it is that this exclusion in spirit from Macbeth is a profound cause of her sleep-walking, of her 'slumbery agitation.' Her 'infected mind' had only her deaf pillows to discharge her secrets to, and the weak solace of tears, it would seem, was not for her. It is surely more than a coincidence that the last words of her sleep-walking are a reminiscence of the last words that we hear Macbeth say to her, 'Come, we'll to sleep.' Lady Macbeth leaves us muttering, 'To bed, to bed, to bed,' a last poor memory of the vanished hours when she and Macbeth were safe and were together, husband and wife, in the comfortable dark, before she craved for lights continually in her solitude.

For Macbeth she is now her Doctor's patient; her 'thick-coming fancies' were for him to 'cure her of that.' And at the very end this tragedy of Lady Macbeth is consummated with a great crying-out of women within; she is dying, still alone, with her unblessed tapers burning. When Macbeth hears the news he has already 'supped full with horrors.'

> SEATON: The Queen, my lord, is dead.
> MACBETH: She should have died hereafter,
> There would have been a time for such a word.

'She would have died some day, sooner or later, when I might have known and felt what it was to lose a wife. But death is upon us all. Mortality makes a mock of all human affairs, and love *is* Time's fool. I am tied to a stake, and so are all men, and all women.' So in a mood of black despair he goes on to that dreadful comment upon life and human love which is made so much more deeply tragic when we recall the moment and the cause of its utterance. In the very rhythm of this speech, if truly heard or justly spoken, we hear the slow measured beat of a passing-bell for Lady Macbeth, and we are appalled by so disastrous an epitaph upon her passing. It is also a passing-bell for Macbeth, and an epitaph upon himself.

The operation of justice, both human and divine, is manifest in the course of the catastrophe of this play, and it is unquestioned, without mitigation of sentence or plea for mercy. We may not distinguish between the two protagonists and seek to plead for Macbeth because of his courage or for any other reason. Both are involved in an equal condemnation, from which there is no appeal. On behalf of human justice, Malcolm passes judgment, the voice as also the instrument of that public justice which has been delegated to him as rightful King of Scotland and which lawfully triumphs over Macbeth in his hands. No other conclusion could be tolerable, unless the estate of the world were to be undone, to use Macbeth's own phrase. His crimes are deadly, regicide, murder, usurpation, and tyranny. Lady Macbeth is accessory before and after his crimes, and shares with him in their fruits full partner at all points. She never comes to that justice, taking her own life and anticipating her certain fate.

There is no room for pity here, it would seem. And none for mercy in the application of divine justice either, despite the potent instigation of the powers of evil. The Elizabethans were accustomed to a theological approach to the problems of life, and were well informed in the main truths of their Christian faith. They were aware, and Shakespeare was aware, that while the Devil had permission to tempt man, yet no man might be tempted beyond his powers of resistance. The choice to yield or to resist remained his own responsibility, and by his free choice he was judged.[5] Macbeth's yielding, upon the further pressure of Lady Macbeth, was a sin as well as an error, inasmuch as submission to a woman's will went contrary to the divinely established order of the universe. As for Lady Macbeth, theologically at least the weaker vessel and by her nature more subject to dangerous thoughts, herself inviting and invoking evil spirits, her obstinacy not only helped to damn Macbeth but fought against her natural adviser and stay, her husband.

So we see in both classical examples of the development of evil in human life, in all its recognised stages. After consent and commission come use and habit, and finally the culminating stage of despair, the deepest of sins. And all these stages are plainly portrayed in action and dialogue in the play. It has been suggested by Professor Hardin Craig[6] that in Lady Macbeth's sleep-walking we see the operation of God's judgment falling upon her, a visitation of God. But it is abundantly explained in the natural order of her life. Both know well enough where they stand. 'Hell is murky,' says Lady Macbeth. And Macbeth has given his eternal jewel to the common enemy of man. He has lost his soul and his hope of salvation. Neither is even capable of repentance at the eleventh hour. The twelfth hour awaits them irrevocably. This is not felony, it is damnation.

Are Macbeth and Lady Macbeth then portrayed in this play as moral *exempla?* Does the heart of the tragedy lie in the pity and terror evoked by the fall of a dead butcher and a fiend-like queen? Are we purged of these emotions solely by the spectacle of public justice in satisfactory operation, and by the prospect of the divine judgment to come? It is most manifestly not so. There is no place for pity in such a spectacle. And there is no recognisable form of *katharsis* in the mere ravening of the hunters after wild beasts at bay. Pity and terror alike reside here in the corruption of a man and a woman of whom we had every reason to look for great and good things. Their downfall is due no less to their qualities than to their defects, to all that makes each complete and full man and woman, to Macbeth's high spirit, to the power and complexity of his intellect and imagination, to the depth of Lady Macbeth's single-minded merging of her desires in the advancement of her husband, and to the absorption of their love one for another. That such fair and good traits of nature should come to such a pass is matter indeed for pity and terror in the general mind surveying their history. It might appear that the universe has gone awry, that the stars are not fixed in their spheres. But in the end, as pity and terror increase, the certainty grows with them that the ancient pillars of justice, upon which the universe rests, are immovable. 'O that a man might plead for a man with God, as a man pleadeth for a neighbour,' cried Job. We are content even in our perturbation not to plead for Macbeth and Lady Macbeth, either at the bar of public justice or at the mercy-seat of divine judgment.

But they *were* our neighbours, it seems, before they became estranged from us as from each other. And they not our neighbours still at the end, as Iago is not, and Richard the Third and Goneril are not? We think we know the absolute Macbeth, and there is something of the changeling in the Macbeth presented to the world in desperate career. He is transformed despite himself by the power of evil, though that power, as always, draws into its stream of influence his own strength, his great spirit, his honour, his imagination. But he is still in all essentials the Macbeth we first met. Even when tied to a stake, at the very end, he would fain be merciful to Macduff, being certain of overcoming him, rather than add to his guilt of blood.

A star may be observed increasing in magnitude and light into a portent of brightness in the night sky, then vanishing, destroyed by its own explosion. But the sky is the poorer for its disappearance from among the strong unchanging stars which never shot madly from their spheres. To the understanding eye there is no spectacle of greater awe, and to the understanding heart none of more moving pitifulness.

NOTES

[1] Bradley no less coolly dismisses her many significant comments upon his character: 'his wife . . . did not fully understand him' (p. 351), in the interests of his own interpretation.

[2] I. vii. 1. (1608).

[3] W. Perkins, 'A Treatise of Predestination,' *Works* (1613) II, pp. 635–6.

[4] It is a rare instance of insensitiveness in Bradley that he observes merely that 'they drift a little apart.' (p. 350).

[5] It is this, if nothing else, that makes impossible Bradley's interpretation of Banquo as also ensnared by the Weird Sisters. 'The Witches and his own ambition have conquered him.' But his attitude is consistent throughout with firm resistance. Whatever truth may appear to lie in their prophecies, he will for himself keep 'My bosom franchised and allegiance clear.' He stands 'in the great hands of God.' Early in the play, late at night, when he is heavy with sleep, a time for evil thoughts assaulting the best of men, he calls upon divine power for help. The need he feels is ominous of the stream of evil directed at another, at Macbeth, that night and in that place. The business of the Weird Sisters is with Macbeth, as they plainly say. Macbeth's attitude is strongly contrasted with Banquo's. He can contemplate jumping the life to come, even before he consents to his fatal crime. It is, moreover, relevant that Banquo was the ancestor of King James, who saw the play.

[6] *The Enchanted Glass* (1936) p. 120.

Elizabeth Nielsen

MACBETH: THE NEMESIS OF THE POST-SHAKESPEARIAN ACTOR

When one comes away from a twentieth-century production of *Macbeth,* one has an uneasy feeling that something is amiss. No actor since Shakespeare's time seems to have made a name for himself playing the part of Macbeth, although one can remember some famous Lady Macbeths. There also have been many Hamlets, Othellos, Iagos, and even Benedicks—but Macbeths? Rarely, if at all. Famous men have played the role, but they have gained their fame elsewhere first. Yet in Shakespeare's time, Macbeth, and not his Lady, was certainly the principal figure. Women's roles, as we know, were played by boys whose voices had not yet changed. In fact, Thomas Whitfield Baldwin[1] gives us the name of the dark, handsome, little lad who played Lady Macbeth, a John Edmans, who had played only a few bit parts until playing that of Lady Macbeth, who played only one more role after that, and who then dropped into oblivion. It might seem that little John wasn't even good enough to graduate into male roles as many other young lads did. And he could not have been as dominating physically, or as experienced an actor, as the great Richard Burbage, a man great in size and talent, who played the warrior roles of Othello, Coriolanus, and Antony as well as that of Macbeth. In the seventeenth century, the buxom ladies began taking over the women's roles, and since that time many actresses have become famous Lady Macbeths, dominating the play physically, mentally, and emotionally, a domination which Shakespeare never intended and actually never put into the lines of the play, as one can see if the lines are studied carefully and with historical fact in mind.

For example, some of Shakespeare's plays written about actual historical figures are called tragedies and some are not, but *Macbeth,* written about a real king of Scotland, is called a tragedy with, it seems to us, very good reason, because the Macbeth in the play is a true tragic hero. The actual data according to Scottish history can be briefly stated. Macbeth ruled Scotland from around 1040 A.D. to 1058 A.D., when he was killed and at which time the law of tanistry,[2] in effect from 843 A.D., ended. The practice of this law meant that no son of a king on the throne could succeed his father immediately; instead, the first ranking adult member of the

From *Shakespeare Quarterly* 16, No. 2 (Spring 1965): 193–99.

nearest or junior branch of the family should, by election, succeed the enthroned king, acting, until his own succession, as military leader of all the king's forces (as Macbeth did in the play), and, in turn, that king's successor would be the first ranking adult member of the preceding senior branch of the family. In other words, the line of succession was not direct but alternating and elective between the branches of the "blood royal". Now, both Macbeth and the woman who became Lady Macbeth were of the royal family and had claim to the throne through this law. In fact, Lady Macbeth by a former husband who had been killed in battle had had a son who would have been next in line to the throne had he not been killed by the alternating branch of the family to keep him from that throne. Scottish kings, as Lady Macbeth and Macbeth both knew from personal experience, sat on the throne in a sea of blood, killing and being killed for the honor of being called king. These facts have been referred to by many Shakespearian scholars, although ignored by the theater since the seventeenth century, and there are a number of reasons for our assuming that Shakespeare knew of these data, not the least of which is the fact that at the time of the writing of the play England had just imported a Scottish king to sit on the English throne and therefore all England would be conscious of Scottish history. In fact, scholars have long known that Shakespeare wrote the play with this new king in mind. They have known also that Shakespeare read the chronicles of his time, including that of the chronicler who "invented" Banquo. But even more important, perhaps, is the fact that one of Shakespeare's contemporaries, Edmund Spenser, wrote of the law of tanistry as it applied in Ireland.[3] Spenser even adds the fact that some believe the law originated in the law of the Danes although others think not. But an eye-opening association to make with this information is that when Shakespeare wrote a play about a Dane, *Hamlet*, he wrote about a prince who did not inherit from his kingly father.

Keeping this law of tanistry in mind, then, we can see the entire opening of the play take on a far from usual aspect. First, we hear of a noble and good, not evil, warrior, Macbeth, through a description of him in battle wherein he and his kinsman Banquo almost alone destroy an army, but it is about Macbeth that the most noble, heroic, colorful, and affectionate terms are used both by the witnesses and the king (Act I, scene ii). Further on, when Macbeth is hailed by the witches as king "that shalt be", a "horrid image" fills his mind, and his heart pounds at the thought of "murder". Why? Because Scottish kings had killed and had been killed! Will he have to kill and be killed like the preceding kings in order to have what is rightfully his, not only through his own lineage but also through the lineage of his wife? He is not wicked, does not wish to kill and be killed among his kinsmen, although he can slaughter enemies in battle without a qualm, and even hopes that if "chance" will have him king, "chance" may crown him without his turning a hand—and the evil precedent surrounding kingship in Scotland will then be broken. Even his Lady in Act I, scene v, when she hears of the prophecy, soliloquizes about his goodness and his nature, saying, "It is too full of the milk of human kindness to catch the nearest way. Thou wouldst be great, Art not without ambition, but without the illness [meaning wickedness, which she knew from bitter experience] should attend it. What thou wouldst highly, That wouldst thou holily. . . ."

So we see a great, kind, heroic soldier who wants what is rightfully his without having to commit evil to get it. But his idealistic hopes are dashed almost immediately in Act I, scene iv, when King Duncan, after telling Macbeth that he cannot repay him enough for what Macbeth has done for him and Scotland, proceeds to repay Macbeth harshly by ignoring the law of tanistry and saying,

> We will establish our estate upon
> Our eldest, Malcolm, whom we name hereafter
> The Prince of Cumberland. . .

after which the shocked Macbeth says to himself,

> The Prince of Cumberland! That's a step
> On which I must fall down or else o'erleap,
> For in my way it lies.

Macbeth would have had no right to be shocked or even dismayed at this decision had such an announcement been accepted practice in his time, but it was not. It defied the law of tanistry, and from this moment on, Macbeth knows what his course must be if he is to obtain what is rightfully his. In fact, he knows it so surely that when he returns to his wife from battle and says, "My dearest love, Duncan comes here tonight", and she replies, "And when goes hence?" as any good housewife would do, he does not respond with the one word "tomorrow", but, "Tomorrow, as he purposes." When she looks up into his face at this, she reads what, she warns him, all the world can read there—murderous intent—and tells him that he must control his outward appearances better.

Other lines which take on deeper color when this historic law and the evils surrounding it are kept in mind are found in Act I, scene viii, when Lady Macbeth, describing a parental love which she has experienced but which Macbeth has not as yet so done, attempts to help her husband gain courage for action and says,

> I have given suck, and know
> How tender 'tis to love the babe that milks me.

Macbeth, knowing she is referring to her first-born son who was eventually murdered, as were her father and two brothers before, certainly would listen intently to his Lady telling of a tender love which had brought her also agony. And the lines which follow, when Lady Macbeth has given him a seemingly successful plan of action, show us a Macbeth who has not only been given that courage and support, but also a bounding, confident ambition as he cries out,

> Bring forth men-children only,
> For thy undaunted mettle should compose
> Nothing but males.

He is not only going to have children by his beloved Lady, but men-children, and he himself is going to be king! But Macbeth has accepted the plan of his wife, in spite of his scruples against killing his kinsman, only because he is convinced that now he can avoid being known as the killer and thus the precedent of "kill and be killed" can be broken in his case, leaving him free to reign in peace. His mind is convinced, though not his conscience, and thus the tragedy unfolds, a tragedy of a great but very human man who is willing to take a chance on the understanding and compassion of the Judge in the world to come, since there is a certain amount of justice in his own act, if he can just avoid the even-handed justice in this world which "commends the ingredients of our poisoned chalice to our own lips."

Macbeth knows, however, the very second that he has killed Duncan that he has not broken the precedent, but has merely joined the long procession of kings who have killed and been killed—and his despair at this knowledge, when he goes out to his wife after the killing, is a pitiful agony to watch. His Lady does not understand the despair at all, and she treats him as her child, telling him to wash his hands and put on his nightgown, yet fails to tell him that she herself, when she was alone with Duncan, could not have killed the king. To admit that to her husband would be to increase his despair, and this she must not do. It is at this point, too, that one should observe that Macbeth never once blames his Lady for the deed. Why not, if she has goaded him into it? The simple truth is that she has not goaded him into anything that he did not himself want to do. In fact, when he says to her before the deed that he thinks maybe they should put off the business, she loses patience because this is what he had done before. The lines spoken about it in Act I, scene vii, are really their first discussion since Macbeth's return and indicate many previous discussions about the throne, particularly when Lady Macbeth (ll. 35–45) impatiently chides Macbeth and says that he must either get the desire, the yearning, for the throne out of his mind, or be a man about it and go after what he wants. What is more, these lines prove that Lady Macbeth is innocent of being the instigator of the idea of murder when she finally says to him, "What beast was it then That made you break [reveal] this enterprise to me?" Macbeth does not deny this statement at all and admits finally that what deters him is the possibility that the enterprise might fail. It is then that Lady Macbeth gives him the plan which elates him and makes him believe in the success of the deed to the point of going forward into it with all speed. So we see that Macbeth not only has no right to blame his Lady for his act, but loving her as he does, he does not even think of blaming her. He knows that he alone is responsible for his desires as well as his acts, and gradually, as he becomes aware that his Lady is incapable of comprehending just what he has done with her help, he shields her from further knowledge of his plans. Looking at Lady Macbeth from this point of view, we can perhaps see her as a disillusioned sister of Shakespeare's other women, a breed of women who have wanted only to help their menfolk, women like Calpurnia and Portia in *Julius Caesar*, and that stronger Portia in *The Merchant of Venice*, who is willing and able to come forth as the most brilliant lawyer in the land only to aid her husband and then return happily to her home to carry on her wifely duties. Shakespeare's women almost without exception are gentle souls who exist only to give peace and comfort and aid to their loved ones,[4] and Lady Macbeth may be no exception to this ideal although her own bitter experience makes her capable of saying harsh things that she is at the same time incapable of carrying out. Her lines in Act II, scene ii, prove this when she says of Duncan and her chance to kill him, "Had he not resembled my father as he slept, I had done it." One even more revealing scene occurs when, as she hears that Macbeth has killed the guards, she faints, a weakness that not only Macduff but also Banquo notice and pay heed to (II. iii. 122–132). She is not prepared for this additional killing. The killing of Duncan had a certain justification (even though, as she says, she had to take some wine to make herself bold), but the guards were merely to be made drunk. Drunkards could neither admit nor deny guilt. Nothing could thus be proved or disproved about the murder of Duncan, and this was the excellent quality of the plan. Others could assume and guess, but no one could prove or disprove. But conscience-stricken Macbeth mars the plan himself, in his overzealous pretense of horrified rage over the king's murder, and kills the guards without any justification—and Lady Macbeth can take no more. She faints—the effects of her wine cannot carry her further. After this show of weakness, as we have said before, Macbeth never tells her again of any of his plans. He refrains out of love for her as the lines in Act III, scene ii, reveal, but she does not understand completely this strange aloofness on his part. All that she seems to realize is that he keeps alone, apart from her, that he has nightmares when he does try to sleep, and that the throne has brought them neither peace nor joy—nor does she any longer share his confidence. Just before the banquet scene when he has by this time been made king, they speak endearingly to one another, as she tries to tell him to forget what is done and enjoy himself at this party. He promises to do so, telling her to be most gracious to Banquo, yet hinting at something more to be done. When she is startled by that into questioning him, he replies, "Be innocent of the knowledge, dearest chuck"—and then concludes by explaining to her quietly, "Things bad begun make strong themselves by ill." Their course has been set, wrong though it is, and he must carry on with it alone to the bitter end. At the feast, however, he forgets for a moment that she does not know of Banquo's murder, and wonders why her cheeks are not as white as his when he sees Banquo's ghost and she does not—but it does not lessen his love for her, nor does he scold her or blame her in any way. And when he says that he is "stepped in blood so far" that returning would be as tedious as going on, she answers, without understanding the depth of his trouble, that he needs sleep. His answer to her? "Come, we'll sleep"—and then—"We are yet but young in deed." The love between them is still there, but understanding is gone. Two hurt, lonely, but still loving souls go off to bed. This is the last we see of Lady Macbeth until her sleep-walking scene, when she appears with a broken mind as well as a broken heart. Just what has caused her final breakdown we are not told, but the murders that show up in her tortuous cries are those of Duncan, Banquo, and finally Lady Macduff and her children. This last may have touched her most deeply because of her own son, but the pitiful thing to note, first and last, is that her now uncontrolled mind always returns to the night of Duncan's murder when she and her husband were still one in body, mind, and spirit, and she calls repeatedly to him, "Come, come, come—." She is a broken woman, still in love with her husband as she was in the beginning of the play, but still incapable of understanding the depths of tragedy which her great-minded warrior-king-husband sees so clearly.

Macbeth, also still in love with his wife, knows that he cannot block up his conscience, knows that he has chosen the wrong course of action, knows that he cannot undo the wrong, knows that he must travel the course to the end without blaming anyone but himself, and knows, too, that the throne will probably be fought over by his kinsmen[5] after he is killed. Then why, really, does he seek out the witches again, those creatures whom no one else has seen except Banquo? Being a man who does not accept defeat, he seeks any and all avenues for a solution to his dilemma. He sees himself moving inexorably to his death and hopes to salvage something of good from somewhere. But again he does not deceive himself. His wife is now under a doctor's care; the forces from England are tying him to his stake, and none of his line will ever inherit the throne again. His angry and broken-hearted disgust with himself when he evaluates his own life so honestly as the English and Scottish forces surround him show us a man who knows his acts have been evil and who would give his live to undo them. "I have lived long enough", he says, "My way of life is fall'n into the sear, the yellow leaf, And that which should accompany old age, As honor, love, obedience, troops of friends, I must not look to have . . . ", and again later, he leaves no doubt in anyone's mind including that of the doctor that he links his wife's sickness of mind with the sickness of his land in the throes of war and knows that this sickness is beyond the cure of any physician, as the doctor himself has stated (Act IV, scene iii). An even greater self-realization occurs when he hears the cry of the women (Act V, scene v), and says that he has almost forgotten the taste of fears because he has "supped full with horrors". That cry and the subsequent announcement of the death of his queen bring him to ultimate despair as he realizes that, now, he is not only without honor, love, obedience, and troops of friends but also without the one great love of life—the one redeeming remnant of a once promising great existence—his beloved wife. Life, to Macbeth now, is a tale "told by an idiot, full of sound and fury, Signifying nothing."

But the saddest lines of the play are yet to come. Macbeth has made up his mind to "die with harness" on his back even though the woods are moving to Dunsinane. As he fights young Siward and kills him, he gains confidence in the prophecy that at least he will not die of any man born of woman. Then he meets Macduff. Believing himself invincible in hand to hand conflict, having just killed Siward, he nevertheless turns away from Macduff. His agony at losing his own wife causes him to realize for the first time the unforgivable evil he has done to Macduff in killing Macduff's wife and children. As he turns from him in saddest remorse, he says, "Of all men else I have avoided thee. But get thee back, my soul is too much charged With blood of thine already" (Act V, scene viii). The rest of the play is anticlimactic after these lines. Macbeth pleads with Macduff to fight with someone else, even explaining the prophecy to Macduff in order to persuade Macduff to desist. But when Macduff explains that even that prophecy has played him false, Macbeth for a moment confesses to cowardice—but only for a moment. Then Macbeth realizes he has one thing left: his ability as a soldier. He resolves to make Macduff earn his victory as he cries his final words, "Lay on, Macduff, And damned be him that first cries 'Hold, enough.' " Then he is killed as he knows he will be, and the tragedy ends there for Macbeth and his Lady.

All the lines quoted above take on great importance in the play when interpreted through the historical data presented. It would be good to see a production of this play today that would present a Macbeth as strong and as tragic as Shakespeare's lines show him to be, a good, talented, even noble man of great promise, who through vaulting ambition rationalized himself into a wrong act to offset an injustice, an error common as humanity itself. Without this interpretation, some of the lines have no meaning at all, while others actually work against the traditional interpretation which conceives of Macbeth as an evil man dominated by an even more evil woman. There is beauty in this play, and the beauty is that Macbeth loves his lady at the opening of the play as she loves him, and the love is still there in them both as they meet death—it is a love that is still there through all the agony. But the greater agony is Macbeth's when his lady dies, this one remaining light of his life goes out, and he is left to face the inevitable retribution alone. There is pity for the waste of this potentially great leader who looks on his own degeneration with such sorrow, who never once blamed another for his own rationalized action, and who even at the end blames no one but himself, a trait most uncommon to humanity. This surely is the stuff of which tragedies are made and the reason that many scholars consider *Macbeth* one of Shakespeare's greatest tragedies.

NOTES

[1] Thomas Whitfield Baldwin, *The Organization and Personnel of the Shakespearean Company* (New York, Russell and Russell, 1961).

[2] W. H. Thomson, *Shakespeare's Characters: A Historical Dictionary* (Altrincham, England: John Sherratt and Son, 1951).

[3] Edmund Spenser, *The Works of Edmund Spenser: A Variorum Edition,* ed. by E. Greenlaw, C. G. Osgood, F. M. Padelford, R. Heffner (Johns Hopkins Press, 1949), IX, 49–52.

[4] Agnes Mure Mackenzie, *The Women in Shakespeare's Plays* (Garden City, New York: Doubleday, 1924).

[5] It is Banquo's issue, not that of Malcolm or Donalbain, that alternately inherit the throne (IV. i).

Robert B. Heilman

THE CRIMINAL
AS TRAGIC HERO

I

The difficulties presented by the character of Macbeth—the criminal as tragic hero—have led some critics to charge Shakespeare with inconsistency, others to seek consistency by viewing the initial Macbeth as in some way morally defective,[1] and still others to normalize the hero by viewing the final Macbeth as in some way morally triumphant. Perhaps a recollection of Lascelles Abercrombie's enthusiastic phrase, 'the zest and terrible splendour of his own unquenchable mind' (1925), and of Wilson Knight's comparable 'emerges at last victorious and fearless'[2] (1930), helped stir L. C. Knights to complain (1933) that 'the critics have not only sentimentalized Macbeth—ignoring the completeness with which Shakespeare shows his final identification with evil—but they have slurred the passages in which the positive good is presented by means of religious symbols.'[3] Even after this, so unflighty an editor as Kittredge could say that Macbeth 'is never greater than in the desperate valour that marks his end'.[4] On the other hand, the editor of a *Macbeth* meant for schools describes Macbeth as a 'bold, exacting and presumptuous criminal, ... bent on destruction for destruction's sake', 'the champion of evil', 'a monster', giving 'the impression ... of some huge beast who ... dies lashing out at everyone within range'.[5] But if intemperateness of eulogy or condemnation is exceptional, the opposing impulses are not altogether reconciled; if to many critics Macbeth is damned, there is hardly consensus about either the way down or the mitigating circumstances or how good the bad man is. 'Damned, but' might be a title for an anthology of critical essays.

The problem of character, which is no more than quickly sketched by this sampling of judgments, becomes intertwined with the problem of generic placement, a standard, though rarely decisive, evaluating procedure. If the play changes from the study of a complex soul to the history of good men's victory over a

From *Shakespeare Survey* 19 (1966): 12–24.

criminal and tyrant, has it not dropped from the level of high tragedy to that of political melodrama? This seems harsh, and we can evade it either by discovering unmelodramatic complications in Macbeth as king (a method approached by Neilson and Hill when they acknowledge that Macbeth 'proved a desperately wicked man' but add, with mild confidence, '. . . we are reassured that he was more than the mere butcher the avenging Malcolm not unnaturally calls him'),[6] or by minimizing the importance of character and insisting that the play is a great dramatic poem (as in that anti-Bradleyism which can be traced at least from Knights's 1933 essay). When we look, as many critics do, at the poetic-dramatic structure, we find, among other things, that the nadaism of Macbeth's 'Tomorrow and tomorrow and tomorrow' speech is not Shakespeare's but Macbeth's and that the play contains numerous images of good kingship and affirmative life; Macbeth is regularly in contrast with the norms of order and hope. The trouble with abstracting a meaning—'Crime doesn't pay' or 'The way of transgressors is hard'—and regarding character as principally a buttress of that meaning[7] is that it has consequences for the placement of drama. Kenneth Muir faces the consequences when he says, 'We may, indeed, call *Macbeth* the greatest of morality plays . . . '.[8] However, Muir is understandably diffident about the term 'morality play'; so he not only says 'greatest' but adds a weighty series of codicils intended to cushion to the utmost, or even counteract, the implicit demotion from 'tragedy' to 'morality play'.

The critical uneasiness with the character of Macbeth is different from the usual feelings—uncertainty, attentiveness, curiosity, passion to examine, and so on—stirred by an obscure or elusive character, because it springs from a disturbing sense of discrepancy not evoked, for instance, by Shakespeare's other tragic heroes. We expect the tragic protagonist to be an expanding character, one who grows in awareness and spiritual largeness; yet Macbeth is to all intents a contracting character, who seems to discard large areas of consciousness as he goes, to shrink from multilateral to unilateral being (we try to say it isn't so by deflating the Macbeth of Acts I and II and inflating the Macbeth of Acts IV and V). The diminishing personality is of course not an anomaly in literature, whether in him we follow a gradual decrease of moral possibility or discover an essential parvanimity, but this we expect in satire (Fielding's Blifil, Austen's Wickham, Meredith's Sir Austin Feverel, Eliot's Lydgate), not tragedy. This source of uneasiness with Macbeth, however, is secondary; the primary source is a technical matter, Shakespeare's remarkable choice of point of view—that of this ambitious man who, in Muir's words that sum up the contracting process, 'becomes a villain'. We have to see through his eyes, be in his skin; for us, this is a great breach of custom, and in the effort at accommodation we do considerable scrambling. When we share the point of view of Hamlet, we experience the fear of evil action and of evil inaction; when we share the point of view of Othello and Lear, we experience passionate, irrational action whose evil is not apprehended or foreseen; but when we share the point of view of Macbeth, we have to experience the deliberate choice of evil. Hence a disquiet altogether distinguishable from the irresoluteness of mind before, let us say, some apparent contradictions in Othello.

The problem is like that which usually comes up when readers[9] must adopt the point of view of a character in whom there are ambiguities. Unless structure is based on contrasts, point of view ordinarily confers authority; but discomforts, which invariably lead to disagreements, arise when authority apparently extends to matters which, on aesthetic, rational, psychological, or moral grounds, the reader finds it difficult to countenance.[10] 'Disagreements', of course, implies studious recollection in tranquillity, or rather, untranquillity; what we are concerned with in this discussion is the immediate, unanalysed imaginative experience which precedes the effort to clarify or define. We are assuming that the person experiencing *Macbeth* is naturally carried into an identification with Macbeth which, if incomplete, is still more far-reaching than that with anyone else in the play. This should be a safe working assumption,[11] whatever the modifications of sensibility that qualify the immediate unanalysed experience and hence lead to alternative explanations of Macbeth in retrospect. Surely Muir is right in saying of our response to Macbeth that 'we are tempted and suffer with him'.[12]

Behind our condemnation of trivial literature, whether we call it 'sentimental', 'meretricious', or something else, lies the sense that the characters whom for the moment we become give us an inadequate or false sense of reality, call into action too few of our human potentialities. Hence 'tragedy' tends not simply to designate a genre, in which there may be widely separated levels of excellence, but to become an honorific term: it names a noble enterprise, the action of a literary structure which compels us to get at human truth by knowing more fully what we are capable of—'knowing', not by formal acts of cognition but by passing imaginatively through revelatory experiences. In a morality we see a demonstration of what happens; in tragedy we act out what happens, undergoing a kind of kinaesthetic initiation into conduct we would not ordinarily acknowledge as belonging to us. The problem is how far this process of illuminating induction can go without running into resistance that impedes or derails the tragic experience, without exciting self-protective counter-measures such as retreating from tragic coexistence with the hero to censorious observation of him from a distant knoll.[13] *Macbeth* at least permits this way out by its increasingly extensive portrayal, in Acts IV and V, of the counterforces whom we see only as high-principled seekers of justice. Do we, so to speak, defect to them because Macbeth, unlike Lear and Othello, moves into a greater darkness in which we can no longer discern our own lineaments? Do we, then, turn tragedy into melodrama or morality?

I I

That, of course, is a later question. The prior question is the mode of our relationship with Macbeth when he kills Duncan; here we have to consent to participation in a planned murder, or at least tacitly accept our capability of committing it. The act of moral imagination is far greater, as we have seen, than that called for by the germinal misdeeds of Lear or the murder by Othello, since these come out of emotional frenzies where our tolerance, or even forgiveness, is so spontaneous that we need not disguise our kinship with those who realize in action what we act in fantasy. Yet technically Shakespeare so manages the situation that we become Macbeth, or at least assent to complicity with him, instead of shifting to that simple hostility evoked by the melodramatic treatment of crime. We accept ourselves as murderers, so to speak, because we also feel the strength of our resistance to murder. The initial Macbeth has a fullness of human range that makes him hard to deny; though a kind of laziness makes us naturally vulnerable to the solicitation of some narrow-gauge characters, we learn by experience and discipline to reject these (heroes of cape and sword, easy masters of the world, pure devils, simple victims); and correspondingly we are the more drawn in by those with a large store of human possibilities, good and evil. Macbeth can act as courageous patriot (I, ii, 35ff.), discover that he has dreamed of the throne ('. . . why do you start . . . ?'—I, iii, 51), entertain the 'horrid image' of murdering Duncan (I, iii, 135), be publicly rewarded by the king (I, iv), be an affectionate husband (I, v), survey, with anguished clarity, the motives and consequences of the imagined deed; reject it; feel the strength of his wife's persuasion, return to 'this terrible feat' (I, vii, 80); undergo real horrors of anticipation (II, i, 31ff.) and of realization that he has actually killed Duncan (II, ii, 14ff.). Here is not a petty scoundrel but an extraordinary man so capacious in feeling and motive as to have a compelling representativeness; we cannot adopt him selectively, feel a oneness with some parts of him and reject others; we become the murderer as well as the man who can hardly tolerate, in prospect or retrospect, the idea of murder. The suffering is so great that the act is hedged about with penance; unless we are neurotic, we cannot pay such a price without earning it; murder belongs, as it were, to normalcy—to us in our normalcy. Furthermore, the anguish is so powerful and protracted, and the 'terrible feat' so quickly done, that it marks only a brief failure of moral governance; we seem to sacrifice only a mite of the sentience that we instinctively attribute to ourselves. That, too, after solicitations whose power we feel directly: 'Vaulting Ambition', indeed, but also challenges to our manly courage, the promise of security, and, behind these, the driving strength of another soul not easy to disappoint or even, when the other speaks for a part of ourselves, to resist. These persuasions, in turn, are a supplement to 'supernatural soliciting' (I, iii, 130), to 'fate and metaphysical aid' (I, v, 26). Finally, Shakespeare affords the reader one more aid in accepting his alliance with the murderer: that alteration of ordinary consciousness that enhances the persuasiveness of deviant conduct by the 'good man'. From the first prophetic phrases Macbeth has been 'rapt', a word applied to him thrice (I, iii, 57, 142; I, v, 5), and when the knocking is heard Lady Macbeth adjures him,

> Be not lost
> So poorly in your thoughts;   (II, ii, 71–2)

there are also his dagger-vision speech before the murder (II, i, 33ff.), and after it the hallucinatory impressions that make Lady Macbeth use the word 'brainsickly' (II, ii, 46). The note of 'unsound mind' helps make the murderer 'one of us', to use Conrad's term, rather than a criminal-outsider.

If it be a function of tragedy, as we have suggested, to amplify man's knowledge of himself by making him discover, through imaginative action, the moral capabilities to which he may ordinarily be blind, then Shakespeare, in the first two acts of *Macbeth*, has so managed his tools that the function is carried out super-latively well. He leads the reader on to accept himself in a role that he would hardly dream of as his. If it be too blunt to say that he becomes a murderer, at least he feels murderousness to be as powerful as a host of motives more familiar to consciousness. Whether he knows it or not, he knows something more about himself. It may be that 'knows' takes us too far into the realm of the impalpable, but to use it is at least to say metaphorically that the reader remains 'with' Macbeth instead of drifting away into non-participation and censure. Shakespeare's drama-turgic feat should not be unappreciated.

III

That behind him, Shakespeare moves ahead and takes on a still greater difficulty: the maintaining of identity, his and ours, with a character who, after a savage initial act, goes on into other monstrosities, gradually loses more of his human range, contracts, goes down hill.[14] Surely this is the most demanding tech-nical task among the tragedies. Othello and Lear both grow in knowledge; however reluctantly and incompletely, they come into a sense of what they have done, and advance in powers of self-placement. With them we have a sense of recovery, which paradoxically accompanies the making of even destructive discoveries. Re-nouncing blindness is growth. Macbeth does not attract us into kinship in this way; his own powers of self-recognition seem to have been squandered on the night of the first murder and indirectly in the dread before Banquo's ghost. Nevertheless there are passages in which he has been felt to be placing and judging himself. There may indeed be something of tragic self-knowledge in the man who says that he has 'the gracious Duncan . . . murder'd' and

> mine eternal jewel
> Given to the common enemy of man;   (III, i, 65, 67–8)

yet he is not saying 'I have acted evilly', much less 'I repent of my evil conduct', but rather, 'I have paid a high price—and for what? To make Banquo the father of kings.' Macbeth is not so simple and crude as not to know that the price is high, but his point is that for a high price he ought to be guaranteed the best goods; and in prompt search of the best goods he elaborates the remorselessly calculating rheto-ric by which he inspirits the murderers to ambush Banquo and Fleance. Again, he can acknowledge his and Lady Macbeth's nightmares and declare buried Duncan better off than they, but have no thought at all of the available means of mitigating this wretchedness; the much stronger motives appear in his preceding statement 'We have scorch'd the snake, not kill'd it' and his following one, 'O, full of scorpions is my mind . . . that Banquo, and his Fleance, lives' (III, ii, 13, 36–7). The serpents of enmity and envy clearly have much more bite than the worm of conscience.

> I am in blood
> Stepp'd in so far   (III, iv, 136–7)

encourages some students to speak as if Macbeth were actuated by a sense of guilt, but since no expectable response to felt guilt inhibits his arranging, very shortly, the Macduff murders, it seems more prudent to see in these words only a technical summary of his political method. In 'the sere, the yellow leaf' lines Macbeth's index of the deprivations likely to afflict him in later years (V, iii, 23ff.) suggests to some readers an acute moral awareness; it seems rather a regretful notice of social behaviour, such as would little trouble the consciousness of a man profoundly concerned about the quality of his deeds and the state of his soul. Finally, in Macbeth's battlefield words to Macduff—

> my soul is too much charg'd
> With blood of thine already—   (V, viii, 5–6)

some critics have detected remorse. It may be so, but in the general context of actions of a man increasingly apt in the saguinary and freed from refinement of scruple, there is much to be said for the suggestion that he is 'rationalizing his fear';[15] possibly, too, he is unconsciously placating the man who has most to avenge and of whom the First Apparition has specifically warned him (IV, i, 71).

Since different Shakespearians have been able to find in such passages a continuance of genuine moral sensitivity in Macbeth, it is possible that for the non-professional reader they do indeed belong to the means by which a oneness with Macbeth is maintained. If so, then we have that irony by which neutral details in an ugly man's portrait have enough ambiguity to help win a difficult assent to him. However, a true change of heart is incompatible with a retention of the profits secured by even the temporarily hardened heart, and the fact is that once Macbeth has become king, all of his efforts are directed to hanging on to the spoils of a peculiarly obnoxious murder. Shakespeare has chosen to deal not only with an impenitent, though in many ways regretful, man, but with one whose crime has been committed only to secure substantial wordly advantages (in contrast with the wrongs done by Lear and Othello). Perhaps what the play 'says' is that such a crime has inevitable consequences, that worldly profit—goods, honour, power—is so corrupting that, once committed to it, the hero can never really abjure it, can never really repent and seeks ways of spiritual alteration, though he may cry out against the thorns and ugliness of the road he cannot leave.[16] However far such a theory can be carried, it is plain that Macbeth, once he has taken the excruciatingly difficult first step on the new route, discovers in himself the talents for an unsurrenderable athleticism in evil.

The artist's problem is that for a reader to accompany such a character and to share in his intensifying depravity might become intolerable; the reader might simply flee to the salvation of condemning the character. This does not happen. For, having chosen a very difficult man to establish our position—to give us shoes and skin and eyes and feeling—Shakespeare so manages the perspective that we do not escape into another position. As with all his tragic heroes, Shakespeare explores the point of view of self, the self-defending and self-justifying motions of mind and heart; alert as we are to self-protectiveness in others, we still do not overtly repudiate that of Macbeth. That is, Macbeth finds ways of thinking about himself and his dilemmas that we find congenial, and, even more than that, ways of feeling which we easily share. The dramatist can rely somewhat, of course, on that ambiguous sympathy with the criminal that human beings express in various ways; even an artist who is not romanticizing a criminal can count on it up to a point if he protects it against counter feelings. Suppose, for instance, that we had seen a great deal of Duncan at Macbeth's castle or that the murder were done on the stage or that Macbeth did not undergo the agonies depicted in II, ii; he would already have lost his role as erring humanity, and we ours as secret sharer. Suppose, also, that he then took the throne by blunt force, or were grossly shameless, or rapped out lies which everyone knew to be lies. But he does not drive us away by such methods; instead, our murderer is a man who suffers too much, as it were, really to be a murderer; he agonizes more than he antagonizes. After the murder, we next see him in a painfully taxing and challenging position—the utter necessity of so acting in public, at a moment of frightful public calamity, that neither his guilt will be revealed nor his ambition threatened. The pressure on him shifts to us, who ought to want him caught right there. Can he bring it off? Can we bring it off? In some way we become the terribly threatened individual, the outnumbered solitary antagonist; further, our own secret self is at stake, all our evil, long so precariously covered over, in danger of being exposed, and we of ruin. But we miraculously come through, our terrible anxiety somehow transmuted to strength under fire; we say the right things ('Had I but died an hour before this chance', II, iii, 89), have the presence of mind to be carried away by 'fury' and kill the chamberlains and turn suspicion on them, and still to 'repent' the fury (105). Relief, perhaps triumph. This statement may require more delicacy and precision, but it should indicate the way in which Shakespeare instinctively approaches the task of enticing us into collusion. We remain the murderer in part because the pressure of other motives makes us forget that we are. What we forget we do not deny.

Macbeth is in danger of degenerating from Everyman into monster, that is, of pushing us from unspoken collusion to spoken judgment, when he coolly plots against Banquo. But Shakespeare moves Macbeth quickly into a recital of motives and distresses that invite an assent of feeling. Macbeth's important 25-line soliloquy (III, i, 47–71) is in no sense a formal apologia, but it has the effect of case-making by the revelation of emotional urgencies whose force easily comes home to us. There are three of these urgencies. The first is fear, that especial kind of fear that derives from insecurity: '. . . to be safely thus' (48) is a cry so close to human needs that it can make us forget that the threat to safety is made by justice. The fear is of Banquo, a man of 'dauntless temper', of 'wisdom' (51, 52); we can credit ourselves with Macbeth's ability and willingness to discriminate at the same time that, unless we make an improbable identification with Banquo, we can enter into the lesser man's sense of injury and his inclination to purge himself of second-class moral citizenship. The second great appeal is that to the horror of being in a cul de sac, of feeling no continuity into something beyond the present: all that we have earned will be nothing if we have but a 'fruitless crown', 'a barren sceptre', 'No son' (60–3). It is the Sisters that did this; 'they' are treating us unfairly, inflicting a causeless deprivation. Our Everyman's share of paranoia is at work. Yet the price has been a high one ('vessel of my peace', loss of 'mine eternal jewel'); it is as if a bargain had been unfulfilled, and we find ourselves sharing the third emotional pressure—resentment at a chicanery of events which need not be borne.

The anxiety in the face of constant threats, the pain at being cut off from the future, the bitterness of the wretched bargain—these emotions, since they may belong to the most upright life, tend to inhibit our making a conscious estimate of the uprightness of the man who experiences them. This may be a sufficient hedge against our splitting away from Macbeth when he is whipping up the Murderers against Banquo. But since Macbeth can trick us into the desire to 'get away with it', or into discovering that we can have this desire, it may be that even the subornation of murder evokes a distant, unidentified, and unacknowledgeable compliance. Here the appeal would be that of executive dispatch and rhetorical skill in a difficult cause; it is satisfying to use against another the method before which one has been defenceless earlier, the appeal to manliness (91ff.), to hint the grave danger to oneself (115–17), to claim a meritorious abstention from 'bare-fac'd power' (118), though the power is legitimate. Then quickly, before we have time to cast off the spell, to catch ourselves tricked into a silent partnership in crime and to start backing away from it, we are enthralled in another way: again, this time with both Macbeth and Lady Macbeth, the terrible fear, the sense of constant menace, the 'affliction of these terrible dreams', the 'torture of the mind' (III, ii, 18, 21). Afflictions and tortures: we have our own, and we do not stop, step to one side, and think that ours are more just and noble than those of the wretched royal pair. Macbeth's language, in a brilliant touch, even makes the usurpers weak victims, such as we sometimes like to be: threatening them is a 'snake', cut in two, but reuniting to extend the 'danger', against which we offer but 'poor malice', that is, feeble op-position (14–15). Here is one of the subtler of the series of verbal and dramatic means by which we are held 'with' Macbeth and the queen; we are with them as long as we do not turn and say, 'But what do you expect?' And as long as we do not say that, we have not shifted to the posture invited by melodrama and morality play.

At the banquet scene the courtesy and breeding of the host and hostess hardly seem that of vulgar criminals, from whom we would quickly spring away into our better selves. But before the Ghost appears, Macbeth learns of the escape of Fleance, and he speaks words that appeal secretly to two modes of responsiveness. He introduces the snake image from III, ii, 14: as for Banquo. 'There the grown serpent lies', but then there's Fleance:

> the worm that's fled
> Hath nature that in time will venom breed. (III, iv, 29–30)

It is not that we rationally accept Macbeth's definition of father and son, but that we share his desperateness as destined victim; and his image for the victimizing forces, as long as it is not opposed openly in the context, is one to evoke the fellowship of an immemorial human fear. This, however, tops off a subtler evocation of sympathy, Macbeth's

> I am cabin'd, cribb'd, confin'd, bound in
> To saucy doubts and fears.   (24–5)

The new image for fear, which we have already been compelled to feel, is peculiarly apt and constraining: it brings into play the claustrophobic distress that can even become panic. We do not pause for analysis, stand off, and say, 'It is the claustrophobia of crime'; rather the known phobia maintains our link with the criminal. Then, of course, the moral responsiveness implied by the appearance of the Ghost and by Macbeth's terror make a more obvious appeal, for here the traditional 'good man' is evident. Not only does he again become something of a victim, but the royal pair draw us into their efforts to save a situation as dangerous as it is embarrassing and humiliating. They are in such straits that we cannot now accuse them, much less triumph over them. Macbeth's demoralizing fear, finally, works in a paradoxical way: fear humanizes the warrior and thus brings us closer to him, while his inevitable reaction from it into almost hyperbolic courage, with its conscious virility ('Russian bear', 'Hyrcan tiger', etc., 99ff.), strikes a different chord of consent. From now on until the end, indeed, Macbeth is committed to a bravery, not unspontaneous but at once compensating and desperate—a bravura of bravery—that it is natural for us to be allied with.

The danger point is that at which the admired bravery and its admired accompaniment, resolution (such as appears in the visit to the Witches, IV, i), are distorted into the ruthlessness of the Macduff murders. Here we are most likely to be divorced from Macbeth, to cease being actors of a role and become critics of it. At any rate, Shakespeare takes clear steps to 'protect' Macbeth's position. That 'make assurance double sure' (IV, i, 83) has become a cliché is confirmatory evidence that the motive is well-nigh universal; getting rid of Macduff becomes almost an impersonal safety measure, additionally understandable because of the natural wish to 'sleep in spite of thunder' (86). We come close to pitying his failure to grasp the ambiguity of the oracles, for we can sense our own naiveté and wishful thinking at work; and his disillusionment and emptiness on learning that Banquo's line will inherit the throne, are not so alien to us that Macbeth's retaliatory passion is unthinkable. Shakespeare goes ahead with the risk: we see one of the cruel murders, and the next time Macbeth appears, he is hardly attractive either in his almost obsessive denying of fear (V, iii, 1–10) or in his letting his tension explode in pointless abuse of his servant, partly for fearfulness (11–18). Still, the impulses are ones we can feel. Now, after Macbeth has been on the verge of breaking out into the savage whom we could only repudiate, things take a different turn, and Macbeth comes back toward us as more than a loathsome criminal. He is 'sick at heart' (19)—words that both speak to a kindred feeling and deny that the speaker is a brute. He meditates on approaching age (22ff.), with universality of theme and dignity of style teasing us into a fellowship perhaps strengthened by respect for the intellectual candour with which he lists the blessings he has forfeited. Above all he has a desperately sick wife: pressed from without, still he must confer with the doctor and in grief seek remedies for a 'mind diseas'd', 'a rooted sorrow', 'that perilous stuff/Which weighs upon the heart' (40–5). Shakespeare makes him even extend this humane concern, either literally or with a wry irony that is still not unattractive, to the health of Scotland:

> find her disease,
> And purge it to a sound and pristine health.   (51–2)

Along with all of the troubles that he meets, more often than not with sad equanimity, he must also face crucial desertions: 'the thanes fly from me' (4). Like us all, he tells his troubles to the doctor. He has become an underdog, quite another figure from the cornered thug, supported by a gang of sinister loyalty, that he might be. This athlete in evil, as we called him earlier, has had to learn endurance and endure, if we may be forgiven, the loneliness of the long-distance runner. Against such solitude we hardly turn with reproof.

Macbeth opened the scene crying down fear; he goes on with three more denials of fear, one at the end (32, 36, 59); now we are able to see in the repetition an effort to talk down deep misgivings, and the hero again approximates Everyman, ourselves. When Macbeth next appears, just before the battle, it is the same: he opens and closes the scene literally or implicitly denying fear, even though the prophecy of his end seems miraculously fulfilled (V, v, 1–15, 51–2). Meanwhile the queen's death is reported, and the warrior, moved but finely controlled, turns grief into contemplation, with the seductiveness of common thought in uncommon language. The closing battle scene is a series of denials of fear, appealing to both pity and admiration. Some details are instinctively ingratiating. 'They have tied me to a stake; I cannot fly' (V, vii, 1)—oneself as the victim of others bent on cruel sport. 'Why should I play the Roman fool . . . ?' (V, viii, 1)—no moral retreat, no opting out of adversity. 'I will not yield' (27)—the athlete's last span of endurance, fight against all odds.

IV

My intention has been, not to offer a full study of Macbeth or a fresh account of his moral alteration, not to argue that he is a worse man than some have thought (though some analyses seem not to catch what Knights called 'the completeness [of] his final identification with evil') or a better man than other men have thought (though he is remarkably endowed with aspects of personality not ordinarily expected in a man committed to evil), but to describe the apparent impact made upon the imagination by certain deeds, thoughts, and feelings of his. Since there is hardly a need to demonstrate that Macbeth is a villain and that villains ordinarily repel us, the emphasis has naturally fallen upon those elements in him that tend to elicit, in whatever degree, fellow-feeling, pity, favour, or even admiration. Macbeth possibly establishes a subtle kinship by setting in motion certain impulses which we would rather not admit—anomalous siding with the criminal, aggressive ambition, envy, the pleasure of getting away with it (which includes leaving the 'it' unexamined). More frequently the appeal to allegiance is that of states or situations which are neutral in that they may come to good or bad men but which, without analysing the merits of the figure involved, we find it difficult not to fear or pity—the threat of exposure, the anxieties of a perilous position, relentless enclosure by men and circumstances, nightmares and insomnia of whatever origin, the pressing need for greater safety, the pain of miscalculation and the gnawing sense of a bad bargain, any enlargement of the penalties of advanced age, desertion, the unequal struggle, the role of the underdog. Finally, and more important, Macbeth early gives every sign of having a conscience, and later he exhibits qualities and abilities that normally elicit respect or admiration—resourcefulness under severely taxing stresses, readiness for intolerable difficulties, resolution, the philosophic cast of mind, endurance, bravery.

If the general demonstration, as it is summarized here, has merit, it opens the way to several others points. For one thing, it should help explain some rather enthusiastic accounts of Macbeth: that which binds us to him, either the painfulness of what he endures or the qualities that he shares with men we admire, so overwhelms the sense of the ruthless tyrant that we either let this slip out of operative consciousness or take it for granted as not requiring further discussion, and proceed then to erect a rational form for all the feelings of kinship or approval. Shakespeare has so thoroughly attacked the problem of keeping a villain from being a mere villain that at times it has apparently been easy to lose sight of his villainy. On the other hand, the endowing of Macbeth with the power to attract fellow-feeling and even approval makes it unlikely that 'the sympathies of the audience are switched to his enemies'.[17] This is a crucial matter. For if such a switch does take place, then the play does not hold us in an essentially tragic engagement, but carries us into a relationship like that with *Richard III* (a play often used to illustrate *Macbeth*).

To be convinced of Macbeth's retention of our sympathy may seem to imply a denial of our sympathy to Malcolm, Macduff, and the conquering party. By no means: obviously we share their passions whenever these control the action, and we may even cheer them on. Yet we do not remain fixedly and *only* with them, as we do with Richmond and his party in *Richard III,* and with such forces in all dramas with a clearly melodramatic structure. When the anti-Macbeth leaders occupy the stage, we are unable not to be at one with them; but the significant thing is that when his point of view is resumed, Macbeth again draws us back, by the rather rich means that we have examined, into our old collusion. After III, vi, when we first see committed opposition to Macbeth ('. . . this our suffering country, / Under a hand accurs'd!'—48–9), the two sides alternate on the stage until they come together in battle. In one scene we have the rather easy, and certainly reassuring, identification with the restorers of order; in the next, the strange, disturbing emotional return to the camp of the outnumbered tyrant. We move back and forth between two worlds and are members of both. As a contemporary novelist says of a character who is watching fox and hounds, 'She wanted it to get away, yet when she saw the hounds she also wanted them to catch it'.[18]

Macbeth, in other words, has a complexity of form which goes beyond that normally available to melodrama and morality play, where the issue prevents ambiguity of feeling and makes us clear-headed partisans. Whether Macbeth goes on beyond this surmounting of melodramatic limitations to high achievement as tragedy is the final problem. It turns, I believe, on Shakespeare's treatment of Macbeth, that is, on whether this retains the complexity that cannot quite be replaced by the kind of complexities that Macbeth does embrace. Here, of course, we are in the area of our mode of response to character, where all is elusive and insecure, and we can only be speculative. What I have proposed, in general, is that, because of the manifold claims that Macbeth makes upon our sympathy, we are drawn into identification with him in his whole being; one might say that he tricks us into accepting more than we expect or realize. If it is true that we are led to experience empathy with a murderer and thus to come into a more complete 'feeling knowledge' of what human beings are like (tragic experience as the catharsis of self-ignorance), then Shakespeare has had a success which is not trivial. Yet there remains a legitimate question or two. Let us try this approach. It is not the business of tragedy to let man know that he is only a scoundrel or devil (any more than its business is to let him know that he is really an angel); it is obvious enough that such an experience would be too circumscribed to gain assent to its truthfulness. In so far as he pushes us in that direction, Shakespeare makes the indispensable qualifications. Yet the felt qualifications can be expressed in ways that are less than satisfactory; for instance, 'Macbeth is a villain, but there's also this to be said', or, still more, 'Macbeth is a wonderful man. Oh yes, a villain, of course.' Such flip statements are not found literally in Macbeth criticism, but they do represent the tendency to make a unitary assessment and then add an afterthought, that is, to pull the constituent elements apart unevenly instead of holding them together in a fusion not so simply describable.

It is possible that Shakespeare's basic method encourages this tendency. Shakespeare first chooses a protagonist who in action is worse than the other main tragic heroes, and then tends to make him better than other tragic heroes, in effect to make him now one, and now the other. Shakespeare had to protect Macbeth against the unmixed hostility that the mere villain would evoke; perhaps he overprotected him, letting him do all his villainies indeed, but providing him with an excess of devices for exciting the pity, warmth, and approval which prompt forgetfulness of the villainies. If critics have, as Knights protested, sentimentalized Macbeth, it may be that the text gives them more ground than has been supposed, that Shakespeare's own sympathy with Macbeth went beyond that which every artist owes to the evil man whom he wants to realize. We may be driven to concluding that Shakespeare has kept us at one with Macbeth, in whom the good man is all but annihilated by the tragic flaw, by making him the flawed man who is all but annihilated by the tragic goodness—that is, the singular appeal of the man trapped, disappointed, deserted, deprived of a wife, finished, but unwhimpering, contemplative, unyielding. If that is so, Shakespeare has kept us at one with a murderer by making him less than, other than, a murderer.

This may seem a perverse conclusion after we have been pointing to the 'risks' Shakespeare took by showing Macbeth lengthily arranging the murder of Banquo and by having the murder of Lady Macduff and her children done partly on stage. The risk there, however, was of our separation from Macbeth as in melodrama; the risk here is of an empathic union on too easy grounds. For what is finally and extraordinarily spared Macbeth is the ultimate rigour of self-confrontation, the act of knowing directly what he has been and done. We see the world judging Macbeth, but not Macbeth judging himself. That consciousness of the nature of the deed which he has at the murder of Duncan gives way to other disturbances, and whatever sense of guilt, if any, may be inferred from his later distresses (we surveyed, early in section iii, the passages sometimes supposed to reveal a confessional or penitent strain), is far from an open facing and defining of the evil done—the murders, of course, the attendant lying, and as is less often noted, the repeated bearing of false witness (II, iii, 99; III, i, 29ff.; III, iv, 49). Of Cawdor, whose structural relationship to Macbeth is often mentioned, we are told that

> very frankly he confess'd his treasons,
> Implor'd your Highness' pardon, and set forth
> A deep repentance. (I, iv, 5–7)

Macduff, with rather less on his conscience than Macbeth, could say,

> sinful Macduff,
> They were all struck for thee—nought that I am;
> Not for their own demerits, but for mine,
> Fell slaughter on their souls. (IV, iii, 224–7)

Cawdor and Macduff set the example which Macbeth never follows; or, to go outside the play, Othello and Lear set examples that Macbeth never follows. Part of Hamlet's agonizing is centred in his passion to avoid having to set such an example. Macbeth simply does not face the moral record. Instead he is the saddened and later bereaved husband, the man deprived of friends and future, the thinker, the pathetic believer in immunity, the fighter. These roles are a way of pushing the past aside—the past which cries out for a new sense, in him, of what it has been. If, then, our hypothesis about the nature of tragic participation is valid, the reader ends his life with and in Macbeth in a way that demands too little of him. He experiences forlornness and desolation, and even a kind of substitute triumph—anything but the soul's reckoning which is a severer trial than the world's judgment. He is not initiated into a true spaciousness of character, but follows, in Macbeth, the movement of what I have called a contracting personality. This is not the best that tragedy can offer.[19]

NOTES

[1] See, for instance, Wolfgang J. Weilgart, 'Macbeth: Demon and Bourgeois', *Shakespeare Society of New Orleans Publications* (1946), and its citations, as well as the citations in Kenneth Muir's Introduction to the Arden *Macbeth* (1951ff.), pp. xlviiiff. Weilgart's ill-written essay, based on Karl Jaspers's *Psychologie der Weltanschauungen* is not uninstructive.

[2] For fuller quotations and appropriate comments, see Muir, op. cit. pp. lixff. The Abercrombie quotation is from *The Idea of Great Poetry*, the Knight from *The Wheel of Fire* (Knight carried the idea further in *Christ and Nietzsche*, 1948).

[3] *How Many Children Had Lady Macbeth?* (1933), pp. 54–5.

[4] Introduction to his edition of *Macbeth* (Boston, 1939), p. xiv.

[5] George Clifford Rosser, Critical Commentary, *Macbeth* (1957), pp. 38, 39, 40, 44. This work might be compared with a Catholic schoolboy manual, the Rev. R. F. Walker's *Companion to the Study of Shakespeare:* Macbeth (1947). The often useful application of Catholic doctrine unfortunately keeps giving way to sermons.

[6] William Allan Neilson and Charles Jarvis Hill (eds.), *The Complete Plays and Poems of Shakespeare* (Boston, 1942), p. 1183.

[7] Cf. Gogol's *Inspector General*, where the meaning 'The way of transgressors is hard' is conveyed exclusively through characters acting in character.

[8] Op. cit. p. lxxiv.

[9] For convenience I shall use the word 'readers' to denote literal readers, spectators at the theatre, viewers, all those who see the play on stage or in print or in any other medium. I use 'we' to denote the hypothetical possessor of characteristic responsiveness.

[10] Some critics always defend apparent authority; others redefine the character who has it; still others look for artistic signs that the apparent holder of authority has been subtly disavowed. Thus, one school accepts Gulliver's view of himself and of the Houyhnhnms; another argues that the total structure of Book IV turns the satire against Gulliver. The readers who accept Moll Flanders's view of things resort to various shifts to deal with her inconsistencies; the opposite way out is to treat Moll as a product of confusions in Defoe's own mind.

[11] Even when an over-valuing of Brecht's theories puts something of a halo upon the *Verfremdungseffekt* and of a shadow upon *Einfühlung*. The inevitability of *Einfühlung*, whatever its precise character, is indicated by Brecht's having to rewrite to try to prevent it after it had appeared in responses to his own work. Perhaps, however, we need a new term like 'consentience' to suggest more than 'sympathy' but less than 'identification' or 'empathy', which suffer from popular overuse.

[12] *Shakespeare: The Great Tragedies,* Writers and Their Work No. 133 (1961), p. 35. Cf. his statement that 'the Poet for the Defence... can make us feel that we might have fallen in the same way' (Introduction, Arden edition, p. 1, and similarly on p. lvi).

[13] Gorki's *Lower Depths*, Ibsen's *Wild Duck*, and O'Neill's *Iceman Cometh* are remarkably alike in their portrayal of the need of self-protective illusions; in effect they deny the possibility of the tragic experience of illumination. But recent playwrights like Osborne, Pinter, and Albee choose an opposite course: they make the reader identify with one evil or another by giving him nowhere else to go. They permit no illusions of saving virtue (though they may foster illusions of irremediable defectiveness). This is of course the way of satire, which aspires to much less than the tragic range of personality.

[14] This difficulty will of course not exist for critics who believe that Macbeth, though a lost soul, has wrenched some sort of moral triumph from his career.

[15] Muir's note on the passage (Arden edition, p. 165).

[16] Among the accounts of Macbeth's descent one of the most interesting is that of W. C. Curry, *Shakespeare's Philosophical Patterns* (Baton Rouge, Louisiana, 1937).

[17] Muir, *Shakespeare: The Great Tragedies*, p. 36. However, Muir uses the words rather incidentally to name one of the factors that may account for the difficulty of presenting the play successfully on the stage. He may not be strongly convinced that sympathies do switch. At any rate, his words conveniently summarize a point of view probably held widely.

[18] Veronica Henriques, *The Face I Had* (1965), p. 38.

[19] As Muir says, '... the last two acts are not quite on the level of the first three' (*Shakespeare: The Great Tragedies*, p. 36). This is a passing comment, however, again in the context of the actability of the play. Cf. G. B. Harrison, '... Macbeth is in some ways the least satisfactory of Shakespeare's mature tragedies. The last Act falls away...' This is from the Introduction to the Penguin *Macbeth* (1937), p. 17. But Harrison uses this statement to introduce the subject of revisions in the text.

Besides the comparisons that have been made, there is another that has elucidatory value. Garrick added to Macbeth's lines a closing speech which in content might have been inspired by the same sense of shortcoming that prevails in the present essay, but which is in the common rhetorical vein of eighteenth-century improvements of Shakespeare:

'Tis done! the scene of life will quickly close.
Ambition's vain delusive dreams are fled,
And now I wake to darkness, guilt, and horror;
I cannot bear it! let me shake it off—
It will not be; my soul is clog'd with blood—
I cannot rise! I dare not ask for mercy—
It is too late, hell drags me down; I sink,
I sink,—my soul is lost for ever!—Oh!—Oh!

(Quoted in Arden edition, p. xlvi, n. 2.) One wonders whether Garrick was remembering Marlowe's *Dr Faustus*, which *Macbeth* resembles, notably in the great ambition of the hero, in the enormous struggle at the time of the first decisive step, and in the phenomena of psychic strain. Garrick's last four lines might be a précis of Faustus's final hundred lines. But this striking fact underscores the difference in the treatment of the two heroes: Faustus sees the whole truth of his career with utmost clarity, but because of a 'block', as we would say, cannot take advantage of the grace he rightly feels is offered; Macbeth, on the other hand, lacks this clarity and hence is hardly able to advance to the next stage, where the issue is spiritual despair.

Wilbur Sanders

"AN UNKNOWN FEAR":
THE TRAGEDIE OF
MACBETH

IV

In what sense ⟨...⟩ is Macbeth free? ⟨...⟩ By his handling of the prophecies, Shakespeare has set us wondering about the very possibility of freedom. He has called into a play a self-doubt which lies in the path of any close scrutiny of one's own 'free' action—the despairing suspicion that it could not have been otherwise, and is therefore meaningless. It is Macbeth's suspicion as he nears the end of his road—either that it could not have been otherwise (that he has been 'paltered with'), or else that the choice offered was only one between equally 'idiot' alternatives, and thus no real choice at all. Yet there is about the famous soliloquy, I think, a very strong sense that it is not a philosophical position so much as an intellectual by-product of behaviour: Macbeth has not thought his way to this position—it has thought him. And we may wonder whether the sensation of fatality is not equally something proceeding indirectly from choice.

It is well to be clear, though, that free-will is not a 'problem' to which Shakespeare is propounding an answer. Rather it is a problematic nexus in human experience to which, as a dramatist, he is naturally drawn. On an obvious level Macbeth is free to refrain from murdering Duncan. On an only slightly less obvious level he was bound to do it. One does not have to opt for one of these versions of the play, for they are both intolerably superficial. What Shakespeare makes us feel, and feel inwardly, is the extremely tenuous division between the 'free' act and the 'determined' one, and the imaginative possibility of a world in which the balance has been imperceptibly tipped towards evil, so that man writhes and sprawls vainly on a greased slope that ends in perdition. The unbalance resides precisely in the problematic nature of the Will.

From *The Dramatist and the Received Idea: Studies in the Plays of Marlowe and Shakespeare* (Cambridge: Cambridge University Press, 1968), pp. 282–307.

In every willing there is first of all a multiplicity of feelings: the feeling of a condition to get *away* from, the feeling of a condition to get *to*; then the feeling of this 'away' and 'to'; furthermore, an accompanying muscular feeling which, from a sort of habit, begins a game of its own as soon as we 'will'—even without our moving our 'arms and legs' . . . Secondly, there is thinking: in every act of the will there is a thought which gives commands—and we must not imagine that we can separate this thought out of 'willing' and still have something like will left! Thirdly, the will is not merely a complex of feeling and thinking but above all it is a passion—the passion of commanding . . . A man who *wills* is giving a command to something in himself that obeys, or which he believes will obey. But now let us note the oddest thing about the will, this manifold something for which the people have only one word: because we, in a given case, are simultaneously the commanders *and* the obeyers and, as obeyers, know the feelings of forcing, crowding, pressing, resisting, and moving which begin immediately after the act of the will: because, on the other hand, we are in the habit of glossing over this duality with the help of the synthetic concept 'I'—for these reasons a whole chain of erroneous conclusions, and consequently false valuations of the will, has weighted down our notion of willing . . .[1]

Macbeth, in Act I, knows the 'feelings of forcing, crowding, pressing' that Nietzsche evokes so well here. He is not the commander, but the obeyer, of forces that present themselves as bodily insurrection, anarchy of soul beyond the possibility of conscious control:

> Why doe I yeeld to that suggestion,
> Whose horrid Image doth unfixe my Heire,
> And make my seated Heart knock at my Ribbes,
> Against the use of Nature? Present Feares
> Are lesse then horrible Imaginings:
> My Thought, whose Murther yet is but fantasticall,
> Shakes so my single state of Man,
> That Function is smother'd in surmise,
> And nothing is, but what is not.   (I. iii. 136)

The 'yeelding' is already fact. The hideous impulsion of the 'horrid Image' overbears all resistance, moral and rational (the thought of murder is the murder of Thought), by its own superior actuality. Its hideousness is indeed part of its power, as anyone knows who has stood at the brink of a sheer drop and felt that uncanny and powerful urge to throw himself down. If we attend carefully to Macbeth's voice here, there is a haunting suggestion that the only answer he can give to his 'Why doe I yeeld?' is to evoke for himself the full fascinating horror of the gulf that yawns below him. A few scenes later, he can assign no motive for a deed which becomes increasingly loathsome the nearer he approaches it, except an 'ambition' which, even as he names it, he depicts as an exhibitionist's vanity, futile and self-defeating:

Vaulting Ambition, which ore-leapes it selfe,
And falles on th'other.   (I. vii. 27)

'Then why do I yield?' comes the tormenting and unanswerable question. The 'fine truth of the Macbeth-conception: a deep, poetic, psychology or metaphysic of the birth of Evil' may lie, as Wilson Knight suggests, in the fact that there is no answer to this question.[2]

Of course it is possible to be sunnily rationalistic about this speech: to point out how he is confusing actuality with reality, fact with truth, to deplore his 'muddled conscience', concluding that he is 'a man who fails to think clearly on a moral issue'.[3] And it is undeniable that Macbeth still calls the image of the murder 'My Thought'—the wedge has not yet been finally driven between the commander and the obeyer in him. But I cannot help feeling that A. P. Rossiter was nearer the heart of the matter when he spoke of 'the upthrust of the essentially guilty undertow of the human mind', something eternally present in consciousness and eternally menacing.[4] Macbeth's 'muddle', in any case, is not so intense as to prevent him seeing precisely what is happening to him—he knows what is and what is not, and knows that they have become inverted. No, there is something much more awesome here than a failure of reason to make necessary discriminations—it is the discovery, too late to prevent it, that one has lost one's footing and that there is nothing now but the long helpless fall into the abyss.

This is not to minimise the truth of Coleridge's contention that Macbeth's is a mind 'rendered *temptable* by previous dalliance of the fancy with ambitious thoughts'.[5] This is plain enough in such things as the self-deluding arithmetic of

Glamys, and Thane of Cawdor:
The greatest is behinde   (I. iii. 116)

(Glamis—one point, Cawdor—one point; Witches—two out of three) when in a very obvious sense the greatest is still *before*. There is a manifest will to self-deception here and elsewhere in the third scene, which prompts Banquo to some fairly pointed observations. But the important point is the impossibility of tracing this guilt to an origin. Macbeth is simply falling in space.

During the descent we have ample time to ponder the nature and the causes of that first false step. All that one feels at this stage is that it has already been taken. And immediately on its heels comes the onset of disintegration. 'Freedom of the will', as Nietzsche observes, 'is the word for that manifold pleasurable condition of the willer who is in command and at the same time considers himself as one with the executor of the command . . .'[6] It is an unimpeded translation of desire into act, unity of being. But with the intrusion of this image which is both horrid *and* desired, the divisive principle is released in Macbeth's nature; his *'single'* state, that is, his state of unity, pureness of purpose, harmony of parts ('if the eye is *single,* the whole body is filled with light'), is shaken, and 'Function' must be parted, divided up, one organ functioning in dissociation from another:

> The Eye winke at the Hand; yet let that bee,
> Which the Eye feares, when it is done, to see.   (I. iv. 52)

The kingdom of the body has become a prey to faction and division, and as a direct consequence we cannot talk simply of Macbeth's 'free-will' any more—for he is not one man. For the rest of the play he seeks to find that singleness again, trying to become 'perfect', as he puts it.

Yet there is another sense in which, though not perhaps freely, Macbeth has now willed the evil which seemed to violate him earlier: .

> Starres hide your fires,
> Let not Light see my black and deepe desires.   (I. iv. 50)

To know the desires to be 'black and deepe' and still to desire them, to recognise the 'Hand' and then to 'winke', is to implicate oneself in the evil by a willing immersion in the 'horrid Image'.

Bradley showed an awareness of all this baffling doubleness when he saw, as the essential Shakespearian insight in the play, not a lesson in 'the misery of a guilty conscience and the retribution of crime' (or as a nineteenth-century critic primly put it: 'an unparalleled lecture in ethical anatomy'), but a deep feeling for 'the incalculability of evil'—

> that in meddling with it human beings do they know not what. The soul, he seems to feel, is a thing of such inconceivable depth, complexity, and delicacy, that when you introduce into it, or suffer to develop in it, any change, and particularly the change called evil, you can form only the vaguest idea of the reaction you will provoke. All you can be sure of is that it will not be what you expected, and that you cannot possibly escape it.[7]

This may seem an oddly agnostic and negative foundation for something I am claiming as a great tragedy, but the interpreters who by-pass the obscure and the incalculable in Macbeth in favour of light and clarity always seem to me to offer a shrunken play. Shakespeare had met these well-meaning rationalists in his day:

> They say miracles are past; and we have our philosophical persons, to make modern and familiar, things supernatural and causeless. Hence it is that we make trifles of terrors, ensconcing ourselves into seeming knowledge, when we should *submit ourselves to an unknown fear.*[8]

There is a danger of *resolving* things in Macbeth which Shakespeare deliberately left unresolved—one of them being the question of Macbeth's freedom. Shakespeare could easily have given us an untroubled, pre-prophecy Macbeth, who possessed, instead of perpetually desiring, 'a clearenesse', who moved by perceptible degrees into the self-divided state of the criminal. But instead, Macbeth walks, on his first entry, right into the arms of the waiting Witches, his whole consciousness before this encounter being narrowed to one prosy remark about the weather, which is itself instinct with the equivocal—'So foule and faire a day I have not seene'. If

Shakespeare had been interested in the crucial act of pure volition which commits a man to annihilation (a pact with Lucifer, for instance), he would have shown it; but that would have initiated a drama in which the moral issues were as perspicuous as they are in *Faustus*. It is a different kind of guilt with which he is concerned— something so obscure in its origins as to appear to have none, a guilt opaque to moral explication.

One senses this opacity in Macbeth's arguments with his wife. Lady Macbeth's skilful manipulation of her husband plays upon his inability to name a time when he was not haunted by the image of the murder. She asks him to accept as his real nature something so close to the truth that it seems pedantic to deny it. She asks him to see himself as the kind of man who murders for ambition, as if the crucial decision were already taken. And it is because Macbeth suspects it *is* already taken, that he has no answer except 'We will speake further' and 'If we should faile?'. When she charges him with 'breaking the enterprise' to her, he is again paralysed by the near-accuracy of her accusation. For he cannot, except on the most literal level, deny that he has broached the matter in that letter to his 'dearest Partner of Greatnesse', when 'nor time, nor place' adhered. Lady Macbeth has merely taken as a proposition what was not yet so fully formed.[9] In Macbeth's guilty silences in these two scenes (I. v and I. vii) we have a powerful presentation of the helplessness of guilt before that which reflects, and thus magnifies, its image. He has silently conceded her claim to know him better than he knows himself. The relationship is summed up, at their first stage meeting, in a few lines of brilliant dialogue:

MACBETH: My dearest Love,
Duncan comes here to Night.
LADY MACBETH: And when goes hence?
MACBETH: To morrow, as he purposes.
LADY MACBETH: O never,
Shall Sunne that Morrow see.
Your Face, my Thane, is as a Booke, where men
May reade strange matters. . .   (I. v. 58)

Lady Macbeth's Gioconda smile converts the innocent announcement so subtly into guilty innuendo, that Macbeth is no longer certain that it was ever innocent. Immediately he is fumbling. The exchange culminates in that long, pregnant pause (I. 61) during which the black contamination rises to the surface of Macbeth's eyes, and after which his wife can interpret him to himself without fear of contradiction. There is a real sense in which she has here created Macbeth's guilt, and we know that, despite the brilliant and witty insight into her military husband displayed earlier in the scene, she is misreading the 'Booke' here. Yet, as with the crucial issue of the nature of manhood, Macbeth finishes by accepting her view—that to wish is the same as to act, and that he has already determined on the deed.

His capitulation, however, uncovers a central failure in Macbeth's nature—a failure of self-knowledge. His wife's misinterpretation of his genuine scruple as a mere cat's timorousness leaves him powerless because he has no better knowledge of his own real motivation. In a similar way he is paralysed by the shadow of his own potential evil when it rises like a ghost across his path, because he cannot acknowledge it as his own. Its power to tyrannise over his better nature is dependent on his inability to recognise it. If he could say, with Prospero, 'this thing of darkness I / Acknowledge mine', its power to appal and master him would be partially broken. Not being able to say this, yet seeing the evil rising demonstrably from his own 'horrible Imaginings', he is torn asunder, divided against himself, thrown into despair. Because he never acknowledges his potential evil, it perpetually terrifies him in shapes of external coercion.

It is this kind of congenital resistance to the contemplative and the inward which makes almost all his soliloquies involuntary acts of mental laceration rather than purposive reflection. What he wants is medicine—'some sweet Oblivious Antidote' to 'Cleanse the stufft bosome, of that perillous stuffe / Which weighes upon the heart' (and that repeated 'stuffe' indicates how vague is his conception of his own malady). A clean external operation of plucking or razing, a potion, a scientific cure which does not involve himself, but merely operates *upon* the self—this is what he wants. And when the Doctor abandons his mission as scientist and turns theologian ('... the Patient / Must minister to himselfe') Macbeth dismisses the matter with a sourly sardonic laugh:

Throw Physicke to the Dogs, Ile none of it.   (V. iii. 47)

The excuse that springs to his lips in Act I, Scene iii, when he has to account for his abstraction—

My dull Braine was wrought with things forgotten—

embodies a profound unconscious truth: the sea of desires and dreams from which he is now emerging is the neglected underside of his own moral nature—'things forgotten' indeed.

We may go further, and say that the very attempt to transmute himself into King Macbeth is just such a flight from self-knowledge.

When the ambitious man whose watchword was 'Either Caesar or nothing' does not become Caesar, he is in despair thereat. But this signifies something else, namely, that precisely because he did not become Caesar he now cannot endure to be himself. So properly ... it is not the fact that he did not become Caesar which is intolerable to him, but the self which did not become Caesar is the thing that is intolerable; or, more correctly, what is intolerable to him is that he cannot get rid of himself. If he had become Caesar he would have been rid of himself in desperation, but now that he did not become Caesar he cannot in desperation get rid of himself. Essentially he is equally in despair in either case, for *he does not possess himself, he is not himself*...

A despairing man wants despairingly to be himself ... [Yet] that self which he despairingly wills to be is a self which he is not (for to will to be that self which one truly is, is indeed the opposite of despair); what he really wills is to tear his self away from the Power which constituted it. But notwithstanding all the efforts of despair, that Power is the stronger, and it compels him to be the self he does not will to be . . .

> . . . to have a self, to be a self, is the greatest concession made to man, but at the same time it is eternity's demand upon him.[10]

At the root of all Macbeth's despairing restlessness, his fruitless search for 'a clearenesse', for 'perfection', lies this failure to *possess himself,* a doomed attempt to tear himself away from his real nature in a 'strange and *self*-abuse'. Yet we should not forget that this breakdown, like the guilty imagining of the murder, is not shown in process of formation, but is one of the pre-existent conditions of the drama; and, as such, it is not insisted upon. The driving energy of the drama lies elsewhere, encouraging us to accept Macbeth's sense of violation and coercion as real. The rational and moral explanation of this sensation, like Duncan's goodness, lies on the fringes of consciousness as something to which we may return later, but not yet.

Meanwhile the initial misdirection brings on a chain of consequences. In the murder sequences, Shakespeare renders the anarchy of Macbeth's whole nature primarily through its bodily manifestations: the man who has warped and dislocated nature in order to produce the tension that will discharge the bolt of murderous desire ('I am settled, and bend up / Each corporall Agent to this terrible Feat') is seen blundering round the stage snatching ridiculously at the phantasmal products of his own delirium and uttering lines as absurdly melodramatic as they are grotesque (II. i. 33f.). Macbeth's spasms of alternate attraction and terror at the hallucination are so disjointed, syntactically and emotionally, as to suggest incipient insanity. And again 'Function' is self-divided ('Eyes are made the fooles o' th' other Sences'). The key changes, but the effect is only intensified as he steadies himself for the murder:

> Now o're the one halfe World
> Nature seemes dead, and wicked Dreames abuse
> The Curtain'd sleepe: Witchcraft celebrates
> Pale Heccats Offrings: and wither'd Murther,
> Alarum'd by his Centinell, the Wolfe,
> Whose howle's his Watch, thus with his stealthy pace,
> With Tarquins ravishing strides, towards his designe
> Moves like a Ghost. Thou sure and firme-set Earth
> Heare not my steps, which way they walke, for feare
> Thy very stones prate of my where-about . . .   (II. i. 49)

Here there is a preternatural sensitivity, especially to sound, an unnatural stillness in which one hears dreams, hears the stealthy pace which thinks to pass unheard, or hears sounds so distant from habitation as to be normally inaudible—the witches' sabbath, the wolf—a silence in which the over-strained hearing would make the very earth cry out. And combined with this, a suggestion that the senses, the body itself, has become detached from the observing mind, a strange disembodied somnambulism in which Macbeth, as in a dream, watches himself moving 'like a Ghost', beyond possibility of control or recall.

The same 'present horror' persists in the next, connected scene, as Lady Macbeth registers the night-sounds with a quick panicky intake of breath— 'Hearke'—followed by the long sigh of relief—'Peace'; or notes the snores of the grooms become suddenly audible as Macbeth opens the doors. But her self-possession, which goes with an ability to localise every sound, simply heightens our awareness of the antithetical condition in Macbeth, who can no longer distinguish inner from outer, 'does not know . . . what voices are these that groan and cry within and about him'.[11] The voice that cries modulates without a break into his own inward crying;[12] the objective event is swallowed in his apprehension of it—he is not listening *to* the fear of the two awakened sleepers, he is 'listening their fear', hearing it within himself, just as, with the same transitive construction, Lady Macbeth speaks of *thinking* these deeds. The body refuses service—he calls out and does not know it, his tongue rebels and the dry throat will not utter ('Amen / Stuck in my throat').

And then the self-division takes its most terrifying shape:

What Hands are here? hah: they pluck out mine Eyes.   (II. ii. 58)

The eye, no longer able to wink at the hand, sees the blood-stained nails descending cruelly to destroy vision itself. The deed, which was his own, has now acquired a life of its own and it threatens the tenderest quick of his being. He does not know whose hands they are: his deed has created a reality of evil outside himself. Yet it is the fact that he also knows them for his own that provokes this frantic desire for blindness, that he may not have to contemplate his deed.

But the self so desperately divided against itself cannot sustain the tension for long, and by the end of the scene Macbeth has moved forward to grasp the only solution that presents itself:

        To know my deed,
'Twere best not know my selfe.   (II. ii. 72)

There is, he sees, no possibility of knowing (grasping the true nature of, and coming to terms with) his deed and also knowing (living amicably with, recognising) himself. It is an absolute antinomy. If he continues to know himself (the self he has been) the deed is incredible and monstrous. If he grasps the reality of the deed he is alienated from himself and can no longer recognise the bloody hand as his own. (It is in the nature of the evil act to drive this wedge between deed and doer, so that acceptance of the deed involves estrangement from the self.) Very well, he will know his deed. He will make his peace with it, build his life around it, accept it as fact. What he will not do is *own* the deed—acknowledge it as the work of the general, Macbeth, loyal vassal of the gracious Duncan. To that self he bids an anguished farewell in these lines, beginning the construction of a new 'self' whose premiss is murder.

V

With this decision, one would expect no more to follow than an extended study in the logic of degeneration, a drawing out of the consequences of total commitment to an act which is irredeemably evil. And this, indeed, is one way (though not the most interesting) of looking at the second half of the play. There is brutalisation, sure enough. The Macbeth who bullies the Murderers in a vain attempt to elicit a hatred for Banquo which will make the murder theirs and not his (III. i); the Macbeth so deeply committed to instrumentalism that men, like dogs, are for him only 'valued' in so far as they will subserve his murderous intent, and who, nevertheless, will 'make love' to the assistance of such 'Mungrels, Spaniels, Curres'; the Macbeth who can answer the Murderer's 'My Lord his throat is cut, that I did for him', with

> Thou art the *best* o' th' Cut-throats,
> Yet hee's *good* that did the like for Fleans:
> If thou did'st it, thou art the *Non-pareill*   (III. iv. 16)

in a tone naïvely innocent of irony—this Macbeth is a man who is rapidly passing out of the range of any very intense sympathy. The Macbeth of the Banquet scene, too, may be mastering his terrors better than he could before, but he does so on such a shabbily rhetorical level, assisted by the hoary clichés of 'rugged Russian Beare' and 'Hircan Tiger', and the vaunt and swagger of martial defiance, that the claim 'Why so, being gone, / I am a *man* againe' rings very hollow indeed (III. iv. 98–107).

This man, one senses, is in pursuit of total insensibility. Nothing is to make his 'firme Nerves' tremble, or to shake his deep and dreamless sleep.

> Strange things I have in head, that will to hand,
> Which must be acted, ere they may be scand.   (III. iv. 138)

He has discovered the secret that actions, once performed, will help to deaden and cauterise that inner sensitivity which is his greatest torment. Since the mind, he learns, has a knack of accommodating itself to that to which it has been accessory, he will act first, and thus surgically remove the sensitised zone of self-doubt and self-accusation, which the performed action will burn out in any case. This technique is 'hard use'—the breaking of a young sensitive animal, by systematic and graduated brutality, to force it into 'maturity'; and it ensures 'sleepe':

> Come, wee'l to sleepe: My strange & self-abuse
> Is the initiate feare, that wants hard use:
> We are yet but yong in deed.   (III. iv. 141)

The prophetic voice that cried to all the house was wrong: Macbeth has found his anodyne.

With the insensibility, perhaps because of it, there goes a willing embracement of evil, known as such:

> I will to morrow
> (And betimes I will) to the weyard Sisters.
> More they shall speake: for now I am bent to know
> By the worst meanes, the worst, for mine owne good,
> All causes shall give way.   (III. iv. 131)

This is the germ of the proceedings against Macduff's family, which we have noted as a turning-point in Macbeth's relations with himself and with the audience, and the sense of dismal finality is strong in the lines. Macbeth has settled his allegiances in favour of hell.

The chosen evil leads naturally to an imaginatively debauched surrender to the forces of annihilation loose in his own mind. All restraint is to be broken, the winds untied, destruction indulged to the point of utter surfeit. It is the wild dream of a cosmic anarchy where his own internal anarchy will be swallowed up in the roar and shriek of universal disintegration. He projects upon nature his own thirst for the confounding of all distinct sensation and apprehension (which is his torment) in a cataclysm of *general* evil:

> Though the treasure
> Of Natures Germaine, tumble altogether. . .   (IV. i. 58)

We cannot grant imaginative patronage, however qualified, to this. The man must be ripped out of the world.

And yet, the sequence in which the evil insensibility is most clearly envisaged and enunciated—Macbeth's late-night colloquy with his wife (III. iv. 121f.)—is also one of the points in the play where we are most conscious of Macbeth's barbarian energy and courage. 'What a frightful clearness of self-consciousness in this descent to hell,' writes Bradley, 'and yet what a furious force in the instinct of life and self-assertion that drives him on!'[13] Improbable though it may seem, that word *life* is the right word. No interpretation which fails to reckon with the essential am- bivalence of our reaction to the 'criminal' Macbeth can hope to do justice to the depth and subtlety of Shakespeare's conception in this play. And those critics who would have us choose between a moral repudiation of the man, and a self-deluding 'justification' of something which is essentially unjustifiable, are simply neglecting the capacity of the mature Shakespeare to encompass extremes of imaginative insight in the one aesthetic experience. The tragic experience transcends both repudiation and justification.

Consider what is happening in the following lines:

> I am in blood
> Stept in so farre, that should I wade no more,
> Returning were as tedious as go ore.   (III. iv. 135)

It is the point of no return for the man of blood. Macbeth is presented here, paused in mid-stream—note the momentary pondering suspension of the conditional clause which is also a question ('should I wade no more')—knowing he must move soon (since a stream is something one either crosses or does not cross) yet overwhelmingly aware of tedium and of his heavy, impeded movement through the water-blood. It is that imperceptible inter-tidal hiatus when choice presents itself in such a form that there seems no choice—and yet the choice is real and damnable: Macbeth envisages 'returning' and 'going ore' as two equally weighted alternatives, each equally 'tedious', and he does not explicitly opt for either; and yet the decision is there, implied in that indefinable tonal nuance which effectively prefers the tedium of 'going ore' to that of 'returning', and makes its choice within a construction which denies the reality of choice. No simple moralisation will fit the complex reality of this verse, not even the ready-to-hand explanation that Macbeth's freedom has been impaired by his violation of the 'natural law' engraved in his own nature. For while this is a truth the play makes us aware of, it is only one truth. With this passage—and its *modus operandi* is fairly typical of the most gripping things in *Macbeth*—our 'judgment', which might otherwise pronounce univocal sentence on Macbeth, is enclosed within a larger act of imaginative recognition, which says, 'Yes, it is so. That is the way of Mind. This man comes of our stock.' The mystery of will, which is at once *causa sui* and subject to other pressures, presents itself as a problematic nexus at the heart of experience which imagination and intelligence can only bring to this fine focus—never resolve.

It is this capacity of the verse to *imply* judgment without being constricted by it, which makes it possible for Shakespeare to suggest a positive energy of 'life' in the damned Macbeth. For if we look hard at the 'insensibility' Macbeth pursues, it reveals itself, from another angle, as a quest for 'perfection', a declaration of war on the divisive forces his own act has released. The sense of contraction, constriction, of being 'cabin'd, crib'd, confin'd', is one of the primal modes in which we recognise and define evil, and this restriction of potentiality is instinctively felt as malign; whereas the free play of impulse, talent, imagination—'broad, and generall, as the casing Ayre'—is equally instinctively grasped as a good (III. iv. 20–4). It is delusion to think to achieve it by murder, but we do recognise the essential importance of Macbeth's objectives as he wrestles blindly in his own soul:

> But let the frame of things dis-joynt,
> Both the Worlds suffer,
> Ere we will eate our Meale in feare, and sleepe
> In the affliction of these terrible Dreames,
> That shake us Nightly: Better be with the dead,
> Whom we, to gayne our peace, have sent to peace,
> Then on the torture of the Minde to lye
> In restless extasie.   (III. ii. 16)

At whatever cost he will recover that integrity of impulse and action, that unobstructed discharge of personal energy in which life delights. And something in us responds to these fighting words: for survival, these things must be fought. Macbeth's challenge to Fate, which follows, is in one sense a determination not to succumb to the complete mental collapse that is figured in the dreams, the image of the rack, the 'restless *extasie*'. And even the 'firstlings' of action, which are so demonically inhuman, are also felt dimly, and at the same time, as the desperate paroxysms of a nature threatened with a madness of self-alienation. It is true that the campaign proceeds on the assumption that there can be no *returning*, but do we ever really *feel* (as distinct from believing on extraneous grounds) that 'turning back' and 'repentance' (the two senses of the word) are real alternatives for Macbeth? Bradley's enigmatic remark about Lady Macbeth is worth pondering for Macbeth too: 'regarding her from the tragic point of view, we may truly say she was too great to repent'.[14] Doesn't this, however startling it may be theologically, 'correspond to the imaginative effect'?

We might make the same double judgment about the rhetoric by which Macbeth fights off his terrors: it is shallow, yet it embodies a kind of resonant, contemptuous courage:

> Why what care I, if thou canst nod, speake too.
> If Charnell houses, and our Graves must send
> Those that we bury, backe; our Monuments
> Shall be the Mawes of Kytes.   (III. iv. 69)

And where else can we find such unmanning and appalling terror mastered and focused in intense, fascinated scrutiny, as in the Macbeth of these lines?—

> Avant, & quit my sight, let the earth hide thee:
> Thy bones are marrowlesse, thy blood is cold:
> Thou hast no speculation in those eyes
> Which thou dost glare with.   (III. iv. 92)

Even in its minor manifestations—'The divell damne thee blacke, thou creamfac'd Loone . . .'—Macbeth's energy of defiance is a force to be reckoned with, something to which we assent at the same time as we recognise its futility. 'It is not merely that he becomes more daring and resolute in action, the more desperate his affairs become', writes Lascelles Abercrombie; '*the whole vitality of the man becomes incandescent.*'[15] It is as if the Shakespeare who knew that the meek must, and do, inherit the earth, also saw from a different point of view (Nietzschean, Lawrencian) what a disaster it would be for the earth if they did, and preserved at the very core of his conception of evil an awareness of dynamism and power: for

> There is a soul of goodness in things evil
> Would men observingly distil it out.   (*Henry V*, IV. i. 4)

I am insisting on the 'soul of goodness', not merely in the reaction that evil provokes, nor even as generating an additional poignancy and sense of waste— though it does have this effect—but at the heart of evil itself, because there are certain masterly things in the play which cannot be received except on this understanding. Chief among them is Lady Macbeth herself.

It is interesting to reflect on the extent to which this astonishing portrait may have taken its rise from an act of historical imagination. Here is Holinshed on the characteristics of Scottish women:

> In those daies also the women ... were of no lesse courage than the men; for all stout maidens and wives (if they were not with child) marched as well in the field as did the men, and so soone as the armie did set forward, they slue the first liuing creature that they found, in whose bloud they not onelie bathed their swords, but also tasted therof with their mouthes ... When they saw their owne bloud run from them in the fight, they waxed neuer a whit astonished with the matter, but rather doubling their courages, with more eagernesse they assailed their enemies ...[16]

Whether he read this passage, or whether, as he might, he deduced Lady Macbeth from the various accounts of bloody viragoes that Holinshed provided, the fact remains that she represents a staggering attempt on Shakespeare's part to feel his way into a kind of womanhood which was barbarian and foreign—an effort of historical projection. (He did much the same kind of thing when he drew the figure of Coriolanus.) So powerful was this faculty of imaginative projection, however, that it gave to Lady Macbeth a kind of validity and potency, even at those points where she most directly affronts all conventional notions of the feminine or even the human.

It may not be the kind of thing that the super-ego readily approves, but do we not find ourselves, in the theatre, over-awed and startled into a kind of terrified admiration by her unconditional blasphemy against the natural?

> I have given Sucke, and know
> How tender 'tis to love the Babe that milkes me,
> I would, while it was smyling in my Face,
> Have pluckt my Nipple from his Bonelesse Gummes,
> And dasht the Braines out, had I so sworne
> As you have done to this.   (I. vii. 54)

Like the leap from the vertiginous precipice, this violation of the infinitely vulnerable is so exquisitely possible as to transfix the mind that once contemplates it. These are the things one does not dare speak aloud, for fear speech should give them reality. And yet determination in this woman has been fanned to such white heat that she can not only say it, but contemplate the unnameable with an overwhelming actuality. As Coleridge observed, the whole conception derives its alarming power from a knowledge of just 'how tender 'tis to love'.[17] And yet she forces herself to a meticulously precise evocation of the particularities of the deed, right down to the 'Bonelesse Gummes'. The taut intensity of will strained beyond belief is presented in that shocked shuddering pause after 'dásht the Bráines óut ...'.

Macbeth is not the only one who is emotionally overborne, and fishes about on the surface of a terrified consciousness for some random reply to words which, it seems, could neither have been spoken nor heard, muttering, 'If we should faile?' Nor is his horrified attraction-repulsion unintelligible when he cries hoarsely,

> Bring forth Men-Children onely:
> For thy undaunted Mettle should compose
> Nothing but Males.   (I. vii. 73)

There is an appalling grandeur in Lady Macbeth's complete subjugation of nature. The sheer resplendence of will has a kind of magnificence which cannot be 'placed' or gainsaid. For the moment the stabbing of an old man in his bed has *become* 'our great quell'.

The same Shakespearian capacity to feel the validity of alien states of mind explains the strange way in which the Macbeths' pagan lightness of conscience—a conscience for which 'things without all remedie / Should be without regard' and 'what's done, *is* done'—comes to seem inevitable. He is creating a barbaric Scottish world in which to unseam a man 'from the Nave to th' Chops' and to 'bathe in reeking Wounds' *is* to be a 'worthy Gentleman' (I. ii. 22f.). In this world, the grave is peace:

> After Lifes fitfull Fever, he sleepes well,
> Treason has done his worst: nor Steele, nor Poyson,
> Mallice domestique, forraine Levie, nothing
> Can touch him further.   (III. ii. 23)

Macbeth envisages no hell; nor does Shakespeare envisage it for him. It was a singularly inept notion of Garrick's to have the dying Macbeth declaim, like a pasteboard Faustus,

> my soul is clog'd with blood—
> I cannot rise! I dare not ask for mercy—
> It is too late, hell drags me down; I sink,
> I sink,—my soul is lost for ever!...[18]

This is completely foreign to Shakespeare's conception (to say nothing of the execution). Shakespeare's Macbeth lays down the terms of his own damnation—

> Heere,
> But *heere*, upon this Banke and Schoole of time,
> Wee'ld jumpe the life to come. But in these Cases,
> We still have judgement *heere* . . .—   (I. vii. 5)

and in these terms he receives his 'Justice'—his own 'poyson'd Challice'. Even if the pagan could impose his own pagan naturalism on the universe, as Shakespeare in some measure permits Macbeth to do, he still has 'judgement heere'. Even within this life, the succession of events in sequence, the endless 'consequence' cannot be trammelled up. The ocean laps round the shoal/school of time. One cannot set a terminus to action; it is never 'done'. And Macbeth's willingness to 'jumpe the life to come' cannot free him from the monstrous menace of an infinity and circularity which is as real within time as beyond it. The Justice that works, the Providence in things is a natural one. Shakespeare does not need to demand a Christian repentance of Macbeth; he lets him have damnation on his own terms. The effect is to make it possible for us to grant the pagan frame of reference at the same time as we sense its limitations—as Macbeth himself does when 'Amen' sticks in his throat. There is a breaking down of theoretical and dogmatic barriers as the play enlarges its imaginative frontiers.

Some effect of this kind is necessary, too, to account for the powerful emotional forces released in sequences like the Sleepwalking scene. Pity seems too weak a word for the response this scene evokes. It is something nearer awe. Like the Doctor we 'thinke, but dare not speake', can only murmur 'God, God forgive us all'. The sympathetic movement of feeling fills out our sense that Lady Macbeth has received her profoundly ironic fulfilment, with something less sharply moral. There is a tenderness, a compassion in her, which calls up the equivalent feeling in us:

> Come, come, come, come, give me your hand: What's
> done, cannot be undone. To bed, to bed, to bed.   (V. i. 63)

The tendency of this movement of feeling, as far as one can define something so fragile and elusive, seems to be to free us from the burden of past horror, permitting us to accept this new feminine solicitousness and protective affection as a self-subsistent reality—even though it is woven out of the stuff of past violations of affection. Her sorrow for 'the old man', while also hopeless horror, is, as Mary McCarthy remarks, real 'contrition—sorrowing with. To ask whether, waking, she is "sorry" for what she has done is impertinent. She lives with it and it kills her.'[19] The movement of pity and awe in the audience coalesces in an act of imaginative identification which is not extenuation, but simply true judgment.

This is not an isolated moment in the play either. Macbeth's anguished cry, 'O, full of Scorpions is my Minde, deare Wife', with its enactment of the agony, not of a blunt blow producing insensibility, nor a searing wound that may yet heal, but of pain that enters the very marrow of sensation and heightens it, pain moreover shut in upon itself, inescapable and armed with innumerable stings—this cry deepens 'judgment' until it becomes 'recognition'. So does the sequence with which this scene opens, which Granville Barker characterises as 'Lady Macbeth's wan effort to get near enough to the tortured man to comfort him', an attempt in which 'the royal robes, stiff on their bodies—stiff as with caked blood—seem to keep them apart'.[20]

> How now, my Lord, why doe you keepe alone?
> Of sorryest Fancies your Companions making,
> Using those Thoughts, which should indeed have dy'd
> With them they thinke on . . .   (III. ii. 8)

As we watch this timorous compassion receive a rebuff—'Be innocent of the knowledge, dearest Chuck . . .'—and then an embracement which is, in its context, more terrible than rejection—'So prythee go with me'—the moral levee-banks which withhold sympathy are broken and feeling flows freely between stage and audience.

The greatness of *Macbeth* lies in its capacity to encompass so many apparently contradictory ways of feeling about the same phenomena. But such greatness, of course, makes it singularly difficult to say anything clear-cut without resort to paradox: the paradox of an evil which is both primary and unreal; the paradox of a goodness which is supremely real yet does not prevail; the paradox of a Fate which is both prescriptive and binding, *and* powerless to fetter the will; the paradox of a freedom of soul which is both betrayed by its possessor, and subject to external violation; the paradox of an absolving pity which is also a judgment. I know no way of eliminating these paradoxes without minimising Shakespeare's achievement at precisely those points where it is most magnificent, nor without making 'trifles of terrors' and 'ensconcing ourselves into seeming knowledge' when we should be submitting ourselves to the mystery of things. For each paradox represents an approach to central regions of uncertainty and mental anguish in experience, regions where explanation is more likely to be impertinent than illuminating. *Macbeth* is not the play it is because it offers explanations, but because it enables us to contemplate these agonising cruces with steadiness and courage.

All the same, the instrinsic doubleness is perhaps at its most disturbing in the last act. For here Macbeth achieves his 'perfection' and his destruction, the forces of goodness in their moment of triumph seem most empty, and the whole dramatic movement resolves on a single flat note which both concludes, and is desperately inconclusive:

> So thankes to all at once, and to each one,
> Whom we invite, to see us Crown'd at Scone.   (V. ix. 40)

What is happening in Act V?

VI

Right at the beginning of the act we are given a moralised Macbeth:

ANGUS: Now does he feele
His secret Murthers sticking on his hands . . .
. . . Now does he feele his Title
Hang loose about him, like a Giants Robe
Upon a dwarfish Theefe.
MENTEITH: Who then shall blame
His pester'd Senses to recoyle, and start,
When all that is within him, does condemne
It selfe, for being there.   (V. ii. 16)

Now this, I suggest, is rather what we feel *must* be the case, than what we see on the stage. The Macbeth we see can claim, with some justice, that 'Direnesse . . .

cannot once start me', and Angus's horrifying image of congealed blood, and nightmare paralysis in which the loathed substance will not come free of the hand, is rather a thematic recapitulation, than a preparation for what is to come. We are not to forget the bloody-handed butcher, but neither are we to be limited to this view of Macbeth. For with the arrival of the invading army and the advent of daylight, a load seems to fall from Macbeth's shoulders. Wilson Knight is one of the few critics who has noticed the positive tendency in Macbeth's development now:

> He has won through by excessive crime to an harmonious and honest relation with his surroundings. He has successfully symbolised the disorder of his lonely guilt-stricken soul by creating disorder in the world, and thus restores balance and a harmonious contact. The mighty principle of good planted in the nature of things then asserts itself, condemns him openly, brings him peace. Daylight is brought to Macbeth, as to Scotland, by the accusing armies of Malcolm. He now knows himself to be a tyrant confessed, and wins back . . . integrity of soul.[21]

'Harmonious contact' is putting it strongly, but the point is valid. The invading generals may insist on the relief of the approaching martial resolution—

> The time approaches,
> That will with due decision make us know
> What we shall say we have, and what we owe—   (V. iv. 16)

but so does Macbeth:

> this push
> Will cheere me ever, or dis-eate me now.
> I have liv'd long enough: my way of life
> Is falne into the Seare, the yellow Leafe,
> And that which should accompany Old-Age,
> As Honor, Love, Obedience, Troopes of Friends,
> I must not looke to have: but in their steed,
> Curses, not lowd but deepe, Mouth-honor, breath
> Which the poore heart would faine deny, and dare not.   (V. iii. 20)

This is not despair, nor the self-condemnation of 'pester'd Senses'. It is nearer acceptance—a submission to seasonal mellowing (autumn *not* winter, observe) and a recognition of his fitness for death. It is worth noting that, although the opening lines envisage two possible outcomes of 'this push'—'cheere' *or* 'dis-eate'—the next clause tacitly discounts the first alternative, and prepares for the second—'I have liv'd long enough . . .' Nor is it a lament for lost felicity: there is something tougher, less self-indulgent, further from contrition about it than that. Logically, at least, the forfeited joys of 'Old-Age' are only invoked to fortify his acquiescence in being 'disseated'. He no longer hungers for these things; they are simply what he 'must not looke to have' (note the prosaic cadence). The pathos of loss is what *we* bring to the speech. Macbeth himself is simply reckoning courageously with a shrunken reality, and recording with scrupulous fidelity—the curses are 'not lowd' it is true, 'but deepe' nevertheless—the realities of his situation. And he is sufficiently accommodated to its ironies to be able to spare a wry pity for the unwilling servant who dares not speak his 'poore heart'. Macbeth, 'sick at heart' though he is, has achieved an honesty as criminal that he never had as a man of honour.

There is the same detached self-observation when, surprised by a breath of supernatural fear at the 'cry of Women', he reflects on the rarity now of such feeling—'I have almost forgot the taste of Feares...' (V. v. 9f.). He compares the flat deprivation of feeling which is real crime with the stirring, horrific crime of anticipation, like a patient intrigued by his own symptoms, even relishing them a little. There is a faint flicker of the old terror as he recalls his hideous, dinner-table familiarity with evil—' I have supt full with horrors'—but the main effort is to hold his own state steadily before him—to know his deed, and to know what it has done to him.

It is on this basis of known and faced reality that he can achieve the bantering humour of his interview with the Doctor, as he gently ribs the man with the inadequacy of his mystery to 'scowre these English hence', or, in a moment of despairing candour, confesses his grotesque plight—'Doctor, the Thanes flye from me'. The exuberant and exasperated wit of his assault on the Servant in this scene (V. iii) or the grotesquely comic business with the armour combine to give a near jocularity to Macbeth's address to the world. It is the levity of real courage faced with irredeemable catastrophe—sober, yet very much alive. The Doctor responds to the lightened atmosphere with a piece of very ordinary, day-to-day humour:

> Were I from Dunsinane away, and cleere,
> Profit againe should hardly draw me heere. (V. iii. 6)

But the ordinariness is the point. The portentous world of blood, night and crime has resumed its daylight proportions.

Yet, like all the achieved things in this play, Macbeth's self-possession is under assault. The stasis is temporary. And with the news of Lady Macbeth's death his acceptance gives way to a new tone:

> To morrow, and to morrow, and to morrow,
> Creepes in this petty pace from day to day,
> To the last Syllable of Recorded time:
> And all our yesterdayes, have lighted Fooles
> The way to dusty death. Out, out, breefe Candle,
> Life's but a walking Shadow, a poore Player,
> That struts and frets his houre upon the Stage,
> And then is heard no more. It is a Tale
> Told by an Ideot, full of sound and fury
> Signifying nothing. (V. v. 19)

This speech presents special difficulties to interpretation. Its direct and powerful effectiveness is manifest, but the range of embodied emotion, and the variety of

responses evoked within this brief space, makes critical formulation a very precari-
ous business—hence the flat disagreements: is there 'a touch of tragic grandeur'
about this Macbeth, as Bradley suggests?[22] or is it simply 'an abject collapse, where
the would-be dominator of the world can see that world only as a procession of
fools by candle-light . . .'?[23] Or is there a triumph of knowledge in the very defeat,
as Abercrombie argues?

> He has staked everything and lost; he has damned himself for nothing; his
> world suddenly turns into a blank of imbecile futility. And he seizes on the
> appalling moment and masters even this: he masters it by *knowing* it absolutely
> and completely, and by forcing even this quintessence of all possible evil to live
> before him . . . Tragedy can lay hold of no evil worse than the conviction that
> life is an affair of absolute inconsequence. There is no meaning anywhere: that
> is the final disaster; death is nothing after that. And precisely by laying hold of
> this and relishing its fearfulness to the utmost, Macbeth's personality towers to
> its loftiest grandeur . . . For we see not only what he feels, but the personality
> that feels it; and in the very act of proclaiming that life is 'a tale told by an idiot,
> *signifying nothing*', personal life announces its virtue, and superbly *signifies
> itself.*[24]

This is to record only a tiny sample of the divergent readings one is offered.

We might begin by noting the prevailing tone of the speech—the impotent
irritation, almost pique, of 'Creepes' and 'petty pace', the slightly over-emphatic
generality of 'Fooles', modulating to a bitter acquiescence with 'Out, out, breefe
Candle' followed by *faux conforts* of negation. But the most powerful effect is
reserved for the last gesture of renunciation—and this can only be described as
savage, a kind of ferocious ennui. The shrillness of tone directs our attention to a
constriction of Macbeth's vision, and, as I suggested earlier, to the truth that he is
now reaping what he has sown, and cannot, finally, make his peace with its utter
negativity. And yet the tone is not merely shrill: it is also, at moments, passionate.

So I don't think it is just the persuasiveness of Abercrombie's prose that makes
me feel that he has grasped something important. If we compare Macbeth's fierce
brand of nihilism with Richard II's, a difference of temper becomes apparent. There
is nothing tearful or self-indulgent about this. It is sternly dry-eyed and rigorous.
One does not feel that the negation is an escapist's passivity: rather that it is the only
vision left to Macbeth—and he will not blink it. More than this. That it has the sort
of validity that derives from strenuousness and rigorousness of imagination—and
this is particularly true of the image of the strolling player, 'the walking Shadow',
transient apparition upon makeshift stages, himself a mere projection of flickering
candle-flame. Here the opening pettishness has gone, and the savagery has not yet
supervened, and we contemplate something that looks very much like an imaginative truth to nature. In any case, the movement of feeling in the rest of the speech
towards, and away from, this apprehension is so much a flux, a continuum, that
gestures of dismissal, like Rossiter's 'abject collapse', simply won't do.

I want, in short, to avoid separating the act of judgment which *sees through*

Macbeth, from the act of imagination which sees the world *with* him; and to exclude at the same time the guillotine criterion of philosophic respectability, which would make Macbeth's sentiments appear self-condemned in the very utterance. 'Something might be true,' wrote Nietzsche, 'even though it is harmful and dangerous in the greatest degree; it might in fact belong to the basic make-up of things that one should perish from its recognition.'[25] This kind of truth fixes Macbeth with its basilisk eye, and he stares back unflinchingly. It is another of the moments in the play when we contemplate the actuality of evil, without being overpowered by it.

All the same, 'nothing' is Macbeth's last word, and as he plunges into the violence of battle, the nothingness seems to gain on him. Death, for Duncan, was a thing of ghastly beauty, a ceremonious rite—'Silver skinne, lac'd with . . . Golden Blood'. Thereafter, once 'Renowne and Grace is dead', it becomes a thing of insane brutality. Banquo dies in an abrupt and overwhelmingly violent crescendo, beginning with the whispered consternation of the Murderers—'A Light, a Light'—rising to Banquo's conversationally-pitched commonplace, and then suddenly blaring forth in 'Let it come down'. A few seconds later all is silent but for the panting of the assassins. But that interval has been filled with the frenzy of 'twenty trenched gashes'—a spectacle of sudden, demonic, ugly brutality—essentially meaningless. Banquo's last healthful words are the most banal in the play, suggesting a pitiful, helpless inconsequentiality about the whole affair (III. iii).

Young Macduff's death (IV. ii) is in the same vein. The word 'traitor', which has hung over the whole scene as something huge, menacing and vague, and which Lady Macduff uses as a vent for her private sense of betrayal, is a mystery to the child. Yet the boy who does not know what a traitor is dies, absurdly, for denying his father to be one. The very ordinary prosiness of the domestic conversation, in the rich poetic fabric of this play, combines with the violent rapidity of a catastrophe ungarnished with words, to produce an effect almost unbearably flat and stark.

Macbeth's death, too, has this blunt-ugly meaninglessness. In the closing scenes of battle, his rhetoric of defiance is increasingly hollow, and Shakespeare permits it to phrase itself in doggerel and jingle:

> But Swords I smile at, Weapons laugh to scorne,
> Brandish'd by man that's of a Woman borne.   (V. vii. 12)

(This after the slaying of a beardless and untried youth.) Or

>   Before my body,
> I throw my warlike Shield: Lay on Macduffe,
> And damn'd be him, that first cries hold, enough.   (V. viii. 32)

This is not clumsy writing, 'silly and resourceless', as Shaw once claimed,[26] but a portrait of sham courage—the rant of the rattled gambler playing his last card, or, in Macbeth's metaphor, the grotesque rage of the baited bear. The man is an empty man.

The attempt to make these final moments wholly satisfying to admirers of Macbeth's heroic stature are wilful. With the appearance of Macduff, something snaps in him. He alternates between a black fatalistic remorse, which has a component of shrinking fear—

> Of all men else I have avoyded thee:
> But get thee backe, my soule is too much charg'd
> With blood of thine already—   (V. viii. 4)

and a puerile vaunting which has an edge of hysterical exaltation—

> As easie may'st thou the intrenchant Ayre
> With thy keene Sword impresse, as make me bleed:
> Let fall thy blade on vulnerable Crests...   (V. viii. 9)

(This is the hysterical Richard II of the 'God for his Richard hath in heavenly pay / A glorious angel' phase.) And when Macduff reveals his birth, Macbeth is reduced to a 'cow'd' and muttering renegade who refuses to fight. It is only the threat of extreme degradation—exhibition in a mountebank's booth—that finally induces him to take up his sword and 'try the last'. There is a kind of courage here, but it is animal rather than human. Plainly, for Shakespeare, Macbeth is finished before this moment.

Yet the effect is to make the final settlement somehow empty. With Macbeth's fallen and diminished stature since he took the field, the play-world too seems to shrink. We do not completely lose sight of Macduff's role as the impersonal executor of a justice larger than revenge—

> If thou beest slaine, and with no stroake of mine,
> My Wife and Childrens Ghosts will haunt me still:
> I cannot strike at wretched Kernes, whose armes
> Are hyr'd to beare their Staves...   (V. vii. 15)

—but we do see the inherent brute meanness and meaninglessness of the act of retribution itself. Viewed from a certain angle, the victory of Malcolm and Macduff is a triumph, and a necessary one. But at close range, the killing has the disturbing ambivalence of all acts of violence. This is death in battle rigorously contemplated. It is grotesque and sickening.

It would take more than the conventionalities of Malcolm's final speech to remove this taste from our mouths—even if there were not the mention of 'this dead Butcher, and his Fiend-like Queene' to ensure that we retain it to the end. Malcolm is, of course, right. But the dramatic focus is wide enough to include his kind of rightness within a much larger truth. For Malcolm's callous remark shocks us into a recognition of Macbeth's potential greatness—a greatness that can endure solitude:

> Very few people are capable of being independent; it is a privilege of the strong. And whoever tries it, however, justified, without *having* to, proves that he is probably not only strong but bold to the point of complete recklessness. For he walks into a labyrinth; he increases a thousandfold the dangers which

are inherent in life anyway. And not the smallest of his dangers is that no one can witness how and where he loses his way, falls into solitude, or is torn to pieces by some troglodytic minotaur of conscience. When such a man perishes, it happens so far from human understanding that other men have no feeling for it, no fellow feeling. But there is no return for him—not even a return to human compassion![27]

This is one half of the truth about the final moments of *Macbeth*.

The other half concerns the muted counterpoint which talks of 'planting newly', of 'loves', 'kinsmen', 'Friends' and 'the Grace of Grace'. It is, however, very definitely muted. The mature Shakespeare would not, for instance, have undercut an invocation of 'Grace' with a slightly frivolous word-play of this kind, unless he were deliberately holding something in check. He did not write the triumphant paean of restored humanity that he could have written: first, because this is Malcolm, not Duncan, and destruction has had very much its own way; and second, because the shadow of a vast evil that the play casts still broods over the consciousness. A burst of facile optimism in the Richmond vein would be drastically out of place. Instead Shakespeare permits the mind to play wonderingly over the events of the drama, questioning and probing, toying with words like 'Grace' or 'measure, time, and place', trying to find a meaningful order in it all:

> It is not only the pious believer who bends to the will of God, and to Providence which has so disposed when he sees the triumphant and unrestrainable outbreak of vitality, but every serious mind aware of the laws of reality disdains useless regrets and abstains from undue judgments, because no one can say that things would have turned out better if such an event, painful and destructive as it was, had not happened. We ourselves, who suffer from it, would not be what we are without it, and we would not necessarily be better, purer, more intelligent . . . Then, when the cycle has been completed, and the sky is more serene, the mind tries to find out whether, in all these raptures, follies . . . and mania of destruction, if there is no human and moral reasonableness, yet there may be . . . a concealed intention on the part of nature . . .[28]

We are left with an awed sense of the overwhelming potency and vitality of evil, and with a subdued question about this concealed intention of nature. It is not a resolution, but a tremulous equilibrium between affirmation and despair, in which we submit ourselves to an unknown fear.

NOTES

[1] F. Nietzsche, *Beyond Good and Evil*, tr. M. Cowan (Chicago, 1955), pp. 20–1.
[2] See G. Wilson Knight, *The Wheel of Fire* (London, 1930), p. 133.
[3] A case argued with some conviction by C. G. Clarke, 'Darkened Reason in "Macbeth" ', *Durham University Journal*, XXII (1960), 11–18.
[4] *Angel with Horns* (London, 1961), p. 215.
[5] *Shakespearean Criticism*, ed. T. M. Raysor (Everyman) (London, 1960), I, 61.

[6] *Beyond Good and Evil*, tr. M. Cowan, p. 22.

[7] *Shakespearean Tragedy* (London, 1904), p. 386.

[8] Lafeu in *All's Well*, II, iii, 1–6 (my italics). Amongst my other debts to Wilson Knight, it was he who first made me ponder the relevance of this passage to *Macbeth*: see *The Wheel of Fire*, p. 173.

[9] I am unconvinced by Dover Wilson's theory (*Macbeth* (Cambridge, 1960), pp. xxxiv–xxxviii) about the lost scene where Macbeth 'broke the enterprise' to her; and since a single, puzzling reference to an off-stage conversation is unlike mature Shakespearian workmanship, I conclude that the remark refers to what we do know (the letter, which was a compromising enough document, if he knew his wife's propensities) or to the unspoken understanding that is common between people who know each other well. Bradley (*Shakespearean Tragedy*, pp. 480–4) has a very sensible discussion of the matter.

[10] Søren Kierkegaard, *The Sickness unto Death*, tr. W. Lowrie (New York, 1953), pp. 152–4 (my italics).

[11] R. Walker, *The Time Is Free* (London, 1949), p. 66.

[12] Editorial head-scratching about the correct place to close the inverted commas is thus beside the point. For this effect only Elizabethan punctuation (or the lack of it) will serve.

[13] *Shakespearean Tragedy*, p. 362.

[14] Ibid. p. 378.

[15] *The Idea of Great Poetry* (London, 1925), p. 176 (my italics).

[16] The 'description of Scotland' prefixed to *The Historie of Scotland* (London, 1585), p. 21.

[17] *Shakespearean Criticism*, ed. T. M. Raysor, II, 221.

[18] Quoted by H. H. Furness, Variorum *Macbeth* (Philadelphia, 1873), p. 295.

[19] 'General Macbeth', *Harper's Magazine*, CCXXIV (June 1962), pp. 36–7.

[20] Quoted by Kenneth Muir in the Arden *Macbeth*, p. 84.

[21] *The Wheel of Fire*, pp. 171–2.

[22] *Shakespearean Tragedy*, p. 365.

[23] A. P. Rossiter, *Angel with Horns*, p. 227.

[24] *The Idea of Great Poetry*, pp. 176–8.

[25] *Beyond Good and Evil*, tr. M. Cowan, p. 46.

[26] G. B. Shaw, *Our Theatres in the Nineties* (London, 1932), III, 3.

[27] F. Nietzsche, *Beyond Good and Evil*, tr. M. Cowan, p. 36.

[28] Benedetto Croce, *History as the Story of Liberty* (London, 1941), p. 62.

Alan Hobson

THIS EVEN-HANDED
JUSTICE

The question whether there could ever be a man so resolute in evil as Richard III is raised by Anne's remark about those 'timorous dreams'. Must there not in any real villain be disturbances of mind that make him hesitate? Would he not have moments of horrified realisation? Margaret, as we have seen, has cursed Richard with the words:

> No sleep close up that deadly eye of thine,
> Unless it be while some tormenting dream
> Affrights thee with a hell of ugly devils!   (I. iii. 225–7)

But, until the final act, Shakespeare does not create the inwardness of Richard's life or show whether the curse is being fulfilled. The play affirms that evil deeds produce evil consequences; and, even if we did not know the story, we should foresee Richard's end as surely as we foresee the end of any villain of melodrama. In plays, bad people can always be brought to a bad end. When the play is convincing, the bad end is seen to have arisen directly from earlier events and from the nature of the people involved. If the play is a genuine study of the nature of evil in man, the villain need not die; for, in life, the wicked prosper, or seem to prosper. A play in which poetic justice is meted out cannot be a genuine study of the nature of evil unless there is some sense in which evil does in fact recoil upon its perpetrator. The forces that kill Richard are forces that his own cruelties have raised against him, but then Richard is an extreme villain. Conclusions about the generality of wickedness drawn from the extreme instance may be questionable. The meaning of evil is not most effectively conveyed to an audience by the presentation of a wholly evil being: we are not wholly evil, and cannot identify sufficiently with such a figure, though we can be impressed by the horror of it. It is when evil is seen in one more like ourselves that it convinces most powerfully. We have already seen a number of ways in which Richard *is* ourselves, but it is the sudden appearance of the 'good' impulses, the partial recognition of the truth about himself, and the human fear, all elicited by the dream, that make us feel *within* Richard and that

From *Full Circle: Shakespeare and Moral Development* (London: Chatto & Windus, 1972), pp. 124–49.

impart tragic awe which his mere death would not impart. We are now no longer merely watching; we are beginning to enter his inner life and thus to experience those consequences of evil that really do seem to be inevitable. In the inner life, we feel, a person is less likely to be able to escape the effects of his own evil choices than in the external world, though he may still remain, at any rate for a long time, unaware of those effects. The revelation of the horrors of Richard's inner world has been prepared, not by the full poetic realisation of his previous inner experience, but by hints of terrible forces within him, by curses and prophecies of dreadful things to come, by the impossible series of wicked triumphs that compels us to expect a reversal, and by the rhythmical iteration of the sufferings of the women, who generate such pity that we come not merely to desire but to expect a terrible vengeance in the soul as well as on the body of Richard.

This is mighty, but less mighty than a comparable realisation of the destructive power of evil in the inner life of one who, like us, has his virtues and his weaknesses, and with whom we can live through the experiences of conscience, of moral choice, and of the raging inner turmoil and the desert of hope and feeling created by deliberate wickedness. Such a one is Macbeth.

At every stage in Macbeth's development, or rather degeneration, we have the experience of choice. Equally, we have the sense of inevitability. This is very true to life, for every deliberate act can be viewed by one philosopher as an act of free will and by another as wholly determined, and the chooser himself can feel about his own choice, not merely in either way, but in both ways at the same time. The witches, the powers of evil, seek Macbeth and prophesy that he will be king. He starts and seems to fear, as if the thought is already in his mind. The uneasy feeling that Macbeth may be doomed has, in any case, started with the mention of his name by the witches in the opening scene. However, when his thoughts are revealed shortly after the prophecy, we find that grammar, rhythm and imagery express his state of indecision. His ambition impels him towards 'the swelling act of the imperial theme', the great drama in which he sees himself as king of Scotland; but his good conscience fills him with horror at the means to the crown which his ambition, stimulated by the witches, has offered:

> This supernatural soliciting
> Cannot be ill; cannot be good:
> If ill, why hath it given me earnest of success
> Commencing in a truth? I am Thane of Cawdor:
> If good, why do I yield to that suggestion
> Whose horrid image doth unfix my hair,
> And make my seated heart knock at my ribs,
> Against the use of nature?   (I. iii. 130–7)

Macbeth is a visualiser; the prophecy has brought before his mind's eye the body of King Duncan as if already murdered. Macbeth is not a man whose heart knocks against his ribs at the sight of physical horrors or in the presence of immediate danger. In the thick of battle, when he is fighting honourably and loyally for Scotland

and his king, he wades through the slaughter 'nothing afeard' of the 'strange images of death' he makes with his own sword, and freshened rather than dismayed by the sight of enemy reinforcements increasing the already heavy odds against him. To Macbeth

> Present fears
> Are less than horrible imaginings.

But the 'imaginings' that terrify him are not of physical, but of moral and spiritual danger; and, whereas physical danger stimulates him to heroic action, moral horror—the horror of doing a terrible evil—threatens his identity and paralyses him:

> My thought, whose murder yet is but fantastical,
> Shakes so my single state of man,
> That function is smothered in surmise
> And nothing is, but what is not.   (I. iii. 139–42)

Such is the power of Macbeth's imagination that the body of the murdered king in his mind's eye seems more real than the objects and the people around him. And, for the moment, the very image that the witches' suggestions have called up deters him. He seems to put aside the temptation:

> If Chance will have me King, why, Chance may crown me
> Without my stir.   (I. iv. 144–5)

Or at least defers the decision:

> Come what come may,
> Time and the hour runs through the roughest day.

When next we see him, an event, the declaration of Malcolm as Scotland's rightful heir, seems to bring him to the point of decision; but, even as he makes his resolve, the stars, the light, and the light of the body, which is the eye, condemn him:

> Stars, hide your fires!
> Let not light see my black and deep desires;
> The eye wink at the hand; yet let that be,
> Which the eye fears, when it is done, to see.   (I. iv. 50–3)

The expression 'yet let that be' leaves a doubt about the firmness of the decision, and the vivid counter imagery shows a powerful and living conscience warning him against the deed. We remain in suspense, for Macbeth has not yet consciously and irrevocably chosen evil; yet we feel a strong and steady movement towards evil that seems to be bearing him along. The horrid image now does *not* unfix his hair as it did on first appearance, and, though he fears it will when made flesh, he is already hardening himself against it.

When the experience of choice is sharpened by indecision, this is how it feels. There is the sense of great helplessness, the knowledge that sooner or later the choice will be made, and it will be made according to which of the forces pressing on the nervous system will prove most powerful; yet there is also the weight of personal responsibility, as if 'I', and in the last resort 'I' alone, can regulate those forces, giving the overbalance of power to one or another. By the poetic realisation of this state of indecision prior to moral choice, Shakespeare gives us an insight into moral experience and the working of conscience. Richard's immediate and outright rejection of conscience cannot be explored, except by its consequences. The decision itself is a matter of a moment. Only by presenting it, as it were, in slow-motion can Shakespeare live through it and discover its meaning. The more aware the chooser can be of the implications of his choice, the more powerful will be our grasp of its import.

In *Richard III* there is much that stimulates reflection on the *origins* of conscience, whether Shakespeare intended this or not. In *Macbeth* we know nothing of the hero's childhood or family or previous history, and though there are signs of immaturity both in his lust for power and glory and in his dependence on Lady Macbeth, his conscience as a mode of knowledge is highly developed, and as a motivating power by no means undeveloped. The powerful lusts, the touches of weakness and the distinct vision of what ought and ought not to be are given data and together make up the image of a truly human being who, by virtue of his aspiration and his insight, might well have been a very great human being. Macbeth longs to be king, but he also longs to be good; hence his special horror of murder, but not of slaughter in a noble cause. His powerful imagination shows him the horror of evil in visual terms. When we say that Macbeth 'knows' he is doing wrong in murdering Duncan, we do not mean merely that he has thought it out. Shakespeare presents him as knowing it by at least three modes of knowledge: the rational, the emotional and the sensory. In the soliloquy quoted above, the grammar of Macbeth's argument with himself and the objectivity of his self-analysis show him assessing the position rationally. However, the rhythm and the antitheses of the opening altercation with himself and of the final line, 'And nothing is but what is not', convey the emotional tension. The diction and images have powerful emotive force: 'swelling' for example expresses his rising hope and pride as well as intimations of royal grandeur. But every thought and feeling is experienced in his body, not only directly in the unfixed hair and the unseated heart, but through his imagination when the mere image of murder 'shakes' so his 'single state of man'. We cannot say that Macbeth knows with his 'head' and not with his 'heart' the horror of committing this crime, and therefore lacks motive for rejecting the temptation. Shakespeare makes Macbeth know it with head and heart and body. Unfortunately heart and body also know 'the swelling act of the imperial theme'. This is the dream of grandeur that will require the direct translation into life and act of the daydream of murder, which the head condemns and the body shrinks from.

Probably for everyone 'I ought' or 'I ought not' follows upon some imagined scene in which an obligation to do or not to do is dramatised as in a dream or day-dream, whether or not it is also being reasoned out. Everything depends on how, or whether, we live out the dreams. By the 'horrid image' of murder, Macbeth's conscience warns him against the very evil that it dramatises. Should he act according to the *meaning* of his vision, he would live it out by *rejecting* the image and refraining from the deed. That would be to affirm his rational judgement and accept the warning. In the event, he lives out the murder, which is the 'suggestion' of the witches, and rejects his good conscience.

That Macbeth's conscience is good and not merely a cowardly self-interest set against the self-interest of ambition is shown in his next long soliloquy, where every kind of self-interest, both noble and ignoble, is present. Richard knows conscience only as an interfering nuisance or as a terrifying threat to which only a coward would submit. Hamlet does himself the injustice of stigmatising his conscientious scruples as cowardice. Macbeth is restrained from committing the murder by two kinds of fear: one is fear of being murdered in his turn; the other is fear of doing evil. The second is the fear we find in saints and martyrs, and we do not call it cowardice. Ironically, it is cowardice that finally drives him to resolve upon committing the murder: he is too cowardly to endure the name of coward from his wife. This, however, is only the last straw and is partly occasioned by his unbounded admiration for Lady Macbeth.

It must be noted that, though Lady Macbeth plays on his own weakness by calling him coward when she is pressing him to do the murder and when she is trying to revive his manhood in the presence of Banquo's ghost, this is not how she describes him when she reflects alone upon those qualities that might prevent him from committing murder. These are her thoughts about him:

> Yet do I fear thy nature:
> It is too full o' th'milk of human kindness,
> To catch the nearest way. Thou woulds't be great;
> Art not without ambition, but without
> The illness should attend it: what thou woulds't highly,
> That would'st thou holily; would'st not play false
> And yet would'st wrongly win; thou'dst have, great Glamis,
> That which cries, 'Thus must thou do,' if thou have it;
> And that which rather thou dost fear to do
> Than wishest should be undone.   (I. v. 16–25)

Macbeth himself has already confirmed the truth of the last two lines, but it is her description of the nature of his fear that is important in expressing the quality of his conscience. What she knows he fears is 'illness', unholiness and playing false. 'Illness' in Shakespeare's day did not mean sickness, but evil or wickedness; here is suggests the cruelty in murder. And he fears these things because he is 'too full' of positive good. Lady Macbeth, like Goneril, despises this good, but whatever she may think in her barbarous mood, the 'milk of human kindness' is a virtue that life soon teaches her to long for. When Lady Macbeth calls upon the powers of evil to turn her milk to gall, she is not merely repudiating her feminine nature, she is desecrating the most sacred bond of kinship and of tender care, and defiling the very sources of life in her. Her husband, she believes, has not only too much gentleness in him to be a murderer but also too strong a sense of the sacredness of life. If 'kindness' has the same meaning as our word today, then 'milk' will be an intensifier and the worst that Lady Macbeth can be saying is that he has too much kindness to serve his own interests. Those who admire crime will condemn him for it and say that 'milk' refers to cowardice that masquerades as kindness. But the word 'kindness' must, in Shakespeare, have associations with 'kindred' and 'nature' and thus the phrase implies the gentleness that is a bond between man and man. This meaning is confirmed by Malcolm when, pretending that he will be a worse tyrant than Macbeth has become, he says it will be his delight to

Pour the sweet milk of concord into Hell   (IV. iii. 98)

Macbeth, then, according to his wife is one who feels strongly the bonds between man and man, one who has too much love in him to do a cruel deed—except, as we have seen, in the way of duty to his king and country. What Macbeth fears is to defile these bonds, to do wrong. This is not a personal and immediately selfish fear; it comes from reverence for life and for concord.

In the scene from which these words of Lady Macbeth are taken we are being shown what it is in Macbeth that causes the horrid image of murder to unfix his hair, and the passage quoted is only part of the impression we receive of Macbeth as one in whom the bonds of nature and of kinship are strong. He himself has few words in the scene and the strength of the bond between him and Lady Macbeth is shown more perhaps by her words than by his. Lady Macbeth's dominance suggests a possible weakness in him, a boyish dependence perhaps, but there is also a tenderness. In the passage quoted, Lady Macbeth shows how well she under-stands him; she has just read a letter in which he has imparted news relating to their secret. His language in the letter is that of a tender sharing:

This have I thought good to deliver thee (my dearest partner of greatness) that thou might'st not lose the dues of rejoicing, by being ignorant of what greatness is promis'd thee. Lay it to thy heart, and farewell.   (I. v. 10–15)

It is a great mistake to read Lady Macbeth's reflections upon the news in this letter as if she were Goneril, who indeed cannot use the word 'milk' without contempt and who really does despise the 'milky gentleness' of her husband, Albany. There is never any sign of gentleness or love in Goneril nor any real bond between her and any other person (unless her lust for Edmund be cited). Lady Macbeth is all solicitude for her husband. She rejoices in his greatness, and greets him ecstatically:

Great Glamis! worthy Cawdor!
Greater than both by the all-hail hereafter!

If he hesitates and has doubts, she will bear the burden of decision and preparation:

Leave all the rest to me.

Indeed, part of the preparation is her advice and encouragement, in which the tone is one of intimate sharing even in—or rather especially in—its sinister irony:

> Your face, my Thane, is as a book, where men
> May read strange matters. To beguile the time,
> Look like the time; bear welcome in your eye,
> Your hand, your tongue: look like th'innocent flower,
> But be the serpent under 't. He that's coming
> Must be provided for; and you shall put
> This night's great business into my dispatch;
> Which shall to all our nights and days to come
> Give solely sovereign sway and masterdom.   (I. v. 62–70)

There is the possessiveness and solicitous condescension of a mother, the common understanding and the shared aspiration. Her terrible repudiation of her woman-hood and all tenderness is already belied by this bond between her and her husband, as it will continue to be belied by subsequent behaviour. The tragic irony of their story is that the gentleness in Macbeth really is killed by the course of action upon which Lady Macbeth urges him, while her own gentleness reasserts itself as the accuser that disturbs her sleep and drives her to suicide. There is a sad contrast between Macbeth's words at her death and his first gentle greeting with its shared secret:

> My dearest love,
> Duncan comes here tonight.

The structure of Macbeth is like St. Andrew's cross, with Macbeth moving along one diagonal, Lady Macbeth along the other: their positions are reversed at the end of the play. At the beginning, Lady Macbeth is dominant. Her conscience is thoroughly repressed—that is, like Richard she does not know that it exists—and she has not the imagination to realise either the horror of evil or the probable consequences of murdering the king. These are the lineaments of bravery. Macbeth, on the other hand, is dependent and hesitating, because his vivid imagination and his active conscience make the decision to do evil very nearly impossible, and immediately after it is done drive him almost to distraction with fear and shame. At the end, Macbeth has 'supp'd full with horrors' and has learned by 'hard use' to contemplate them with indifference; his imagination is dead and his conscience hardly speaks. Lady Macbeth, however, is tormented by guilt and remorse to the point of suicide. Virtue repressed—virtue which she thought weakness—takes vengeance upon her. She who has thought that she could dash her baby's brains out finds that she cannot kill an old man because he resembles her father and that she feels so strongly for that old man and for a murdered lady that she cannot cleanse herself of their blood or keep them out of her dreams. Throughout all the period after the murder of Duncan both she and Macbeth suffer bitter remorse, but she suffers in silence and, as before the murder, is solicitous only for him.

> LADY MACBETH: Nought's had, all's spent,
> Where our desire is got without content:

'Tis safer to be that which we destroy,
Than by destruction dwell in doubtful joy.

(*Enter* Macbeth)

How now, my Lord? why do you keep alone,
Of sorriest fancies your companions making,
Using those thoughts, which should indeed have died
With them they think on?   (III. ii. 4–11)

He, on the other hand dwells on his own suffering:

O! full of scorpions is my mind, dear wife!

Until after the murder of Banquo, however, the bond between them remains
tender and strong:

LADY MACBETH: Come on:
Gentle my Lord, sleek o'er your rugged looks;
Be bright and jovial among your guests tonight.
MACBETH: So shall I, Love; and so, I pray, be you.

There is all the tenderness of shared suffering and mutual pity in these lines, as in
their first endearments there was the shared hope. But the sharing is to end:
Macbeth does not confide to her his secret intention to murder Banquo:

Be innocent of the knowledge, dearest chuck
Till thou applaud the deed.

And she can only marvel at hearing from him strange words she does not understand. After the murder of Banquo they still appear at first a perfect team as they
pronounce the welcome to the guests, and Lady Macbeth is his 'sweet remembrancer' when anxiety makes him forget to 'give the cheer' to his guests. When the
ghost appears, Lady Macbeth is at his side trying to brace his courage by the sharp
rebuke that was once so effective in moving him to a determined purpose; but we
soon realise that he is hardly conscious of her presence. There is very great pathos
in the quiet moments after the 'good meeting' has been broken 'with most admired
disorder'. It is as if, after the expenditure of all her strength in his behalf, a great
weariness falls upon Lady Macbeth. This is conveyed in two brief replies to questions which Macbeth addresses to her in the midst of broodings that are almost
soliloquies:

What is the night?
LADY MACBETH: Almost at odds with morning, which is which.
MACBETH: How say'st thou, that Macduff denies his person
At our great bidding?
LADY MACBETH: Did you send to him, Sir?   (III. iv. 125–8)

But Macbeth is brooding deeply on his own fears and upon a new resolve. He
hardly seems aware of her presence, but she listens to his broodings and in one

single line expresses all her care for him, while the burden of her own suffering cannot be shared:

> You lack the season of all natures, sleep.

He replies to her:

> Come, we'll to sleep.

but his next word is about himself—and it is the resolve to harden himself by further dreadful deeds. The bond is breaking between them, or rather withering on Macbeth's part. We do not see them together again, but when we next see Macbeth he has lost all power of tender feeling. Not so Lady Macbeth! When next we see her the close pent-up guilts rive their concealing continents as she walks in her sleep and relives her experience in nightmare. Even here, apart from the overwhelming and inescapable guilt and remorse, her predominant emotion is solicitude for her husband, still expressed in bracing rebuke. To this are now added agonising regrets that she and her husband have, putting it euphemistically, felt no solicitude for Duncan and Lady Macduff, either in love or in duty. It is this awareness of others that gives pathos to this dramatic re-enactment of their agonies of guilt and fills the audience with tragic pity and fear rather than with mere triumph over a 'fiend-like queen'. She 'did not know what she was doing' when she tried to 'unsex' herself and dispel all 'compunctious visitings of nature'. Her violated nature, whose disposition was and still is towards love, now reasserts itself to her infinite suffering, self-condemnation and finally self-destruction. Lady Macbeth's tragedy is the waste of love.

We have seen that, unlike Lady Macbeth, Macbeth does know, in at least three senses of the word, what he is doing when he decides to murder Duncan. The divided conscience and the implications of moral choice are yet more fully explored by Shakespeare in the soliloquy of Macbeth at the very point of decision on the night of the murder:

> If it were done, when 'tis done, then 'twere well
> It were done quickly: if th' assassination
> Could trammel up the consequence, and catch
> With his surcease success; that but this blow
> Might be the be-all and the end-all—here,
> But here, upon this bank and shoal of time,
> We'd jump the life to come—But in these cases,
> We still have judgement here; that we but teach
> Bloody instructions, which, being taught, return
> To plague th' inventor: this even-handed Justice
> Commends th' ingredience of our poison'd chalice
> To our own lips. He's here in double trust:
> First, as I am his kinsman and his subject,
> Strong both against the deed; then, as his host,

Who should against his murtherer shut the door,
Not bear the knife myself. Besides, this Duncan
Hath borne his faculties so meek, hath been
So clear in his great office, that his virtues
Will plead like angels, trumpet-tongu'd, against
The deep damnation of his taking-off;
And Pity, like a naked new-born babe,
Striding the blast, or heaven's Cherubins, hors'd
Upon the sightless couriers of the air,
Shall blow the horrid deed in every eye,
That tears shall drown the wind.—I have no spur
To prick the sides of my intent, but only
Vaulting ambition, which o'erleaps itself
And falls on th' other—

                    Enter Lady Macbeth   (I. vii. 1–28)

As in the soliloquy examined earlier, we see here the form and grammar of argument suggesting rational thought. At the same time, nothing could suggest the wish and the fear, the tension between urgency and indecision, more effectively than the rhythm and grammatical shape of the opening lines. He speaks boldly, as if he would risk eternity for the crown, but he hesitates in fear of more immediate retribution. If this hesitation is cowardice, it is also prudence and, in so far as it shows a realistic grasp of the nature of things, it is wisdom. The subsequent course of events confirms the existence of a moral 'law' by which an evil choice does bring evil consequences upon the chooser—not only the consequences that Macbeth appears to be thinking of here, but the inner consequences of moral, emotional and spiritual destruction. Richard would have despised Macbeth for hesitating to take the risk of retribution in this life or any other. So does Lady Macbeth in the ensuing lines. We may approve his wisdom or condemn his fear, or both; but after line 12 a very different motivation appears and we see at work what most of us would call a good conscience or a better nature. For five lines Macbeth thinks only of the bonds that bind him to Duncan and the obligations that a noble host and a loyal kinsman and subject would fulful. Here there is no threat, only the attraction of love and duty. Not that there is any sign of personal affection: that is not the meaning of 'love' in this context. Duty is the formal aspect of love, expressing co-operation and respect within a harmonious social framework—that is how Shakespeare normally uses the word, and the word 'love' often appears with it in the plays to emphasize the strength of the bond. Macbeth's words about Duncan show that he is aware of the bond and values it. Here is the love-conscience working, but without strong feeling for the individual person.

But Macbeth's awareness is wider and deeper than this. Contemplating Duncan's great virtues as a man and as a king, and showing his intense appreciation of them by the degree adverbs, he sees them, and his own projected crime in the context, not of a particular act alone, nor of society merely, but of the universe; and he, like the universe in his imagination, overflows with pity. The pity and the tears are in Macbeth, and so are the angels that plead against the murder: this is *his* vision, and it is decisive:

> We will proceed no further in this business: (I. vii. 31)

Macbeth's conscience, allowing the admixture of selfish fear, may not be perfect, but if the function of conscience is to guide and direct us beyond immediate interest to that 'long-term desire to remain on good terms with others' and beyond that to the achievement or even the preservation of a harmonious order in the universe, then Macbeth's conscience is of a high order and we might well weep with him at the thought of a deed that would run counter to it and bring so much unhappiness.

Very sadly, however, the words in which he first rejects the idea of murder are regretful and indecisive:

> I have no spur
> To prick the sides of my intent,

and it is as if he despises himself for his failing ambition. Lady Macbeth enters: she will be the spur. In the face of her heroic malignity, his conscience is silenced and he makes his feeblest and most contemptible objection:

> If we should fail?

With the disorganisation of his own moral being, he does indeed show the cow-ardice that Lady Macbeth has accused him of. Here, as earlier, he seems vulnerable to her suggestion. His own kind of courage is now to be replaced by a new kind infused into him by her, which will destroy them both.

> I dare do all that may become a man
> Who dares do more, is none.

gives way to

> I am settled, and bend up
> Each corporal agent to this terrible feat.
> Away, and mock the time with fairest show;
> False face must hide what the false heart doth know.   (I. vii. 80–3)

Rationally, he knows that murder is unmanly and that he will be less than man if he commits it, but lust for 'the ornament of life', fear to be called a coward, and admiration of an intrepid woman overcome both reason and conscience, and he takes his first decisive step on the road to misery and damnation.

His conscience, however, is not silenced. On the contrary it troubles him with added power and in a new way. The attractions of goodness now disappear and only the warning and the threat remain. We have seen the link between imagination and conscience. The horrors of murder that Macbeth formerly saw with the mind's eye now materalise before him in the shape of an 'air drawn dagger' that seems to lead him to Duncan's chamber. It does not lead him: it marshals him the way that he is going. It does not even speed him there, for he awaits the signal to approach the chamber. But, on its blade and dudgeon, gouts of blood warn him that he will be one with murderers and ravishers and the powers of evil. This, the final warning, is by its visual manifestation more vivid than previous ones; but, being a mere threat it is weaker in its effect. The vision of Pity and the attraction of goodness almost deterred him; this horror he sweeps aside contemptuously.

After the deed is done, the conscience that gave warning against cruel deeds and appealed on behalf of love and duty changes again. Now it becomes the terrible accuser: it condemns and punishes with remorse and guilt, and also with fear of the 'even-handed Justice'. Now Macbeth sleeps in the affliction of terrible dreams that shake him nightly; hands reach from the air to pluck out his eyes, for he has looked on the murdered king; a voice cries 'sleep no more', for he has murdered one who slept; each night, 'on the torture of the mind' he lies 'in restless ecstasy'. The rejected conscience takes vengeance. At the same time, the conscience once rejected is more easily rejected a second time. As Richard suspects his subjects, so Macbeth suspects Banquo. Banquo is murdered—by hired murderers: there is a degeneration even in forms of murder. But Macbeth's visualising conscience is still strong. From his royal banquet one guest is absent. He pays an ironic compliment:

> Here had we now our country's honour roof'd,
> Were the grac'd person of our Banquo present;   (III. iv. 39–40)

At the name, Banquo's ghost appears 'with twenty trenched gashes on his head'. Macbeth is 'quite unmanned' and betrays himself before his guests. Yet, when the ghost disappears, he tries to recover himself with the same vaunting irony. At once the ghost is present again. We know Macbeth as one who has only to think of an abomination to see it. This is the third and last of the visible projections of his conscience, and this time the audience see it too. For Shakespeare's audience this would not be merely a psychological phenomenon: they did not think—and we should be foolish to be confident—that conscience has no origins beyond the mind of man. However that may be, the ghost confirms Macbeth's vision of the angels pleading trumpet-tongued against the murder of Duncan: Macbeth has violated the universal order. Just before the murder of Banquo he has uttered the first of his three invocations of chaos, blood-curdling to Shakespeare's contemporaries:

> But let the frame of things disjoint, both the worlds suffer,
> Ere we will eat our meal in fear, and sleep
> In the affliction of these terrible dreams,
> That shake us nightly.   (III. ii. 16–19)

Ghosts presage disjointing of the frame of things. An audience that feared ghosts and feared chaos, and grasped the link between the two, would be drawn into Macbeth's experience, and feel the power of the accusing conscience, by seeing the apparition that he sees but is not seen by others.

Macbeth can no longer endure the torment of conscience and the fear that 'blood will have blood', his blood. He makes his second major choice and takes an even more firm step down what the Porter euphemistically calls 'the primrose path to the everlasting bonfire'. There have been no primroses on Macbeth's path, and now there is nothing to gain but escape from remorse and escape from the vivid knowledge of his true situation. Twice before, we have been with him in states of acute indecision, living through the experience of choice. In the first he did not choose, but hoped the choice would be made for him (I. iv. 144–5). In the second he made the decision that Lady Macbeth persuaded him to reverse (I. vii. 31). In each, we were with him, hesitating before the act of choice. After Banquo's ghost has disappeared and the banquet has ended in disorder we are taken again into his thoughts for, though Lady Macbeth is present, he seems not to be addressing her but brooding upon his situation. He sees himself standing deep in a river of blood. Should he continue to wade across, or not? This time the decision comes *before* the image of division, and the image is given as the reason for the choice that has already been made. He has decided that conscience must be killed: there must be no hesitation about doing wrong or injuring others:

> For mine own good
> All causes shall give way: I am in blood
> Stepp'd in so far, that, should I wade no more,
> Returning were as tedious as go o'er.   (III. iv. 135–8)

This assessment of the situation is more consistent with his wish than with reality. His subsequent development, if that is the word, will show that he is not in a river or a pond, but in a sea. There is no wading through to the other side: he will be engulfed. The image of a possible return is a reminder of the only true way to come to terms with his conscience, namely to repent, to relinquish his crown and all the effects for which he did the murder.[1] Externally the penalties would be severe, but the inner life would be redeemed. The possibility is there, but he chooses a different way to quieten the conscience, namely 'by custom of fell deeds':[2]

> My strange and self-abuse
> Is the initiate fear, that wants hard use:
> We are yet but young in deed.   (III. iv. 141–3)

Now Scotland will become a place where

> Each new morn
> New widows howl, new orphans cry: new sorrows
> Strike heaven on the face.   (IV. iii. 4–6)

The innocent Lady Macduff and her children will be slaughtered so that Macbeth may sleep. But what now happens to Macbeth is what he partly foresaw would happen:

> this even-handed Justice
Commends the ingredience of our poison'd chalice
To our own lips.

The consequences of his evil choice are first and most terribly experienced within himself.

In *Richard III* there is no such exploration of the experience of conscience and of choice as we have observed it here in *Macbeth:* Richard is an unhesitating sinner. The theme of retribution, however, is common to both plays. In each, usurpation and murder bring the kingdom near to chaos. In each, the usurper is killed by the forces that his own evil deed has roused against him, and peace is restored only after his death. In each, the protagonist suffers the consequences of his evil within himself. The difference lies in the depths to which the inner life is explored.

The full effect of inner changes for the worse, brought about by the denial of conscience and the choice of evil can be felt in Macbeth so much more strongly because he is not a villain from the start. He is not, like Richard, a man denied the experience of love and duty; and he is highly honoured by 'all sorts of people'. Though a man of ruthless boldness in fight, he is capable of tenderness and pity and he desires a good conscience and a stainless reputation. All this we have seen. Finer feeling and imaginative realisation strive in him against the murder of Duncan. That murder being committed, the next comes more easily, and the next. At first the powers of evil have to visit Macbeth and urge him on to the evil he has already contemplated or to which his ambition predisposes him; but, after the appearance of Banquo's ghost, he does what Lady Macbeth did at the very first: he seeks the powers of evil, calls upon the witches. The Macbeth who visits the witches of his own free will is already a changed man; there is a wildness and a domineering violence in his speech that were not heard before the appearance of Banquo's ghost, and resemble more his rages in Dunsinane castle during the final war, when it is said of him:

> Who then shall blame
His pester'd senses to recoil and start,
When all that is within him does condemn
Itself, for being there?   (V. ii. 22–5)

All *consciousness* of inner conflict has gone, but we have the sense of fearful tensions at play beneath the surface. Yet, after he has seen the apparitions from the witches' cauldron and heard the reassuring (but deceptive) prophecies which convince him that he bears a charmed life, he sees 'no more sights' and is devoid of fear and remorse. No longer does he hesitate to do evil—though he cannot decide whether to put his armour on, and his servants scurry hither and thither in obedience to his violent commands and countermands. None serve him now but 'constrained things, whose hearts are absent'. The honour that he so coveted he must not look to have, nor other rewards of age that might well have been his:

> I have liv'd long enough: my way of life
> Is fall'n into the sere, the yellow leaf;
> And that which should accompany old age,
> As honour, love, obedience, troops of friends,
> I must not look to have; but in their stead,
> Curses, not loud, but deep, mouth-honour, breath,
> Which the poor heart would fain deny, and dare not.   (V. iii. 22–8)

The language in which he requests the Doctor to cure Lady Macbeth gives the impression that he himself still knows what it is to suffer from 'a mind diseased' and to bear in the memory 'a rooted sorrow'; but his ungovernable rages alternating with black despair mark the unbalanced mind in which self-awareness is fitful and uncertain.

The final state of mind of one who has made Macbeth's choices and whose conscience has been killed by the 'hard use' of evil deeds is presented in his famous speech on the meaninglessness of life. A cry of women is heard, and we are reminded how the knocking at the gate startled him on the night of Duncan's murder. Now, 'direness', familiar to his slaughterous thoughts, cannot once start him. The queen is dead. Macbeth's comment is

> She should have died hereafter:
> There would have been a time for such a word—

These terrible words express at once his need to sorrow for another and the horror of his incapacity to do so. They recall a bond that once existed and a shared dream that has not been realised; but neither here nor in the preceding or ensuing lines does Shakespeare give Macbeth one word of tenderness. In the scorched earth of his mind, love cannot revive: it is his own disappointments on which he dwells, and his bitter contempt for a life that has no hope, no joy, no meaning for him. To Cleopatra, on the death of Antony, 'All's but naught' and 'there is nothing left remarkable beneath the visiting moon'; but Cleopatra forgets herself in thoughts of Antony, and learns love as she has not known it before. Shakespeare fills her speeches with him both at his death and ever afterwards. From Macbeth's speeches, on the other hand, Lady Macbeth is most dreadfully absent. Their final separation is the signal for an outburst, not of grief, but of cynicism, in which his private chagrin is inflated to a solemn affirmation of the worthlessness of life in general:

> Tomorrow, and tomorrow, and tomorrow,
> Creeps in this petty pace from day to day,
> To the last syllable of recorded time;
> And all our yesterdays have lighted fools
> The way to dusty death. Out, out, brief candle!
> Life's but a walking shadow; a poor player,
> That struts and frets his hour upon the stage,
> And then is heard no more: it is a tale

> Told by an idiot, full of sound and fury,
> Signifying nothing.   (V. v. 19–28)

The passage is preceded by a speech of angry defiance; it is followed by a scene of desperate fury. The one who struts and frets and whose life has been full of sound and fury and lunatic violence is Macbeth. The world Macbeth sees and condemns is a projection of himself. His words describe, not the external world or the nature of man, but the last state of one who has lived the life Macbeth has lived and made the choices Macbeth has made. Shakespeare is observing a process—a process human beings have a disposition to ignore. Either, like Lady Macbeth, we lack the imagination to foresee the consequences of evil; or, like Macbeth, we put aside the knowledge. But the process is ineluctable.

Cynicism is a mode of self-defence. If one blames the world, or the nature of man, one need not blame oneself. If one makes a general exaggeration of faults, either in the world or in oneself, one can avoid a true assessment of oneself. One may then, like Jaques or Timon, maintain a pose of superiority even while viewing human nature with *defensive* contempt. Every cynic has, in one form or another, made Macbeth's choice,

> For mine own good,
> All causes shall give way.

He is a disappointed egoist, often one, like Timon of Athens, whose egoism has been disguised as altruism till the counterfeit altruism has ceased to bring in immediately pleasing returns. Cynicism breeds equally in the disappointed idealist and the thwarted opportunist. Macbeth is something of both, and his feeling that life is meaningless is the more intense.

To ensure that we continue to feel Macbeth's fate as to some extent our own, Shakespeare retains our sympathy for him, partly by his desperate bravery to the last, partly by pity as the witches' prophecies fail him, but much more by one moment in which his bravery falters, but his almost obliterated conscience revives in a genuinely altruistic impulse. He meets Macduff, whose family he has slaughtered:

> Of all men else I have avoided thee:
> But get thee back, my soul is too much charg'd
> With blood of thine already.   (V. viii. 4–6)

This and his magnificence preserve a sense of his worth and preclude any acceptance of his own assertion that life means nothing. What Macbeth might have been, another man might be; for different choices can be made. The choice that Macbeth has made leads to despair; but he very nearly made the opposite choice, and here at the end is the voice of the conscience that might have saved him and created happiness through love and duty.

Macbeth has chosen murder, but the life has gone out of *him*. He has practised cruelty and has cultivated indifference, and love has died in him. He has violated the bonds of order, and he himself has become a chaos. He has committed moral suicide, and this one last altruistic impulse is the final gush of his life-blood. All things but one that give meaning to his life he has annihilated; that one is his dream of the secure enjoyment of 'solely sovereign sway and masterdom'. That dream having proved an illusion, he dismisses life as 'signifying nothing'. But he does not commit suicide:

> Why should I play the Roman fool, and die
> On mine own sword? whiles I see lives, the gashes
> Do better upon them.   (V. viii. 1–3)

His life continues to mean destruction and murder. Yet the pang of conscience immediately follows these words and reminds us how love and duty once attracted him. His life, that has lost meaning for him, is profoundly meaningful to us.

Macbeth reads like a dramatic exposition of two sayings from Scripture. One is St. Paul's dark summary of the moral law:

> For the wages of sin is death.

The other is in the words of Jesus:

> For whosoever will save his life shall lose it.

But neither of these sayings is complete, and each of them implies its sequel. St. Paul continues:

> but the gift of God is eternal life.

The whole range of the passage from Matthew's gospel reads:

> For whosoever will save his life shall lose it: and whosover will lose his life for my sake shall find it.
> For what is a man profited, if he shall gain the whole world, and lose his own soul?

Like both these sayings, Macbeth affirms the worth of the human soul, and by its terrifying imitation of despair, arouses hope and a longing for abundant life. The hope is encouraged by the spectacle of Macbeth's grandeur—though ruined—and the realisation of human potential conveyed by this and the reappearance of a conscience that could not quite be killed. And hope ends the play, with the return of the rightful king and the beginning of a new order which is also the recovery of the old order.

The question whether Shakespeare intended to deliver a moral exhortation or preach a Christian sermon through the implications of this play is not so easy to answer as was once assumed.

The last statement of the recurring theme that first appeared in the opening scene with 'Fair is foul and foul is fair' has the *form* of a 'moral' pronounced by one who, above all others, should know:

And be these juggling fiends no more believ'd,
That palter with us in a double sense;
That keep the word of promise to our ear,
And break it to our hope.   (V. viii. 19–22)

Though its meaning is not to be summed up by this or any other single quotation, the play is certainly a representation of what happens when a man and a woman hearken to the promises of the 'Fiend'. Shakespeare compels us to identify with that man and woman, even though they be mightier, more heroic, more influential than we. The deeds they do, we probably will not do; but the choice they make we have often made, and may make again. It is true that the play delineates a process; it would be difficult to maintain that it does not also offer an evaluation. An evaluation of a process in which I see myself an actor does in practice imply a prescription or prescriptions.

It will be observed that the sayings of Jesus and St. Paul, quoted above, are not exhortatory in their form; each, whether true or false, is in the form of description, or statement of fact, comparable to 'He who puts his finger in the fire will get it burnt'. The second premise, 'I do not want my finger burnt', or, in the case of *Macbeth* and the two scriptural sayings, 'I do not want to suffer death or despair, or meaninglessness, or an emotional and spiritual desert' can be taken for granted either in this or in its positive form, 'I want my finger painless and healthy' or 'I want life and hope and significance and a "well of water springing up into eternal life." '. The conclusion follows: 'I must not put my finger in the fire', 'I must not live as Macbeth lived'—and so forth. Exhortation, then, is implicit. In the case of the scriptural sayings, everyone would assume this. *Macbeth* has a moral point. It says, 'These are the ways to misery; you do not want misery; so avoid these ways;' or, 'There are numerous indications in the play of a road to happiness that Macbeth did not follow; you want happiness; so take the road Macbeth did not take.'

However, it may be objected, the so-called 'moral' of a play or story may be really a counsel of prudence, not a statement about right and wrong about moral good and moral evil. If the exhortation to avoid Macbeth's ways and follow those he rejected is basically an appeal to our self-interest (because we want happiness, not misery) then it is a counsel of prudence and not strictly a moral exhortation at all, it might be asserted.

The first part of the answer to this is that the play, like the passages from Jesus and St. Paul, does not acknowledge the distinction. In studying the play, we have observed in Macbeth different and conflicting forms of self-interest. Egoism, or selfishness is pleasing oneself in the comparatively short term or in a narrow context and thus regardless of the interests of others. Altruism or unselfishness is pleasing oneself by having regard to the long term and the universal context, and thus of the interest of others, and ultimately of all. In Shakespeare's plays the first is both condemned as bad, at least in many of its forms, and seen to lead to unhappy endings in most, perhaps in all, of its forms. Altruism is both approved and seen to be the means to happiness. We have observed much of the language and the imagery that stigmatises Macbeth's egoism as evil and his altruism as good. This moral approval and condemnation is embodied in a metaphysic expressed in images of a universe in which evil and unhappiness are inseparable and both are pleaded against by angels. The philosopher's distinction between moral and prudential considerations would appear to be inapplicable to Macbeth unless the word 'prudential' be taken to mean 'prudent in the short run or in a narrow context' (i.e. expedient) and 'moral' taken to mean 'prudent in the long run or in a universal context'. Indeed, Shakespeare's plays *as a whole* seem to demonstrate that what is good is also generally advantageous even in the short run and in the individual life; and *Macbeth* shows the destructiveness of evil within the nature of the one who does evil. A Macbeth will bring suffering upon the innocent and the good; a Prospero will save the wicked from the destruction that would otherwise fall upon them; but this does not alter the general Shakespearean picture of the moral and natural order, or the general impression that virtue pays and vice does not.

The second part of the reply to the assertion that in so far as *Macbeth* is exhortatory it urges counsels of prudence, not moral imperatives, would involve a discussion of whether moral prescriptions are not always in some sense prudential. This, however, is not necessary for our purpose, which is to observe that Shakespeare's plays, like the Sermon on the Mount, link goodness with happiness and evil with misery inextricably, and that all these are operative within a context of order and disorder in which the second is evil but subordinate to the first and capable, like Satan, of being exploited to good ends, as in the regeneration of King Lear. That order prevails in *Macbeth* has been obvious since Bradley pointed it out, but from the disruption in the play no good issues. This emphasises how much it is in man's interest to subserve the universal order; and that is also his moral duty.

NOTES

[1] Cf. Claudius (*Hamlet:* III. iii. 54).
[2] *Julius Caesar:* III. i. 270.

P. Rama Moorthy

FEAR IN *MACBETH*

The ambiguity of Macbeth's character is likely to be perpetuated as long as we identify the imaginative truth of the play with its moral faith. The play is, in an important way, more than its preoccupation with good and evil; its imaginative complex extends beyond its moral intention. There has been a certain romanticising of evil in *Macbeth* criticism. In calling the play 'a statement of evil'[1]—'*Macbeth* defines a particular kind of evil—the evil that results from a lust for power'[2]—L. C. Knights has made it morally central and, in doing so, abridged the work's imaginative scope and freedom. This approach has led to the diminution of both the play and its protagonist apparent in statements like—'We may indeed call *Macbeth* the greatest of morality plays';[3] '(Macbeth) though a tragic hero, (is) yet a criminal';[4] and 'to all intents (Macbeth is) a contracting character'.[5] Such a magnification of its moral structure results in a dwarfing of the spiritual, non-moral content of the tragedy, and diminishes the imaginative complexity of Macbeth's character. What has been lost is a certain vital mystery that relates Macbeth, amorally, to the bear (to which Macbeth compares himself) that 'must fight the course'.

The play, before it is about evil, is about something anterior to evil, something of which evil is a reductive part—an elemental ground that creates the kind of world that Macbeth inhabits and also is a product of. It is a world *in extremis* and of elemental turmoil, of thunders and lightning, and of the utterness of blood, blackness and death. It is a world that has jumped its nature and norms—a world of aberrations (like the witches), of unnatural happenings (like the horses eating each other), and of inversions (like unsexing, unmanning). It is a world of doubleness of character, incident and action; of the doubleness of language—of equivocation, ambiguity and anthithesis. In it there is a confusion of values, a mixing of opposites—fair and foul. It generates dreams and nightmares, vision and voices and in it 'nothing is but what is not'. It is on the verge of life and death, and crisis is its norm.

The tension that holds Macbeth and his world is the tension of fear. Fear is the medium and also the material of the play. Lady Macduff, in her anguished utterance,

From *Essays in Criticism* 23, No. 2 (April 1973): 154–66.

states the theme: 'All is the fear, nothing is the love'. Fear, like the elemental happenings strikes both the innocent mother and the child. Fear has its own diabolic operations and it creates what it apprehends. The gruesome murder of Lady Macduff and her child come as the apalling fulfilment of her own fears: 'When our actions do not, our fears do make us traitors.' Fear wills its own sinister creation, supplanting the natural one.

What Macbeth is combatting beneath the haze of ambition and moral scruple, is fear—or death that fear symbolises. The thought of murdering Duncan throws up an image of fear that threatens Macbeth's vital being. He is himself a bewildered witness of fear

> Whose horrid image doth unfix my hair,
> And make my seated heart knock at my ribs,
> Against the use of nature.   (I. ii. 135–7)

The horror is so dire that Macbeth fears a division in his 'single state of man'. Nevertheless he dares it, and in spite of his vision and voices, holds himself together, while his wife, deeply affected by the horror of the deed, breaks down, suffers a division, and dies. It is the peculiar fate of Macbeth that he is condemned to begin, to dwell, and to endure where Mr. Kurtz (*Heart of Darkness*) ended crying—'The horror, the horror!' It is Macbeth, therefore, that speaks, most obsessively, the word fear and its synonyms (there are about fifty of them in the text)—two out of every three invocations of fear being Macbeth's, and the third one, almost always, Lady Macbeth's. Haunted by fear they both go through the travail of life like the condemned. Lady Macbeth succumbs to fear before long; but Macbeth rides it until the death of a soldier puts an end to his tragic career.

Macbeth's first reflex at the suggestion of the crown by the witches is, significantly, a startle—a fright: 'Good Sir,' asks Banquo in surprise, 'why do you start and seem to fear Things that do sound so fair?' It is important to examine whether in his first soliloquy the suggestion of the crime comes to him as sin, a disgusting act of moral depravity, a fall, or as sheer horror which the image of retribution, a daring of the forbidden, engenders. Is it horror as revulsion, as in Oedipus, or horror as fear, as in Mr. Kurtz, or both? Here is a confession of Macbeth's nature by himself when he hears the cry of women:

> I have almost forgot the taste of fears.
> The time has been, my senses would have cool'd
> To hear a night-shriek; and my fell of hair
> Would at a dismal treatise rouse, and stir,
> As life were in't   (V. v. 9–13)

No moral question is involved in this. Yet 'a night-shriek' or 'a dismal treatise' disturbs Macbeth as deeply as does the thought of murdering Duncan. The reaction in both the cases is identical.

Examining Macbeth's susceptibility to fear in the passage above, A. C. Bradley observes that Macbeth's fear is 'a native disposition',[6] and 'that it belongs to a time

before his conscience was 'burdened'.[7] The word 'native' in the phrase appropri-
ately identifies the origin and depth of Macbeth's fear, but we have to consider
whether the 'horrid image' of murdering Duncan carries in it an element of 'conscience burdened'.

'Most readers have felt', affirms L. C. Knights, 'that after the initial crime there
is something compulsive in Macbeth's crimes'. But the germ of the compulsiveness
is already there in him and his 'initial crime' is itself the result of the compulsiveness
we discern in Macbeth's killings in the battlefield. Macbeth who

> Unseam'd him from the nave to the chops,
> And fix'd his head upon our battlements   (I. ii. 23–4)

and who 'didst make Strange images of death' betrays, in the relished violence,
excess and picturesqueness of his killings, a compulsiveness of which the 'initial
crime' is a further dramatisation. 'Strange' is a keyword here, suggesting elements
of both the unnatural ('I have seen Hours dreadful and things strange'—II. iv. 3) and
the obsessional ('strangely-visited people, All swoln and ulcerous'—IV. iii. 150). This
is a streak peculiar to Macbeth's mind and Macbeth's confessions of his mental state
further reinforces it: ' My strange and self-abuse Is the initiate fear, that wants hard
use' (III. iv. 141–2)—mark the word 'initiate'. Are not both Macbeth and his wife
speaking the truth when Lady Macbeth says in the Banquet scene—'My Lord is
often thus, And hath been from his youth'? Macbeth confirms it by saying 'I have a
strange infirmity which is nothing To those who know me'.

Fear has been the most trying, deeply unsettling ordeal that Macbeth is fated
to go through. Rather than dare it, he would avoid it, seek excuses to be exempted
from it. Perplexed and helpless he hopes, almost childishly, that somehow 'Chance',
'Time and the hour' will resolve the problem for him: 'If Chance will have me King,
why, Chance may crown me without my stir'. He seeks, in desperation, the support
and help of Banquo by frequently reminding him of his share in the prophecy: 'Do
you not hope your children shall be kings . . . ?', 'Think upon what hath chanc'd', 'It
shall make honour for you'. In writing the letter to his wife about the prophecy he
betrays his need for strength and encouragement from his 'dearest partner of
greatness'.

The 'horrid image' of murdering Duncan symbolises for Macbeth a terrible
daring fraught with fatal consequences. He is himself taken aback by the image that
suddenly springs into his consciousness. He asks incredulously, 'why do I yield to
that suggestion', as if it is an involuntary happening of which he has no control.
Macbeth's responses here are clearly the reflexes of a terrified man. The issue is,
crucially, of life and death, whatever else it may be later to his rational thinking.

It is in the soliloquy 'If it were done . . . ' that the state of Macbeth's mind and
the truth of his motivations are clearly revealed. The beginning of the passage is
conditional, the mood subjunctive, and the tone is defensive and argumentative, and
even veiledly apologetic—there are two 'ifs' and five 'but's' in the passage. The
whole passage of 28 lines, except for the last two and half lines, is lopsidedly
devoted to the issue of why the deed should *not* be done, which suggests that

Macbeth is already emotionally decided on the issue and that he is seeking intellectual and moral support for his disinclination. First, it is the practical aspect of the issue that occupies his mind and then, to reinforce it, comes the moral question which, turning to religion, rouses the horror image of outraged pity. The moral question, in its order of occurrence, and position in the passage, suggests its auxiliary nature, its importance as a reinforcement of the claims of practicality and prudence—for there is no feeling on Macbeth's part, either before or after the deed, of a kinsman, host, or subject towards Duncan, and there is no revulsion towards himself either of having violated those bonds. It is, for Macbeth, only the 'deed'—'I have done the deed', a doing or a daring for the 'soldier', for the 'man'. But what acts as an *effective* deterrent or support for his unwillingness is the image of horror in the guise of pity:

> And Pity, like a naked new-born babe,
> Striding the blast, or heaven's Cherubins, hors'd
> Upon the sightless couriers of the air,
> Shall blow the horrid deed in every eye
> That tears shall drown the wind   (I. vii. 21–5)

But how subsidiary the question of morality or even consequence is to Macbeth is brought home to us in the image of the 'intent' as horse ('I have no spur To prick the sides of my intent'). This 'horse' has to oppose the 'horse' of the new-born babe ('Striding') and the heaven's Cherubins ('hors'd') who 'shall blow the horrid deed in every eye, That tears shall drown the wind'—the power suggested in those words symbolising the power of the 'horse' to be opposed. And in relation to the 'horse', Macbeth's ambition is a 'rider' ('Vaulting ambition'), and is on par with 'spur'. There is regret in the words—'I have no spur', 'but only'—and Macbeth is, deep down, deploring his helpless condition. But the 'horse' of the intent is there in its vitality (mark, also, the tension the word *intent* suggests), and it is Lady Macbeth that provides the 'spur'.

It is the 'male' and the 'man' in Macbeth, that his wife prods and rouses to action. But to rouse the 'elemental' male in Macbeth, she has to be herself the elemental female, a possessed Agave tearing her child to pieces, in the frenzied passage:

> I would, while it was smiling in my face,
> Have pluck'd my nipple from his boneless gums,
> And dash'd the brains out   (I. vii. 56–8)

Lady Macbeth's words have the desired effect on Macbeth. Macbeth's words witness the response of the 'male', the 'man' in Macbeth:

> Bring forth men-children only!
> For thy undaunted mettle should compose
> Nothing but males   (I. vii. 73–5)

Macbeth has to be his elemental biological self, the male, to deal with the elemental fear. And, what is more, Lady Macbeth also seeks to be 'Unsex'-ed, to be the 'male' or 'man'. They both repeat the word 'man' so frequently and obsessively that the word itself becomes a kind of chant to charge them into that state.

For Macbeth, being a soldier is not a mere profession. It is bound up with the fact of his fear—'native disposition'—and his consequent obsession with being 'man'. His soldiership is his self-expression and his style of dealing with fear. How else would Macbeth, except as a soldier dramatise his fears in making 'Strange images of death' and thus reassure himself of his bravery? Lady Macbeth knows that her words go home and draw the proper response from Macbeth when she says in the sleep-walking scene: 'Fie, my Lord, fie, a soldier, and afeard?' So intimate is the role of a soldier for Macbeth that it is almost indistinguishable from his character. Macbeth is more soldier than Lear is king. Towards the end, when Macbeth feels that there is no possibility of hope for him and the thought of suicide occurs to him, he asks:

> Why should I play the Roman fool, and die
> On mine sword? Whiles I see lives, the gashes
> Do better upon them   (V. viii. 1–3)

Macbeth cannot abdicate his role, in life or in death, for to do so is to falsify what is obviously his life-time involvement with fear. It is in the role of a soldier he lives most vividly, and though he knows, on confronting Macduff, that Macduff 'hath cow'd my better part of man', yet he cannot but be a soldier—'before my body I throw my warlike shield'—and there is the final challenging of death by Macbeth in his cry:

>   lay on, Macduff;
> And damn'd be him that first cries,
> 'Hold, enough!'   (V. ix. 33–4)

Fear, therefore, is both the destiny and the fate of Macbeth. It whets him where it hurts him. It is through fear—fear which is the tension between life and death—that Macbeth apprehends life as vividly as he does death. Referring to Macbeth's daring of death in the Banquet scene ('approach thou like the rugged Russian bear . . .'), Bradley observed: 'These, when they arise, hold him spell-bound and possess him wholly, like a hypnotic trance which is at the same time the ecstasy of the poet.'[8] Macbeth's horror does have the vividness and vitality of a poet's vision. When he speaks of the 'taste of fears', there is a poet's relish of the emotion. In the passage:

> I have almost forgot the taste of fears
> The time has been, my senses would have cool'd
> To hear a night-shriek . . .   (V. v. 9–11)

there is regret that he has 'almost forgot the taste of fears' and a nostalgia in the tone.

Macbeth's fear is also his measure of sensitivity, his test of being alive. Macbeth needs fear for his conviction of the reality of life and death. It is the peculiar medium of his acute perceptions. To take away fear from him is to take away his *taste* of both life and death. Twice Macbeth is 'rapt' in the dream of kingship—once when the witches prophesy it ('He seems rapt withal'), and again when Ross announces the new honour ('Look, how our partner's rapt'). Macbeth himself confesses his ecstasy to his wife—'I stood rapt in the wonder of it'. 'Rapt' and 'wonder' are the apt terms that identify the poetic sensibility of Macbeth for whom life in its joy strikes as a vision just as death in its horror affects him as a nightmare. The ecstasy is a lived dream, a dream that holds him in a trance as he experiences it in the exquisite phrase—'the swelling act of the imperial theme', the expansion ('swelling') into the grandeur of supreme power that Rome ('imperial') symbolises. Macbeth who has been pursued by death and is desperately seeking freedom from it, and the power to secure that freedom, realises in that phrase both freedom ('swelling', 'cabin'd, cribb'd, confin'd') and supreme power ('imperial theme')—his beatific vision of life, which the words 'rapt' and 'wonder' precisely identify.

It is in vivid sensuous concretes that the experiences of life—and death—come to Macbeth. The 'wine of life is drawn' from a life without significance; age is 'days fallen into the sere, yellow leaf'; sleep is 'the balm of hurt minds, sore labour's bath', death is sleep 'after life's fitful fever'; murdered Banquo shakes his 'gory locks'; murdered Duncan has his 'silver skin lac'd with the golden blood'. There is also a certain largeness and richness to Macbeth's conception of life. A rich life is 'honour, love, obedience and troops of friends', to drink happily is to 'Be large in mirth' and to ask to 'Give me some wine, fill full', and freedom is to be 'broad and general as the casing air'.

And because life is so rich and sensuous, death which is an annihilation of this, strikes Macbeth as horror—horror which is apprehensible to the senses, vivid and dire, to his poetic sensibility. The horror is 'the naked new-born babe, Striding the blast'; fear is 'gory locks'. But the horror or the fear, while it deters him, also draws out the soldier in him. He responds to the challenge with the verve and dash of a soldier—the 'bravura of bravery',[9] to use Robert B. Heilman's phrase. It is the warrior that leaps to the defence of the poet—and Macbeth is, in a profound sense, a 'warrior poet'.

Macbeth is 'king'—in taste ('swelling act of the imperial theme'), valour ('valour's minion') and royal blood ('I am his kinsman'). It is only the law, the law of morality, that stands in his way. It does not seem 'unreasonable' that he should desire to be king. His vital impulses are such that it seems almost inevitable that he should do what he is doing in order to realise them. There is behind his doings a subtle force of a claim, a compulsion which a claim induces, a sense of obligation ('an appalling sense of duty'[10] as Bradley put it), a vital impulse beneath what is apparently a criminal compulsion. Therefore, the moral issue in the problem does not strike Macbeth as 'true', and when he talks of the moral implications of the deed before murdering, he is not 'really' there: he is 'rationalising' his fear.

To dare the 'terrible feat' Macbeth has to be part of what he is daring; he has to work himself into the state of horror. In the soliloquy before the murder of Duncan ('Is this a dagger . . .') the imagery points to the charged state of Macbeth before he proceeds to murder Duncan. Macbeth sees a vivid vision of a dagger— 'thy blade, and dudgeon, gouts of blood' (mark the apostrophising 'thy' which further dramatises the 'reality' of the dagger)—invokes the diabolism of 'Pale Hecate's Off'rings' and the lust of 'Tarquin's ravishing strides', and hopes that no distraction takes 'the present horror from the time which suits it'. And he proceeds, as the bell strikes, in the 'present horror', to do the murder.

A certain incredibility or a kind of possessedness goes with Macbeth's murdering of Duncan. Macbeth had to do what was to him the ultimate in his daring. Both in that *he* did it because he must, and in that, perhaps, *something else* did it through him, Macbeth has to feel 'innocent' about the deed. Naturally, immediately after the murder, he asks, perplexed and anguished: 'But wherefore could not I pronounce "Amen"? I had most need of blessing.' The word 'wherefore' has a greater force than 'why' and acquires further emphasis when followed by 'but', for Macbeth knows that there is no culpable *'there'* to his 'crime' to account for a 'therefore' in it for the denial of 'blessing' to him. (And, further, when Macbeth says 'Glamis hath muther'd Sleep, and therefore Cawdor Shall sleep no more, Macbeth shall sleep no more!', he is pointing to the apparent illogicality of 'Cawdor' and 'Macbeth' being punished for the crime of 'Glamis'—implying thereby that what he did as Glamis has no more culpable bearing on him than if he had done it in a state of possession or trance.) In saying that he had 'most need' of blessing, he not only implies his innocence as to the guards, but emphasises a greater deserving or need of protection against the external evil than them, for he has been haunted by it more than they. There is deep anguish in his persistent dwelling on it in spite of his wife's attempts to dissuade him from it.

It is significant that Macbeth, unlike Othello who, in a similar situation of murder, invites damnation—'whip me ye devils, From the possession of this heavenly sight. Blow me about in winds. Roast me in sulphur'[11]—regards himself as an innocent victim of it and agonises over the fact that the blessings of God are denied to him. Othello sees and recognises his guilt, but Macbeth cannot; his involvement in the deed is of a different dimension. So much so, that after the knocking, seeing his own hands of blood, he asks incredulously, 'What hands are here?' and agonises: 'Ha! They pluck out mine eyes.' Macbeth cannot pluck out his eyes like a sinner who has seen his sin, for unlike Oedipus he is not there in the sin. It is not because he is too close to the crime, and too dazed to recognise his guilt. It is just that the nature of his involvement and responsibility is of a different kind, for long after the crime he could still say, with innocence:

They have tied me to a stake: I cannot fly,
But, bear-like, I must fight the course   (V. vii. 1–2)

Nor is there any statement of remorse on his part, anywhere in the play, as from a sinner or a criminal: there is anguish and agony, but Macbeth does not see them as something that he deserves. He is a victim in a hostile universe and he is fighting, 'bear-like . . . the course'. When he learns, towards the end, that 'Macduff was from his mother's womb Untimely ripp'd' he finds that 'it hath cowed my better part of man' and says 'I'll not fight with thee', but, nevertheless, with the better part of him cowed in him, he still dares to fight him with a challenging cry—'lay on . . . '. Where there is a suggestion of regret, remorse or a sense of guilt, there is a curious process of rationalisation. The Macbeth who says

> Of all men else I have avoided thee:
> But get thee back, my soul is too much charg'd
> With blood of thine already.   (V. viii. 5–7)

is either 'rationalising' or 'placating' Macduff, as Kenneth Muir and Robert B. Heilman suggest. Quoting Chambers who thinks that it is 'the only touch of remorse in Macbeth'—mark the word *only*—Muir asks: 'Or is he rationalising?';[12] Heilman adds: 'Possibly too, he is unconsciously placating the man.'[13] To authenticate re- morse or a sense of guilt on the part of Macbeth it would be necessary to establish Macbeth's recognition of the crime and his moral responsibility in regard to it. The problem is bound up with Macbeth's integrity as 'man' of which his being a soldier is the self-expression. It is his nature—'yet do I fear thy nature'—that determines the kind of involvement he has in his conflict with the world. Macbeth has to fight, he is condemned to fight, and in his fighting he has his peculiar being.

But Macbeth cannot kill himself. To destroy something, the preservation of which has been his life-time obsession, would be to falsify the fight, his relation to the world and, above all, the truth of his being. It has been given to Macbeth to look into the face of Horror and begin his career where Mr. Kurtz's ended: Mr. Kurtz comes to Horror corrupted, and the Horror he looks into spells his death. Mac- beth's peculiar privilege is to face it, combat it and thus achieve the vital dignity that fighting confers on the fighter—the bear, that must 'bear-like . . . fight the course'. In comparing himself to the bear Macbeth identifies the vital streak in his character. Macbeth in being 'man', is being vividly himself when he is fighting soldier-like or dying soldier-like on the battlefield. And in this battle, Macbeth's sorrow is still in vital terms. His sorrow in this struggle is not his realisation of the outrage of human morals, but the tragic awareness of his dwindling energy, age and battle fatigue—'I have liv'd long enough: My way of life Is fall'n into the sere, the yellow leaf . . . '; time stretches endlessly for him and there is no end, no respite of death: 'To-morrow, and to-morrow, and to-morrow, Creeps in this petty pace from day to day . . .' and 'I 'gin to be aweary of the sun And wish th'estate o'th' world were now undone . . . '.

Macbeth has to be judged in terms of the ethics that govern his own involve- ment in life. To induct the play's moral prejudice into Macbeth's vital consciousness, and consequently into the imaginative consciousness of the play, is to destroy the autonomy of Macbeth's vital—and the play's imaginative—integrity. The play is bifocal: the moral truth in the play is subjacent to its imaginative one. Illustratively Macbeth is evil; but experientially Macbeth is life-in-death. The 'evil Macbeth' points to himself: the 'vital Macbeth' points to something that issues beyond himself, something that sustains him and what he fights, both the perplexed Ahab and his intangible whale. His anguished cry 'But wherefore could not I pronounce "Amen" ' is taken beyond society, to the realm of religion, and his very protest is the establishment of his 'innocence' before God.

NOTES

[1] L. C. Knights, *Explorations*, London, 1958: p. 18.
[2] L. C. Knights, *Some Shakespearean Themes*, London, 1959: p. 120.
[3] Kenneth Muir, *Macbeth*, London, 1964: p. lxxii.
[4] Ibid., p. lix.
[5] Robert B. Heilman in *Shakespeare Survey 19:* (Ed.) Kenneth Muir, Cambridge, 1966: p. 13.
[6] A. C. Bradley, *Shakespearean Tragedy*, London, 1961: p. 296.
[7] Ibid., p. 296.
[8] Ibid., pp. 296–7.
[9] *Shakespeare Survey 19*, p. 19.
[10] A. C. Bradley, op. cit., p. 300.
[11] *Othello*: V. vii. 278–9.
[12] Kenneth Muir (Ed.), *Macbeth*, p. 165.
[13] Robert B. Heilman: *Shakespeare Survey 19*, p. 16.

Carolyn Asp

TRAGIC ACTION AND SEXUAL STEREOTYPING IN *MACBETH*

Almost without exception people feel constrained to play roles in accordance with what they believe to be the expectations of others. The individual suspects that he can only become a part of his society through performing roles which are defined by both negative and positive sanctions of law, custom, and accepted norms of behavior. A stereotype is an intensification of a role which typifies in an unvarying pattern a conception, opinion, or belief concerning appropriate modes of behavior. Stereotypes frequently narrow the expression of human personality and the range of authentic sexual identity by embodying a conventional and superficial view of the roles men and women are to play in social interaction and even in their perceptions of themselves. They not only make self-knowledge difficult; they impede authentic communication and create a society in which fixed ideas and modes of response are accepted and even admired. Because stereotypes focus on one aspect of the personality and disregard or denigrate others, they create models which, ironically, are almost impossible to embody because they fragment and narrow the personality rather than unify or express it.

The examination of sexual stereotyping is one of Shakespeare's enduring interests, and is found in plays as diverse as *Much Ado About Nothing* and *Antony and Cleopatra.* In *Macbeth* the phenomenon of such stereotyping is highly developed and central to the tragic action. Lady Macbeth consciously attempts to reject her feminine sensibility and adopt a male mentality because she perceives that her society equates feminine qualities with weakness. The dichotomy between role and nature which ensues ends with her mental disintegration and suicide.[1] Macbeth's case is more complicated. In the play the male stereotype is associated with violence made socially and ethically acceptable through the ritual of warfare. Under the urging of his wife, Macbeth not only accepts the narrow definition of manhood that the stereotype imposes but he agrees to act that role for self-aggrandizement. Unlike his wife's role-assumption, Macbeth's is not in conflict with his nature; rather, it is an expression of a certain aspect of it. It tempts him to exercise godlike power through the violence it calls courage and aspire to freedom from consequences and

From *Studies in Philology* 78, No. 2 (Spring 1981): 153–69.

invulnerability from mortal danger. But because it releases anarchic forces within him and allows him to give full play to his intense egoism, it seals his doom both psychologically and socially.

When the play opens, Macbeth is presented as the most complete representative of a society which values and honors a manliness and soldiership that maintain the cohesiveness of the tribe by extreme violence, if necessary. Even before he appears on stage he is admiringly described as the quintessential warrior, the upholder of tribal unity in the face of rebellion. The account of his battle with Macdonwald is meant to portray him as a man of fearless courage whose valor is the very symbol of his manhood, yet the description of the traitor's disembowelment emphasizes cruelty and violence rather than courage. In the eyes of his peers and his sovereign, however, he is the "brave" and "noble" Macbeth. In such a world, as Edmund says in *King Lear*, "to be tender minded/Does not become a sword" (V.iii.31–2). Ironically, it is the "gracious" Duncan who is the only man in the play who could be called "tender minded." Thanking his generals, he exclaims, "My plenteous joys/Wanton in fullness, seek to hide themselves/In drops of sorrow" (I.iv.33–5).[2] Duncan's sentimental joy over the bloody victory emphasizes the fundamental weakness of a warrior society that condones and rewards in its heroes a violence that, unregulated by ritual or power, can turn against it. The conviction that valor is the whole of virtue (*virtus*) can displace the values of peace with those of war and cause the metamorphosis of the human into inhuman being.

Among the warriors expressions of tenderness are considered either degrading or counter-productive. When Rosse is moved to tears by Lady Macduff's complaints, he says, "I am so much the fool, should I stay longer,/It would be my disgrace, and your discomfort" (IV.ii.28–9). Anguished by the news of his family's massacre, Macduff tries to repress his tears, admitting that they make him "play the woman." Urged by Malcolm to "dispute it like a man," he at first rejects the stereotypical response and tells the prince, "I must also feel it like a man," that is, like a complete human being who can integrate both feminine and masculine responses. It is significant that at this major turning point in the action Shakespeare emphasizes the full humanity of Macduff, the pre-ordained instrument of retribution. If only for a moment he transcends the stereotype. Then under the pressure of Malcolm he converts his "feminine" grief to manly revenge, crying out: "front to front,/Bring thou this fiend of Scotland and myself!/Within my sword's length set him" (IV.iii.235–7). Only a fully human warrior can confront and conquer the "fiend" that Macbeth has become.

The manly stereotype in this play exceeds the limits of soldierly valor and embraces the extreme of retaliatory violence. This attitude permeates society from noble to bondsman. On one end of the scale Macduff's cry "He has no children!" voices his frustration at being balked of complete vengeance. On the other end, the murderers whom Macbeth suborns to kill Banquo assert, "We are men, my liege" when Macbeth asks them if they will suffer Banquo's "crimes." Macbeth agrees that "in the catalogue ye go for men" (III.i.91), yet he makes a distinction between the catalogue of men and the "valu'd file": there is no basis for identity as a man merely in declaring one's male gender or membership in the human race. In Macbeth's mind manhood is not a constant, fixed quality but one which must continually be proved by manly deeds. So he asks them to define themselves further: "Now if you have a station in the file/Not i'th'worst rank of manhood, say't" (III.i.101–2). One declares that the vile buffets of the world have incensed him to recklessness; the other, weary with disasters, would set his life on any chance. Both men dare to take the course of their lives into their own hands and prove their manhood in violently self-assertive action. Under Macbeth's questioning, a sophistical syllogism emerges from the conversation: the valued man is the courageous man; the courageous man will dare even murder to right the wrongs done to him; therefore, the valued man is he who will dare to commit murder. By this reasoning, Macbeth justifies himself as well as his agents.

Although a definition of manhood in terms of qualities such as daring and ruthlessness is not totally invalid, it is incomplete,[3] as Macbeth knows in his deepest being. Initially he rejects his wife's call to violence, emphasizing the limits that circumscribe human/humane action: "I dare do all that may become a man,/Who dares do more is none" (I.vii.46–7). He fears the inhuman, godlike power that overstepping the limits implies; he fears to lose his humanity in the exercise of "manly" deeds. Macbeth has an inchoate grasp of the idea that being human means accepting the limits imposed by social interconnectedness, by one's rank and role. He cherishes the "golden opinions" he has won from his peers by circumscribed action. Although he seems unsure of his own relationship to the concept of true manhood, he can recognize in Banquo a complete man whose "royalty of nature" and sexual potency he fears yet admires. Macbeth admits that Banquo, like himself, "dares much," yet

> . . . to that dauntless temper of his mind,
> He hath a wisdom that doth guide his valour
> To act in safety.   (III.i.49–51)

As Eugene Waith comments: "True manhood is a comprehensive ideal, growing out of the familiar Christian concept that man is between beasts and angels in the hierarchy of creation. To be worthy of this station, a man must show more than physical valor which characterizes the soldier and traditionally distinguishes the male of the species."[4]

A major part of Macbeth's agony is created by his recognition of what constitutes full manhood and his conflicting acceptance of an incomplete stereotype. Why, knowing what he does, does he accept it? Because he succumbs to the temptation that faces every tragic hero set within a world of limits, the temptation to override those limits and establish himself as an omnipotent center of reference. The stereotype gives Macbeth a role whereby to act out a species of godlike power which manifests itself in the ability to take human life with impunity. The tragic irony of his situation, of which he gradually becomes aware, is that in the actualization of this "godlike" potential he becomes inhuman, less the man, in the full understanding of the word.

The text indicates that Macbeth is an effective killer on the battlefield, but as a representative figure, he is no more violent than any man could be, nor is he any more of a killer than the warriors who are his peers. What differentiates Macbeth from other males in the play is his intense awareness of the potential for violence within him and his willingness to entertain *unrestricted* fantasies as to how that potential might be used. Immediately after his first encounter with the Weird Sisters he asks himself:

> ... why do I yield to that suggestion
> Whose horrid image doth unfix my hair,
> And make my seated heart knock at my ribs
> Against the use of nature?   (I.iii.134–7)

Later he bids the stars hide their fires lest his dark desires be exposed to even a glimmer of light. He is a man terrified yet fascinated by the power within him. This is why he initially seeks limits, calling upon the restraints that morality and society can impose upon him. When his wife describes him as "too full of the milk of human kindness," she bases her interpretation of his character on those energies of restraint (fear, human respect, conscience) to which he conforms his outward behavior. Understanding his fascination with violence but not his terror of its effects, she forces him to ask himself whether or not he dares to risk acting out the potential that is in him in order to objectify the possibilities of his self. If he does not dare, will he ever know himself and his possibilities? The question he must ask himself is whether or not the consequences of purely self-defining action will destroy his humanity. Macbeth senses that once he enacts his deep desires he will be radically transformed. Inhuman energy will be generated from this commitment to self-realization uninhibited by responsibility. He, even more than his wife, realizes clearly that "what is done, is done/And cannot be undone." Since the effort to be inhuman is essential to the service of Mars, the limited definition of manhood associated with soldierly valor is perfectly suited to Macbeth's project of self-divinization.

In Macbeth's Scotland, violence and its accompanying qualities are limited to the male. Women are subordinate to men and divorced from political influence because they lack those qualities that would fit them for a warrior society. Rosse, describing Scotland's dire state, says that the crisis is so unnatural it would "make our women fight" (IV.iii.187). This comment suggests that Shakespeare took liberties with his source in order to create an artistic world in which he could examine male and female stereotypes. Holinshed actually writes of this period that "in these daies also the women of our countries were of no lesse courage than the men; for all stout maidens and wives (if they were not with child) marched as well in the field as did the men, and so soone as the armie did set forward, they slue the first living creature that they found, in whose bloud they not onlie bathed their swords, but also tasted thereof with their mouthes."[5] The stereotypical role of women in the play, however, defines them as weak, dependent, non-political, incapable of dealing with violence except to become its victims. After Duncan's murder, when Lady

Macbeth demands to know "what's the business," Macduff describes the typical feminine reaction to such news:

O gentle lady,
'Tis not for you to hear what I can speak:
The repetition in a woman's ear,
Would murther as it fell.   (II.iii.84–6)

Macduff, like Hotspur, refuses to share his political life with his wife; instead, he leaves for England without a word to her.[6] She resents his departure and interprets it as a desertion. Rosse, in a patronizing manner, counsels her to "school" herself, excusing Macduff's behavior on the grounds that her husband is "noble, wise, judicious," in political life and must, as a result, be a good husband and father. Even though Macduff and his wife seem to be the normative couple in the play, their communication with and understanding of each other fall far short of that exhibited between Macbeth and his wife early in the action. Until he is bowed by calamity, Macduff lacks the capability for sympathetic communion that Macbeth possesses: he fails to foresee his wife's sorrow and anger and he seems unaware of the real danger to which he has exposed his family by his absence. The action of the play proves his wife's complaints to be justified. Significantly, Macduff and Lady Macduff never appear on the stage together.

In his conversation with Malcolm, Macduff exhibits a condescending attitude toward women, whom he separates into saints and whores. When Malcolm claims to be an arch-voluptuary, Macduff cynically assures him:

We have willing dames enough; there cannot be
That vulture in you, to devour so many
As will to greatness dedicate themselves.   (IV.iii.72–4)

On the other hand, he approves of the fact that Malcolm's mother was "oftener upon her knees than on her feet,/Died every day she liv'd" (IV.iii.110–13), a royal hermitess rather than an imperial jointress.

In a society in which femininity is divorced from strength and womanliness is equated with weakness, where the humane virtues are associated with womanliness, the strong woman finds herself hemmed in psychologically, forced to reject her own womanliness, to some extent, if she is to be true to her strength. Lady Macbeth is such a woman, worthy of the equality her husband bestows upon her early in their relationship when he calls her "my dearest partner of greatness." Macbeth here shows himself remarkably free from the chauvinistic attitudes that dominate his society. It certainly seems his intent to share power with her and establish a kind of joint-rule that would fly in the face of custom. It is obvious that she is attracted by the prospect of wielding power in her own right, but there is no evidence to indicate that she wants royal status for herself alone. Convinced that she must work through her husband if they are both to attain greatness, she scrutinizes his weaknesses and determines to "chastise with the valour of [her] tongue/All that impedes [him] from the golden round" (I.v.29–30). Her valor throughout the play is, as she describes it here, primarily rhetorical. Her role, as she perceives it, is to evoke her husband's "noble strength" so that he can act in accord with his desires. To do this she must appeal as a woman to his manliness as well as channel her energies into maintaining a persona of masculine courage. As Rosenberg observes, masculine and feminine impulses are at war within her; she is unable either to fuse them or to polarize them.[7]

Lady Macbeth has so internalized the stereotypes of her society that she is convinced that she must divest herself of her femininity if she is to have any effect on the public life of her husband. She calls upon the "murdering ministers" to turn her maternal milk to vengeful gall, to "unsex" her so that she may become "the fierce and terrible instigator of murder."[8] Yet, in spite of her dire invocations, her conscious desire to take on a male psyche, her fundamental, even unconscious femininity breaks through the surface of her arguments with her husband before Duncan's murder. In these arguments she wages a sexual assault which can only be successful if Macbeth perceives her as intensely female.[9] When she describes him as a husband/lover who, like his hope of glory, has become "pale," "green," and "waning," she challenges an essential element of his self-image, that of potent male, which is the foundation of all his other roles. To be the heroic warrior, to be king, he must first act the man with her. When this role is threatened by her scorn, when the symbol of his whole enterprise is found to be flaccid or unacceptable ("from this time,/Such I account thy love" I.vii.38–9), the collapse of what might be called the male ego is imminent. She implies that she *will* find him unacceptable if he is afraid "to be the same in [his] own act and valour/As [he is] in desire" (I.vii.40–1). Only if he dares to do the deed will he be a man, and so much more the man, in her esteem. The whole argument to murder is couched in sexual terms: she accuses him of arousing her expectations and then failing to follow through with action. What man would not try to disprove that accusation?

What potency is to the male, maternity is to the female. Lady Macbeth plays on both of these physical/psychological states that are fundamentally associated with the sexual stereotypes in the play. On the one hand, she taunts her husband to show his potency in performance; on the other, she offers to negate her own maternal power as an example of her dedication. While her rhetoric of violence convinces her husband to move beyond the limit and take on the role of "manly" murderer, the images she uses refer directly to her physical femaleness: "I would . . ./Have pluck'd my nipple from his boneless gums" (I.vii.56–7). Macbeth's admiring command ironically affirms the very maternal instinct she boasts of denying:

> Bring forth men children only!
> For thy undaunted mettle should compose
> Nothing but males. (I.vii.73–5)

Finally, she assures him of invincibility. When he hesitates, entertaining the possibility of failure and discovery, she merely asks contemptuously: "We fail?" She affirms that daring and courage will overcome all obstacles, an idea later echoed by the prophecies: "Be bloody, bold and resolute" (IV.i.79).

In spite of her pragmatic and ruthless rhetoric, it is obvious that the gall in her breasts has not been sufficient to unsex Lady Macbeth.[10] She admits that she has relied on wine to make her bold and give her fire, qualities normally associated with the masculine temperament. When Macbeth appears after the murder she calls him "my husband," the only time in the play she addresses him by that familiar title that emphasizes the sexual bond between them. It connotes a certain desired reliance on his strength, indicating that she is not as independent as the stress of her role demands. The staccato rhythm of her speech preceding and just after her husband's entrance betrays an anxiety that not even the wine can mitigate. It is only when she realizes that her husband is losing control that she resumes the dominant role she would much rather he played.

Ironically, her assumption of a masculine role does not create partnership; rather, it distances Lady Macbeth from her husband. As long as he retained elements of so-called feminine sensibility, he was susceptible to her appeal: there was a "weakness" in him that responded to her challenge. After he fully assumes the stereotype she urges upon him, there is nothing in him she can manipulate. Her dream of being partner to his greatness is doomed by the very means she has used to insure that greatness. By making him "manly" she has guaranteed that he will think of her as subordinate and unworthy of truly sharing power. Her action shares with his a peculiarly self-defeating thrust.

After Duncan's murder Lady Macbeth begins to admit the breakdown of congruence between the role she is playing and the person she is; alone, she admits: "Nought's had, all's spent, / Where our desire's got without content" (III.ii.4–5). A dawning realization of the self (her repressed dimension of womanliness) behind the mask is essential to her tragic identity.[11] When Macbeth morosely enters she resumes the mask and acts the strong companion. Unmoved, her husband echoes her internal apprehensions:

> Better be with the dead,
> Whom we, to gain our peace, have sent to peace,
> Than on the torture of the mind to lie
> In restless ecstasy.   (III.ii.19–22)

Although united in the same embrace of misery, each is isolated in a separate world of suffering. "The affliction of these terrible dreams / That shake us nightly" (III.ii.18–19) drives the partners apart even in the marriage bed.

It is ironic that throughout this scene Macbeth addresses his wife in terms of intimacy and affection, calling her "love," and "dearest chuck," while at the same time, he deliberately deceives her about the murder of Banquo. It is evident that she is no longer in his confidence, for when she asks "what's to be done?" he tells her "be ignorant of the knowledge . . . till thou applaud the deed" (III.ii.45). His refusal to answer her question parallels Macduff's earlier reluctance to answer her when she inquired "What's the business?" It can be argued that Macbeth deceives his wife to protect her from implication in Banquo's murder, yet in spite of this overtly good motive, his attitude reveals a patronizing and stereotyped point of view. In their conversation it is almost as though Macbeth is testing his wife's reactions. When he remarks in a seemingly casual way that "Banquo and his Fleance lives" her answer comes up to the mark: "But in them Nature's copy's not eterne" (III.ii.38). It is a subdued response, lacking her earlier vehemence and conviction. It cannot be that Macbeth wishes to protect her from the *fact* of the murder since he drops too many hints as to the nature of the deed. His tactic seems geared deliberately to impress upon her that it is he who has planned and initiated the action that will result in Banquo's death, that he has internalized her "bloody instructions" so successfully that he no longer needs her. When he perceives that she "marvels" at his words, he lamely justifies his conduct by telling her "Things bad begun make strong themselves by ill" (III.ii.55).

The last time we see Macbeth and his wife together is during the banquet scene as they attempt to preside over the festivities. As the scene opens Macbeth reiterates certain norms that guide human and humane conduct: "You know your degrees," (III.iv.1) he tells his guests, emphasizing the structure of hierarchy and limit that governs responsible social interaction. The banquet itself is an archetypal human situation which involves feasting and communality: it symbolizes that "living with" or conviviality that is the keynote of humane behavior. Macbeth can only play at being a part of the human scene: "Ourself will mingle with society/And *play* the humble host" (III.iv.4–5 [italics mine]). Lady Macbeth significantly "keeps her state," remaining apart from the group. When the inhuman world breaks in upon him in the form of Banquo's ghost, his wife, oblivious to the phenomenon, berates him for not even acting "the man." Her failure to see the ghost indicates that she has no real affinity with the realm of the inhuman. Macbeth, on the other hand, seems to have the power not only to communicate with this realm but actually to conjure it. The ghost appears only after Macbeth hypocritically wishes that Banquo were present. When Lady Macbeth asks him the old question "Are you a man?," he affirms the stereotype: "Ay, and a bold one, that dare look on that/Which might appall the Devil" (III.iv.58–9). It is obvious then that Macbeth does not fear the ghost itself but what the ghost signifies: the extent and limits of his own power. This encounter is a moment of truth in which Macbeth clearly sees his affinity with and power over the inhuman world; his ability to summon the ghost, even inadvertently, proves how far he has stepped beyond the limits of humanity. In this confrontation he hysterically resorts to violent physical prowess as his standard of courage: "What man dare, I dare" (III.iv.98), he boasts.[12] Like the old Macbeth, he longs to prove himself in single combat: "Be alive again,/And dare me to the desert with thy sword" (III.iv.102–3); but Banquo represents a realm of existence with which Macbeth is engaged but which he cannot confront with a sword. At the same time that the ghost affirms Macbeth's alienation from the human community it also manifests the limits that plague his ambition to act with impunity. The role of manliness may allow him to act with imagined godlike freedom but it cannot guarantee that the deed will be done when it is done. The ghost is a reminder that although Banquo may be dead, Macbeth cannot escape the consequences of that death. It thrusts the very conditions of his humanness into his face:

> ... the time has been
> That, when the brains were out, the man would die,
> And there an end; but now they rise again,
> With twenty mortal murders on their crowns,
> And push us from our stools.   (III.iv.77–81)

As Macbeth had conjured up the apparition so he dismisses it, calling it an "unreal mockery," asserting that "it being gone/I am a man again" (III.iv.107). For Macbeth, "being a man" has become synonymous with being invulnerable to conscience, fear, or compassion, in a word, with assuming to himself godlike qualities and powers. Throughout the banquet he is almost completely divorced from the human situation of which he is the center; he creates "most admir'd disorder" by his obsessive engagement with the realm of the inhuman. The feast disintegrates, bonds of fellowship and rank are disregarded, and Lady Macbeth commands the guests, "Stand not upon the order of your going,/But go at once" (III.iv.118–19).

Just as Macbeth was oblivious to his guests during the banquet, so he is oblivious to his wife after it. Focused intensely inward, he plots in solitude his future schemes. The distance between husband and wife is accentuated by the formal "Sir" with which she addresses him. As in Act II, scene ii, the action concludes with Lady Macbeth's invitation to bed: "You lack the season of all natures, sleep" (III.iv.140), a subtle hint expressing her need for the intimacy of the boudoir. Macbeth, however, is preoccupied with his determination to seek out the Weird Sisters: "now I am bent to know,/By the worst means, the worst" (III.iv.133–4). Preternatural knowledge means control, domination; it is an intrusive, penetrating activity, a kind of masculine sexual equivalent. His wife's invitation to literal sexual consummation pales before the intensity of Macbeth's psychic need. The ravenous desire to control futurity, to reinforce his invincible image, drives him to move actively towards these representatives of the inhuman realm. By the end of this scene Macbeth has taken a significant step away from his own humanity: he is content that his actions be mechanical, unreflective, untouched by considerations of conscience. "Strange things I have in head," he boasts, "that will to hand,/Which must be acted, ere they may be scann'd" (III.iv.138–9).

In the human realm knowledge of events is the male prerogative; in the preternatural realm, on the contrary, it belongs to the sexually ambiguous Weird Sisters. In a perverse way they suggest a debased image of the hermaphroditic figure, a figure to whom sexual stereotypes are simply not applicable. Can we say that the inhuman, as represented by these creatures, is also the sexually undifferentiated? They are mysterious and powerful not only because of their knowledge but also because of the spontaneity and unpredictability that freedom from stereotypes allows. They come and go as they please; they will not be interrogated or commanded. Macbeth tells his wife: "When I burn'd in desire to question them further, they made themselves air, into which they vanish'd" (I.v.4–5).

When the Weird Sisters first encounter Macbeth they present him with a vision of his destiny that tempts him to create his own future through an action that can only be performed if he accepts a false stereotype of manliness: murder becomes the means he must use to create actively his destiny and he can only commit murder by linking the image of the murderer to that of the male.[13] They show him what he could be. The question is: will he aggressively create himself or will he passively let events work their way? At first he resolves: "If chance will have me king, why, chance/May crown me without my stir" (I.iv.143–4). Yet Macbeth has always shaped his life by will and action; he is by nature one who takes the significance of his existence into his own hands. Finally, he rejects passivity and takes control of his future. In his second encounter with the Weird Sisters he demands that the prophecies be presented by the "masters," presumably demons who assume the shapes of the apparitions. These prophecies enkindle in him the false certainty that he can eliminate limitations, restrictions, and ultimately the threat of his own mortality if only he intensifies the male stereotype: "Be bloody, bold and resolute"; "be lion-mettled and proud" (IV.i.79; 90). The promise of security is his greatest enemy because it blinds him to the truth of his contingent status as a human being. If no man of woman born shall harm Macbeth, then he has achieved a godlike invulnerability which allows him to act without restraint or fear: "the very firstlings of my heart shall be the firstlings of my hand" (IV.i.147–8). It is this very type of action, however, that dooms him to destruction under the sword of Macduff.

As Macbeth strives to emulate "marble-wholeness," his wife splits apart psychically under the pressure of his indifference and her remorse. Her agony of spirit and deep dividedness burst forth without her conscious awareness in the sleep-walking scene. On the one hand she exhibits fearless determination: "What need we fear who knows it, when none can call our power to account?" (V.i.36). She uses the plural "our" when she speaks of power, indicating that it had been her desire and intent to share, a fantasy she can only live out in nightmares. On the other hand, she exhibits a horror of the deeds and their consequences: "What, will these hands ne'er be clean?" (V.i.42). Significantly, in her sleep she relives the mastery over her husband she no longer has: "Fie, my lord, fie, a soldier and afeard?" (V.i.36). Her final words, however, are a pathetic expession of her need for comfort and union: "come, give me your hand . . . To bed, to bed, to bed" (V.i.68). As in the early scenes of the play, she both despises her husband's "weakness" and desires to lean on him for support.

As Lady Macbeth collapses under the onslaught of an infected mind, Macbeth succumbs to the assaults of external foes. When Seyton brings his word that the queen is dead, his response is terse and ambiguous: "She should have died hereafter" (V.v.17).[14] Significantly, Lady Macbeth's demise is announced by the wailing of her women. At the end of the play she is completely removed from the masculine world she so desperately wanted to enter and which so effectively has excluded her. A victim of her "thick-coming fancies," she, like her husband, loses touch with her humanity except within the ambiance of a dream world.

In the battle scenes at the end of the play, Macbeth, who channeled all his energies into being a "man," is visually and linguistically surrounded by boys until his final encounter with Macduff, the man of no woman born. It seems as though the feminine principle, removed by the sequestration and suicide of Lady Macbeth, transfers itself to the persons of these young males whom Macbeth considers inferior to himself. He disparagingly refers to Malcolm as a "boy"; he bullies Seyton, calling him "lily-liver'd boy"; and when young Siward challenges him to combat, he can hardly condescend to battle such an adversary. Although Macbeth seems invincible on the battlefield, we must remember that his "valor" is being exercised upon males unequal to him in strength and experience. In terms of courage, and according to the laws of Macbeth's society, young Siward does prove himself a man by paying "a soldier's debt"; in his case, manliness does not confer invulnerability. It is, rather, a willingness to confront death and take the consequences:

> He only liv'd but till he was a man;
> The which no sooner had his prowess confirm'd,
> In the unshrinking station where he fought,
> But like a man he died.   (V.ix.6–9)

Siward achieves a form of manhood, but the structure of the play demonstates the limitations of the definition set forth in the eulogy.

During the final action, the very humanity that Macbeth has tried so hard to escape forces itself upon his consciousness. He feels acutely his alienation from human society:

> . . . my way of life
> Is fall'n into the sere, the yellow leaf;
> And that which should accompany old age,
> As honour, love, obedience, troops of friends,
> I must not look to have.   (V.iii.22–6)

A strange remorse afflicts him when he confronts Macduff:

> Of all men else I have avoided thee:
> But get thee back, my soul is too much charg'd
> With blood of thine already.   (V.viii.2–4)

He sees with tragic clarity that in having striven to become more than a man he has become less than one: "bear-like I must fight the course" (V.vii.2). Deprived of preternatural assurance by Macduff's revelation, Macbeth begins to "pull in resolution," suddenly losing that false valor created by the illusion of his own immortality. He briefly falters, and in that faltering, an echo of his former martial courage is heard once more. It is as though Shakespeare forces us to remember Macbeth as the warrior-hero whose true valor is the emblem of his manhood.[15] Threatened with humiliating captivity, Macbeth refuses to yield; like young Siward, he fights on, knowing he is doomed.

At the end of the play the action of the opening scenes finds remarkable parallels,[16] indicating society's continued acceptance of the values and stereotypes that paradoxically both threaten it and guarantee its continuation. The false claimant to the throne is destroyed by superior force, this time embodied in Macduff, who, ironically, performs the same task that had previously been Macbeth's. He walks on stage with Macbeth's severed head, a brutal gesture that recalls Macbeth's own ruthless execution of Macdonwald. The same emphasis on repression of pain and tender feeling, the same equation of soldierly valor and manhood are reiterated in the discussion of young Siward's death. Malcolm, a subdued, more Machiavellian version of Duncan, distributes thanks and rewards using the same imagery of planting that his father before him had used, but unlike the former king's, Malcolm's thanks are brief and measured, his tears merely promised. The warm, golden blood of Duncan shows colder, less bright, in his son. The prince, in a performance convincing enough to have deceived Macduff, claimed that he could, had he the power, "pour the sweet milk of concord into Hell" (IV.iii.97). Now that he is king, there is no guarantee that he, like Macbeth, could not be seduced into actually carrying out that claim. Society has not changed; it has merely eliminated two extremists who pushed the stereotype of manliness beyond the limits it was established to serve.

The verdicts levelled against Macbeth and his wife by their society, "butcher," and "fiend-like Queen" do partial justice, if that, to the richness of their characters or the universal dimensions of the seductions to which they are exposed and to which they succumb. The tension which raises them to the level of tragedy in the eyes of the audience is created by the conflict between the roles they think they must play to actualize the self and achieve their destiny and the limits imposed by both nature and society. On the one hand, there is the ancient temptation: "ye shall be as gods"; on the other, there is the profound awareness (especially on Macbeth's part) of the inviolable limits which keep men human. As Macbeth accepts a false masculinity that simultaneously fosters the illusion of his godlike power and diminishes his total human development, he is alienated from the very society that inculcates the stereotype. Although Lady Macbeth strives to share in the male world by consciously renouncing her femininity, neither she nor we are allowed to forget that "little hand" that cannot, finally, wield the knife. As his "dearest partner" she was to have shared in the "golden round" and the "greatness promised"; instead, she shares only in the dehumanization and nothingness Macbeth faces as his end.

NOTES

[1] Marvin Rosenberg in *The Masks of Macbeth* (Berkeley, 1978) discusses various interpretations of the character which have emphasized either the defeminized "terrible woman" aspect of the character or the sexually attractive, cunning, "loving wife" side (pp. 160–95).

[2] Shakespeare, *Macbeth*, ed. Kenneth Muir (London, 1970). All further references to the play will be made to this edition and cited in the text.

[3] Robert Heilman, "Manliness in the Tragedies," in *Shakespeare 1564–1964* (Providence, 1964), pp. 28–31.

[4] Eugene Waith, "Manhood and Valor in Two Shakespearean Tragedies," *ELH*, XVII (1950), 263.

[5] Holinshed, *Chronicles of Scotland* (ed. 1587), in *The Arden Shakespeare: Macbeth*, ed. Kenneth Muir (London, 1970), p. 188.

[6] D. W. Harding, "Women's Fantasy of Manhood: A Shakespearean Theme," *Shakespeare Quarterly*, XX (Summer, 1969), 249. Harding describes Lady Macduff's attitude as "the woman's feeling that

although she is helpless in the world of action a man should be able to cope with anything." The major complaint Lady Macduff voices, however, is her disappointment at being kept in ignorance. She construes her husband's secrecy as lack of trust and love. In an earlier tragedy, *Julius Caesar*, Portia argues that she can only be a true and loyal wife to Brutus if she shares in the totality of his life, including his politics; otherwise she dwells but in the "suburbs" of his pleasure.

[7] *The Masks of Macbeth*, p. 159.

[8] Rosenberg, p. 160.

[9] For a contrasting view see Moelwyn Merchant, "His Fiend-like Queen," *Shakespeare Survey*, XIX (1966), 75–81. Merchant argues that Lady Macbeth becomes literally possessed by demons, an opinion that lessens her considerable complexity and interest. Walter Clyde Curry, *Shakespeare's Philosophical Patterns* (Baton Rouge, 1959), pp. 58–61, argues substantially the same position.

[10] From gall springs both a desire for revenge and the courage which inflames a man for action; it is frequently associated with the masculine sex because it is the source of the irascible instinct and the choleric humor, both traditionally ascribed to the male. Hamlet, for example, berates himself for lacking manly action: "for it cannot be/But I am pigeon-liver'd and lack gall/To make oppression bitter...." (II.ii.576–8). For a more extended discussion of Renaissance physiology in relation to sexual characteristics, see Ruth Anderson, *Elizabethan Psychology and Shakespeare's Plays* (Iowa City, 1972).

[11] Rosenberg, p. 170.

[12] Heilman, in the article previously cited, asserts that "modern man finds a remarkably complete Shakespearean prototype in Macbeth when he is terrified of Banquo's ghost. What is in the forefront of Macbeth's mind is the necessity of asserting his manly valor, or insisting that his confusion and terror do not make him less a man. 'What man dares, I dare' is his self-rehabilitating vaunt.... Bears, tigers, duels to the death are all better than ghosts and impalpable dangers, all substantial, faceable, reassuring man that he is man" (p. 37).

[13] Peter Ure in *Elizabethan and Jacobean Drama* (Liverpool, 1974) argues that Macbeth plays an alien role of murderer. His argument breaks down, however, after his discussion of the appearance of Banquo's ghost. He fails to account for "the new brutality and directness of Macbeth's resolution" and complains that "we are not shown the antecedents of the transformation" (pp. 58–9). He fails to see how "[Macbeth] can suddenly alter [his] character and devise a new, more brutal ... approach to murder" (p. 59). These problems are resolved if we take the position, as this essay does, that Macbeth's role as murderer is not alien to him at all.

[14] L. C. Knights in *Some Shakespearean Themes* (Stanford, 1959) is of the opinion that "the point of the line lies in its ambiguity. Macbeth is groping for meanings, trying to conceive a time when he might have met such a situation with something more than indifference..." p. 141.

[15] Matthew Prosser takes much the same view of Macbeth's final moments. See his *The Heroic Image in Five Shakespearean Tragedies* (Princeton, 1965), p. 90.

[16] Howard Felperin comments that the final scene is an "eerie and unsettling repetition of an earlier scene in the play." *Shakespearean Representation* (Princeton, 1977), p. 135.

Lisa Low

RIDDING OURSELVES
OF MACBETH

But where there is danger,
There grows also what saves.   —Hölderlin

Unlike most tragic heroes, Macbeth is much less sinned against than sinning, which makes him a strange candidate for our affections.[1] He does not fall prey to infirmity like Lear, nor is he ignorant of what he does like Oedipus. He is not like Romeo, well-intentioned but too hasty; nor is he like Hamlet, Romeo's inverse, too cool. Too hot to stop, too cool to feel, Macbeth is no Romeo and no Hamlet. He is a fiend and a butcher. Standing before him, we cannot but be paralyzed with fear.

And yet, almost against our wills, we are drawn to Macbeth. We should not be, but we are. We are with him in his darkest hours and though we cannot especially hope for his success, we share with him the uncomfortable feeling that what must be done must be done and that what has been done cannot be undone. Banquo, who we come to feel is a threat to ourselves, however good, must be eliminated. So must Fleance, Macduff's wife and children, or anyone else who stands in the highway of our intense progress. Thinking that "to be thus is nothing, but to be safely thus," and wishing with "barefaced power" to sweep him from our sights, we straddle the play repelled by, but irresistibly drawn to Macbeth.

We listen to Macbeth as we listen to the beatings of our hearts. Engaged in the play, we think our hands are up to the wrists in blood and we startle at the knockings at our doors. Watching Macbeth, we suspect the height and depth of our own evil, testing ourselves up to the waist in the waters of some bloody lake. Allowed to do that which we must not do, guaranteed that we shall suffer for it, we watch Macbeth by laying our ears up against the door where our own silent nightmares are proceeding. There we see ourselves projected, gone somehow suddenly wrong, participating in the unforgivable, pursued by the unforgiving, which is most of all, ourselves.

Why should this be? Why are we so drawn to Macbeth by whom we must be at last repelled? Two reasons suggest themselves. First, we identify with Macbeth because identification is the condition of the theatre, especially in a nearly expressionistic play like *Macbeth* where the stage is the meeting ground between the hero's psyche and ours. Second, we pity Macbeth because, like us, he moves within breathing distance of innocence.

From *Massachusetts Review* 24, No. 4 (Winter 1983): 826–37.

As moral obscurity is the world in which Macbeth stands at the beginning of his play, so it is the world in which we are seated watching the play, for the stage is both an extension of Macbeth's mind and the field of our imaginations. There in the domed, dimly lit theatre we watch like swaddled infants, this two hour's traffic, this our own strutting and fretting upon a bloody stage. Before us the Macbeths move like shadowy players, brief candles, little vaporous forms sliding behind a scrim. As if standing in Plato's cave, we see, but at one remove, we listen, but only to echoes, until we find ourselves fumbling along the corridors of our own dark psyches. There, supping on evil, dipped to the waist in blood, we watch the Macbeths go out at last in a clatter of sound, pursued by furies. The play over and the brief candles out, night flees, vapors vanish, and light is restored.

We identify with Macbeth because the theatre makes us suffer the illusion that we are Macbeth. We pity him because, like us, he stands next to innocence in a world in which evil is a prerequisite for being human. Macbeth is not motivelessly malicious like Richard III or Iago. He savors no sadistic pleasure in cruelty. Rather, set within reach of glory, he reaches and falls, and falling he is sick with remorse.

To have a clear conscience is to stand in the sun. To have a clouded conscience, one hovering between good and evil, between desire and restraint, is to stand where most of us stand, in that strange and obscure purgatory where the wind is pocketed with hot and cool trends, where the air is not nimble and sweet but fair and foul. This is the world of choice where thought and act and hand and eye are knit, but in a system of checks and balances.

Set within reach of triumph, who is not tempted to reach? And who, plucking one, will not compulsively and helplessly pluck every apple from the apple tree? For the line dividing self-preservation from ambition is often thin and we walk as if on a narrow cord above an abyss. We have constantly to choose, almost against our wills, for good, for as it is easier to fall than fly, so it is easier to be like Satan than God. We identify with Macbeth because we live in a dangerous world where a slip is likely to be a fall; but in the end, we must rip ourselves from him violently, as of a curse, as of an intolerable knowledge of ourselves. Through him we pay our chief debts to the unthinkable and are washed, when we wake, up onto the white shores of our own innocence. Macbeth is an ironic Christ who absorbs our sins that we may return "striding the blast." Redeemed through him, we ourselves must become the redeemers.

II

I have said that our sympathy for Macbeth is provoked by at least two factors: 1) the obscurely lit stage which is the meeting ground of Macbeth's imagination and ours; and 2) the condition of evil above which most of us manage to stand, but only by hard choice. I would like in the second portion of this essay to say something more about Macbeth's function as a restorer of the redemptive imagination and to describe the condition of terror into which, for our sakes, Macbeth falls.

Macbeth's damnation comes of a willed failure of the imagination. He permits himself, in spite of conscience, to kill his King. His eyes "wink" at his hands and in that dark moment all cruelties become possible:

> Stars, hide your fires;
> Let not light see my black and deep desires.
> The eye wink at the hand; yet let that be
> Which the eye fears, when it is done, to see.

Conversely, our redemptive victory over Macbeth and over ourselves results from the strengthening of the empathetic imagination which our participation in Macbeth's fall affords. The play restores in us pity which

> . . . like a naked new-born babe
> Striding the blast, or heaven's cherubin horsed
> Upon the sightless couriers of the air,
> Shall blow the horrid deed in every eye
> That tears shall drown the wind.

In short, we live and die by our imagination's willingness to comprehend and we comprehend with our eyes. The play is an acting out before our mind's eyes of ourselves participating in and then eschewing evil.

In *Babi Yar*, Andrei Kuznetsov writes that he did not hate the Nazis, it was only that they lacked imagination. Not feeling the sympathy which retards cruelty or the empathy which prevents it, the German soldiers at Babi Yar severed hand from eye and act from conscience in order to carry out daily rounds of slaughter. Day after day, Russian Jews were lined up along precipices and shot. Murder required only blankness of mind.

If sympathy retards cruelty, empathy prevents it. To be in someone else's skin is to startle at pain, to recoil with human pity from unkindness. Foolish enough to think it possible to commit black deeds and not to be held "to accompt" for it, Macbeth permits his imagination to fail. Considering himself outside his own human skin, Macbeth severs himself. He calls for darkness, commits evil, and is walled-in afterwards in the windowless dungeon of his imagination. A cord yanked from its socket, a chicken with its head cut off, Macbeth shrieks and jerks his way down the corridors of his maimed psyche into death's private cell.

Since cruelty depends upon the imagination's willingness not to see, it is best carried out in darkness. Night obscures witness, prevents the compassionate eye, the organ of pity, the cherub at the gate of sense, from mutinying against the hand. So Macbeth calls for night to cloak Duncan's murder with "Stars, hide your fires," and so he prepares for Banquo's death with "Come, seeling night." The world of the play is so black that light is a contradiction:

> Thou seest the heavens, as troubled with man's act,
> Threatens his bloody stage. By th' clock 'tis day,
> And yet dark night strangles the travelling lamp.

The sun is no more than a "travelling lamp" for Macbeth's birth-strangled mind, travelling in self-willed darkness, troubles even the heavens. After flickering tapers, brief candles, and stars in heaven blown out, the "tomorrow" speech "memorize[s] another Golgotha," finally confirming the bloody stage as a sunless habitation where by the light of lamps, by the light of his own dimming intelligence, Macbeth's crimes have occurred. Macbeth has stood titanic in the way of his own sun and ours.

Darkness has its consequences. Once commit yourself to darkness and you are no longer eligible for light's sanctuary. Macbeth calls on darkness to prevent witness to his crime; he wills his eyes to "wink" at his hands, but when he does so, he slits his own wrists and throat. He blacks out.

Shakespeare explores this slitting, this recession into darkness, with physiological metaphors. The cords Macbeth severs—the umbilical one that runs from himself to his kingdom—and the veins and arteries that connect his brain and soul to his body—are the ones which allow him to thrive. Having cut these Macbeth travels through the play as death-in-life—blind, suffocating, stiffening in *rigor mortis*—toward his actual decapitation. Cut off, running beheaded, Macbeth loses internal and external equilibrium. Circulation and communication stop; his body survives, but only briefly, as a body will survive on the impulse of shock, when it has been severed from its head.

Shock has two countermotions: wildness and paralysis. Macbeth's wild power decreases inversely as he seeks to increase it; the larger the sweep of his hand, the more cribbed and cabinned his soul; the greater the space about his feet, as a throned king, the less room his mind has to run about in. Macbeth's reason is pushed from its stool and his body is repelled by the mind that commands it. His mind, in a "restless ecstasy," tries to hold onto the wooden mask it no longer fits and his body scrambles within clothes it cannot shape. Mind and form stand at odds as a crown tilts lopsidedly on a brow for which it was not meant. Time is pushed from its center and runs elliptically. Eye and hand, moving and fixed are jarred and confused by fits and starts until, "as two spent swimmers that do cling together / And choke their art," spirit is wrenched from body and stutters from sublimity to silence.

Decapitation's "restless ecstasy" is succeeded by its counter motion *rigor mortis*, the gradual turning to stone. Because the dark plain Macbeth's mind rides is full of "strange images of death," of "new Gorgon[s]" to destroy sight, Macbeth becomes himself a Gorgon. At the idea of murdering Duncan Macbeth's heart leaps, knocking at his ribs, and his hair stands on end:

> Why do I yield to that suggestion
> Whose horrid image doth unfix my hair
> And make my seated heart knock at my ribs
> Against the use of nature?

This Medusa-like image of "unfixed hair" is repeated. Imagining Banquo has risen again with "twenty mortal murders on [his] crown[ ]," Macbeth gasps at the image he sees: "Thou canst not say I did it. Never shake / Thy gory locks at me." Banquo's hacked hair stands up in the same snaky Medusa locks that Macbeth's hair had at the prospect of killing Duncan. We see the same head in the murdered Duncan. Announcing the King's death to the castle walls Macduff cries: "Approach the chamber and destroy your sight / With a new Gorgon."

Were the person next to you in the theatre to knock your sleeve at this point and ask you the time, your eyes would be transfixed, comprehending nothing, as if you had been in another man's dream. Watching the play you are as the dead, for the eyes of the dead have no speculation, perhaps because they dream another dream. So Macbeth shrinks at his vision of Banquo:

> Avaunt, and quit my sight! Let the earth hide thee!
> Thy bones are marrowless, thy blood is cold;
> Thou hast no speculation in those eyes
> Which thou dost glare with!

More than any other feature the eyes connect us to this world. They are the windows to the soul and the soul's windows to the world. Speak to someone's eyes and you will know who you speak to. Macbeth's eyes are as if rolled up into his skull for, dreaming a vision no one in his kingdom can dream, he is far away. Intoxicated, mad, trapped, Macbeth gazes permanently into the bloody narcissus pool of his own mind.

So does Lady Macbeth. She who chided her husband by saying

> The sleeping and the dead
> Are but as pictures. 'Tis the eye of childhood
> That fears a painted devil.

becomes herself a painted devil. Sleepwalking, haunted by her crimes, her "eyes are open . . . but their sense are shut." Like Macbeth's, her mind has closed down around itself, admitting no light, and she sees only the blood upon her hands which, for all her rubbing, for all her "out, damned spot[s]," will not rub away. A "little water" cannot clear her of her deeds, nor can she wash the "filthy witness" from her eyes. Instead, the very water with which she tires to rinse her hands free will turn red, proclaiming she is a murderer.

The Macbeths run fast but not far. Macbeth's, unlike Lear's, is an eye for an eye world where to kill a king is to commend "th-ingredience" of the "poisoned chalice" back to the lips of the murderer. Thus, Macbeth's own body revolts against him as he considers the image of a dead Duncan. He wills his eyes to "wink" at his hands; later he wills his hands to "pluck out" his eyes. The smiling babe that Lady Macbeth promises to yank from her milkless breast returns striding the apocalyptic blast. The dead are nature's *enfants terribles,* rising again to push Macbeth from his stool:

> The time has been
> That, when the brains were out, the man would die,
> And there an end. But now they rise again,
> With twenty mortal murders on their crowns,
> And push us from our stools.

The dead Banquo's face is mirrored in a prodigious series of child kings to come, and the trees at Birnam Wood, cut off at the root, walk toward Dunsinane to defeat Macbeth. The witches' riddles invert as Macduff strides not "of woman born" to behead the beheader. As the dead infant shrivels to a counterfeit, the screaming infant, hanging on its bloody root, the umbilical cord, becomes the world restorer.

III

I have said in Part One that we are drawn to Macbeth, almost against our wills, both because the theatre makes us dream we are Macbeth, and because, a villain against his will, he walks near innocence, anguished by remorse. In Part Two I have said that Macbeth is our ironic Christ who, absorbing our sins, allows us to be redeemed. In Part Two I have also described the conditions of darkness into which the damned Macbeth falls. I have described what it is like to commit terrible sins against the race and have hinted at the restorative powers of the redeeming imagination in a world where "blood will have blood." It should be clear by now that *Macbeth* is a play which moves neither in the land of evil nor in the present, but rather in the land of good and in the future. In these last two brief sections I would like to describe the damned and the redeemed imagination, for we come to *Macbeth* and are entangled, but we leave *Macbeth* released, having learned not what we are, but what we must become.

The imagination is not bound by formal laws of nature. It can pass through walls, enter heaven, drive down into hell. It can make a villain of a hero, and a hero of a villain. When Macbeth stands at the beginning of his play in the fair and foul air of his private thoughts, he is standing between two such large ideas as heaven and hell. As it is heavenly to have new honors sitting upon the brow, so it is hell to stuff the mouth of praise with a dagger. It is hell, too, to be tied to the stake of one ambitious thought until flesh is hacked from bone.

Macbeth stands in the murky, chiaroscuro world of conscience and conscientiousness, between good and evil, a step toward heaven and a slip toward hell. There is but a thinly scratched line between right and wrong, between a sword smoking in a villain's blood and a villain smoking in the blood of a king. Here to "unseam" a man "from the nave to th' chops" may be either a moment of barbaric inhumanity or patriotic fervor. Here if death to the left is laudable, to the right it is enough to throw the self off balance, to push it from its stool and into the blackest abyss of hell. If Hamlet leans upon a question mark, Macbeth rides into an "if." For this we empathize when we watch Macbeth "upon this bank and shoal of time . . . jump the life to come." For this we feel pity as Macbeth does not "trammel up" but rather unravels "the sleave of care."

Thoughts pass in the mind like crows to rooky woods. To catch at a thought, to snag it, to blow it up and become oppressed by it, is to subordinate the reason, the healthy remainder of the mind, to a static picture. It is to eat of "the insane root / That takes the reason prisoner." Life stops. Instead of extirpating the "insane root" obsession, Macbeth cultivates it. Thereafter all else is choked out and the kingdom of his mind becomes not as it should be, a mass of impressions taken in from without, mingled with history and memory, but instead one single knotted mass. The mind's fundamental will, its overriding flexible complexity, cannot be so tethered and survive. The mind as a breathing organism in equilibrium with the world and with the social order stops. Or, infected with itself, it invents its own world.

Macbeth approaches the expressionism to which Shakespeare did not have access. Pressing up against the boundaries of its medium, the play explodes with the pressure of Macbeth's mind. Its language is clotted and heat-oppressed. As Macbeth's mind is "full of scorpions" so is the play's. As Büchner's *Woyceck,* Munch's *The Scream,* and Van Gogh's self-portraits present minds on the verge of madness, so does *Macbeth.* Shut off from the country of health Macbeth's brain, like a poison bag, distends and bursts, infecting its world. When Ross says,

> But cruel are the times when we are traitors
> And do not know ourselves; when we hold rumor
> From what we fear, yet know not what we fear
> But float upon a wild and violent sea
> Each way and none

we recognize that the play occurs inside the upset equilibrium of Macbeth's panicking mind.

The mind is the deepest recess within the castle walls of the face; it is private, isolated, and vulnerable. We feel this play as we test electricity with one finger in water, or as if electric wires were tapping against the skull. Because we never feel, even for a moment, Macbeth's safety; because we hear him breathe in our ears his bloody imaginings, we watch the play, as we look at a late Van Gogh, as if we were studying a mind from inside out. In this *Macbeth* most moves and terrifies us. Watching the play, we voyage on "a wild and violent sea" of a mind made mad by its own cruelty. The terror of this passage:

> What hands are here? Ha! they pluck out mine eyes,
> Will all great Neptune's ocean wash this blood
> Clean from my hand? No, this my hand will rather
> The multitudinous seas incarnadine
> Making the green one red

is immense because, for him, all is unredeemable. Macbeth, having shut his eyes to pity, having "rapt" himself in turbanned darkness, is condemned to a plain darkened by the red seas of his own guilt. The water with which he tries to rinse his hands clean will condemn him. Macbeth is a painted devil before a mirror and the play, until he is decapitated, is his self-portrait and ours.

IV

We come to the play and our imaginations are tethered to Macbeth as to our own guilt. We leave the play, after having ripped ourselves free of him, with imaginations redeemed. The play teaches us how to become what we can become, for we live, like Macduff, not ultimately within Macbeth's imagination, but within the greater imagination of God—within the greater will to goodness in ourselves. When the play is done, when vapors vanish and light is restored, Macbeth lies, titanically defeated, within the vast circumference of the audience's redeemed and redeeming imagination.

In this last section I would like to say something about the providential vision toward which Shakespeare is moving. The nature of his vision in this pivotal play is oddly Miltonic. That is, good wins because good is the life force, the *élan vital*. Evil, to the contrary, can only mimic good, feed off of its motifs parasitically. In the end, ripped free of good, evil withers at the root. The function of drama, of *Macbeth*, is to have evil painted upon a pole underscored as "the tyrant." Through witnessing evil we are exorcised of it, becoming good. Ultimately we rise free not only of Macbeth, but of death, as if by our willing it, death itself could die.

If Macbeth's mind is earthly, a globe where fair and foul, welcome and un-welcome vapors are mixed, it is also limited. Macbeth's imagination stands within the greater imagination of miracle, the providential vision toward which, as O. B. Hardison and Emrys Jones have recently demonstrated, Shakespeare is moving. The play is acted out within the compressed and dark quarters of an earthly hell, but it moves finally toward the city of infinite good. Macbeth's Satanic mind, eyes, hands, and touch are contained within the supranatural forces of Macduff who was from his "mother's womb untimely ripped"; of Duncan, whose unearthly blood is like gold laced upon silver skin; and of Edward the Confessor, whose touch has "such sanctity" from heaven that he can heal victims of the bubonic plague. If there is a special poignance to Malcolm's dramatically ironic comment to Macduff, "He hath not touched you yet," there is an ending to it and to the jurisdiction of the tyrant's grasp. For this play stands not in Macbeth's hand but in "the great hand of God."

In *Macbeth* evil feeds off of good. Sin and death, here as in *Paradise Lost* and *Paradise Regained*, are not self-invented, but parasitic. Duncan enfolds, embraces, enriches and plants; he is the Christ-like incarnation of the Biblical blessing on human sexuality, "Be fruitful and multiply." The Macbeths, conversely, are sterile. They can neither be fruitful, nor multiply; instead they can only shrink, melt down, as the witch does in *The Wizard of Oz* and as Satan does in *Paradise Lost*. Macbeth shrinks within his armor. By his end he is a clanging bell of doom, a great clatter upon the stairs, a suit of armor that has become an echo chamber because it is hollow. Thus Macduff knows Macbeth by his sound, "That way the noise is. Tyrant, show thy face!" and "There thou shouldst be:/ By this great clatter one of greatest note/ Seems bruited."

As the "juggling fiends . . . palter" with Macbeth in a "double sense" so does time. Foul meets fair and evil good. Eyes without speculation, rolled up, shut as if eternally inside, roll down at the sound of the apocalypse:

> Awake, Awake!
> Ring the alarum bell! Murder and treason!
> Shake off this downy sleep, death's counterfeit,

> And look on death itself. Up, up, and see
> The great doom's image. Malcolm! Banquo!
> As from your graves rise up and walk like sprites
> To countenance this horror. Ring the bell!

The dead are avenged, raised from graves to bear witness to the eternal damnation of the damned. The good wake to see the bloody Macbeth, the birth-strangled babe, death itself.

When Macduff reveals himself to Macbeth as the man who not "of woman born" was from his "mother's womb untimely ripped" Macbeth knows what we already know, that though he will fight until his flesh is hacked from his bones, he will be defeated. As Macduff raises his sword he proclaims Macbeth's role for us as redeemer,

> Then yield thee, coward,
> And live to be the show and gaze o' the' time.
> We'll have thee, as our rarer monsters are,
> Painted upon a pole, and underwrit
> 'Here may you see the tyrant.'

That Macbeth will be the "show . . . o' th' time" puns on the complex emotional effects which drama and visual art have upon us. Beheaded, gored, terrified, and terrifying, Macbeth shall "live" before an audience who shall know through him the true fruit of sin.

In a world of good where "stones . . . move and trees . . . speak" evil depends, for its lifeblood, upon good. The bloody babe from the womb, this play's Christ-like *deus ex machina,* makes of the birth-strangled babe a counterfeit. Because evil has of itself no godliness, because it cannot reproduce but only copy, borrowing for its temporary life blood and babes and roots, it can only be the inverse of live. Uprooted, severed, dependent, the bad is marrowless. If this is true, around random weeds the world will root itself, restore itself infinitely in an ecstasy of green, out of a bath of blood. Around the mask of evil the audience humankind will press, celebrating the exorcism of the devil from the self.

Because in the end "where there is danger, / There grows also what saves," we rid ourselves of our Macbethness by necessity. Having merged ourselves with Macbeth in the private obscurity of the dimly lit stage, having said not, "This castle hath a pleasant seat," but, "The raven himself is hoarse / That croaks the fatal entrance of Duncan / Under my battlements," we have learned empathy; we have learned to bear the pain of others as if it were our own. In the end we rise naked and trumpeting above the gray trembling earth, shaking off "this downy sleep, death's counterfeit." Lifted up bodily toward Malcolm and Macduff, we are within reach of Duncan. With trumpets to our lips and wings to support us, we stand like bloody generals for good and for God. Darkness and devils having been torn from us at last, the earth vanishes and we stand in eternity's light. For cruelty in us is a painted thing, life's counterfeit, a blight to be shaken off at the end of unredeemed time. These are the good "blood instructions" of plays and players. Through *Mac-*

beth we learn what monsters are, what a monstrous thing it is to kill a king, God's infant man. When the play is done we shake off the "strange images of death" we have become to be the selves of our hereafter, seeing evil, even death, as Macbeth is: dominionless—a gored mask, a painted devil, a head of unfixed hair upon a post.

NOTES

[1] All quotations from *Macbeth* are taken from Alfred Harbage's *William Shakespeare: The Complete Works* (Baltimore: Penguin Books, 1970). I would like to thank Normand Berlin for his enthusiastic support of this essay.

Kay Stockholder

STEALTHY LOVERS
IN *MACBETH*

Macbeth storms the barricade Othello attempted, seizes the woman with whose help he crowns himself king of the nightmare realm on the margins of which Hamlet delayed. By defining himself as husband, Macbeth becomes conscious of the emotions and associations that other protagonists avoided. In the process he creates a polarity between domestic and social harmony and sexual passion. Rather than being the source of procreation and love, Macbeth's relation to his wife is fulfilled in the murder of Duncan, who represents for Macbeth legitimate authority, gentle fathering, maternal nurturing, social accord, and childlike trust. His murder constitutes a psychological holocaust that is also the climax of Macbeth's erotic passions.

Macbeth is not only pervaded by dreamlike occurrences, but Macbeth experiences himself in a dreamlike state. As a consequence of the different levels of dreaming involved, this play more explicitly than others involves connections between internal and external experience. The introductory sequence of action parallels the full sequence of earlier plays in which the protagonist comes to experience as emotions what previously he confronted as external circumstance. But most of the action reverses that process to render a figure transforming his own dreamlike state into what he later confronts as external reality.[1]

The world Macbeth inhabits contains, besides himself, only three defined figures, two of whom he eliminates in short order. The remaining figures with whom he peoples his world, all in some degree shadowlike, fall into two categories. Those relatively realistic but thinly characterized figures who extend from Banquo and who slowly become inimical to Macbeth represent royal authority. The other more dreamlike figures extend from Lady Macbeth to seduce Macbeth into the depths of nightmare. They include the witches, Hecate, and, in the imagery, the country itself as well as the owls, rooks, ravens, and all the extensions of Lady Macbeth's language that compose almost the entire lurid landscape on which Macbeth moves, more real to him than the pallid remnants of the more present-oriented figures.

From *Dream Works: Lovers and Families in Shakespeare's Plays* (Toronto: University of Toronto Press, 1987), pp. 100–117.

We encounter Macbeth in a state of transition, indicated by the male figures who acclaim him as 'Valour's minion' (I.ii.19) in images of violence and blood and those who couple his name with that of the traitor thane of Cawdor. Both Cawdor's treason and the blood of battle are associated with Macbeth's role as husband when he is called 'Bellona's bridegroom.' The drama of Macbeth's emerging redefinition of himself is enacted when Duncan gives Cawdor's title to Macbeth while he reflects that 'There's no art / To find the mind's construction in the face: / He was a gentleman on whom I built / An absolute trust' (I.iv.11–14). Macbeth momentarily resists donning the 'borrowed robes' of Cawdor's treachery, but his inner readiness generates the witches' prophecies. In the 'horrible imaginings' that appear to his inner eye instead of images of the 'imperial theme, ' he reveals that his desire to kill Duncan, only vaguely suggested before, has suddenly coalesced into an identification of himself with Cawdor's treachery.[2] Cawdor's defection was as mysterious to him as is the image of Duncan murdered by his own hand that fills his inner vision and obscures what previously constituted both his external reality and his self-definition, so that now 'nothing is but what is not.'

Macbeth's previous and fading self-definition appears in his characterization of and relation to Duncan. Duncan as king occupies a paternal realm, which Macbeth emphasizes when he says, 'our duties / Are to your throne and state, children and servants; / Which do but what they should, by doing everything / Safe toward your love and honour' (I.iv.24–7). Duncan's paternal role, which Lady Macbeth emphasizes when she says that the sleeping Duncan reminds her of her father, also appears in Duncan's praise of Macbeth's heroism: 'The sin of my ingratitude even now / Was heavy on me,' and 'More is thy due than more than all can pay' (I.iv.15–16, 21). Duncan's lament that he cannot adequately reward Macbeth becomes ironic when Duncan in the next breath names Malcolm as successor to the throne. In a subtle way Macbeth casts himself as a slighted 'worthiest cousin' rather than eldest son. In doing so he expresses his feeling that he is unworthy of the mantle of authority, and he fuels a sense of grievance that derives from his having interpreted as betrayal his ambition for paternal authority and the maturity it represents. Hearing himself praised as his country's saviour is then a strategy by which he justifies the betrayal that is already taking shape.[3] Already hidden within the initial configuration is the image of himself as a 'dwarfish thief' in the process of acquiring a 'giant's robe' (V.ii.21–2).[4]

However, the paternal image that excites Macbeth's divided feelings carries distinctly maternal colouring, in a way that makes more explicit Hamlet's merger of maternal and paternal figures. In praising Macbeth, Duncan says, 'I have begun to plant thee, and will labour / To make thee full of growing, ' and wishes to 'bind us further to you' (I.iv.28–9, 43). Even while Macbeth reflects on his 'black and deep desires,' Duncan associates himself with nurturing and food: 'he is full so valiant, / And in his commendations I am fed; / It is a banquet to me' (I.iv.51, 54–6). The association of Duncan with nurturing fertility is elaborated when he approaches Macbeth's castle: 'This castle hath a pleasant seat; the air / Nimbly and sweetly recommends itself / Unto our gentle senses' (I.vi.1–3). While Macbeth plans to murder Duncan as king and father, he surrounds him with an aura of creaturely warmth.

The only figure with whom Macbeth identifies is Banquo. They are companions in battle, in encountering the witches, and in earning Duncan's praises. Macbeth completes the isolation of himself and Lady Macbeth when he moves Banquo into Duncan's orbit by associating him with the images of children from which he begins to remove himself. After the witches vanish Macbeth observes that Banquo's 'children shall be kings, ' and immediately upon learning that he is thane of Cawdor he says, 'Do you not hope your children shall be kings' (I.iii.86, 118). Macbeth's association of Banquo with children also associates him with Duncan, who, after having promised to make Macbeth 'grow,' has more intimate words for Banquo: 'let me enfold thee, / And hold thee to my heart' (I.iv.31–2). Banquo becomes for Macbeth a figure fused with Malcolm as a more legitimate successor than he to the mantle of authority, when Banquo adds to Duncan's praises of Macbeth's castle his observation that

> The temple-haunting martlet, does approve,
> By his loved mansionry, that the heaven's breath
> Smells wooingly here: no jutty, frieze,
> Buttress, nor coign of vantage, but this bird
> Hath made his pendent bed, and procreant cradle:
> Where they most breed and haunt, I have observ'd
> The air is delicate.   (I.vi.4–10)

His association of Macbeth's castle, within which Macbeth and Lady Macbeth plan a different kind of birth, with images of fertility and tender nurturing contrasts this external image of Lady Macbeth to her interior, which she describes in a different bird image when she says, 'The raven himself is hoarse / That croaks the fatal entrance of Duncan / Under my battlements' (I.v.38–40). Macbeth generates the two opposed images of femininity; he exposes the latter but distantly expresses in Banquo's words haunting regret for the realm of nurture, fidelity, affection, and procreation, which is for him in opposition to his marital intimacy with Lady Macbeth.

Having defined his desires for becoming father and king as illegitimate, Macbeth has reversed the classical Oedipal paradigm in which the son in order to marry the mother wishes to kill the father. Rather, he has married the mother, and included the implied sexuality in the project of killing the father. Becoming Bellona's bridegroom meant for him forgoing Banquo's 'bosom franchis'd, and allegiance clear' (II.i.28), and eating of the 'insane root, / That takes the reason prisoner' (I.iii.84–5), so that he may with her aid enter, as Hamlet did not, the Vulcan's stithy of his own imagination.

Macbeths attitudes towards women appear first in the figures of the witches and Hecate. As non-realistic figures they represent emotions from past configurations that have not been integrated into present circumstances. The sense of depth in this play derives largely from these figures and the resonant imagery that surrounds them and spreads to other figures. Unlike most plays, *Macbeth* contains no reference to any circumstance or event prior to the action we witness, but the sense of pastness is suggested by the entranced or dreamlike state into which the witches draw Macbeth. In their first appearance, remote from himself, Macbeth reveals the feelings he has aroused in himself in the process of casting himself as husband. Their plan to waylay him expresses his fear of women's devious strategies, and the surrounding 'fog and filthy air' expresses his moral confusion in which 'fair is foul, and foul is fair.' He casts himself as the object of women's nefarious designs, and in interpreting these women, most unseductive in appearance, as preternatural, he reveals the gap between his self-conception and the seductive desires that have generated these fateful figures. In the image of the 'blasted heath' on which they appear Macbeth associates women with all that is the reverse of the gentle nurturing suggested in the images with which Banquo and Duncan describe the exterior of Macbeth's castle.[5] That the first and second appearances of the witches sandwich the voices that declare his martial heroism suggests that these bubbles of the earth are the opposite side of the coin on which is stamped his self-image as bloodily heroic.

The meaning of the witches for Macbeth unfolds later in the action as more associations cluster around them. Through their relation to Hecate they are associated with murder, but more important, despite his initial revulsion, Macbeth links them to the sensuous images with which he anticipates murdering Banquo when he says,

> Ere the bat hath flown
> His cloister'd flight; ere to black Hecate's summons
> The shard-born beetle, with his drowsy hums,
> Hath run Night's yawning peal, there shall be done
> A deed of dreadful note.   (III.ii.40–4)

These images of the night creatures that are radically opposed to legitimate daylight activities evoke a kind of dark ease that overwhelms and cancels the moral horror that is the overt content. Macbeth savours the theoretically horrifying deed when he continues, 'Light thickens; and the crow / Makes wing to th'rooky wood; / Good things of Day begin to droop and drowse, / Whiles Night's black agents to their preys do rouse' (III.ii.49–52). The language with which he invokes Hecate associates sensuous darkness with moral outrage ('Fair is foul and foul is fair') and adds a more specifically sexual note when 'Night's . . . agents' rouse their prey. These lines that precede Banquo's murder show Macbeth swooning into an anticipation of erotic violence that he interprets as supernaturally induced.

In the witches and Hecate Macbeth evokes a distanced and diabolically defined version of an offended mother. Hecate scolds the witches like erring daughters, Macbeth's sisters rather than his mother, and sounds like a neglected and resentful parent when she rebukes them for having favoured 'a wayward son, / Spiteful and wrathful; who, as others do, / Loves for his own ends, not for you' (III.v.11–15).[6] In Hecate's words Macbeth expresses his sense of himself using women for his own ends, and of them in reprisal manipulating him through an equivocal seduction that will 'palter with us in a double sense; / That keep the word of promise to our ear, / And break it to our hope' (V.viii.20–2). All of the images that compose these remote actualizations of feminine figures are also associated with Lady Macbeth.[7] These unrealistic and dreamlike forms in their wavering reality and supernatural attributes depict emotional components from a past or infantile level out of which Macbeth assembles the more present figure that he espouses in his wife. Her figure merges with theirs when she awaits Duncan as the witches did Macbeth, and calls upon the spirits that 'tend on mortal thoughts' to

> unsex me here,
> And fill me, from the crown to the toe, top-full
> Of direst cruelty! make thick my blood,
> Stop up th'access and passage to remorse;
> That no compunctious visitings of Nature
> Shake my fell purpose, nor keep peace between
> Th'effect and it! Come to my woman's breasts,
> And take my milk for gall, you murth'ring ministers,
> Wherever in your sightless substances
> You wait on Nature's mischief! Come, thick Night,
> And pall thee in the dunnest smoke of Hell,
> That my keen knife see not the wound it makes,
> Nor Heaven peep through the blanket of the dark,
> To cry, 'Hold, hold!' (I.v.39–53)

The images of 'thick night' and 'dunnest smoke of Hell' recall the earlier 'fog and filthy air,' and the croaking raven is the first of the crows, owls, bats, and rooks that reach deep into the later murky depths. Lady Macbeth's desire that 'direst cruelty' should fill her 'from the crown to the toe' recalls the figure that Macbeth 'unseam'd . . . from the nave to th'chops' (I.ii.22), and 'make thick my blood' leads to the images of blood that flow through the play. More explicitly than the witches, she opposes herself to the nurturing that defines Duncan. Banquo will grow in Duncan's bosom, but no nourishment will flow from her breasts, and in wanting freedom from any 'compunctious visitings of Nature,' she relates herself to the barren infertility of the 'blasted heath.'[8]

Her scorn of the weak, milky-natured nurturing aspect of Macbeth, which is associated with the benign and foolishly trusting Duncan, extends through associated images to infants and mothers. She separates children from the sexuality that generates them by relating sexuality to her murderous desire that Duncan, who reminds her of her father, should pass beneath her battlements. The raven that will herald him, along with bats, beetles, rooks, is associated with owls when Lady Macbeth says during the murder, 'It was the owl that shriek'd, the fatal bellman, / Which gives the stern'st goodnight' (II.ii.3–4). Lady Macduff, blaming Macduff for leaving his family unprotected, says, 'for the poor wren / The most diminutive of birds, will fight / Her young ones in her nest, against the owl' (IV.ii.9–11). Macbeth himself becomes the child-killing owl when Macduff says, 'O Hell-kite! All? / What, all my pretty chickens, and their dam, / At one fell swoop?' (IV.iii.219–21). Ross and the Old Man include in the portents on the night of the murder 'A falcon, towering in her pride of place, / Was by a mousing owl hawk'd at and kill'd' (II.iv.12–13). Since a falcon image underlies Macbeth's invocation, 'Come, seeling Night / Scarf up the tender eye of pitiful Day / And with thy bloody and invisible hand / Cancel, and tear to pieces, that great bond / Which keeps me pale!' (III.ii.47–50), the falcon killed by the mousing owl comes to represent a fusion of regal pride with infantile tenderness and pity. Though a prideful falcon may seem an unlikely image for an infant, it coheres with Macbeth's image of Pity, like a new-born babe, riding the blasts. These clustering images, which are implied in Lady Macbeth's croaking raven, fuse infanticide into the aura of erotic violence in which Duncan's murder is anticipated.

Lady Macbeth's denied maternity is associated with perverse sexuality through another cluster of images that relates her to the witches, and casts Macbeth as child to her. On the witches' second appearance, one says that she has been 'killing swine' (I.iii.2), and when Macbeth wishes to consult the witches' masters the witch says to pour in their cauldron 'sow's blood, that hath eaten / Her nine farrow' (IV.i.64–5). Lady Macbeth, when planning the murder with Macbeth, says that when Duncan's attendants are 'in swinish sleep / Their drenched natures lie, as in a death, / What cannot you and I perform upon / Th'unguarded Duncan?' She calls them 'spongy officers' (I.vii.68–71, 73), and while she awaits Macbeth's return she says, 'The surfeited grooms / Do mock their charge with snores' (II.i.5–6). Her scorn is a bit unjust, since it was she who 'drugged their possets,' but the image of swinish sleep merges with that of drunkenness. She associates swinishness with drink and sleep, and connects the grooms to her revulsion at Macbeth's softer nature when she rebukes him, 'Was the hope drunk, / Wherein you dress'd yourself? Hath it slept since' (I.vii.35–6). When she says that Duncan's resemblance to her father stopped her hand, she responds lovingly to that maternally tinged father image, but that image merges with those of the swinish grooms who arouse her murderous revulsion, so that she can without difficulty smear their faces with Duncan's blood. Through Lady Macbeth, Macbeth expresses his fear of woman's scorn for male passivity, seen as swinishly sodden.

A more specific form of the implied sexual impotence is evoked through the Porter, who is a version of Hamlet's grave-diggers. Though more remote from Macbeth's consciousness than is the grave-digger scene from Hamlet's, like the grave-diggers, the Porter's grotesque comedy makes explicit what is elsewhere vaguely implied when the Porter says, 'Much drink may be said to be an equivocator with lechery: it makes him, and it mars him; it sets him on, and it takes him off; it persuades him, and disheartens him; makes him stand to, and not stand to: in conclusion, equivocates him in a sleep, and, giving him the lie, leaves him' (II.iii.30–5). The parallels between equivocating drink, the equivocating witches, and Lady Macbeth's equivocating femininity as expressed in the opposing images of her castle relate Macbeth's experience of feminine duplicity to male impotence, explicitly associated in the Porter's words with the drunken swinishness of the sleeping grooms. That image completes an emotional circle in which Macbeth defines women as cruel and mocking, fears them therefore, joins them in order to safeguard himself and to use them against paternal authority, in the process wedding aggression to eroticism and becoming impotent in ordinary ways. As a consequence, he fears even more the mocking voices of women.[9]

Lady Macbeth also shares her ambiguous sexual definition with the witches, whose beards cast doubt on their sex, and with Duncan, who carries feminine attributes. She asks to be unsexed, and she imagines herself in a sexually dominant role when she wants to 'pour my spirits in thine ear, / And chastise with the valour of my tongue / All that impedes thee from the golden round' (I.v.26–8), and in her attribution to Macbeth of the 'milk of human kindness' that she denies in herself. Her language binds in a single cluster images of denied nurturing, barrenness, cruelty, and role reversal, and joins that cluster to an aura of sexualized violence when she desires that Heaven not 'peep through the blanket of the dark' to see the wound made by her 'keen knife.' Her words, ringing in the same register as Macbeth's, 'let that be, / Which the eye fears, when it is done, to see' (I.iv.52–3), gather and focus the implications that have already shadowed his figure.

In Lady Macbeth Macbeth has wedded himself to a figure on whom he projects his own eroticized violence, with all the related ideas that are suggested by the imagistic associations that condition the language of the entire play. But he also projects onto her the spurs 'to prick the sides of [his] intent' (I.vii.26), so that he may experience himself in part as passive to women's force ('he loves for his own ends / Not for you'). Despite the many images and structural forms that relate Lady Macbeth to the witches and Hecate, she is on a different dream level from the other feminine figures. Like a dream figure who appears identical to one in waking life, she carries a full sense of present reality. Macbeth, at whatever cost, has generated a female figure who complements his own, and has succeeded in envisioning a mutually loving relationship, though the nature of the shared enterprise that defines their love also carries back to the more dreamlike experiences from which these dark lovers and childless parents have arisen.[10] As their relationship takes shape it also brings to a more presently defined adult level the full implications of the surrounding suggestiveness. Therefore I will consider some of the passages already discussed in that more adult context in order to see how the associations from a deeper past, suggested by the more fantastic configurations, shape Macbeth's love for his wife.

The letter Macbeth writes to Lady Macbeth in its suggestive brevity reveals an intimacy that substantiates the lovingness expressed in its close: 'This have I thought good to deliver thee (my dearest partner of greatness) that thou might'st not lose the dues of rejoicing, by being ignorant of what greatness is promis'd thee' (I.v.10–14). Their loving intimacy is further suggested by her instant intuition of Macbeth's excited fear, and her similar assumption that circumstances alone will not fulfil the witches' prophecy. As Macbeth immediately envisioned Duncan's murder rather than himself enthroned, so she will 'catch the nearest way.' She surrrounds the projected murder with perverse sexual intimacy, and associates her genitals with cruelty when she imagines Duncan entering her castle. She turns impulses of 'compunctious tenderness' to 'murthering ministers,' and evokes tender sexual feelings, associates them with mothering, and negates them even as they arise when she asks them to 'take my milk for gall.' She equates Duncan's murder with rejecting both her own normal sexuality and mothering. Macbeth expresses his desire to kill Duncan through the image of her cruelty, giving her the 'keen knife' that will make the death wound beneath the 'blanket of the dark' in the atmosphere of an intimate sexuality. A vague image of a sexual act begins to form, in which the hostility Macbeth feels for the paternal Duncan imbues his imagination of woman's violence. But he also associates himself with Duncan remotely when Lady Macbeth describes his nature as full of the 'milk of human kindness,' so that the anticipated murder includes an image of himself as passive victim of her sexualized violence.[11]

When Macbeth enters this aura of perverse sexuality she tells him that, having been transported by his letter beyond the ignorant present, she feels 'the future in the instant.' The previously denied procreative power now generates images of power in her allusion to his new title, which promises him the throne. Macbeth defines his love within his wife's unspoken thought when he responds, 'My dearest love, / Duncan comes here to-night' (I.v.57–8). The mutually intuitive understanding of their exchange drains the impact from Macbeth's vacillating demur 'We will speak further' (I.v.71). The accord of her mind to his shows that in writing to her he relied on her resolve to steady his, a naturalistic extension of what the images have suggested, and so in his passivity to her he can 'wrongly win' that which he would not 'play false' to attain.

Their relationship to each other provides a rhythm by which each excites the other to the point of action. The first movement occurred in Macbeth's sending the letter, in Lady Macbeth's response, and in his collusive reaction to her. The second begins when Macbeth for a moment enters a meditation, like that of Hamlet, on this 'bank and shoal of time' between life and death. Like Hamlet, he shrinks from the dreams that may arise in the 'undiscover'd country' (Hamlet, III.i.79) of the 'life to come' that he cannot jump. But Macbeth has defined himself as Claudius rather than Hamlet, and so envisions himself as victim rather than instrument of the 'even-handed Justice [that] / Commends th'ingredience of our poison'd chalice / To our own lips' (I.vii.10–12). That thought rouses his more filial feelings as Duncan's 'kinsman and his subject,' as well as his host. The image of himself as host arouses his protective feelings so that he envisions himself guarding the gentle Duncan, who has 'borne his faculties so meek.' From that double image of gentleness violated is born the image of 'Pity, like a naked new-born babe, / Striding the blast,' riding the winds in vengeance against him, before which he falls back from his 'vaulting ambition.' But even as he generates an image of a natural child, he turns it against himself, for he has already chosen his Gertrude and eliminated any Ophelia against whom to unpack his heart with words.

As previously Macbeth came, as though called, at the end of Lady Macbeth's soliloquy, now she comes, as though called, to do in fact what she and Macbeth had anticipated she would. By chastising 'with the valour of my tongue / All that impedes thee from the golden round' she draws his enraptured vision into his ordinary reality and daily life, where 'Time and the hour runs through the roughest day' (I.iii.148). He initiated the integration of the past to the present level of his reality in writing the letter. She overcomes the impeding pity by equating his murderous desire to his sense of manliness, and his pity, with all its accumulated associations, to cowardice, and by implication in view of the swinish grooms, to sexual impotence. In her Macbeth generates the voice he needs to join his desire, first experienced through the witches, to his 'own act and valour' (I.vii.40). He permits himself a fleeting resistance, looking for an alternative equation between manliness and seemliness, but her words carry his deeper impulses when she argues that Macbeth's pledge to her is more binding than a mother's love for her child. Given the strong metaphorical equation generated throughout the play of the kingdom to a family, in asserting that Macbeth's pledge to her supersedes his bonds to kind and country, she opposes the love between herself and Macbeth to the encompassing scale of creaturely accord that extends from sucking infants to social harmony. When she says 'From this time / Such I account thy love' (I.vii.38–9) she defines their love as a world apart from ordinary reality, like that between Romeo and Juliet. However, in the idyllic romance of the earlier play the violence appeared as external to the lovers. That violence, seeping into the love of Hamlet and Ophelia, Desdemona and Othello, kept them apart. Here it invades and defines love, rendering it inimical to familial and social harmony when Lady Macbeth confirms Macbeth's purpose by saying.

> I have given suck, and know
> How tender 'tis to love the babe that milks me:
> I would, while it was smiling in my face,
> Have pluck'd my nipple from his boneless gums,
> And dash'd the brains out, had I so sworn
> As you have done to this. (I.vii.54–9)

In generating Bellona for his bride Macbeth has expressed his hatred and fear of his own child self—weak, vulnerable, in his eyes despised by woman as swinishly ineffectual. Therefore Lady Macbeth's image of destroying her child does not repel him, but rather persuades him to murder the gentle Duncan. He implicitly associates her image of the sucking babe with Duncan's murder when he responds, 'if we should fail?' He completes their secret collusion in acknowledging the role he has assigned her in saying, 'thy undaunted mettle should compose / Nothing but males' (I.vii.74–5), and prepares to take her keen knife into his hands when he advises her as previously she had him: 'Away, and mock the time with fairest show / False face must hide what the false heart doth know' (I.vii.82–3).

As he approaches the murder the two levels of Macbeth's awareness draw together. Defining the airborne dagger as a 'false creation / Proceeding from a heat-oppressed brain' (II.i.38–9), he gives it a reality midway between the dagger Lady Macbeth imagines herself wielding, and the dagger with which he will kill Duncan. Pointing to Duncan's room, it preludes the murder, and then stained with 'dudgeon gouts of blood,' it marks a transition from the past to the future, and a stage in the process by which Macbeth congeals free-floating emotion into images of reality. As he follows the dagger to Duncan's bedroom the perverse sexuality that has been dimly associated with the murder comes closer to his awareness:

> Now o'er the one half-world
> Nature seems dead, and wicked dreams abuse
> The curtain'd sleep: Witchcraft celebrates
> Pale Hecate's off'rings; and wither'd Murther,
> Alarum'd by his sentinel, the wolf,
> Whose howl's his watch, thus with his stealthy pace,
> With Tarquin's ravishing strides, towards his design
> Moves like a ghost.   (II.i.49–56)

Having stilled the compunctious visitings of nature, Macbeth with deep self-reflectiveness defines himself as a wicked dream that disturbs both Duncan's and his own 'curtain'd sleep.' The logic of the sentence then becomes discontinuous, but in the sequence he identifies with Hecate and offers the murder to the celebrating witches. Abandoning the female identification, he personifies himself as Murder, but that image elides with that of 'Tarquin's ravishing strides.' The passage moves from a negative female image of witchcraft and Hecate to a negative male image of Murder represented as a wolf's howl, a distant image that suddenly transforms into the more immediate one of Tarquin. But Tarquin was not pacing towards a murder, as is Macbeth, but rather towards the rape of Lucrece. Macbeth's sudden identification with Tarquin associates the dagger penetrating Duncan to sexual penetration of a woman.[12]

The total configuration is composed of two sets of fused images. Macbeth's image of himself as a wicked dream contains both female and male ranges, and the sleeping Duncan fuses beneficent paternal with feminine and maternal associations. With his self-image fused with the image of Hecate, Macbeth gets revenge on the unmanly, swinish paternal figure 'drenched in sleep,' who 'loves for his own ends, not for you,' while as Tarquin he interprets his dagger as a bloody phallus with which he violently penetrates the equivocating and seductive woman, and revenges himself on the passive paternal figure loved by the woman, as well as on this version of his own unmanly self. In a remote Oedipal configuration Macbeth's erotic drive towards the mother has blended both with his fear and horror of it and with rage at the interfering father, so that Macbeth in a single configuration expresses the active and passive ranges of his desire, since, identified with Duncan, he is also penetrated. But in espousing the active range he opens the wound in images of father, nurturing mother, and more remotely the children associated with her, the sexual woman, and those aspects of his own emotional capacities represented by those figures. 'Who would have thought the old man to have had so much blood in him?'

Neither our eyes nor Macbeth's peep through the blanketed dark to the invisible bedroom in which Macbeth and Lady Macbeth consummate their love. But what Macbeth does not wish to see or be seen, he wishes both to hear and to be heard. For having envisioned the sexuality implied in his association of women with malicious manipulation, illegitimate authority, and violence, he calls into action representatives of the legitimate authority he has violated. Through them he both maintains his self-definition as evil—for he can be evil only in terms of some concept of virtue—and generates the agents of his own punishment.

The punitive powers that will finally overwhelm him are first dimly heard in the knocking at the Porter's gate, the sound of which links the interior of Macbeth's castle where Macbeth hears it to the exterior where the Porter describes all equivocating professions being drawn into the interior hell. In this remote form Macbeth defines his castle as an underworld that draws into itself the surrounding social world. In a reverse movement he then envisions the devastation from the bedroom encompassing the cosmos when Macduff says, 'up, up, and see / The great doom's image!—Malcolm! Banquo! / As from your graves rise up, and walk like sprites / To countenance this horror!' (II.iii.76–9). That image of doomsday joins with Lady Macbeth's 'hideous trumpet [that] calls to parley / The sleepers of the house' (II.iii.80–1), both of which were implicit in Macbeth's earlier vision of Duncan's virtues pleading 'like angels, trumpet-tongu'd against him.'

Hamlet associated Gertrude's sexuality with doomsday in images of the risen dead and of heaven's face 'thought sick' at witnessing Gertrude's 'act.' In a complex image Macbeth calls for his own punishment in evoking the Judgement Day, but also associates it with images of birth when Ross describes the 'obscure bird' that 'prophesying with accents terrible / Of dire combustion and confus'd events, / New hatch'd to th'woeful time . . . Clamour'd the livelong night' (II.iii.56–9). As well, he associates himself with a birth of another kind when he says that 'Augures, and understood relations, have / By magot-pies, and choughs, and rooks, brought forth / The secret'st man of blood' (III.iv.122–5). That combination turns the doomsday image into one of the death of himself as a swinish swiller in the milk of human kindness and the birth of himself first as a usurping tyrant and then as a fiend. He also generates the opposing forces by which he can so define himself, thereby preserving in his world a vision of the good, protective paternal force, figured first in the images of the avenging babe and later in the avenging paternal figures whose forces are gathering. As well, in a remote form he satisfies perverse desires by distancing them into images of a country deprived of food, sleep, and peace. Secretly colluding with the avenging forces of legitimate authority by the self-defeating ways in which he pursues those creature pleasures, he also gradually separates himself from Lady Macbeth, even as he is reborn as the man she wanted him to be.

In Macbeth's new state his barren sceptre and fruitless crown deny the child-like and creaturely feelings that he fears. In what he defines as a means to restore natural pleasures, he repeats in externalized and remote ways the infanticide that deprived him of them. Having failed to kill Fleance, and having Hecate's assurance that no man 'of woman born' can kill him, he murders Macduff's wife and children. Since their murder in no way secures the peace of mind for which he says he commits it, the action becomes an image of his perverse relation to domestic tenderness. At the same time children become messengers of reprisal, from the image of Pity as an avenging babe, to the bloody child who gives him false security, and the crowned child who shows him Banquo's progeny.[13] Consciously in search of relief from the 'affliction of these terrible dreams, / That shake us nightly' (III.ii.17–20), and the 'restless ecstasy' of his nights with Lady Macbeth, he generates images that simultaneously extend and punish his initial perverse act. In order to eat and sleep in safety he murders Banquo, but brings his ghost back to destroy the ceremonial banquet about which Lady Macbeth says, 'to feed were best at home; / From thence, the sauce to meat is ceremony; / Meeting were bare without it' (III.iv.34–6), a punning image that merges the familial and the social realms. Under the guise of seeking peace Macbeth turns his country into an extended image of the original murder. The daggers that killed Duncan are recalled when Lennox says the country weeps and bleeds as 'each new day / A gash is added to her wounds' (IV.iii.40–1), Ross says that it 'cannot / Be call'd our mother, but our grave' (IV.iii.164–6), and Macbeth's determination to eat and sleep in peace is echoed in Macduff's quest in England for succour that will 'Give to our tables meat, sleep to our nights, / Free from our feasts and banquets bloody knives' (III.vi.33–5).

As Macbeth transforms his inner turmoil into images of a waste-land kingdom he also gradually redefines himself in his relation to Lady Macbeth. The collusive intimacy between them fades almost immediately after Duncan's murder, for as Macbeth espouses her image of him as an unthinking man of action he redefines her in a more conventional feminine role. The altered relationship appears in Macbeth's secrecy about his plan to murder Banquo, and in her secrecy about her fears. He projects onto her figure the reflectiveness that previously defined him when she says that all has been for nought 'Where our desire is got without content; / 'Tis safer to be that which we destroy, / Than by destruction dwell in doubtful joy' (III.ii.5–7). But she denies her anxiety by dismissing his when he envies Duncan who 'After life's fitful fever' sleeps well, and he savours the secrecy of his planned murder when he tells her to 'Let your remembrance apply to Banquo' (III.ii.30). Both withdraw from their 'restless ecstasy' with each other to 'make our faces vizards to our hearts / Disguising what they are' (III.ii.34–5). He approaches his plan indirectly, saying 'O! full of scorpions is my mind, dear wife! / Thou know'st that Banquo, and his Fleance, lives.' When she responds that 'in them Nature's copy's not eterne' (III.ii.36–9), he secretly obtains her validation of his unspoken plan. She addresses him as 'gentle, my lord,' and he her as 'love,' but in calling her 'dearest chuck' and withholding knowledge from her he reestablishes the conventional protectiveness of men towards women. The banquet scene despicts in association with each other Macbeth's separation from his wife, his isolation of himself from the realms of creaturely and social pleasures, and his redefinition of himself as a man of action when he says, 'Strange things I have in head that will to hand, / Which must be acted, ere they may be scann'd' (III.iv.138–9). In Banquo's ghost he experiences for the last time an emotionally laden image of his inner state, an image that occasions the last rebuke for lack of manliness he will hear from Lady Macbeth.[14]

He dismisses the ghost as an 'unreal mock'ry,' and starts to empty himself of his resonant inwardness and deep desires, which will remain in his consciousness only remotely when he attributes them to Lady Macbeth, from whom he will have separated himself.

This is the last scene in which Macbeth and Lady Macbeth appear together. Thereafter he allows the presently oriented image of woman defined in Lady Macbeth to sink into the inward sea of blood as he leaves it behind. Simultaneously he revivifies the more distant images of women and families, sups 'full of horrors' at Hecate's cauldron rather than at the banquet table, and then, having made the 'firstlings of [his] heart . . . the firstlings of [his] hand,' kills another image of the family in Macduff's wife and children.

Just as before the regicide he had anticipated the avenging forces that would pursue him, so after it he anticipated the emptiness that would follow from externalizing his emotions into images of a devastated mother country. Earlier, after Duncan's murder, he was the better able to dissimulate for being able to say truthfully that, 'There's nothing serious in mortality; / All is but toys: renown, and grace is dead; / The wine of life is drawn' (II.iii.91–3). Later he says without dissimulation, 'I have liv'd long enough: my way of life / Is fall'n into the sere, the yellow leaf' (V.iii.22–3), and finds himself confronted simultaneously with the avenging armies and with news of his wife's thick-coming fancies / That keep her from her rest,' an image that attributes to her the 'thick night,' thickening blood, and light that previously they had shared. As he dons his manly armour he equates the disease that troubles his wife with the English who trouble his country when he asks, 'What rhubarb, cyme or what purgative drug, / Would scour these English hence? Hear'st thou of them?' (V.iii.55–6). In the conflicting images of Lady Macbeth and of the battle Macbeth expresses his now divided and disowned feelings. When Macbeth feels confidence that 'Our castle's strength / Will laugh a siege to scorn,' the cry of women, as though in mockery, is heard from within that castle—the centre now of disease and corruption. In response he asserts his dry indifference in an image that completes the motif of nourishing food, milk, and human warmth, when he says, 'I have supp'd full with horrors: / Direness, familiar to my slaughterous thoughts, / Cannot once start me?' (V.v.13–15). Macbeth associates his incapacity to feel with his separation from Lady Macbeth in the announcement of her death that immediately follows.

Her death signifies his final retreat from his nightmare of love:

She should have died hereafter:
There would have been a time for such a word.—
To-morrow, and to-morrow, and to-morrow,
Creeps in this petty pace from day to day,
To the last syllable of recorded time;
And all our yesterdays have lighted fools
The way to dusty death. Out, out, brief candle!
Life's but a walking shadow; a poor player,

That struts and frets his hour upon the stage,
And then is heard no more: it is a tale
Told by an idiot, full of sound and fury,
Signifying nothing.   (V.v.17–28)

Since he is preoccupied with reassuring himself of his imperviousness to death in battle, he rejects the knowledge of his own mortality already implied in his wife's death. As well, since she dies immersed in the inner world of fantasy that he has escaped, he tries to dismiss the news of her death with affectless dry weariness when he says, 'She should have died hereafter.' As a strategy to avoid the impact of her death in the present, his mind moves first to the future, and then to the past. But when he has emptied the present of significance, the future stretches ahead, 'To-morrow, and to-morrow, and to-morrow,' partaking of the present emptiness, the 'petty pace' that he presently feels. In that state of mind the prospect of escaping death in battle and living forever can give no joy when all recorded time is composed of the insignificant syllables of meaningless action. But the phrase 'creeps in this petty pace' suggests that infant state that he has violated first in himself and then in the world. With that suggestion his mind swings from the future to the past. He no longer responds to the horror of that past; only the sense of meaninglessness remains that he has already projected onto the future. All those 'yesterdays' from infancy to the present, at one time alight with desire, now appear illusory, leading to a 'dusty death' that is indistinguishable from his former vision of his future. Therefore he wants to extinguish the candle that, by illuminating the past, reveals the meaning of Lady Macbeth's death. He sees instead his inner condition writ large when he calls life 'but a walking shadow,' whereas he is now the walking shadow, the bloodless form of himself without the content of passion. The image of the moving shadow suggests one of the stage, but since the candle has been blown out, it is a darkened stage, a scene like Duncan's bedroom that Macbeth both wants and fears to see. Just as sound replaced sight earlier, so he now hears in the dusty darkness the player who 'struts and frets' upon the 'bloody stage' that he himself has generated, and which, Ross says, the heavens threaten. In turn, this suggests an image of Duncan's bloody bedroom, coloured by Macbeth's desires and revulsion, guilt and rage on which he does not wish to look again. So threatening is his projection of what he might see if he allowed himself to look that he takes a further and final means to distance himself from the vision. He transforms the image of the stage to the less immediate one of a tale; but a tale is told to a child. Despite himself, Macbeth evokes the image of a child, but denies what that child might reveal by attributing the tale to an enlarged and grotesque version of a child—an idiot. In this way he eradicates the meaning of his past, present, and future. But thereby hangs another tale of the process by which Macbeth, in fearing to see the images that reveal the emotional content of his actions, transforms life into a tale 'signifying nothing.'[15]

   Before Macbeth encounters the witches, one of them says that, having been refused chestnuts, she will pursue through the ports of the world the 'rumpfed ronyon's' sailor husband in a sieve;

I'll drain him dry as hay:
Sleep shall neither night nor day
Hang upon his penthouse lid;
He shall live a man forbid.
Weary sev'n-nights nine times nine,
Shall he dwindle, peak and pine:
Though his bark cannot be lost,
Yet it shall be tempest-tost.   (I.iii.18–25)

Macbeth associates himself with that image when he conjures the witches and Hecate to foretell the future 'though the yesty waves / Confound and swallow navigation up; / Though bladed corn be lodg'd, and trees blown down' (IV.i.53–5), and the witches' images prefigure the feelings he later experiences. But the last two lines seem contrary to the play's end, since by any ordinary account Macbeth, called a fiend by Macduff, would seem as damned as man can be. But amid the increasing vilification in which he approaches his death, he also generates purified images of authority. Macduff is not of woman born, and children are referred to in images of wrens, eggs, and nestlings that remind one of those in *Hamlet*. They also are not of women born, and Malcolm evokes and dissociates himself from all of Macbeth's crimes, specifically declaring himself 'unknown to woman' (V.iii.126). Birnam wood, a disembodied female image detached from the 'rooky wood' in which Banquo dies, moves towards Macbeth's embattled tower in which Lady Macbeth lies dead. While on the one hand he claims his wife, though within the sense of evil that comes with the voices who couple them—'this dead butcher and his fiend-like Queen' (V.ix.35)—on the other he sees his head, like Cawdor's earlier, on a stick, without blood, passion, or body. That final stage image seems to flow from Macbeth's earlier words, 'They have tied me to a stake; I cannot fly, / But bear-like I must fight the course' (V.vii.1–2). One might say that in these words he initiates a process by which he denies his body, merges it with the stake to which he feels bound, and completes the process in the image of his bodiless head on a pole. One might speculate further, though it is perhaps far-fetched, that Macbeth's last vision of himself foreshadows Prospero, who has detached himself from his bodily passions, which are contained in the figure of Caliban, and who exercises total control of his domain through his books. Such a speculation gains some credence from the witches' assurance that the sailor's bark cannot be lost, though it can be tempest-tossed.

NOTES

[1] In '*Macbeth:* Drama and Dream,' *Literary Criticism and Psychology,* ed Joseph P. Strelka (University Park: Pennsylvania State University Press, 1976), 150–73, Simon O. Lesser relates the play's dreamlike quality to the murder of the sovereign, the symbol of order in the state and psyche, which touches infantile anarchic desires (172). A. P. Rossiter in *Angel with Horns and Other Shakespeare Lectures,* ed Graham Storey (New York: Theatre Arts Books, 1961), implies an analogy to dreams in saying that the play's meaning resides in its plot, rather than in what characters say about it (229).
[2] J. I. M. Stewart states in *Character and Motive in Shakespeare* (London: Longmans, Green, 1949) that Macbeth is compelled by the 'crime and not the crown' (93).

[3] In line with Freud's comment on the poetic justice of the Macbeths' being childless, Ludwig Jekels in 'The Riddle of Shakespeare's *Macbeth,*' *The Design Within,* ed Melvin Faber (New York: Science House, 1970), thinks the play advocates being a good son in order to be a good father (243).

[4] The image also suggests that beneath Macbeth's fair exterior is a self-image like that of Richard III. In *A Psychoanalytic Study of the Double in Literature* (Detroit: Wayne State University Press, 1970) Robert Rogers argues that Lady Macbeth is both a double for Macbeth and a mother-figure, a configuration that represents Macbeth's failure of individuation (51). Wagner sees her as Macbeth's 'phallic prop' (248).

[5] Marjorie Garber in *Coming of Age in Shakespeare* (London: Methuen, 1981) relates Lady Macbeth's barrenness to the barren world that Macbeth creates around him (153–4).

[6] Despite the general agreement that this scene is not in Shakespeare's 'usual style,' the sequence of the Hecate scenes parallels that of the two witch scenes, and accords with the previous emotional patterns. Here, as elsewhere, it is conceivable that the style reflects Shakespeare's drawing back from the images of terror he generates, leaving figures uninformed by language that flows from full imaginative evocation, even allowing for the interpolation of Middleton's songs.

[7] Dennis Biggins in 'Sexuality, Witchcraft and Violence in *Macbeth,*' *Shakespeare Studies* 8 (1976) 255–77, widens and deepens the significance of the relation between Lady Macbeth and the witches by pointing out that traditionally witches were presumed to be lustful, sexually perverse, and sexually dominant. He also thinks of the murder as a kind of rape.

[8] Jenifoy La Belle in '"A Strange Infirmity": Lady Macbeth's Amenorrhea,' *Shakespeare Quarterly* 31 (1980) 381–6, on the basis of medical terminology of the time, argues that Lady Macbeth literally wants and gets her menstruation stopped, and later suffers the physiological and emotional consequences in the barren sceptre and blood images that substitute for the natural flow (384–5). In 'Lady Macbeth and Infanticide, or How Many Children Had Lady Macbeth Murdered?' *Journal of the American Psychoanalytic Association* 17 (1969) 528–48, Victor Kalef writes that Lady Macbeth's childlessness both punishes her and is part of the crime (539). Vesny Wagner in *'Macbeth:* "Fair is Foul and Foul is Fair,"' *American Imago* 25 (1968) 242–57, states that Macbeth's hatred of his mother leads to his being pursued by children.

[9] In 'Macbeth: Imagery of Destruction,' *American Imago* 39 (1982) 149–64, Joan M. Byles argues that Macbeth's actions are not only in proportion to his guilt, as Freud suggested, 'but rather to the threats on his manhood they represent' (155). Coppélia Kahn in *Man's Estate* (Berkeley: University of California Press, 1981) relates images of milking babes in both *Macbeth* and *Coriolanus* to their protagonists' denial of infantile vulnerability that leads to a dehumanized masculinity (154).

[10] D. S. Kastan in 'Shakespeare and the Way of Womenkind,' *Daedalus* 11 (1982) 115–30, reads *Macbeth* in terms of the the contemporary ideal of equal partnership in marriage. Lady Macbeth 'champions an ideal of manhood that excludes compassion' (124).

[11] In 'The Babe That Milks: An Organic Study of *Macbeth,*' *The Design Within,* 251–80, David B. Barron sees incomplete masculinity rendering Macbeth helpless in a 'nightmare world of women' (265).

[12] Richard Wheeler in *Shakespeare's Development and the Problem Comedies* (Berkeley: University of California Press, 1981) says Duncan's dead body becomes a 'new Gorgon,' both male and female, murdered, raped, and castrated (145). Madelon Gohlke in '"I Wooed Thee with My Sword": Shakespeare's Tragic Paradigms,' *The Woman's Part,* 150–70, says that here as in *Othello* murder is a loving act, and love a murdering one (156).

[13] In 'The Naked Babe in the Cloak of Manliness,' *The Well Wrought Urn* (London: Dobson, 1968), 17–39, Cleanth Brooks first called attention to the significance of Macbeth's war with children.

[14] Carolyn Asp in '"Be Bloody, Bold and Resolute": Tragic Action and Sexual Stereotyping in *Macbeth,*' *Studies in Philology* 78 (1981) 153–69, blames the sexual stereotyping of society for Macbeth's narrow definition of his masculinity, and for his consequent alienation (156).

[15] In *The Dynamics of Literary Response* (New York: Oxford University Press, 1968) Norman Holland gives a penetrating reading of the core fantasy of this speech as though it were an independent poem (106–14). I depart from him in that I relate the speech to the past of the text, rather than to the character's hypothetical past.

Barbara Everett

MACBETH: SUCCEEDING

Macbeth's story is of a man who desires kingship enough to kill for it, and whose action leads him on into proliferating crimes. This desire, which is destructive—a lust mystifyingly cold—requires explanation, as Macbeth can be felt to wish to understand himself. The explanation of Macbeth most often given is that he is an 'ambitious' man. This makes obvious sense. But there are problems. 'Ambition' is in itself a fairly limited and trivial impulse, however large its ends and rewards, and doesn't precisely account for the large imaginative resonances of Macbeth's story. Moreover, the Macbeth of the first two acts behaves so little like an ambitious man as to provide critics with a lasting problem of motivation. It is more as if Macbeth moves blindly, allowing what happens to create motives gradually. Certainly he ends as a far simpler, far more brutal man than he begins—he finishes as a man of nothing but motives.

The play itself offers a concept both less purposive and less limited than 'ambition': one which at least helps to explain what it is that relates Macbeth to his fellow human beings in a fashion at once so cold, so withdrawn and yet so violently engaged. That concept is of *success.* We first meet Macbeth as a successful man. At I. iii Rosse and Angus meet the victorious warriors, Macbeth and Banquo, and they communicate Macbeth's first promotion:

> The King hath happily receiv'd, *Macbeth,*
> The newes of thy successe.

Macbeth then remembers with grave excitement that the Witches who met him on the field of battle foretold such promotion and therefore gave what he calls 'earnest of successe'. Later, reporting back to his wife, named as his 'dearest Partner of Greatnesse' in the letter she is reading when we first meet her, Macbeth proclaims of the Witches: *'They met me in the day of successe: and I have learn'd by the perfect'st report, they have more in them, then mortall knowledge . . . '* 'Success' returns once more and fatefully in scene 7, as Macbeth confronts his desire for the crown, with the old King a guest in his house:

From *Young Hamlet: Essays on Shakespeare's Tragedies* (Oxford: Clarendon Press, 1989), pp. 95–105.

If th'Assassination
Could trammell up the Consequence, and catch
With his surcease, Successe . . .

The writing is interestingly strange here, as if Macbeth were making up intense
obscure knotted runic poems which at once reveal his nature and conceal it:
'surcease' means death, the great pool of blood beneath the old man, and 'Successe'
means to Macbeth something that we cannot see clearly. Macbeth's tragedy is a
coldness, and that coldness is brought about by his absolute response to a concept
whose vagueness in human terms is vital to what Shakespeare is doing in the play.
For the Elizabethans, 'Success' was a word and concept in process of change. Its
original meaning entails the mere happening of one thing after another. 'Success'
begins by meaning simply the way things fall out; just as 'succession' means a son's
following or inheriting from his father. But 'succession' came to hold the special
sense of ascent to a royal father's throne, and 'success' similarly moved upward on
the same worldly path. It was natural for Elizabethans to use 'success' widely, to
cover good and bad happenings alike; if they particularly wanted to distinguish, they
wished each other 'good success' or regretted 'bad success'. This neutral sense is
probably still contained in what Angus and Rosse say to Macbeth, meaning that the
King is pleased with the news of how things have fallen out. And when Macbeth
speaks of the 'Successe' that follows the 'surcease' he is thinking first of stopping
some possible retributive future from happening—he is in will inhibiting the things
that follow on.

The mocking half-rhyme of 'surcease, Successe' involves different meanings
though. Medieval Macbeth is in a sense a very modern character. His infatuation
with the word 'success' eagerly grasps towards the sense that we use it for now.
All these first-act occurrences of the concept show it caught in the drift towards a
peculiar specificity that it was undergoing historically. For us, 'success' has come to
mean in effect that what happens, ought to happen—that whatever goes is good;
and that if a man happens to 'succeed' (in our sense) then plainly he ought to have
succeeded. Our concept of success insists that fortune is fate and even morality.
Because Macbeth has won a battle—a battle whose ugly vertiginous chanciness the
first scenes labour to make clear—he thinks he deserves to sit on a throne; he
thinks that success spells succession.[1] Every time Macbeth hears the word 'success',
he thinks of murder. Thinking so, he moves from a chance victory to a progressive
deformation of all natural laws, the principles of true succession. This is why—to
return to a detail I mentioned earlier—a bird makes wing, alarmingly, to a wood
where it meets itself; and why the Macbeths, who early in the play can think readily
of having children, end the tragedy childless, successionless. For the man of success
there is power but no future, no existence in the natural.

A fascinating and enigmatic feature of Macbeth's career is that he never seems
to agree to do the King's murder; it just gets done. Moreover, responsibility seems
to slither from Macbeth to Lady Macbeth, and then critically from her back again
to him, in a way that puzzles some critics and makes them feel that the play must
have been cut. Lady Macbeth actually asks him 'What beast it was' that made him

get her interested in murder, and so on, when there has been remarkably little time for any such communication. The answer, I think, is that both the Macbeths slide along the channels of success, which are not entirely voluntary. They fold into their world, and the next thing they know, they are killing the King. They start to live, that is to say, in 'the day of successe', and natural succession—laws of true cause and effect—begin to fall away from them.

This is why, as Bradley pointed out long ago, neither of the Macbeths regard themselves as actually pushing a knife into a gentle old man at all; they refer to the murder by a series of runes and euphemisms, as if it were a high but appalling duty. But once Duncan is dead, the play starts its descent into clarity. Macbeth knows with more and more lucidity what it is he is going to do, and he does it. This process is brought about by Macbeth's use of success as an inward criterion. The word obfuscates for him as it does now, and when the mists clear it is too late to change. Some things that are successfully done aren't worth doing, and some are nothing but vicious when they are done. The Macbeths only find out the meaning of words by getting blood on their hands. Macbeth sacrifices all past and future time, all Nature's great objective pattern of true succeeding, a complex of events quite outside the desires of the self, to a present appetite: and his life turns into an infinite present, a 'To morrow, and to morrow, and to morrow / . . . To the last Syllable of Recorded time'. There is something curiously horrible about the fact that Macbeth, having murdered to get into History, in the end can't get out of it.

Why does Macbeth get himself locked up in this way in 'the day of successe'? This is a tragedy of suggestion more than of statement, but the opening of the play is rich in its suggestiveness. A peculiarity of it is the fact that it holds remarkably few characters. A named part is not a character, though some recent productions have clearly tried to make the Witches, for instance, characters, or Angus and Rosse characters. But this is simply against the grain of a work in which even Lady Macbeth (say) doesn't have a first name, and we have to refer to her throughout as Lady Macbeth. The tragedy tends to have, instead of subordinate characters, powerful and explanatory scene-setting. This is particularly strong at the opening. Macbeth is a luminary of Duncan's Court and its chief warrior. With remarkable economy I. ii—whose oddities have made some scholars believe it to be heavily edited—tells us in shorthand what we need to know about this world and its representative, the most gloriously successful man of the hour: whose glory is, however, from the first lines of the play darkened and made even more ambiguous because waiting for Macbeth on the edge of the heroic battlefield are the three Witches.

In I. ii, in a wonderfully strange and deformed speech, the 'bleeding Captaine', the 'bloody man', describes the scene that has made Macbeth what he is. If Macbeth hungers, as we shall find out, for success and succession, for somewhere to climb to, it is because climbing upward is a way of getting out of what the wounded Captain describes. The theatre of war is, he says, 'Doubtfull . . . / As two spent Swimmers, that doe cling together, / And choake their Art'. The Captain further tells the King that when Macbeth saved the day against a frightening successful rival, he

(Like Valours Minion) carv'd out his passage,
Till hee fac'd the Slave:
Which nev'r shooke hands, nor bad farwell to him,
Till he unseam'd him from the Nave to th' Chops,
And fix'd his Head upon our Battlements.

What has worried scholars about this second scene is the fact of its literal confusions—Macbeth apparently defeating two geographically far-distanced enemies on one afternoon, for instance. The scene also describes Macbeth as apparently confronting as the enemy Norwegian King's right-hand-man a Cawdor whose treachery he seems to know nothing whatever about in the next scene. But none of this matters because the Captain's theme is in any case the almost unendurable confusion of war. This confusion actually shapes the Captain's speech. The encounter of King's Man and rebel dissolves into 'He ... him ... he ... him', leaving a real and rather horrible uncertainty as to who exactly unseamed whom instead of politely shaking hands among the butchery. All that clearly arises from the mazed syntax is that the winner seems to be described as 'Valour's minion', a worrying title in itself. Similarly, when Macbeth and the traitor Cawdor meet in battle, someone called Bellona's Bridegroom—whom, again, we take to be Macbeth—

                    lapt in proofe,
Confronted him with selfe-comparisons,
Point against Point, rebellious Arme 'gainst Arme.

The confusions of these lines (editors hesitate over how to punctuate them) help to sum up what they show, all the weak, confused, yet 'heroic' violence of the scene, in which identities, genders, even syntaxes are lost in vertigo. The writing is deep in that irony which rules throughout the play, undermining and reversing meanings. The confusion and irony with which warfare is here described, and the suggested uncertainty of the outcome, become the more important in that Duncan will at I. iv extend it to all politics, all diplomacy, all human relations:

                    There's no Art,
To finde the Mindes construction in the Face.

The battlefield, that is to say, extends into the Court, as the Court into the Castle. Human relations themselves are summoned up in the image with which the Captain opens:

                    Doubtfull it stood,
As two spent Swimmers, that doe cling together,
And choake their Art.

They pull each other down in their frenzy to survive—an image we may later think of in relation to Macbeth and his wife. The 'swimmers' suggest an irreversible pull downwards in existence, a something in human energies that self-destructs as surely as gravity pulls. This is a moral vision which is categorizable under the Calvinistic— Calvin followed the dark vision of Augustinian Christianity, which argued that without God, even human virtue is nothing but splendid vices, 'splendida vitia'. Yet a theology isn't needed to countenance this vision of will-to-corruption. It's alarming, but not surprising, that the Witches probably seem less unbelievable figures now, with the signs of revival of interest in black magics, than they appeared to the eighteenth and nineteenth centuries, when it still seemed possible to believe in a progressive movement in civilization.

Matthew Arnold called up a scene not unlike the opening of *Macbeth* when he wrote in 'Dover Beach' that

> we are here upon a darkling plain
> Swept by confused alarms of trouble and flight
> Where ignorant armies clash by night.

But there is a sense in which Arnold's image is only an epic simile, brought in to intensity the appeal to emotional relationship. Shakespeare's Marguerite is his Witches. The battle is the Court's other place, the arena in which Macbeth embodies the Court's perpetual pathless climb upward. The Witches put that climb in a moral perspective, and direct the climb upward simultaneously downward. They make sure that Heraclitus's 'Way up is the way down'.

They don't effect more than this. Supernaturally speaking, they reveal only two properties in the course of the play. They can vanish, but then so could most people with the aid of Jacobean stage-machinery. And the Witches can tell the future. Or rather, they can tell one thing about the future: 'Haile to thee *Thane* of Glamis /... haile to thee *Thane* of Cawdor. / All haile *Macbeth,* that shalt be King hereafter.' The Witches have the same faculty as regards human success as animals—cats, for instance—have about the smell of cooking kidneys. They can tell it from an amazing distance, and they gather. There is nothing else in the Witches except a pulse-beat of minute, dangerous, absolutely incessant ill will:

> in a Syve Ile thither sayle,
> And like a Rat without a tayle,
> Ile doe, Ile doe, and Ile doe ...

> Ile dreyne him drie as Hay:
> Sleepe shall neyther Night nor Day
> Hang upon his Pent-house Lid:
> He shall live a man forbid ...   (I. iii. 9–22)

None of this is how Macbeth sees it, and writes about it to his wife:

They met me in the day of successe: and I have learn'd by the perfect'st report, they have more in them, then mortall knowledge. When I burnt in desire to question them further, they made themselves Ayre, into which they

vanish'd. Whiles I stood rapt in the wonder of it, came Missives from the
King . . .   (I. v. I–6)

When the witches refer to themselves in the early texts of the play, they call
themselves not 'Weird'—which is the word shared by both Shakespeare's source
Holinshed and modern editions—but 'Weyward', which may be only a contemporary spelling of Weird, or may not. Macbeth sees weyward old women—trivial,
grubby, infinitely malevolent, but apparently fond of animals—and he makes them
'Weird', figures of power, figures of awe.

It's conceivable that we can guess why he does this. *Macbeth* is a tragedy
extremely bare in human relationship: which is what gives that between Macbeth
and Lady Macbeth such intensity, such strength and life. The two Macbeths between them sacrifice every other possibility of relationship that might have opened
around them. But every now and again there is a kind of curtain lifted in the tragedy
and we see one of these lost possibilities. While Macbeth is murdering Duncan Lady
Macbeth tells us, 'Had he not resembled / My Father as he slept, I had don't'. Lady
Macbeth with a father is a troublingly different thing. The Witches have a somewhat
similar effect on Macbeth. Because of his murders, he needs them—he is drawn
into their company, he hunts them out, it is almost an infatuation. He is even, we
might say, like a weak and childish man who is always abandoning his family and
allows himself to be drawn back into the spoiling care and comfort of a collection
of elderly female relatives. The Witches are dingy, bad pre-Volumnias, who locate
in the play the faintest hint of that destructive power-relationship of mother and
son more sharply present in *Coriolanus:* 'Give me, quoth I'. The resemblance is just
enough to make us see how Macbeth lacks that human rootedness as well. Certainly these unreal 'mothers' give him nothing except a form of knowledge he
would in any case have been infinitely better without.

The simplest form of the evil that the Witches do to Macbeth—though the
truth is that he does it to himself—is to draw him away from Lady Macbeth.
Because of the play's marked thinness in terms of character, we feel the coexistence of these two acutely. Though the soul, as it were, of Macbeth's tragedy is the
slow destruction of his inner self—the luminous moral imagination that understands
everything that is happening to him—the heart of his tragedy is the destruction of
his marriage. Lady Macbeth is all relationship to Macbeth—she is his rooting in
human life.

In a recent interview about his production of *Macbeth*, Sir Peter Hall
remarked—and he said it several times, with insistence—that Lady Macbeth is
'very, very sexy'. I find this modish jazzing up of the part saddening; it almost ideally
misses by overshooting the real point of the darkly ironical fact that the Macbeths
are probably Shakespeare's most thoroughly married couple. Not just lecherous
but married: and these aren't the same things. The Macbeths have an extraordinary
community and complicity. Some of the play's most troubling moments are those
which reach ahead through (say) Chekhov and Ibsen and Strindberg, and many
current writers, into 'the woe that is in marriage': the Macbeths become that

terrible couple who appear so early in the play, 'two spent Swimmers, that doe cling together, / And choake their Art'—their love is so corrupted by the struggle to survive as to pull each other down. Macbeth, to put it simply, loves Lady Macbeth;—they love each other; at the painful III. ii, where they first show a marked drift away from each other, each minds. Macbeth addresses his wife with troubled extra care, as 'Love', 'deare Wife', and 'dearest Chuck'. The tragic mutual destructiveness of the marriage is summed up by a simple fact. Married couples invariably, if it is a true marriage, grow like each other. The Macbeths slowly exchange qualities in the course of the play. From the beginning Lady Macbeth has brought to their life a directness, a practicality, an inability to see difficulties in a good cause. Only, she can't see difficulties in a bad cause, either. 'But screw your courage to the sticking place, / And wee'le not fayle.' The crux over what precisely her first 'We faile?' means is interesting: she genuinely can't imagine—she can't cope with ifs; she simply throws Macbeth's phrases back at him. And this practicality moves into Macbeth in the form of brutality—which is why he starts not to need her any more. Lady Macbeth for her part inherits his imagination, but only in the form of nightmare. And she can't live with it: it stops her sleeping ever again.

I want to stress the fact of Shakespeare's depth and seriousness and even tendernesss in depicting their marriage. One of the play's most touching and subtle moments is that which brings Lady Macbeth before us for the first time, and she is reading Macbeth's letter: he exists for her when he isn't there. He exists too much for her when he isn't there, she plans and thinks ahead too much for him, she too much connives, putting her image of Macbeth's future where her conscience should be: as the Doctor says, staring at her wide-open but out-of-touch gaze, 'You have knowne what you should not.' And the Gentlewoman adds, 'Heaven knowes what she has knowne.' Lady Macbeth is Macbeth's 'Dearest Partner of Greatnesse', the tender yet arrogant phrase Macbeth uses to her in his letter, as if the one thing in the world a good marriage were for, were getting a throne. And there begins from that point the insidious corruption of the good which I mentioned earlier:

> yet I doe feare thy Nature,
> It is too full o'th' Milke of humane kindnesse,
> To catch the neerest way . . .

For Lady Macbeth's immediate action, when she knows that the King is coming, is to call to spirits to 'Unsex me here'—to make herself no more a woman. She is sacrificing to Macbeth's success his succession—their hope of children. When the two of them meet at I. vii, it is the hope of children, and the destruction of children, that is a theme of what they say to each other. There is a kind of strange sense in the fact that when finally—in V. v—Lady Macbeth dies, evidently by her own hand, Macbeth feels her death as real, yet as 'signifying nothing'. He has created a present in which there is no time for death. Because he has succeeded, he cannot grieve for the one person he cared for absolutely, the person who was in a strict and technical sense 'his life'.

I have stressed Macbeth's relation with his wife, and spent little time on his more inward and imaginative life in the play, for two reasons. Macbeth's moral disintegration is very superbly articulated in the play; it is not difficult to understand; and in any case has had an enormous amount of critical attention devoted to it. My second reason is even stronger. A problem of the play seems to me how to explain why we mind it so much—why we feel great pain at the end of this savage warrior murderer. One of the most remarkable aspects of Shakespeare's genius is the degree to which in the last act he shows the brutish and external Macbeth—'Hang out our Banners on the outward walls'—and yet retains for him a pure human sympathy, so that we can still associate his fate with our own:

> I have liv'd long enough, my way of life
> Is falne into the Seare, the yellow Leafe,
> And that which should accompany Old-Age,
> As Honor, Love, Obedience, Troopes of Friends,
> I must not look to have: but in their steed,
> Curses, not lowd but deepe, Mouth-honor, breath
> Which the poore heart would faine deny, and dare not.   (V. iii. 22–8)

This is the Macbeth whom Shakespeare has created as the human creature in pursuit of success, and who feels the deepening intensities of the pain of true human failure. We see here, as at moments everywhere through the tragedy, the larger human life that Macbeth and his 'poore heart' might have enjoyed, but which he has failed to understand. This experience Shakespeare sums up in one of the last lines Macbeth speaks before he is swallowed up by his last battle—a line of extraordinary power in its simplicity, and indeed it seems to me one of the very great lines in literature: 'I 'ginne to be a-weary of the Sun.' Murder and tyranny are transmuted into altogether other human simplicities.

NOTES

[1] Emrys Jones draws my attention to the fact that, for a short period spanning Shakespeare's working lifetime, the word *success* could actually mean 'succession of heirs and rulers' (*OED, success*, sense 5).

CONTRIBUTORS

HAROLD BLOOM is Sterling Professor of the Humanities at Yale University and Henry W. and Albert A. Berg Professor of English at the New York University Graduate School. He is a 1985 MacArthur Foundation Award recipient, served as the Charles Eliot Norton Professor of Poetry at Harvard University (1987–88), and is the author of nineteen books, the most recent being *The Book of J* (1990). Currently he is editing the Chelsea House series Modern Critical Views and The Critical Cosmos, and other Chelsea House series in literary criticism.

A. C. BRADLEY held professorships of Modern Literature at the University of Liverpool, of English language and literature at the University of Glasgow, and of Poetry at Oxford. *Shakespearean Tragedy* (1904) established him as the preeminent Shakespeare scholar of the early twentieth century and remains a classic of modern Shakespeare criticism. His *Oxford Lectures on Poetry* were published in 1909, and *A Miscellany* in 1929.

WAYNE C. BOOTH is George W. Pullman Professor of English at the University of Chicago. His first book, *The Rhetoric of Fiction* (1961), is a classic of modern criticism. *Modern Dogma and the Rhetoric of Assent* (1974) and *Critical Understanding: The Powers and Limits of Pluralism* (1979) are excursions into cultural criticism, while Booth's most recent book, *The Company We Keep: An Ethics of Fiction* (1988), is a provocative examination of the ethics of reading.

JOHN HOLLOWAY is Professor of Modern English at Queen's College, Cambridge. Among his many books of criticism are *The Victorian Sage* (1953), *The Charted Mirror* (1960), *Narrative and Structure: Exploratory Essays* (1979), and *The Slumber of Apollo* (1984). Holloway is a distinguished poet, and is known for such volumes as *The Landfallers* (1962) and *Planet of Winds* (1977).

C. J. SISSON, who died in 1966, taught in many universities in France, Egypt, India, and England, most prominently as Lord Northcliffe Professor of Modern English Literature at University College, London. One of the great Shakespeare scholars of his time, he edited Shakespeare's works (1954) and wrote such volumes as *The Last Plays of Shakespeare's Age* (1936) and *New Readings in Shakespeare* (1956).

ELIZABETH NIELSEN was Professor of English at Long Beach State College. She published another article on *Macbeth* in a 1973 issue of *Shakespeare Quarterly.*

ROBERT B. HEILMAN is Professor Emeritus of English at the University of Washington. He has written books on *King Lear* (1948) and *Othello* (1956), as well as *The Ways of the World: Comedy and Society* (1978) and many other volumes. He has edited several critical anthologies, including *Understanding Drama* (1948; with Cleanth Brooks), and critical editions of works by Swift, Hardy, Shakespeare, and others.

WILBUR SANDERS is University Teaching Officer at Selwyn College, Cambridge. Among his volumes are *John Donne's Poetry* (1971), *Shakespeare's Magnanimity* (1978), and *The Winter's Tale* (1987).

ALAN HOBSON was, until his death, Schoolmaster Fellow of English at the University of Wales–Bangor. He wrote *Full Circle: Shakespeare and Moral Development* (1972).

P. RAMA MOORTHY teaches at the University of Mysore in Mysore, India, and has written on *Othello* and other Shakespeare plays.

245

CAROLYN ASP is Associate Professor of English at Marquette University, and is the author of articles on *All's Well That Ends Well, King Lear, Troilus and Cressida, The Winter's Tale*, and Andrew Marvell.

LISA LOW is Assistant Professor of English at Pace University in New York City. Currently she is editing a collection of essays on Milton, the Metaphysicals, and Romanticism.

KAY STOCKHOLDER is Professor of English at the University of British Columbia. She has written *Dream Works: Lovers and Families in Shakespeare's Plays* (1987).

BARBARA EVERETT is the author of *Auden* (1964), *Poets in Their Time: Essays on English Poetry from Donne to Larkin* (1986), and editions of *All's Well That Ends Well* (1970) and *Antony and Cleopatra* (1964). She is Senior Research Fellow and Lecturer in English at Somerville College, Oxford.

BIBLIOGRAPHY

Adam, R. J. "The Real Macbeth: King of Scots, 1040–1054." *History Today* 7 (1957): 381–87.

Adelman, Janet. " 'Born of Woman': Fantasies of Maternal Power in *Macbeth."* In *Cannibals, Witches, and Divorce: Estranging the Renaissance,* edited by Marjorie Garber. Baltimore: Johns Hopkins University Press, 1987, pp. 90–121.

Amneus, Daniel. "Macbeth's 'Greater Honor.'" *Shakespeare Studies* 6 (1972): 223–30.

Anderson, Ruth L. "The Pattern of Behavior Culminating in *Macbeth." Studies in English Literature* 3 (1973): 151–73.

Arthos, John. "The Naive Imagination and the Destruction of Macbeth." *ELH* 14 (1947): 114–26.

Baird, David. *The Thane of Cawdor: A Detective Study of* Macbeth. London: Oxford University Press, 1937.

Bamber, Linda. *"Macbeth* and *Coriolanus."* In *Comic Women, Tragic Men: A Study of Gender and Genre in Shakespeare.* Stanford: Stanford University Press, 1982, pp. 91–107.

Barroll, J. Leeds. *Artificial Persons: The Formation of Character in the Tragedies of Shakespeare.* Columbia: University of South Carolina Press, 1974.

Bartholomeusz, Dennis. *Macbeth and the Players.* Cambridge: Cambridge University Press, 1969.

Baxter, John. *"Macbeth:* Style and Form." In *Shakespeare's Poetic Styles: Verse into Drama.* London: Routledge & Kegan Paul, 1980, pp. 196–220.

Berger, Harry, Jr. "The Early Scenes of *Macbeth:* Preface to a New Interpretation." *ELH* 47 (1980): 1–31.

Bernad, Miguel A. "The Five Tragedies in *Macbeth." Shakespeare Quarterly* 13 (1962): 49–61.

Berryman, John. "Notes on *Macbeth."* In *The Freedom of the Poet.* New York: Farrar, Straus & Giroux, 1976, pp. 56–71.

Birenbaum, Harvey. "Consciousness and Responsibility in *Macbeth." Mosaic* 15, No. 2 (June 1982): 17–32.

Black, James. *"Macbeth:* The Arming of the Hero." *English Studies in Canada* 3 (1977): 253–66.

Bradbrook, M. C. "The Sources of *Macbeth." Shakespeare Survey* 4 (1951): 35–48.

Bradshaw, Graham. "Imaginative Openness and the *Macbeth*-Terror." In *Shakespeare's Scepticism.* New York: St. Martin's Press, 1987, pp. 219–56.

Brooke, Nicholas. "Language Most Shows a Man . . . ? Language and Speaker in *Macbeth."* In *Shakespeare's Styles: Essays in Honour of Kenneth Muir,* edited by Philip Edwards, Inga-Stina Ewbank, and G. K. Hunter. Cambridge: Cambridge University Press, 1980, pp. 67–78.

Brown, John Russell. *"Macbeth."* In *Shakespeare's Dramatic Style.* London: William Heinemann, 1970, pp. 160–91.

———, ed. *Focus on* Macbeth. London: Routledge & Kegan Paul, 1982.

Bryant, Joseph A., Jr. *"Macbeth* and the Meaning of Tragedy." *Kentucky Review* 8, No. 2 (Summer 1988): 3–17.

Bulman, James C. "Bellona's Bridegroom or Dwarfish Thief?" In *The Heroic Idiom of Shakespearean Tragedy.* Newark: University of Delaware Press, 1985, pp. 169–90.

Burton, Philip. "Macbeth." In *The Sole Voice: Character Portraits from Shakespeare.* New York: Dial Press, 1970, pp. 356–79.

Byles, Joan M. "Macbeth: Imagery of Destruction." *American Imago* 39 (1982): 149–64.

Cahn, Victor L. *"Macbeth."* In *The Heroes of Shakespeare's Tragedies.* New York: Peter Lang, 1988, pp. 125–42.

Calderwood, James L. *If It Were Done:* Macbeth *and Tragic Action.* Amherst: University of Massachusetts Press, 1986.

Cartelli, Thomas. "Banquo's Ghost: The Shared Vision." *Theatre Journal* 35 (1983): 389–405.

Clark, Arthur Melville. *Murder under Trust; or, The Topical Macbeth and Other Jacobean Matters.* Edinburgh: Scottish Academic Press, 1981.

Clarke, C. C. "Darkened Reason in *Macbeth." Durham University Journal* 22 (1960–61): 11–18.

Collmer, Robert G. "An Existentialist Approach to *Macbeth." Personalist* 41 (1960): 484–91.

Coursen, Herbert R. "Agreeing with Dr. Johnson." *Ariel* 10, No. 2 (April 1979): 35–42.

———. "A Jungian Approach to Characterization: *Macbeth."* In *Shakespeare's "Rough Magic": Renaissance Papers in Honor of C. L. Barber,* edited by Peter Erickson and Coppélia Kahn. Newark: University of Delaware Press, 1985, pp. 230–44.

Cox, Roger L. "Macbeth Divided against Himself." In *Between Earth and Heaven: Shakespeare, Dostoevsky, and the Meaning of Christian Tragedy.* New York: Holt, Rinehart & Winston, 1969, pp. 96–119.

Creeth, Edmund. "Mankynde in *Macbeth."* In *Mankynde in Shakespeare.* Athens: University of Georgia Press, 1976, pp. 40–72.

Cunningham, Dolora G. "Macbeth: The Tragedy of the Hardened Heart." *Shakespeare Quarterly* 14 (1963): 39–47.

Curry, Walter Clyde. "The Demonic Metaphysics of *Macbeth." Studies in Philology* 30 (1933): 395–426.

———. "Macbeth's Changing Character." *Journal of English and Germanic Philology* 34 (1935): 311–38.

Daalder, Joost. "Shakespeare's Attitude to Gender in *Macbeth." AUMLA* No. 70 (November 1988): 366–85.

Dillon, Janette. " 'Too Absolute': *Macbeth, Coriolanus, Timon of Athens."* In *Shakespeare and the Solitary Man.* Totowa, NJ: Rowman & Littlefield, 1981, pp. 135–45.

Donohue, Joseph W., Jr. "Macbeth and Richard III: Dramatic Character and the Shakespearean Critical Tradition." In *Dramatic Character in the English Romantic Age.* Princeton: Princeton University Press, 1970, pp. 189–215.

Driver, Tom F. "The Uses of Time: The *Oedipus Tyrannus* and *Macbeth."* In *The Sense of History in Greek and Shakespearean Drama.* New York: Columbia University Press, 1960, pp. 143–67.

Egan, Robert. "His Hour upon the Stage: Role-Playing in *Macbeth." Centennial Review* 22 (1978): 327–45.

Elliott, G. R. *Dramatic Providence in* Macbeth. 2nd ed. Princeton: Princeton University Press, 1960.

Empson, William. *"Macbeth."* In *Essays on Shakespeare.* Edited by David B. Pirie. Cambridge: Cambridge University Press, 1986, pp. 137–57.

Enright, D. J. *"Macbeth* and the Henpecked Hero." In *Shakespeare and the Students.* New York: Schocken Books, 1970, pp. 121–52.

Farnham, Willard. *"Macbeth."* In *Shakespeare's Tragic Frontier: The World of His Final Tragedies.* Berkeley: University of California Press, 1950, pp. 79–137.

Fergusson, Francis. " 'Killing the Bond of Love': Ugolino and Macbeth." In *Trope and Allegory: Themes Common to Dante and Shakespeare*. Athens: University of Georgia Press, 1977, pp. 23–48.

Fergusson, Sir James. *The Man behind Macbeth and Other Studies*. London: Faber & Faber, 1969.

Ferrucci, Franco. "*Macbeth* and the Imitation of Evil." In *The Poetics of Disguise: The Autobiography of the Work in Homer, Dante, and Shakespeare*. Translated by Ann Dunnigan. Ithaca: Cornell University Press, 1980, pp. 125–58.

Firkins, Oscar W. "The Character of Macbeth." In *Selected Essays*. Minneapolis: University of Minnesota Press, 1933, pp. 255–80.

Foster, Donald W. "*Macbeth*'s War on Time," *English Literary Renaissance* 16 (1986): 319–42.

French, Marilyn. "*Macbeth*." In *Shakespeare's Division of Experience*. New York: Summit Books, 1981, pp. 241–51.

French, William W. "What 'May Become a Man': Image and Structure in *Macbeth*." *College Literature* 12 (1985): 191–201.

Frye, Roland Mushat. "Launching the Tragedy of Macbeth: Temptation, Deliberation, and Consent in Act I." *Huntington Library Quarterly* 50 (1987): 249–61.

Godshalk, William Leigh. "*Macbeth:* The Round of Sovereignty." In *Patterning in Shakespearean Drama*. The Hague: Mouton, 1973, pp. 116–33.

Goldberg, Jonathan. "Speculations: *Macbeth* and Source." In *Shakespeare Reproduced: The Text in History and Ideology*, edited by Jean E. Howard and Marion F. O'Connor. New York: Methuen, 1987, pp. 242–64.

Greene, James J. "Macbeth: Masculinity as Murder." *American Imago* 41 (1984): 155–80.

Gregson, J. M. "*Macbeth*." In *Public and Private Man in Shakespeare*. London: Croom Helm; Totowa, NJ: Barnes & Noble, 1983, pp. 189–204.

Grenander, M. E. "*Macbeth* as Diaphthorody: Notes toward the Definition of a Form." *Yearbook of Comparative Criticism* 10 (1983): 224–48.

Hapgood, Robert. "Point of View and Viewpoint: *Henry IV, Part One* and *Macbeth*." In *Shakespeare the Theatre-Poet*. Oxford: Clarendon Press, 1988, pp. 41–48.

Harrison, G. B. "*Macbeth*." In *Shakespeare's Tragedies*. London: Routledge & Kegan Paul, 1951, pp. 184–202.

Hartwig, Joan. "Parodic Scenes in *Macbeth:* The Porter, the Murderers, and Malcolm." In *Shakespeare's Analogical Scene*. Lincoln: University of Nebraska Press, 1983, pp. 43–65.

Hawkes, Terence. "*Macbeth*." In *Shakespeare and the Reason*. London: Routledge & Kegan Paul, 1964, pp. 124–59.

———, ed. *Twentieth Century Interpretations of* Macbeth. Englewood Cliffs, NJ: Prentice-Hall, 1977.

Holland, Norman N. "*Macbeth*." In *The Shakespearean Imagination*. New York: Macmillan, 1964, pp. 50–71.

Honigmann, E. A. J. "Past, Present and Future in *Macbeth* and *Antony and Cleopatra*." In *Myriad-Minded Shakespeare: Essays, Chiefly on the Tragedies and Problem Comedies*. New York: St. Martin's Press, 1989, pp. 93–102.

Horwich, Richard. "Integrity in *Macbeth:* The Search for the 'Single State of Man.'" *Shakespeare Quarterly* 29 (1978): 365–73.

Jekels, Ludwig. "The Riddle of Shakespeare's Macbeth." *Psychoanalytic Review* 30 (1943): 361–85.

Jones, Emrys. *"Macbeth."* In *Scenic Form in Shakespeare.* Oxford: Clarendon Press, 1971, pp. 195–224.

Jorgensen, Paul A. *Our Naked Frailties: Sensational Art and Meaning in* Macbeth. Berkeley: University of California Press, 1971.

Kantak, V. Y. "An Approach to Shakespearian Tragedy: The 'Actor' Image in *Macbeth."* *Shakespeare Survey* 16 (1983): 42–52.

Kimbrough, Robert. "Macbeth: The Prisoner of Gender." *Shakespeare Studies* 16 (1983): 175–90.

Kirsch, Arthur. "Macbeth's Suicide." *ELH* 51 (1984): 269–96.

Kirsch, James. "Macbeth's Descent into Hell and Damnation." In *Shakespeare's Royal Self.* New York: Putnam's, 1966, pp. 321–422.

Knight, G. Wilson. "The Milk of Concord: An Essay on Life-Themes in *Macbeth."* In *The Imperial Theme.* 3rd ed. London: Methuen, 1951, pp. 125–53.

———. *Shakespeare's Dramatic Challenge: On the Rise of Shakespeare's Tragic Heroes.* London: Croom Helm; New York: Barnes & Noble, 1977.

Knights, L. C. "How Many Children Had Lady Macbeth?" In *Explorations.* London: Chatto & Windus, 1946, pp. 1–39.

———. *"Macbeth."* In *Some Shakespearean Themes.* London: Chatto & Windus, 1959, pp. 120–42.

Kott, Jan. "Macbeth or Death-Infected." In *Shakespeare Our Contemporary.* Translated by Boleslaw Taborski. Garden City, NY: Doubleday, 1964, pp. 75–86.

Lawlor, John. *The Tragic Sense in Shakespeare.* London: Chatto & Windus, 1960.

Lesser, Simon O. *"Macbeth*—Drama and Dream." *Yearbook of Comparative Criticism* 7 (1976): 150–73.

Llorca, Raymond L. *"Macbeth* and the Use of Appetite in Tragedy." *Silliman Journal* 15 (1968): 151–89.

Long, Michael. *Macbeth.* Boston: Twayne, 1989.

Lyman, Stanford M., and Marvin B. Scott. *"Macbeth."* In *The Drama of Social Reality.* New York: Oxford University Press, 1975, pp. 7–20.

McAlindon, T. *"Macbeth."* In *Shakespeare and Decorum.* London: Macmillan, 1973, pp. 132–66.

McCarthy, Mary. "General Macbeth." In *The Writing on the Wall and Other Literary Essays.* New York: Harcourt, Brace & World, 1970, pp. 3–14.

McElroy, Bernard. *"Macbeth:* The Torture of the Mind." In *Shakespeare's Mature Tragedies.* Princeton: Princeton University Press, 1973, pp. 206–37.

Mackinnon, Lachlan. *Shakespeare the Aesthete: An Exploration of Literary Theory.* New York: St. Martin's Press, 1989.

Manlove, Colin N. *"Macbeth."* In *The Gap in Shakespeare: The Motif of Division from* Richard II *to* The Tempest. London: Vision Press; Totowa, NJ: Barnes & Noble, 1981, pp. 132–57.

Marienstras, Richard. "Macbeth or the Tyrant Sacrificed." In *New Perspectives on the Shakespearean World.* Translated by Janet Lloyd. Cambridge: Cambridge University Press, 1985, pp. 73–98.

Mathur, K. C. "Macbeth and the Will to Power." *Indian Journal of English Studies* 15 (1974): 13–26.

Mellamphy, Ninian. "The Ironic Catastrophe in *Macbeth." Ariel* 11, No. 4 (October 1980): 3–19.

———. "Macbeth's Visionary Dagger: Hallucination or Revelation?" *English Studies in Canada* 4 (1978): 379–92.

Morris, Harry. "*Macbeth:* The Great Doom's Image, II." In *Last Things in Shakespeare.* Tallahassee: Florida State University Press, 1985, pp. 163–204.

Morris, Ivor. "*Macbeth.*" In *Shakespeare's God: The Role of Religion in the Tragedies.* London: George Allen & Unwin, 1972, pp. 310–22.

Nevo, Ruth. "*Macbeth.*" In *Tragic Form in Shakespeare.* Princeton: Princeton University Press, 1972, pp. 214–57.

Norbrook, David. "*Macbeth* and the Politics of Historiography." In *Politics of Discourse: The Literature and History of Seventeenth-Century England,* edited by Kevin Sharpe and Stephen N. Zwicker. Berkeley: University of California Press, 1987, pp. 78–116.

Pack, Robert. "Macbeth: The Anatomy of Loss." In *Affirming Limits: Essays on Mortality, Choice, and Poetic Form.* Amherst: University of Massachusetts Press, 1985, pp. 67–83.

Paris, Bernard J. "Bargains with Fate: The Case of *Macbeth.*" *American Journal of Psychoanalysis* 42 (1982): 7–20.

Parker, Barbara L. "*Macbeth:* The Great Illusion." *Sewanee Review* 78 (1970): 476–87.

Paul, Henry N. *The Royal Play* of Macbeth. New York: Macmillan, 1950.

Prosner, Matthew N. "*Macbeth:* The Manly Image." In *The Heroic Image in Five Shakespearean Tragedies.* Princeton: Princeton University Press, 1965, pp. 51–91.

Rackin, Phyllis. "*Macbeth.*" In *Shakespeare's Tragedies.* New York: Ungar, 1978, pp. 107–22.

Ramsey, Jarold. "The Perversion of Manliness in *Macbeth.*" *Studies in English Literature* 13 (1973): 285–300.

Rauber, D. F. "Macbeth, Macbeth, Macbeth." *Criticism* 11 (1969): 59–67.

Reid, B. L. "*Macbeth* and the Play of Absolutes." *Sewanee Review* 73 (1965): 19–46.

Ribner, Irving. "*Macbeth:* The Pattern of Idea and Action." *Shakespeare Quarterly* 10 (1959): 147–59.

Rogers, H. L. "*Double Profit*" in Macbeth. Melbourne: Melbourne University Press, 1964.

Rosenberg, Marvin. *The Masks of Macbeth.* Berkeley: University of California Press, 1978.

Rossiter, A. P. "*Macbeth.*" In *Angel with Horns and Other Shakespeare Lectures.* Edited by Graham Storey. New York: Theatre Arts Books, 1961, pp. 209–34.

Ryan, Kiernan. "Macbeth: 'For Mine Own Good.'" In *Shakespeare.* Atlantic Highlands, NJ: Humanities Press, 1989, pp. 58–65.

Sanders, Wilbur, and Howard Jacobson. "*Macbeth:* What's Done, Is Done." In *Shakespeare's Magnanimity: Four Tragic Heroes, Their Friends and Families.* New York: Oxford University Press, 1978, pp. 57–94.

Scott, William O. "Macbeth's—and Our—Self-Equivocations." *Shakespeare Quarterly* 37 (1986): 160–74.

Sewell, Arthur. *Character and Society in Shakespeare.* Oxford: Clarendon Press, 1951.

Shakespeare Survey 19 (1966). Special *Macbeth* issue.

Sinfield, Alan. "*Macbeth:* History, Ideology and Intellectuals." *Critical Quarterly* 28 (1986): 63–77.

Slights, Camille Wells. "Equivocation and Conscience in *Macbeth.*" In *Casuistical Tradition in Shakespeare, Donne, Herbert, and Milton.* Princeton: Princeton University Press, 1981, pp. 106–32.

Smidt, Kristian. "Double, Double, Toil and Trouble." In *Uncomformities in Shakespeare's Tragedies.* New York: St. Martin's Press, 1990, pp. 150–62.

Speaight, Robert. "Nature and Grace in *Macbeth.*" *Essays by Divers Hands* 27 (1955): 89–108.

Stachniewski, John. "Calvinist Psychology in *Macbeth.*" *Shakespeare Studies* 20 (1988): 169–89.

States, Bert O. "The Horses of *Macbeth.*" *Kenyon Review* 7, No. 2 (Spring 1985): 52–66.

Stein, Arnold. "Macbeth and Word-Magic." *Sewanee Review* 59 (1951): 271–84.

Stockholder, Kay. *"Macbeth:* A Dream of Love." *American Imago* 44 (1987): 85–105.

Sypher, Wylie. "Duration: *Macbeth."* In *The Ethic of Time: Structures of Experience in Shakespeare.* New York: Seabury Press, 1976, pp. 90–108.

Tomlinson, T. B. "Action and Soliloquy in *Macbeth." Essays in Criticism* 8 (1958): 147–55.

Toppen, W. H. *Conscience in Shakespeare's* Macbeth. Groningen: J. B. Wolters, 1962.

Traversi, D. A. *"Macbeth."* In *An Approach to Shakespeare.* 2nd ed. Garden City, NY: Doubleday/Anchor, 1956, pp. 150–81.

Tufts, Carol Strongin. "Shakespeare's Conception of Moral Order in *Macbeth." Renascence* 39 (1986–87): 340–53.

University of Dayton Review 14, No. 1 (Winter 1979–80). Special *Macbeth* issue.

Ure, Peter. *"Macbeth."* In *Elizabethan and Jacobean Drama: Critical Essays by Peter Ure.* Edited by J. C. Maxwell. Liverpool: Liverpool University Press, 1974, pp. 44–62.

van den Berg, Kent T. "From Community to Society: Cultural Transformation in *Macbeth."* In *Playhouse and Cosmos: Shakespearean Theater as Metaphor.* Newark: University of Delaware Press, 1985, pp. 126–47.

Waith, Eugene M. *"Macbeth:* Interpretation versus Adaptation." In *Shakespeare: Of an Age and for All Time,* edited by Charles Tyler Prouty. Hamden, CT: Shoe String Press, 1954, pp. 101–22.

Walker, Roy. *The Time Is Free: A Study of* Macbeth. London: Andrew Dakers, 1949.

Walton, J. K. *"Macbeth."* In *Shakespeare in a Changing World,* edited by Arnold Kettle. New York: International Publishers, 1964, pp. 102–22.

Watkins, Ronald, and Jeremy Lemmon. *Macbeth.* Newton Abbot: David & Charles, 1974.

[Whately, Thomas.] *Remarks on Some of the Characters of Shakespeare.* London: T. Payne & Son, 1785.

Wilbern, David. "Phantasmagoric *Macbeth." English Literary Renaissance* 16 (1986): 520–49.

Wilson, Harold S. *On the Design of Shakespearean Tragedy.* Toronto: University of Toronto Press, 1957.

Winstanley, Lilian. Macbeth, King Lear *and Contemporary History.* Cambridge: Cambridge University Press, 1922.

ACKNOWLEDGMENTS

"Some Character-Types Met With in Psycho-Analytic Work" by Sigmund Freud from *Collected Papers* by Sigmund Freud, Volume 4, translated by Joan Riviere, © 1959 by The Hogarth Press and The Institute of Psycho-Analysis, London. Reprinted by permission of Chatto & Windus/The Hogarth Press and Basic Books, Inc.

Character Problems in Shakespeare's Plays by Levin L. Schücking, © 1922 by George G. Harrap & Co. Reprinted by permission of Harrap Publishing Group Ltd.

"*Macbeth* and the Metaphysic of Evil" by G. Wilson Knight from *The Wheel of Fire* by G. Wilson Knight, © 1930 by Oxford University Press, © 1949 by Methuen & Co. Reprinted by permission of Methuen & Co.

"Time, Violence and Macbeth" by Stephen Spender from *Penguin New Writing* No. 3 (February 1941), © 1941 by Penguin Books, Ltd. Reprinted by permission.

Shakespearian Tragedy by H. B. Charlton, © 1948 by Cambridge University Press. Reprinted by permission.

"Manhood and Valor in Two Shakespearean Tragedies" by Eugene M. Waith from *ELH* 17, No. 4 (December 1950), © 1950 by The Johns Hopkins University Press. Reprinted by permission.

"*Macbeth*" by Harold C. Goddard from *The Meaning of Shakespeare* by Harold C. Goddard, © 1951 by The University of Chicago. Reprinted by permission of The University of Chicago Press.

"The Operation of Evil: *Timon of Athens* and *Macbeth*" by Irving Ribner from *Patterns in Shakespearean Tragedy* by Irving Ribner, © 1960 by Irving Ribner. Reprinted by permission of Methuen & Co.

"*Macbeth*" by William Rosen from *Shakespeare and the Craft of Tragedy* by William Rosen, © 1960 by the President and Fellows of Harvard College. Reprinted by permission of Harvard University Press.

"*Macbeth*" by Terence Eagleton from *Shakespeare and Society: Critical Studies in Shakespearean Drama* by Terence Eagleton, © 1967 by Terence Eagleton. Reprinted by permission of Chatto & Windus.

"The Voice in the Sword" by Maynard Mack, Jr., from *Killing the King: Three Studies in Shakespeare's Tragic Structure* by Maynard Mack, Jr., © 1973 by Yale University. Reprinted by permission of Yale University Press.

"*Macbeth: Counter-Hamlet*" by James L. Calderwood from *Shakespeare Studies* 17 (1985), © 1985 by The Council for Research in the Renaissance. Reprinted by permission.

"Speaking Evil: Language and Action in *Macbeth*" by Michael Goldman from *Acting and Action in Shakespearean Tragedy*, © 1985 by Princeton University Press. Reprinted by permission.

"The Tyrannical Kingship of Macbeth" by John Turner from *Shakespeare: The Play of History* by Graham Holderness, Nick Potter, and John Turner, © 1987 by Graham Holderness, Nick Potter, and John Turner. Reprinted by permission of the University of Iowa Press.

"Macbeth as Tragic Hero" by Wayne C. Booth from *Journal of General Education* 6, No. 1 (October 1951), © 1951 by The University of Chicago. Reprinted by permission of The Pennsylvania State University Press.

"*Macbeth*" by John Holloway from *The Story of the Night: Studies in Shakespeare's Major Tragedies* by John Holloway, © 1961 by John Holloway. Reprinted by permission of Routledge.

"Public Justice: *Macbeth*" by C. J. Sisson from *Shakespeare's Tragic Justice* by C. J. Sisson, © 1961 by C. J. Sisson. Reprinted by permission of Methuen & Co.

"*Macbeth:* The Nemesis of the Post-Shakespearian Actor" by Elizabeth Nielsen from *Shakespeare Quarterly* 16, No. 2 (Spring 1965), © 1965 by the Shakespeare Association of America, Inc. Reprinted by permission of *Shakespeare Quarterly.*

"The Criminal as Tragic Hero: Dramatic Methods" by Robert B. Heilman from *Shakespeare Survey* 19 (1966), © 1966 by Cambridge University Press. Reprinted by permission.

" 'An Unknown Fear': *The Tragedie of Macbeth*" by Wilbur Sanders from *The Dramatist and the Received Idea: Studies in the Plays of Marlowe and Shakespeare* by Wilbur Sanders, © 1968 by Cambridge University Press. Reprinted by permission.

"This Even-Handed Justice" by Alan Hobson from *Full Circle: Shakespeare and Moral Development* by Alan Hobson, © 1972 by Alan Hobson. Reprinted by permission of Chatto & Windus.

"Fear in *Macbeth*" by P. Rama Moorthy from *Essays in Criticism* 23, No. 2 (April 1973), © 1973 by The Editors, *Essays in Criticism*. Reprinted by permission.

"Tragic Action and Sexual Stereotyping in *Macbeth*" (originally titled " 'Be Bloody, Bold and Resolute': Tragic Action and Sexual Stereotyping in *Macbeth*") by Carolyn Asp from *Studies in Philology* 78, No. 2 (Spring 1981), © 1981 by The University of North Carolina Press. Reprinted by permission.

"Ridding Ourselves of Macbeth" by Lisa Low from *Massachusetts Review* 24, No. 4 (Winter 1983), © 1983 by The Massachusetts Review, Inc. Reprinted by permission.

"Stealthy Lovers in *Macbeth*" (originally titled " 'Blanket of the Dark': Stealthy Lovers in *Macbeth*") by Kay Stockholder from *Dream Works: Lovers and Families in Shakespeare's Plays* by Kay Stockholder, © 1987 by the University of Toronto Press. Reprinted by permission.

"*Macbeth:* Succeeding" by Barbara Everett from *Young Hamlet: Essays on Shakespeare's Tragedies* by Barbara Everett, © 1989 by Barbara Everett. Reprinted by permission of Oxford University Press.

INDEX